DEDICATION

To my partner Snow, who stood by me through the sacrificed weekends, holidays, and birthdays spent writing this book.

—Robert

To Toni, without whom, neither this book, nor any other accomplishment, would be remotely worthwhile.

—Simon

Acknowledgements

As anyone in computer book publishing can tell you, the process of building a new book is hardly a simple—or easy—task. This book has been in development for over a year, requiring more days and weeks than we care to admit. Without sounding too much like an Oscar or Golden Globes acceptance speech, there are several people who made this book a reality—without their involvement, you wouldn't be holding this book in your hands.

We were lucky to have the careful and attentive eye of our editors at Macromedia Press and Peachpit Press. Angela Kozlowski, our acquisitions editor, guided us through the early development period of the book and helped us keep the scope of this book within the expectations of Macromedia designers and developers. Robyn Thomas, this book's development and copy editor, made sure each of our chapters flowed from one to the next, ensuring that you, the reader, would have the best experience while reading each paragraph. Our book's technical editors, Nengshia Ly from Macromedia and Quinn Supplee, kept us honest with all of our assertions and examples. With their help, we were able to make sure that our readers would be able to build each application successfully.

While many computer book authors choose to write without a literary agent, we honestly don't know why. David Fugate and Waterside Productions were the best allies we could have. David has been with us from the earliest proposal stages to the final submission of this book's material. Thank you, David, for all of your encouragement and hope.

Of course, all of the Macromedia MX products are built by the best designers, engineers, and programmers available. We wouldn't have been able to show you the capabilities of each product if it weren't for the help of these people. Of particular note, we would like to thank Peter Ryce, the product manager of Flash Communication Server MX, and those who work with him, including Heather Hollaender, Pritham Shetty, Srinivas Manapragada, Giacomo "Peldi" Guilizzoni, Damian Burns, Eric Negron, and Sarah Allen.

Last but not least, we would like to extend our gratitude to those that helped us in the "little" ways that really make a difference in the end. Graham Pearson, Brian Lesser, and Joey Lott provided insightful comments and feedback throughout the writing of this book. We'd also like to thank countless friends of ours who helped us test each application (and on most occasions, over and over and over again... "Testing 1, 2, 3... Do you hear me? Do you see me?").

BUILDING RICH
INTERNET APPLICATIONS

and Simon Allardice

Macromedia MX: Building Rich Internet Applications
Robert Reinhardt, Simon Allardice

Published by Macromedia Press, in association with Peachpit Press, a division of Pearson Education.

MACROMEDIA PRESS
1249 Eighth Street
Berkeley, CA 94710
510/524-2178
510/524-2221 (fax)
Find us on the World Wide Web at:
www.peachpit.com | www.macromedia.com

To report errors, please send a note to errata@peachpit.com

Macromedia Press Editor: Angela C. Kozlowski
Editor: Robyn Thomas
Technical Editor: Nengshia Ly, Quinn Supplee
Production Coordinators: Connie Jeung-Mills, Judy Zimola
Indexer: Joy Dean Lee
Proofreader: Haig MacGregor
Interior and Cover Design: Happenstance Type-O-Rama
Page Layout: Happenstance Type-O-Rama

ISBN 0-321-15881-4

9 8 7 6 5 4 3 2 1

Printed and bound in the United States of America

Biographies

ROBERT REINHARDT

Robert Reinhardt is a leading Flash expert, who has co-written the best selling *Flash Bible* series, including the recently released *Flash MX ActionScript Bible* (Wiley). He is also co-principal of [theMAKERS] (www.theMakers.com), a multimedia company based in Los Angeles, and is the Director of Multimedia Applications for The Content Project (www.contentproject.com) in Santa Monica, California. He has developed multimedia courses for educational facilities in Canada and the United States, been a speaker at the FlashForward conferences, and presented at FlashintheCan 2002 and SIGGRAPH 2002. With a degree in photographic arts, Robert takes a holistic approach to computer applications for the creation of provocative multimedia. Recent projects have included screen graphics for Sean Penn's film *The Pledge* (2000) and a Flash Web site for the Warner Bros. feature film *Training Day* (2001). Robert also maintains FlashSupport.com (www.flashsupport.com), which features forums, tutorials and Flash resources created by [theMAKERS].

SIMON ALLARDICE

Simon Allardice has been building software applications for over seventeen years, coding everything from database-driven applications and music for computer games to safety routines for nuclear reactors. for clients throughout the US and UK. He has presented seminars on database-driven Flash at several international Web conferences, and has taught workshops on advanced Flash and Web site development at Lynda.com in Ojai, California and at Stanford University's Academy for New Media.

Simon is the author of *Building Database-Driven Web Sites with Dreamweaver MX* (from O'Reilly), and was the technical editor for the *Flash MX Bible* and *Flash MX ActionScript MX Bible*. Simon also created the inaugural Web Graphics program for SIGGRAPH, the premier conference on computer graphics and interactive techniques. Currently, Simon develops database-driven site development resources at www.clingfish.com. He is based in Scottsdale, Arizona.

CONTENTS AT A GLANCE

CONTENTS

III Communicating Between Clients

IV Architecting a Comprehensive Application

Foreword

The Internet provides a powerful canvas for creating content and applications. The raw capability of TCP/IP networks to send data around the world in a fraction of a second enables a whole world of applications that we have not yet dreamed into being. The Internet started out as a place to send text-based messages and quickly evolved into a tool for distributing documents through FTP and the Web. With early versions of Macromedia Flash, we enriched the ability to display graphics, animation, and sound in an interactive form on the Web. This provided a toolset for designers to convey richer information and emotion to a worldwide audience, with the same immediacy that previous flows of data had enabled.

Application servers like ColdFusion expanded the ability to easily create a two-way flow of information over the Web so that users could interact with data-oriented applications through their Web browser. A key innovation of Flash, Macromedia Dreamweaver, and ColdFusion has been to blur the roles of designer and programmer by providing tools that integrate content development with programming. By understanding and supporting the amazing range of capabilities in our users, we have enabled them to integrate information with data and behavior. The integration of design, programming, and data continues to reduce the investment needed for talented and creative individuals and teams to create Rich Internet Applications and to communicate their ideas to a worldwide audience of users. The Macromedia MX family of products represents the synthesis of all we have learned through the first generation of products about how to enable people to build great content and applications.

The MX family also embodies our efforts to enable a whole new generation of content and applications on the Internet. We can bring even more life to the Web by integrating people more closely into expression of information on the Internet. The growth of Blogs is a great example of bringing more life to the Web. Macromedia's own Flash Communications Server Team has focused their efforts for the past couple of years on Flash Communications Server MX. By enabling instant data, audio, and video communications within the Web browser, we enrich and empower the connection between people across the Internet. Our vision is to bring teleportation and time travel to your computer screen. Instant audio and video communication with anyone in the world brings remote communication closer to teleportation, and the ability to effortlessly record and store all forms of communication allows you to travel back in time.

With all these products we provide the tools and technology, but we depend on developers who create great content and applications to complete the vision and make it a reality. This book gives you a great advantage in building the next generation of Rich Internet Applications by teaching you how Flash Communication Server, Flash Remoting, Macromedia Flash, Dreamweaver, and ColdFusion fit together, so you can add your vision to the future of the Internet.

Jonathan Gay

Introduction

Who Should Use This Book

Rich Internet Applications (RIAs). This term is more than just the latest buzz word on the Macromedia Web site—it's the best thing to hit the Web since the introduction of the Flash Player. Regardless of your Web production specialty, you'll likely want to know what the fuss is all about.

While it may seem cliché, this book is for you if you want to learn how to build Web applications with the latest round of authoring and server products released by Macromedia. Collectively, these are known as Macromedia MX products, which can be purchased individually or within a software bundle such as Macromedia Studio MX. If you are a Web designer or developer who wants to build advanced Web applications that deliver truly dynamic and real-time Internet experiences, then this book is for you. Ideally, you should have a working knowledge of Flash MX and Dreamweaver MX. If you haven't built a basic Flash movie with interactive buttons and graphics, you may want to read another Macromedia Press book first. However, you don't need to know the latest versions of Flash and Dreamweaver to build the applications described in the chapters of this book. You don't need any prior experience with databases or server-side functionality to understand the concepts we explore in this book. Even if you are an experienced Flash or ColdFusion developer, the new features introduced by Flash Remoting MX and Flash Communication Server MX in our applications will open your eyes to a whole new world of efficient and mind-blowing Rich Internet Applications. Indeed, Macromedia is synonymous with "What the Web Can Be."

Once you've built the applications in this book, you'll have the skills necessary to build your own Web applications that explore new ways of distributing information and connecting users to one another across the globe.

How to Use This Book

We created this book to address two problems that the average Web developer faces: how do you decide which technology or server-side product to use for a Web application, and what exactly do you need to know of that technology to use it successfully?

As Macromedia and other software companies continue to expand the tools and services available to Web developers, you're faced within an ongoing dilemma: which server-side product is best suited for the problems you need to solve? Several factors will influence your decision, from budgetary concerns to ease of use. For example, while PHP and mySQL are open-source standards employed by many Web sites, how long will it take you to develop a Flash application that retrieves dynamic data with XML? Is it better to use Flash Remoting MX? Is it truly faster? Will you save time (and money) developing with one technology over another? This book explains how each Macromedia MX product can be used to create amazing Rich Internet Applications with the least amount of development time.

The second problem is that of breadth and depth of each product's capabilities. It's not necessary to know every in and out of a product to successfully create real-world and enterprise-level Web applications. This book covers the essential areas of application development with respect to each MX product. This book is not a substitute for the invaluable reference materials already created by Macromedia.

Note Most of the documentation for each product is available as a free download from the product's support area on the Macromedia Web site at www.macromedia.com.

Don't misunderstand though—there's plenty of material in this book that you won't find in any other book. You have the benefit of two masters of Web application development guiding you through the hoops of each product.

Part I—Introducing Macromedia MX

Part I of this book describes how many of the Macromedia MX products fit into a Web application development workflow. Each product has specific capabilities that allow you to build RIAs in a fast and efficient manner.

In Chapter 1, "Flash MX: The Interface Creator," we discuss the importance of Flash Player 6's new features with respect to Rich Internet Application development. You learn how the Flash MX authoring environment has been improved to build RIAs with the latest additions to the ActionScript language and the new development framework enabled by Flash Components.

Chapter 2, "Dreamweaver MX: The Foundation," covers the use of Dreamweaver as a development tool for Rich Internet Applications, with a focus on the features for creating database-driven pages and server-side components, rather than HTML page design.

Chapter 3, "ColdFusion MX: The Application Engine," introduces you to Macromedia's powerhouse application server. You learn how ColdFusion documents are authored with CFML (**C**old**F**usion **M**arkup **L**anguage) and dynamically processed by the server. You also learn how **C**old**F**usion **C**omponents (CFC files), new to ColdFusion MX, enhance Web application service.

Chapter 4, "Databases," explains the role of relational databases in an RIA environment. This chapter is a crash course in modern database systems, covering the concepts behind designing, building, and using databases. You explore the SQL language common to all popular database systems, and examine some available options for implementing a database-driven site.

In Chapter 5, "Web Services," we explore the emerging standards of XML Web Services and discuss how the increased abilities for sharing data and functionality can affect your development of Rich Internet Applications. Web Services are supported by the current generation of application server technologies, including ColdFusion MX and ASP.NET.

Chapter 6, "Flash Communication Server MX: The Switchboard," introduces one of the newest Macromedia MX server products. In this chapter, you learn about the exciting real-time interactive features that this server can add to your Flash movies. FlashCom, or FCS, as it is also called, can simultaneously connect several Web users to one another, sharing audio, video, text, and data in real-time.

Chapter 7, "Flash Remoting MX" ...illustrates how Macromedia's Flash Remoting MX is used to streamlined the process of connectivity between different elements of your application, allowing you to easily integrate Flash movies with application servers, databases, and Web service.

Note Because this book is focused on Web application development, other Macromedia MX products such as Fireworks MX and FreeHand MX are not discussed. You can find other Macromedia Press books that specifically explore these products for Web design and production at www.macromedia.com/support/mmpress.

Part II—Establishing Links to Data

Once you know how each Macromedia MX product can contribute to the development of a Web application, Part II launches into hands-on, practical examples of Rich Internet Application development.

Chapter 8, "Gathering and Saving Data," explains how to build a simple application that ties together ColdFusion MX and Flash Remoting MX to enable you to save database information directly from a Flash movie.

Chapter 9, "Displaying Data," covers the visual representation of dynamic data. One of Flash's strengths over plain HTML is programmatic flexibility for creating informational graphics on the fly. This chapter shows how database information can be retrieved and represented in dynamic charts and graphs, utilizing Flash Remoting MX and ColdFusion Components, which contain complex database queries.

Part III—Communicating Between Clients

While Part II focused on ColdFusion MX and Flash Remoting MX, Part III introduces you to the world of Flash Communication Server MX (also known as FlashCom). In each chapter, you learn how to take advantage of a unique aspect of the server's capabilities.

Chapter 10, "Publishing, Playing, and Recording Streams," introduces you to the basic concepts of FlashCom development: how to connect to a FlashCom application, how to detect a user's camera and microphone, how to publish the output from a user's camera to a FlashCom server, and how to enable other Flash movies (or clients) to subscribe to live or recorded streams.

In Chapter 11, "Sharing Text with Multiple Users," you learn how to use Shared Objects with Flash movies. Both local and remote SharedObject data are discussed in the context of building a live chat room for multiple Flash clients. You also learn how to create more than one application instance on a FlashCom server, allowing a user to join specific chat rooms with other connected users.

After you have learned the fundamental operations of a FlashCom application, you're ready to start building more advanced Web applications.

In Chapter 12, "Directing Streams Between Clients," we show you how to build a talk show application that enables one user (the "speaker") to moderate a live audio/video and text chat with several participants (the "viewers"). You learn how to use several of the Communication Components, which allow you to quickly add enhanced interactive features and controls to your Flash movies.

Chapter 13, "Creating a Stream Archive System," continues your exploration of FlashCom application development. In this chapter, you build two Flash clients: one to record a live audio/video conference between two users, and another to playback the audio/video streams recorded during the live session. This chapter combines many of the concepts introduced in Chapters 10, 11, and 12, while introducing you to new techniques such as building proxied remote SharedObjects and using virtual directories for recorded streams.

Part IV—Architecting a Comprehensive Application

Part IV teaches you integration: it takes all the material covered so far in this book and integrates it into a single, coherent application that uses all the technologies in unison.

Chapter 14, "Integration: Creating a Video Instant Messenger," is an intense hands-on chapter where you create a Video Instant Messenger application, which includes database-driven user authentication and video archival. While building this application, you finish the book by successfully integrating Flash MX, FlashCom, Flash Remoting, a relational database, ColdFusion Components, remote and local sharedObjects, and server-side ActionScript.

Appendixes

Appendix A, "Typical Bandwidth Consumption by Streams," provides several tables demonstrating average bit rates used by audio and video streams published by the Camera and Microphone objects and several of the Communication Components. This appendix reviews the methods of the Camera and Microphone objects that control the bandwidth and quality of published streams.

Appendix B, "Online Appendixes," is a description of appendixes that you can find on the book's Web site at www.mxbook.com.

The CD-ROM

The accompanying CD-ROM contains just about everything you need to build the applications discussed in this book, including:

- Evaluation edition of Macromedia Flash MX.

- Evaluation edition of Macromedia Dreamweaver MX.

- Evaluation and developer editions of Macromedia ColdFusion MX.

- Evaluation edition of Macromedia Flash Communication Server MX.

- Evaluation and developer editions of Macromedia Flash Remoting MX for .NET.

- Source code and databases (as Microsoft Access MDB files) for all the examples in this book.

- Separate code listings (as TXT files) for long code blocks shown in the steps of some exercises. If you see a section of code within a Listing heading, such as Listing 10.1, you can find the same code in the Listing10-01.txt file of the chapter_10 folder of the book's CD-ROM.

Note

For the best learning experience, you should install or have access to a database program or server for some of this book's exercises that involve ColdFusion MX. If you are new to database development, we suggest that you use Microsoft Access. You can also download a time-limited trial version of Microsoft SQL Server 2000 at www.microsoft.com/sql/evaluation/trial. You can also use other databases, such as mySQL or postGreSQL, with ColdFusion MX.

BEYOND THE BOOK

It wouldn't be honest to say that you can learn everything there is to know about Rich Internet Application development within the pages of this book alone. As new techniques are discovered and as product features continue to expand, no hard copy book can be fully 100 percent up to date. As such, we've endeavored to build a dynamic Web site that keeps you on track with the latest developments in the world of Macromedia MX and Rich Internet Applications. You can access the Web site at:

www.mxbook.com

 Note Look at other Macromedia Press books for more information on a particular product. You can find the most current titles at www.macromedia.com/support/mmpress. Both Robert and Simon have written Macromedia MX-related titles for other publishers as well.

We'd also like to hear from you, so that we can make future editions of this book better. Whether you want to tell us about a problem you're experiencing or show us one of your own Rich Internet Applications, you can send your questions and comments to us at:

feedback@mxbook.com

We'll do our best to answer your e-mails within an appropriate time frame.

We also encourage you to submit feedback about Macromedia MX products directly to the folks at Macromedia. If you would like to see a new feature in the next product revision or think you've found a bug with an existing product, fill out the online form at:

www.macromedia.com/support/email/wishform

Macromedia **does** actually read these submissions—your comments will not go unnoticed.

Now that you know where and how to access the resources in (and out) of this book, you're ready to start your journey into the world of Rich Internet Application development with Macromedia MX products. What are you waiting for?

Introducing
Macromedia MX

In This Chapter:

1 Flash MX: The Interface Creator

Every Rich Internet Application needs an interface—something that allows the person using the application to do whatever he needs to accomplish. Using Macromedia Flash MX, you have the power to create fully functional Web applications that can utilize everything from vector or bitmap graphics to runtime JPEG or MP3 files to streaming video and audio. In this chapter, you will learn how Macromedia Flash MX fits into the development process.

INTRODUCING FLASH MX

Throughout this book, you will use Macromedia Flash MX as the primary tool to author the Rich Internet Applications and projects that are discussed. In this section, you will learn about the new capabilities of Flash MX movies and how these features apply to building Rich Internet Applications.

Note

This chapter is not intended to provide a comprehensive working knowledge of the Flash MX authoring environment. If you want to learn more about the Flash MX interface, drawing tools, and animation, refer to the "Jumping to More Flash MX" sidebar at the end of this chapter.

Reviewing a Brief History of the Flash Format

Since 1997, Macromedia has developed its most popular product to date, Flash. Traditionally, Macromedia Director was the authoring tool employed by most multimedia designers and developers to create highly interactive and engaging content for CD-ROMs, kiosks, and the Internet. When Macromedia introduced Shockwave content to the Web in 1995, Web surfers could download the Shockwave Player for either Windows or Macintosh operating systems. The Shockwave Player essentially was (and still is) a Web browser plug-in that uses the playback engine from the projector file created by Director. Once Internet users had the plug-in installed, they could view the "shocked" versions of Director movies on the Web. Shocked movies (DCR or DXR files) are Director files that contain the authoring instructions and compressed media assets required for playback.

Note

A DXR file is a protected version of the Director authoring document, the DIR file. DXR files are not compressed, while DCR files are protected and compressed.

Originally, Flash 1 and 2 content was viewed with the first versions of the Shockwave Player. However, the Shockwave Player was a large download (over 1 MB in its first release), and Flash movies (as SWF files) didn't need the Director engine to play in a Web browser. In 1997, Macromedia released Shockwave Flash Player 2, which could play SWF files authored in Macromedia Flash 2. This player plug-in was much smaller—less than 200 KB! At this point, Flash content was no longer considered Shockwave content. Shockwave was exclusively Director's domain, while Flash content (as SWF files) could be viewed in either the Shockwave Player or the Flash Player. While the Shockwave Player plug-in is only available for Windows and Macintosh computers, the Flash Player plug-in is available for several platforms and devices, from the Pocket PC to Linux.

Today, four versions later, the capabilities of the Flash Player are truly remarkable. No other plug-in or multimedia player can compare to Flash Player 6. While the size of the plug-in installation has jumped to 529 KB (or more, depending on platform, browser, and the specific release of the player), the rewards are worth it. Here is just a short list of what Flash MX and Flash Player 6 can do:

- Play vector and bitmap animations. SWF files are progressively down-loaded into the Flash Player, so animation can begin before the entire file has downloaded.

- Embed fonts that display on any supported system. Flash movies (SWF files) can embed characters from specific typefaces that you use in the Flash authoring document (FLA file). Once embedded, these characters will be seen when any user views the Flash movie.

- Integrate a wide range of media content, from JPEG and GIF files to EPS, FreeHand, and Fireworks (PNG file) documents.

- Display JPEG image files at runtime. Flash Player 6 can download standard JPEG images directly into Flash movies (SWF files) as they play.

- Play MP3 audio files at runtime. Flash Player 6 can download both CBR (Constant Bit Rate) and VBR (Variable Bit Rate) MP3 audio into Flash movies (SWF files).

- Play embedded video content. Flash MX now allows you to import digital video files into a Flash document (FLA file). During import, the digital video is recompressed with the Sorenson Spark codec. This proprietary codec is built into Flash Player 6, Web users do not need to download additional plug-ins such as Apple QuickTime or Real Systems Real One Player to view the video content.

 A codec is a compression/decompression module that optimizes audio and/or video data for storage purposes. On playback, the codec is used to decompress the data.

- Play streaming video and audio content delivered by a Web site running Flash Communication Server MX (aka FlashCom). And when we say, "streaming," we mean streaming—we're not talking about SWF files that contain embedded video content. Using FlashCom or third-party utilities like Sorenson Squeeze or Wildform Flix, you can record or convert digital video into Flash Video files, or FLV files. FlashCom can publish FLV files to several connected users in real time.

Xref

For more information about Macromedia Flash Communication Server MX, see Chapter 6.

- Integrate remote data from application servers, such as Macromedia Cold-Fusion Server MX or Microsoft ASP.NET. Remote data can be formatted in several ways, from URL form-encoded name/value pairs to standard XML. The MX family of products introduces a new data format, AMF (**A**ction **M**essage **F**ormat), which is used by Flash Remoting services built into Cold-Fusion Server MX. Now you can send and receive binary data to and from the Flash Player.

Note

Macromedia Flash Remoting MX is also available for Microsoft .NET, Java, and SOAP-based Web services. For more information about Flash Remoting, see Chapter 7.

- Develop complex interface elements (as components) with less hassle. In previous versions of the Flash authoring tool, the onus was upon the developer to create even the simplest of user interface widgets. Now you can quickly drag scrollbars, window panes, push buttons, and radio buttons onto the stage of your Flash documents. These elements are called Flash UI components, and are installed automatically with the program.

Tip

You can download additional components from the Macromedia Exchange for Flash, at www.macromedia.com/exchange/flash.

- Use Unicode text encoding with data loaded into Flash movies. Flash MX allows you to use UTF-8 encoding with ActionScript (in AS files called with the #include directive). By default, Flash Player 6 treats all text data loaded with loadVariables() or the LoadVars and XML objects as Unicode text. Flash Player 6 can interpret text in UTF-8, UTF-16LE and UTF-BE encodings. Why is this important to you? If you want to create multilingual Flash applications (that is, applications that display a variety of languages, including Japanese characters as well as English characters), you need to be able to load text data that contains special characters. See the following URLs for more information:

www.macromedia.com/support/flash/ts/documents/unicode.htm
www.macromedia.com/support/flash/languages/unicode_in_flmx

Note Most, if not all, of your clients (or your employer) will likely be concerned about the availability of the Flash Player on end users' machines. Read the section "Working with Flash Player 6" later in this chapter for more information.

See **Figure 1.1** for an illustration of assets that can be used with Flash movies in Flash Player 6.

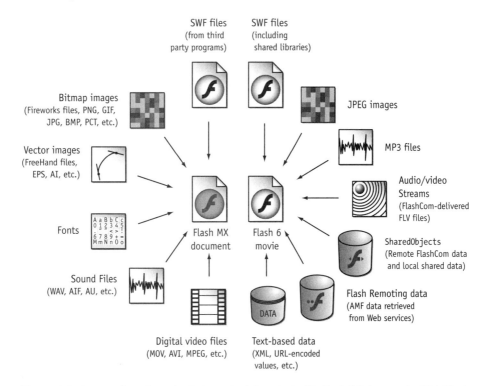

Figure 1.1 An overview of assets that can be integrated with Flash MX documents (FLA files) and Flash movies (SWF files).

As you can see in the previous list, Flash movies can use binary and text-based data from images and video, Web services, and XML text. Flash MX was purposefully designed to build applications. No longer just an animation tool, movies created with Flash MX can connect to a wide range of server-side applications, from Macromedia server products to standard J2EE or ASP.NET servers. As a developer, you have the flexibility to use Flash MX's newly modified Actions panel or another text editor such as Macromedia Dreamweaver MX to write the Action-Script, the code necessary for client- and server-side interactivity.

Looking at the Possibilities

So just what kind of applications can you create with Flash MX? It's easy enough to see how versatile Flash MX can be with several media and data formats, but that flexibility alone won't take you anywhere unless you have a plan that defines the problem (or task) your application will solve. While the majority of this book shows you how to create robust Rich Internet Applications with Flash MX, this section presents various categories of Web applications. This list is just a starting point. Macromedia has created an extensive interconnected architecture for the MX products—it's quite possible that you'll create new ways to create, store, retrieve, and display information in your applications as you become more familiar with the tools.

PORTABLE APPLICATIONS

Flash MX ActionScript allows you to create Flash movies that are "device aware." The new Capabilities object allows you to detect various operating system and display characteristics. As Flash Player 6 becomes available on other non-desktop devices such as the Pocket PC and Nokia PCS phones, you will be able to tailor the content within a Flash movie (SWF file) to the device that is playing it. For example, you can design one Flash movie to reorganize the position and size of user interface (UI) elements on the stage, based on the available screen area of the device (or display).

BANDWIDTH-SENSITIVE APPLICATIONS

One of the long-standing benefits of using Flash movies for Web content is the fact that SWF files can be incredibly small. While some JPEG images on the

Web are easily over 50 KB, you can write an entire application that uses only 6 or 10 KB.

Even graphics-heavy applications can be designed without requiring several hundred kilobytes. Flash MX's native drawing tools are vector-based; you don't have to sacrifice elegance and beauty for vector artwork.

You can also construct your Flash movies to load assets that are customized for the bandwidth of your target audience. For example, you can have low-, medium-, and high-quality JPEGs available to load into a Flash movie. You can also design bitrate-sensitive media streams (containing audio and video) to be delivered from Flash Communication Server MX (aka FlashCom) to your Flash movies.

REAL-TIME COLLABORATION

Since the introduction of Flash 5, ActionScript's XMLSocket object has had the capability to utilize XML data transfers between an application server and a Flash movie. Using third-party socket servers like Xadra's Fortress or Moock.org's UNITY, you could (and still can) create multiuser games and shared environments. With Flash MX, you can design applications that connect multiple users through a Flash Communication Server MX (aka FlashCom). Everything from shared whiteboards to text chats to videoconferencing can be accomplished with the integration of Flash MX and FlashCom.

AUDIO/VIDEO ARCHIVING SYSTEMS

You can design a user interface in Flash MX that allows you to monitor and record the output from a local (or remote) camera and microphone. Or you can convert existing digital video footage into Flash Video (FLV) files that are published by a FlashCom server to multiple users. Using remote SharedObject files, you can store textual data alongside the stored streams to identify and catalog them.

DATA AND E-COMMERCE SYSTEMS

One of the most popular activities on the Web is searching for information using search engines like Google.com. With Flash MX, you can design a front-end client that allows you to enter search terms, send those terms to an application server, and display the server's results within the Flash movie. A practical example of this transaction is a standard e-commerce site, where visitors select items to purchase and securely send their credit card information to your application server. The Flash Player supports SSL (Secure Socket Layer) transfers using the https:// protocol.

DISTANCE LEARNING APPLICATIONS

Distance learning has been a popular catchphrase for the past couple of years. Distance learning is essentially any method of delivering educational content (that is, course material, lessons, and assignments) to a student who isn't physically present in a traditional classroom environment. For years now, many universities and colleges have offered degree programs through the mail. Until recently, though, the use of the Internet to deliver rich media learning materials has been awkward at best—audio/video and collaboration software like CUSeeMe and Microsoft NetMeeting required specific operating systems, drivers, and hardware. More importantly, most of these products use one-to-one peer-to-peer connections, which means that only one person can talk to one other person via a direct Internet (or network) link between two computers.

As mentioned in earlier examples, Flash MX, Flash Player 6, and FlashCom servers allow you to create Flash movies that connect multiple users in real time. You can create a broadcast movie for instructors of a course to send live or pre-recorded material to several students at once. You can create an interface that allows a student to send the audio and video from a microphone and webcam, respectively, to everyone connected to the discussion as well. Because a FlashCom server, and not the Flash Player, manages the connections, the end-user only needs to have Flash Player 6 installed. Better yet, just about any microphone or videocamera is recognized by Flash Player 6—almost all USB and Firewire (IEEE 1394) cameras work flawlessly with the player.

MEDIA PLAYERS

Prior to Flash MX, dynamic media could only be loaded into a Flash movie with the use of Macromedia Generator. In Flash 5 or earlier, you had the ability to create Flash movie templates (SWT files) that contained placeholder elements that Generator would dynamically replace with real data (for example, JPEG images or results from database queries). When Flash MX was released, Macromedia discontinued Generator, largely due to the fact that Flash Player could natively import standard JPEG and MP3 files on the fly, without the use of SWT files or conversion to SWF files. You can create image catalogs or browsers, MP3 jukeboxes, or a streaming video and audio player, just to name a few examples. With these new capabilities, you can effectively create stand-alone media players using a Flash movie as the "shell," or skin, that provides the user interface. Flash MX allows you to publish stand-alone projectors (as EXE or Mac APPL files) that do not require the use of a Web browser with the Flash Player plug-in. You can distribute these projectors on floppy disks, CD-ROMs, DVD-ROMs, or as downloads from your Web site.

MISCONCEPTIONS ABOUT FLASH

If you ask anyone who's not a Web developer about Flash, chances are they won't even know that Macromedia Flash is a rich media plug-in for the Internet. If they have heard of Flash, they'll usually tell you that it's used for Web animation. Or maybe you've had your own doubts, especially if you come from a strict HTML background that has encouraged "vanilla-flavored" design aesthetics in favor of usable interfaces. Indeed, usability design guru Jakob Nielsen once published an article entitled "Flash: 99% Bad." (You can read this article at www.useit.com/alertbox/20001029.html.)

Why have segments of the Web design community seen Flash as an "unusable" technology? Prior to Flash MX, every aspect of interface design was largely the responsibility of the Flash designer or developer—there were no preset buttons, radio buttons, or even scrollbars to add to your Flash movies. However, with the introduction of components in Flash MX (discussed later in this chapter), you'll be able to easily add standard HTML interface elements to your Flash movies. Flash movies can also be accessed by screen readers, which are applications that assist visually impaired users by reading text on the screen out loud. Because of these and other enhancements, the usability experts are gravitating more to Flash as a viable technology for Web deployment. Even Jacob Nielsen has changed his tune. Check out the following URLs about Flash MX and Nielsen on Macromedia's Web site:

www.macromedia.com/macromedia/proom/pr/2002/macromedia_nielsen.html
www.macromedia.com/desdev/mx/blueprint/articles/nielsen.html

Before you can begin production on a Flash project, you'll likely have to convince your employer or your client that Flash is indeed the technology that should be used for the project. Macromedia has gone to great lengths to provide documentation specifically geared to members of the business community. These whitepapers are written with less emphasis on geek speak (that is, you won't find ActionScript source code anywhere in these documents). If you need material to present to your clients or other departments in your company that may not be familiar with Flash, check out the following resources:

www.macromedia.com/resources/business/whitepapers/
www.macromedia.com/resources/richmedia/

Understanding Flash MX File Formats

Before you start to develop Flash applications, you should know how each file format is used within the production process. In this section, you will learn about document formats created by Flash MX, as well as those that can be used in conjunction with Flash movies in Flash Player 6. You will use each of these formats throughout projects in this book. If you come across a project that employs a specific file format, and you're not sure what it is, use this section as a quick reference guide.

FLA

The project file that you create within Macromedia Flash MX is called a Flash document and has an `.fla` file extension, such as `main.fla`. This document is the central file for your Flash production. While you can author an entire project within one single FLA file, we generally recommend that you divide large projects into several FLA files. In this way, several people within your team can work on different project elements simultaneously.

Note

Many Flash designers prefer to construct several scenes within one large FLA file. While there are some cases (such as linear animated shorts) that can benefit from this file structure, an FLA file with multiple scenes usually indicates a large file download for your target audience. It's better to break up your Flash presentation or application into several smaller elements that are downloaded as they are required.

FLA (pronounced "flah" or "F-L-A") files are not uploaded to your Web server for final production and delivery to your target audience. FLA files can be opened only with Macromedia Flash MX. Flash MX has a new feature that allows you to save your Flash document as a Flash 5–compatible FLA file. Some MX-only features like named anchors or accessibility information cannot be saved with a Flash 5–version FLA file. To save a Flash document that can be opened in Flash 5, choose File > Save As in Flash MX and select Flash 5 Document in the Save as type menu.

Tip

If you create large graphic assets or import media files, such as JPEG and MP3 files into a Flash document that are later deleted, you will notice that the size of the Flash document file will not decrease as the assets are removed. You need to save a new Flash document (that is, one with a different name, using File > Save As) in order for Flash MX to compact the contents of a Flash document.

SWF

A SWF (pronounced "swiff" or "S-W-F") file is the Flash movie file that is published from your Flash document in Flash MX. These files have a .swf file extension, such as main.swf. SWF stands for **S**mall **W**eb **F**ile.

SWF originally stood for **S**hockwave **F**lash, but Shockwave is now a term used exclusively for Director content on the Web.

A Flash movie (SWF file) is an optimized version of your Flash document (FLA file). Layer names, Guide layers, frame comments, ActionScript comments, and unused symbols in the Library are not included with a SWF file. Flash MX can also compress Flash 6 movies. With this new option, Flash MX applies compression to vector assets, text elements, and ActionScript code. You can see significant file savings with this new compression option, especially for movies that use Flash UI components and/or have several hundred lines of ActionScript code.

Throughout this book, references to Flash 6 movies should be interpreted as Flash MX movies that have been published for use in Flash Player 6. You can enable the compression option and Flash 6 as the version of your Flash movies in the Flash tab of the Publish Settings dialog box (File > Publish Settings).

With a Flash document (FLA file) open in Flash MX, you can create a SWF file in several ways:

- Choose Control > Test Movie (Ctrl+Enter or z+Enter), Control > Debug Movie (Ctrl+Shift+Enter or z+Shift+Enter), or Control > Test Scene (Ctrl+Alt+Enter or z+Option+Enter). Test Movie creates a SWF file named exactly the same as the Flash document (FLA file), but with a .swf extension. Debug Movie creates the same type of SWF file, but also creates a SWD file, which is a debugging file required for the Debugger panel. Test Scene creates a SWF file of the current scene displayed in the Timeline window; if Test Scene is used while a symbol timeline is open in the Timeline window, a SWF file containing just the elements on that timeline is created.

- Choose File > Publish Preview > HTML, File > Publish Preview > Flash, or File > Publish. Publish Preview not only creates a SWF file of your Flash document but also opens the SWF file in either the default Web browser or the Flash stand-alone player. The name and options of the SWF file are pre-determined in the Publish Settings dialog box (File > Publish Settings).

- Choose File > Export Movie, and select Flash Movie in the Save as type menu. After you enter a name for the SWF file, you can enable the format options (such as JPEG image compression, debugging, etc.) in an Export Flash Player dialog box.

SWD

As mentioned in the previous section, an SWD file is created by Flash MX when you choose Control > Debug Movie to test your movie in the Flash MX authoring environment. An SWD is also created by Flash MX if you select the Debugging Permitted check box in the Flash tab of the Publish Settings dialog box (File > Publish Settings). The SWD file must be in the same directory (or folder) as the Flash movie (SWF file) in order for the Debugger panel to work properly in Flash MX. If you want to remotely debug a Flash movie from your Web server, you must upload the SWD file to the same web folder where the Flash movie resides.

Projectors (EXE and APPL files)

With Flash MX or the stand-alone Flash Player 6, you can create a self-running version of your Flash movie. This type of movie is called a projector, or a stand-alone. Essentially, the Flash movie and the Flash Player engine are combined into one file: an EXE file for Windows playback, or an APPL file (as the file creator type) for Macintosh. Because the projector file contains the Flash Player engine, you do not need a Web browser and a Flash Player 6 plug-in to view the Flash movie. You can distribute the projector files on a CD-ROM or some other type of fixed media, like DVD-ROM.

You can create both Macintosh and Windows projectors regardless of which version of Macromedia Flash MX you use. To create a projector file, choose File > Publish Settings, and select the appropriate projector format. You can select the Windows Projector and/or the Macintosh Projector checkbox. Click the Publish button in the Publish Settings dialog box, or choose File > Publish to create the projector files.

You can also open a Flash movie (SWF file) in the Flash stand-alone player. With the movie open, choose File > Create Projector. Note that this method can only create a projector specific to the operating system you are using.

Tip

You can find the Flash stand-alone player in the `Macromedia\Flash MX\Players` folder inside your programs or applications folder. In Windows, the stand-alone player is named `SAFlashPlayer.exe`. On a Macintosh, the player is named `SAFlashPlayer`. You can find information regarding the most recent release of the Flash Player at `www.macromedia.com/support/flash/ts/documents/flashplayer_r40.htm`.

FLV

The Flash Video format is designated with an `.flv` extension. FLV (pronounced "F-L-V") files are precompressed video and audio files. Any video that has been compressed with the Sorenson Spark codec is in the FLV format. FLV files can be imported into Flash MX documents and published as embedded video in Flash movies (SWF files). However, you can also use Flash Communication Server MX (aka FlashCom) to publish FLV files to several users simultaneously. FLV files can be created or accessed in a variety of ways:

- After you use File > Import to convert digital video to embedded video within a Flash MX document, you can select the embedded video in the Library panel and choose Properties in the options menu of the panel. In the Embedded Video Properties dialog box, you can choose Export to save the video to an FLV file. This way, you can reimport the video into other Flash MX documents without having to recompress the original digital video file again.

- You can use a FlashCom server to record live video and audio to FLV files that reside on the server. The FLV files can be rebroadcast to other users at a later time, or you can import the FLV files into other Flash MX documents. You can script Flash movies to record the video and audio streams from a user's webcam and microphone during a conference call or a remote learning session.

- Third-party utilities such as Sorenson Squeeze (`www.sorenson.com`) or Wildform Flix Pro (`www.wildform.com`) can compress digital video source files into ready-made SWF files or FLV files. The primary benefit of these utilities is that they can compress video in the Sorenson Spark Pro codec. The Pro version of the codec can use Variable Bit Rate (or VBR) encoding, which allows the stream's bit rate to vary from frame to frame. The native encoder for Flash MX is the Sorenson Spark Basic edition, which can only use Constant Bit Rate (or CBR) encoding. VBR-encoded video files look much better and are smaller files than equivalent CBR-encoded video files.

SOL and FSO

The SOL and FSO file formats are associated with local and remote SharedObject data, respectively. The SharedObject object is a new addition to ActionScript in Flash MX. Local SharedObject data is saved in an SOL (pronounced "S-O-L") file, with a .sol file extension. Anytime a Flash movie (SWF file) registers a local SharedObject object, an SOL file is created in the Flash Player preferences folder on the end user's machine. SOL files are stored within folders specific to the Internet domain of the Flash movie (SWF file) that created the SharedObject data. For example, if a Flash movie named main.swf located in a subdirectory named swf from the domain richmediamx.com creates a persistent SharedObject object named navInfo on a Windows XP machine (with a user name of David), an SOL file named navInfo.sol is created with the following directory path:

```
C:\Documents and Settings\David\Application Data\Macromedia\Flash Player\
richmediamx.com\main.swf\navInfo.sol
```

If the same user name on a Mac OS X system accessed the same SWF file, the navInfo.sol file would be created with the following directory path:

```
[Startup Disk]\users\David\Library\Preferences\Macromedia\Flash
Player\richmediamx.com\main.swf\navInfo.sol
```

The client-side ActionScript within the Flash movie (main.swf) would have the following syntax:

```
nav_so = SharedObject.getLocal("navInfo");
```

FSO files are essentially the same file format as SOL files, except that FSO files are created and saved by Flash Communication Server MX (FlashCom). FSO files are stored in the sharedobjects folder of the FlashCom application directory that created the SharedObject data. If you have a development installation of FlashCom within IIS 5.0 or later on a Windows machine, and you created an application named broadcast that creates a SharedObject named userInfo, a file named userInfo.fso would be created with the following directory path:

```
C:\Inetpub\wwwroot\flashcom\applications\broadcast\sharedobjects\_definst_\
userInfo.fso
```

 Note   In a production installation of FlashCom, FSO files are stored in an application folder that is not accessible by the end-user.

Remote `SharedObject` data (FSO files) can be created by client-side or server-side ActionScript. The following client-side code creates a persistent remote `SharedObject` named `userInfo` after a successful connection is made to an application named `broadcast` on a FlashCom server:

```
server_nc = new NetConnection();
server_nc.connect("rtmp:/broadcast");
server_nc.onStatus = function(info){
  if(info.code == "NetConnection.Connect.Success"){
    user_so = SharedObject.getRemote("userInfo", server_nc.uri, true);
    user_so.connect(server_nc);
  }
};
```

Xref

For more information on Flash Communication Server MX, read Chapter 6.

AS

You can save lines or entire blocks of ActionScript code in a text file with a `.as` file extension. When you are developing an extensive Flash application or project, you will likely find it very useful to store frequently used (or edited) ActionScript code in AS files. You can build entire libraries of your own custom functions, objects, and classes in AS files. In this way, you can easily reuse an application's functionality from one Flash document to the next.

Note

AS files can also be stored in the Flash MX application folder. For more information, refer to the "Locating Script Libraries in Flash MX" section later in this chapter.

AS files can be incorporated with a published Flash movie (SWF file) by using the `#include` directive in any event handler within the Flash document (such as a `keyframe`, `Button`, or `MovieClip` object). The following ActionScript inserts the code from a text file named `mainLib.as` into the Flash movie when it is published:

```
#include "mainLib.as"
```

Note that you do not include a semicolon (;) at the end of an `#include` directive. The `mainLib.as` must be in the same folder as the saved Flash document (FLA file) at the time of publishing. You can use relative or absolute directory paths

in an `#include` directive. The following code retrieves the `mainLib.as` file in the parent folder of the Flash document:

```
#include "../mainLib.as"
```

On a Macintosh system, you can use either a / or a : to indicate a relative directory path.

This code retrieves the `mainLib.as` at the root directory of the C: drive on a Windows system:

```
#include "C:/mainLib.as"
```

You can use either a / or a \ in absolute directory paths on a Windows system.

On the Macintosh, you can locate a `mainLib.as` file using a reference to the volume name of the drive:

```
#include "Macintosh HD:mainLib.as"
```

You must use a : for absolute directory paths on a Macintosh system.

AS files can only be added to a Flash movie (SWF file) when it is published or tested—you cannot load AS files directly into a Flash movie at runtime in the Flash Player. You can, however, execute server-side ActionScript files with Macromedia ColdFusion Server MX or Flash Communication Server MX.

You can create AS (client-side ActionScript), ASC (server-side ActionScript for Flash-Com applications), and ASR (server-side ActionScript for Flash Remoting) files with built-in templates and code syntax highlighting in Macromedia Dreamweaver MX.

Media Files

Macromedia Flash MX can import a variety of image and sound formats into a Flash document (FLA file). The following list shows you which import formats are supported by Flash MX's File > Import command:

- Image formats: TIF, TGA, JPEG, GIF, PCT (or PICT), BMP, PSD (version 2.5 or 3), EPS (Photoshop EPS is not supported), AI (Adobe Illustrator 8.0 or earlier), QTIF, SGI, PNG, FH, EMF (Windows only), WMF (Windows only)

- Sound formats: AU, WAV, MP3, SD2, AIF (or AIFF)

- Video formats: AVI, ASF (Windows only), DV, DVI, MPEG, MOV, WMV (Windows only)

As mentioned earlier in this chapter, you can also load files into a Flash movie at runtime, while the movie runs in Flash Player 6:

- Images: You can load standard JPEG images into Flash movies using the MovieClip object's loadMovie() method. Progressive JPEG images cannot be loaded into Flash Player 6.

- Sounds: MP3 audio files can be loaded into Flash movies using the loadSound() method of the Sound object. From our research, both CBR and VBR MP3 files can be loaded into Flash Player 6. Be sure to test the files created by your preferred MP3 encoder before you finalize your Flash project.

- Other Flash movies: You can load other SWF files into a Flash movie that is running in the Flash Player. Use the loadMovie() method of the MovieClip object to load SWF files into existing MovieClip objects within the movie. You can load SWF files into specific levels of the Flash Player using the loadMovieNum() function. Note that you can make SWF files that contain embedded video load video independently of other content used within the Flash application or presentation.

- Video and audio streams: You can play live video and audio from other Flash movies connected to a FlashCom server, or you can access prerecorded video and audio (saved as FLV files) from a FlashCom server.

ACCESSING REMOTE DATA

At runtime, Flash MX movies (SWF files) can retrieve remote data in several ways, and the data can be formatted in more than one way too. As you develop Flash applications, you will likely need to access data outside of the Flash movie (SWF file) in order to provide up-to-date and personalized information for the user. In this section, you will learn how data can be loaded into Flash movies, and what formats can be used for this data.

ActionScript Methods and Objects

The following methods and objects can be used to load data into Flash movies at runtime:

- The loadVariables() method or function can retrieve URL-encoded name/value pairs (discussed later in this section) into Flash 4 (function only), 5, or 6 movies.

- Flash 5 and 6 movies can use the XML and XMLSocket objects to load XML data.

- Flash 6 movies can use the new LoadVars object to retrieve URL-encoded name/value pairs, with greater control and flexibility than the loadVariables() method.

- The new local SharedObject object (discussed earlier in this chapter) allows you to save and retrieve data from a Flash 6 movie on the end-user's machine. The remote SharedObject object allows you to save and retrieve data on a Flash Communications Server MX–enabled domain.

- The new LocalConnection object in Flash MX allows you to access data in other SWF files that are running concurrently with a Flash movie in a Web browser. For example, if you have an HTML frameset with two frames, each containing a SWF file, you can enable each SWF file to talk to one another with the LocalConnection object.

- Flash MX introduces Flash Remoting, which allows Flash MX movies to exchange data with remote services, including ColdFusion components and pages, EJBs (Enterprise JavaBeans), Java classes, and .NET components and pages. You will learn more about the use of Flash Remoting in projects throughout this book.

Tip

Flash MX movies cannot save or retrieve data from any other file on the user's system. If you want to create applications that can read and write data to text files outside of the Player preferences directory, you can use the Macromedia Director and its FileIO Xtra.

Each of these Flash MX features requires a specific format for the remote data. The following sections briefly describe these data formats.

URL-encoded Data

The loadVariables() method and LoadVars object require data to be formatted as URL-encoded name/value pairs, in the following syntax:

```
variable_1=value&variable_2=value&…
```

As you can see, each variable and value (called a name/value pair) is separated by an ampersand (&), and an equal sign (=) separates the variable's name from the value. The names and the values should be URL-formatted as well. URL-formatting converts special characters, such as punctuation (: ; . ?) and slashes (/ and \), into coded escape sequences. For example, a space is converted into %20. The following ActionScript variable declarations would require a different syntax in a remote text file or data source:

```
firstName = "George";
lastName = "Smith";
title = "Director & Producer";
```

In a remote data source, these variables would be presented as the following:

```
firstName=George&lastName=Smith&title=Director%20%26%20Producer
```

The spaces before and after the ampersand of the title value are encoded as %20, while the ampersand itself is encoded with %26. When the Flash Player loads data, it automatically URL-decodes these escape sequences.

All variables loaded from URL-encoded data have a string data type.

XML Data

With the XML or XMLSocket object in ActionScript, you can load XML data into a Flash movie (SWF file) at runtime. XML stands for e**X**tensible **M**arkup **L**anguage, and its syntax is fairly similar to HTML. Using a series of structured tags, you can describe relationships of data. In comparison to URL-encoded data, the benefits of using XML for structured data are immediately apparent. For example, if you had several names and titles of employees or clients that you wished to retrieve from a remote data source (such as a Microsoft SQL Server database), the URL-encoded version could look something like the following:

```
firstName_1=George&lastName_1=Smith&title=Director%20%26%20Producer
&firstName_2=Frank&lastName_2=Jones&title=Director%20of%20Photography
```

Using XML, the returned data from the data source would look like the following text:

```
<?xml version="1.0" encoding="UTF-8"?>
<crew>
  <member fName="George" lName="Smith" title="Director & Producer"/>
  <member fName="Frank" lName="Jones" title="Director of Photography"/>
</crew>
```

As you can see in the first line of this sample XML data, the XML declaration allows you to tell Flash Player 6 how the text within the document is encoded. Remember, Flash Player 6 supports UTF-8, UTF-16LE, and UTF-16BE encoding. You can avoid the use of escape sequences by using Unicode text. The primary advantage, though, of this XML data is that it describes the relationship of the data. In the URL-encoded version, the order of the name/value pairs is arbitrary. In XML, though, each tag (or node) contains related data. The names and titles of each crew member are attributes of the `<member>` nodes. You can think of XML data nodes as `Array` objects in Flash MX ActionScript; each node contains children nodes that relate to one another.

Furthermore, XML has become a data standard for many Web applications. You can share XML data between different applications much more easily than you can URL-encoded name/value pairs. If you have the opportunity to use XML as your data format for Flash MX applications, make every effort to integrate it with your production.

SharedObject, LocalConnection, and Flash Remoting Data

When you use these objects or services to send and receive data from Flash MX movies, you can use all the basic data types: `Array`, `Boolean`, `Number`, `Object`, and `String`. Moreover, this data is sent and received in binary, not as text-based data (such as ASCII). Binary transmissions are usually much smaller (in byte size) than equivalent text-based structures.

EXPANDING ACTIONSCRIPT

Flash MX has implemented some changes to the way in which you can write ActionScript event handlers. There are even new event handlers that were unavailable in Flash 5 or earlier. In this section, you will learn how the Flash MX ActionScript model has changed.

Understanding the New Event Model in Flash MX

In Flash 5 and earlier, you could "catch" events on keyframes, Button instances, and MovieClip objects. Specifically, Flash 5 gave us the onClipEvent() handler, which allowed you to detect nine different events with MovieClip objects. In Flash MX, you can assign these same events to MovieClip objects without using an onClipEvent() handler. Flash MX has also expanded the range of movie events that ActionScript can detect.

MovieClip OBJECTS

Now you can assign the following event handlers directly to MovieClip objects. Some of these handlers can also be assigned to the new Button object as well. The Button objects are designated in the list below with an asterisk:

onData	onMouseMove
onDragOut *	onMouseUp
onDragOver *	onPress *
onEnterFrame	onRelease *
onKeyDown *	onReleaseOutside *
onKeyUp *	onRollOut *
onKillFocus *	onRollOver *
onLoad	onSetFocus *
onMouseDown	onUnload

Take a look at how you can transform the onClipEvent(mouseMove) handler into a new MovieClip.onMouseMove handler. In Flash 5, you would have to place the following code directly on a physical MovieClip instance on the stage:

```
onClipEvent(mouseMove){
  this._x = _root._xmouse;
  this._y = _root._ymouse;
}
```

This code moves the MovieClip instance (this) to the position of the mouse cursor whenever the user moves the mouse. Therefore, the instance follows the mouse cursor. However, if you wanted to use this code with a dynamically attached MovieClip object (using the attachMovie() method), you would have to assign the code to yet another instance nested within the attached instance. In Flash MX, you can assign the same functionality directly in a keyframe:

```
_root.attachMovie("customCursor", "customCursor_mc", 1);
customCursor.onMouseMove = function(){
  this._x = _root._xmouse;
  this._y = _root._ymouse;
};
```

This code is much more flexible; you can assign (or remove) handlers with much less hassle than in Flash 5. To remove the functionality in Flash 5, you would need to remove the MovieClip object from the stage. In Flash MX, you can simply assign a null value to the handler, as the following code demonstrates:

```
customCursor.onMouseMove = null;
```

attachMovie() and createEmptyMovieClip(), a new method in Flash MX, both return a reference to the newly created instance as well. The newObj reference in the following code refers to the customCursor instance:

```
newObj = _root.createEmptyMovieClip("customCursor", 1);
with(newObj){
  lineStyle(1, 0x000000, 100);
  moveTo(0,0);
  lineTo(25, 25);
  lineTo(-25, 25);
  lineTo(0,0);
}
newObj.onMouseMove = function(){
  this._x = _root._xmouse;
  this._y = _root._ymouse;
  updateAfterEvent();
};
```

This code uses the new drawing API that Flash MX added to ActionScript as well. These specific moveTo() and lineTo() methods create a black outlined triangle that follows the mouse. Notice the addition of the updateAfterEvent() function within the onMouseMove() handler. This function forces the Flash Player to update the contents on the stage faster than the movie's frame rate. Try out the code to see the results.

LISTENERS

By far, one of the most powerful additions to Flash MX ActionScript is the ability to assign objects (and their custom event handler methods) to other objects associated with specific events. For example, ActionScript can now detect when the user has resized the Flash Player window (or browser window containing the Flash movie). The new Stage object is associated with this event. Using the addListener() method of the Stage object, you can create objects with the event handler onResize(), which is linked to the event or act of resizing the player window. The following code rotates a MovieClip object named square by 10 degrees each time the user resizes the player window:

```
square.onResize = function(){
  this._rotation += 10;
};
Stage.addListener(square);
```

There are other prebuilt classes in ActionScript that can use listeners as well: Key, Mouse, Selection, FStyleFormat, and TextField. While Key, Mouse, and Selection are static classes (that is, you can't create new instances of them), the FStyleFormat and TextField classes use listeners on an instance level. For example, listener objects for a TextField object can use the onChanged() event handler. Whenever the user changes the text within an Input text field, the listener object's onChanged() handler will execute. In the following code, when the user changes or adds text to the comments_txt object (a TextField object), a trace() action will display the new contents of the field in the Output window:

```
monitorText = new Object();
monitorText.onChanged = function(){
  trace("current content = " + comments_txt.text);
};
comments_txt.addListener(monitorText);
```

This code shows you how even an Object object can be used as a listener. You can pass Object, Button, or MovieClip objects as the argument for the addListener() method. To remove an object as a listener, you can use the removeListener() method. The following code can be assigned to a Button object to remove our monitorText object from the comment_txt object's active listener list:

```
on(release){
  comments_txt.removeListener(monitorText);
}
```

Note   You can actually create a listener event model for any object in Flash MX Action-Script. You can learn more about the undocumented ASBroadcaster() object and methods to create such custom listener objects at www.flashguru.co.uk/000032.php.

You might be wondering how listeners apply to your day-to-day tasks with Flash applications. Listeners allow you to develop application-programming models that *respond* to events, rather than check for them. In older Flash movies, you were required to design frame loops that would search for changes to information or states within the Flash movie. Now you can save valuable processor cycles by employing listeners in your application designs.

Locating Script Libraries in Flash MX

If you installed the trial or commercial versions of Macromedia Flash Communication Server MX or ColdFusion Server MX, your version of Flash MX will have access to several ActionScript source files (AS files) that can be directly referenced within #include directives in the Actions panel, without needing to know the full directory path to the AS files. You can store your own frequently used AS files in this location too. By placing your own AS files in this location, you can make sure that you don't have multiple copies of the same AS file floating around on your system, and you can be certain that any modifications to AS files will propagate throughout any Flash documents that reference them.

If you are using a Windows version of Flash MX, browse to the following directory in Windows Explorer:

    C:\Program Files\Macromedia\Flash MX\Configuration

If you are using a Mac OS X version of Flash MX, go to the following location in the Finder:

    [Startup volume]: Applications: Macromedia Flash MX: Configuration

If you are using Mac OS 9.x or earlier with Flash MX, go to the following location:

    [Startup volume]: Applications (Mac OS 9): Macromedia Flash MX: Configuration

If you haven't installed any Macromedia MX server products, you will not see an Include folder in the Configuration directory. You can make a new folder and name it Include, and place your own AS files in this location. Once you have an AS file(s) in this folder, you can reference the file in the Actions panel. For example, if you created a custom AS file named getMovieSize.as and saved it to the Include folder, you can reference the AS file as follows:

```
#include "getMovieSize.as"
```

If an AS file is located in the Include folder, you do not need to have a copy of the AS file in the same folder as the Flash document (FLA file) with which you are working.

 Note

Throughout the projects constructed in this book, you will learn how to use and access the AS files, such as NetServices.as, that are installed by Flash Remoting and Macromedia ColdFusion Server MX.

GETTING HELP WITHIN FLASH MX

Flash MX has introduced a couple of useful self-help panels within the authoring environment: the Answers and Reference panels. You can open either of these panels by choosing the corresponding name in the Window menu.

The Answers panel features a drop-down menu at the top of the panel. By default, this menu is set to Getting Started. However, if you access this menu, you see that you can access everything from TechNotes to Extensions to the current Site of the Day. Be sure to click the Update Now button in the Settings area to retrieve the latest Answers panel information.

The Reference panel is a built-in ActionScript dictionary that offers detailed information on every object, property, method, and function in the ActionScript language. As you install additional Macromedia MX products and/or third-party extensions, supplemental information pertaining to ActionScript objects and components related to products or extensions appears as additional booklets in the left pane of the Reference panel. You can download extensions to Flash MX at www.macromedia.com/exchange.

If you prefer, you can also access additional Flash MX information by using the commands in the Help menu.

Powering up with Components

Perhaps the most substantial development update to Flash MX is the new component framework. Components are the new version of Flash 5's Smart Clips, which allowed you to create customized Movie Clip symbols that had user-defined settings. Components have extended this ability to create customizable objects within a Flash movie. Components can act as behavior controllers that modify another object's properties (such as fading a MovieClip instance in or out), or they can be complete user interface elements.

As an application developer, you can install or purchase additional Macromedia and third-party components, or create your own components to reuse from one project to the next. While AS files allow you to reuse code from one Flash document to the next, components give you the luxury of dragging and dropping complete functionality—from the GUI (graphical user interface) to the ActionScript code required for them to work—right onto the stage of your Flash document.

Another benefit of components is that you, as a Flash developer, can create sophisticated interactive elements that even a beginner Flash designer or developer can integrate quickly within a production environment. By exposing only the core parameters to the Flash designers who will be using the components, you can hide advanced code and prevent it from being accidentally changed by another Flash developer on your team. To help Flash developers use components within Flash documents, Macromedia added a Live Preview feature, which allows component instances on the authoring stage to display the custom values you entered for the instance in the Parameters tab of the Property inspector (**Figure 1.2**).

An Overview of the Flash UI Components

Flash MX ships with seven user interface (UI) components that you can use to quickly create elegant and user-friendly applications. These components include everything from a basic scrollbar to advanced window panes. In this section, you will learn about the basic functionality of each Flash UI component. Most of these components resemble their HTML counterparts, in both functionality and appearance. You can access the Flash UI components by choosing Window > Components, (Ctrl+F7 or ⌘+F7). See **Figure 1.3** for a list of the UI elements in the Components panel.

Figure 1.2 Live Preview enables component instances to display custom data on the stage of the Flash document in the authoring environment.

Figure 1.3 Flash MX ships with seven Flash UI components that are located in the Components panel.

Note   You will learn about components specific to other Macromedia MX products throughout Part I of this book.

Each component has its own methods and properties. You can learn more about each component's ActionScript features by looking in the Flash UI Components booklet of the Reference panel. Many of these properties and methods are discussed throughout the projects in this book.

Tip   In ActionScript help documents, the class name of each Flash UI component is preceded by an "F," as in FCheckBox.

CHECK BOX

You can add simple check boxes to your Flash movies with this Flash UI component. When you place this component on the stage of a Flash document, you can set the value of the text label and its placement in the Parameters tab of the Property inspector. You can also set the initial value (or state) of the check box. A value of true selects the check box, while a value of false clears the check box.

Almost all of the Flash UI components have a Click or Change Handler setting in the Property inspector. You can set this option to the name of a function that is invoked whenever the user clicks or changes the state of a component instance.

COMBOBOX

This component is a drop-down menu that you can populate with values in the Property inspector or in ActionScript code. Each item in a ComboBox instance can have a label (the text that the user sees in the menu) and a data value (the data that is associated with the menu item). For example, you can populate a ComboBox instance with the label values Red, Green, and Blue, but the data values would be 0xFF0000, 0x00FF00, and 0x0000FF, respectively, to indicate the hexadecimal value for each color. You can also specify how many rows are displayed in the ComboBox instance.

LISTBOX

This component creates a scrollable text area where each line within the field is an active item that has a label and a data value. You can add ActionScript handlers to detect when an item within the list is clicked, and retrieve that item's label and data values.

PUSHBUTTON

As the name implies, this component is a simple gray push button, similar to an HTML submit button. You can change the text that appears on the button via the Label value in the Property inspector.

EXERCISE CARE WITH UI ELEMENTS

When you add Flash UI components to your Flash applications, make sure you match the right element to the functionality you wish to add. Many novice interface designers will inadvertently try to use a series of check boxes when they should use a series of radio buttons, or they may add a single radio button when they should use a single check box. A general rule of thumb to remember is this: If you want the user to choose only one option out of many, use a series of radio buttons. If you want the user to enable (or disable) a single option or setting, use a check box.

RADIOBUTTON

 This component adds a radio button interface element to your movie. You can specify a group name to which a set of radio buttons belongs. The RadioButton component has a built-in event handler that automatically notifies other buttons in the group when one is clicked.

SCROLLBAR

 Did you ever have to script your own scrollbar for a text field in Flash 4 and 5? Flash MX introduces a simple drag-and-drop ScrollBar component. Simply create a Dynamic or Input text field, assign an instance name to the field, and drag a ScrollBar component from the Component panel to the right edge of the text field. Voila! You have a scrolling text field. It doesn't get any simpler than that.

SCROLLPANE

 By far one of the most visually interesting Flash UI components, the ScrollPane component allows you to scroll other linked Movie Clip symbols within a window pane. You can also use ActionScript to dynamically load JPEG images directly into a ScrollPane instance.

Skinning Components

One of the most flexible options for all Flash UI components is the ability to "skin," or modify, the physical appearance of the component instances within your Flash document. Flash MX separates the artwork symbols from the core

ActionScript-driven symbols of a component. When you add a component to your Flash document, Flash MX creates a Flash UI Components folder to the Library, as shown in **Figure 1.4**. Inside of this folder, you can find a nested folder named Component Skins. Within this folder, you can modify the artwork symbols used for individual components, such as those found in the FScrollBar Skins folder. Any symbols that are used throughout several components can be found in the Global Skins folder.

Figure 1.4 Change the appearance of Flash UI components by altering the symbols within the Skins subfolders in the Library.

Not only can you change the look and feel of components directly by editing the skin symbols, but you can also use the FStyleFormat and globalStyleFormat objects to change the appearance of components through ActionScript. For more information on these objects, see the Reference panel in Flash MX.

WORKING WITH FLASH PLAYER 6

Flash Player 6 introduces new features that can be accessed by the user, and protects SWF files from retrieving data in SWF files on separate top-level domains. In this section, you will learn how to access new features of Flash Player 6 and how data between Flash MX movies existing on separate Internet domains is protected.

Accessing Flash Player 6 Settings

When a Flash movie (SWF file) loads into the Flash Player 6 plug-in or ActiveX control of a Web browser, you can right-click (Windows) or Control-click (Macintosh) the movie's stage to open the player's contextual menu, as shown in **Figure 1.5**.

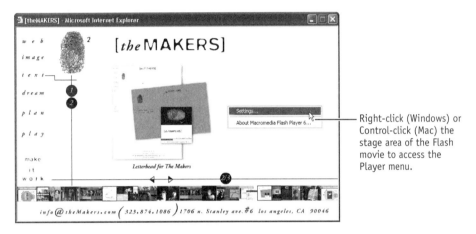

Right-click (Windows) or Control-click (Mac) the stage area of the Flash movie to access the Player menu.

Figure 1.5 Choose Settings in the Flash Player 6 menu to access the player's new features.

From this menu, you can choose Settings, which opens the Macromedia Flash Player Settings dialog box. From left to right, there are four tabs in this dialog box: Privacy, Local Storage, Microphone, and Camera (**Figure 1.6**).

PRIVACY

This tab controls whether the domain from which the Flash movie (SWF file) loaded has the authority to access the user's camera and microphone. The user can choose to either accept (Allow) or reject (Deny) a request to access his/her camera or microphone. If you are developing Flash MX applications that use the `Camera.get()` or `Microphone.get()` methods, the Flash Player will automatically open this tab of the Player Settings when those methods are invoked. You can use ActionScript to open the Player Settings dialog box to this tab directly:

```
System.showSettings(0);
```

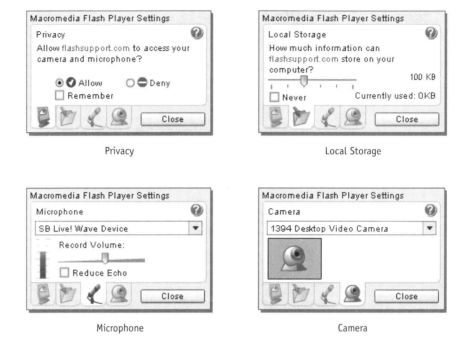

Privacy   Local Storage

Microphone   Camera

Figure 1.6 The Player Settings dialog box has four separate tabs of information.

LOCAL STORAGE

As you learned earlier in this chapter, Flash MX has added a new local SharedObject data object that can store text information on the user's machine. This tab of the Player Settings dialog box allows the user to determine how many bytes of text the Flash movies from a given domain can consume on a system. Acceptable values are None, 10 KB, 100 KB, 1 MB, 10 MB, or Unlimited. By default, 100 KB is enabled for Flash Player 6. The user is not automatically alerted when a Flash movie (SWF file) accesses and stores information locally. This tab will display, however, if a Flash movie attempts to use more disk space that its domain is allowed. You can use ActionScript to open the Local Storage settings directly:

```
System.showSettings(1);
```

MICROPHONE

This tab of the Player Settings dialog box allows the user to control which microphone port on the local machine is used, if one is available. On average, most users will only have access to one microphone. However, Macintosh users with Firewire DV camcorders have the benefit of accessing DV Audio in addition to the traditional microphone. This tab also lets you monitor the current activity on the selected microphone, and you can control the mic's record volume. You can even select the Reduce Echo check box to minimize any echoes picked up by your microphone. To open this tab directly with ActionScript, use the following code:

```
System.showSettings(2);
```

CAMERA

Similar to the Microphone tab, this tab controls which available camera is active. Flash Player 6 recognizes most USB and Firewire (IEEE 1394) cameras. To preview the video output from a camera, click the webcam icon within the tab. You can directly open this tab from a Flash movie by using the following ActionScript:

```
System.showSettings(3);
```

Handling Security Concerns with the Flash Player

In Flash Player 6, it is feasible to load two Flash movies (SWF files) from different Internet domains into the same instance of the Flash Player running in a Web browser window. For example, you can load a movie named `main.swf` from `richmediamx.com` into Level 0 of the Flash Player while you load another movie named `banner_ad.swf` from `flashsupport.com` into Level 1 of the Player. What's different in Flash Player 6 from previous versions is the fact that you can't access any ActionScript variables or objects in a Flash movie that don't originate from the source domain of the Flash movie located at Level 0 of the player.

However, you can specifically allow a Flash movie (SWF file) to be accessed by movies in different domains by using the `System.security.allowDomain()` method. The following ActionScript code added to a SWF file named `main.swf` allows any Flash movies from the domain `richmediamx.com` to access its variables and objects:

```
System.security.allowDomain("richmediamx.com");
```

Tip

As discussed earlier, Flash Player 6 can also use the SSL protocol with URL requests.

JUMPING TO MORE FLASH MX

If you're not familiar with using basic to intermediate Flash MX ActionScript, you may need to read additional material to understand the complexities of the projects discussed within this book. To learn more about Macromedia Flash MX, check out the following books:

Flash MX Bible, by Robert Reinhardt and Snow Dowd, John Wiley & Sons.

Flash MX ActionScript Bible, by Robert Reinhardt and Joey Lott, John Wiley & Sons.

For an up-to-date list of resources, check out this book's Web site at www.richmediamx.com.

SUMMARY

- Macromedia Flash MX can be used to create compelling Rich Internet Applications, which use a wide range of media and data types.

- Flash Player 6 is one the smallest and most versatile multimedia players and plug-ins available today. The Flash Player is available for all major browsers, desktop operating systems, and devices such as the Pocket PC.

- You can add embedded video to Flash movies created for Flash Player 6. Such movies can also play true streaming audio and video delivered by a server running Macromedia Flash Communication Server MX.

- No longer just for Web animations, Flash movies can be used to deliver dynamic content and data. Now you can build advanced applications that retrieve records from databases and connect several users to each other simultaneously.

- Flash MX has added a new event model to the ActionScript language. Event handlers can be defined for `MovieClip` objects without the use of `onClipEvent()`.

- Listeners allow many object types to respond to specific events. When the event is detected by the listener, any other objects subscribed to the listener receive the event as well.

- Components enable you to repurpose and reuse common user interfaces and behaviors from one movie to the next. The Flash UI Components include basic user interface elements such as a scrollbar and a check box.

- The settings of Flash Player 6 can be controlled by the user, who determines which resources a Flash movie can utilize.

In This Chapter:

2 Dreamweaver MX: The Foundation

Macromedia Dreamweaver plays an important part in the Rich Internet Application development process. But perhaps not for the reasons you might expect. This book uses Flash for the majority of front-end application design, simply because of its capabilities that can't be found in HTML.

So while you might have the impression of Dreamweaver as a tool for generating HTML pages, we're mainly interested in the other things it can do. With Dreamweaver MX, you have the capabilities to create XML Web services, database interaction, server-side scripting, JavaScript and DHTML interaction and much more.

And yes, you can use it to create HTML pages, too.

INTRODUCING DREAMWEAVER MX

For many years, Dreamweaver has been the tool of choice for professional Web developers, and the latest release only solidifies that position. While building Rich Internet Applications requires working with several different tools, Dreamweaver can act as the foundation of your Web site, handling the internal structure, creation of both client-side and server-side elements, and the management of assets, including files (such as .swf) it doesn't create itself.

 Note   Like the previous chapter, this chapter does not attempt to teach a full working knowledge of Dreamweaver MX. If you wish to spend time on the Dreamweaver MX interface, please consult the resources listed at the end of this chapter.

Dreamweaver History

Dreamweaver has changed dramatically since version 1.0 was released at the end of 1997. It was originally developed as a WYSIWYG (What You See Is What You Get) HTML design tool and is still often perceived that way. However, it has become far more than that.

Over the years, the growing technical demands of Dreamweaver users, along with the growth of Web standards, meant that while HTML design remained the cornerstone of Dreamweaver, other development features became as—if not more—important. These include:

- Cascading Style Sheets (CSS) support
- Site management features: FTP, check in/check out, site synchronization
- Dynamic HTML and JavaScript

It was these features that helped solidify its reputation. After all, if you just want to write HTML, you can do that with MS Notepad or Apple SimpleText or TextEdit. But basic text editing programs aren't ideal in these more demanding times, when you're likely to be required to create XHTML compliant pages, which are design driven by CSS, meeting Section 508 guidelines and supporting client-side JavaScript behaviors and image maps.

Note

Occasionally, you come across people with the "purist" approach that insists that all HTML should be done in text editors. Sometimes this is almost a "religious" issue, and there is not much you can do about this. But often, this notion is a result of a misconception that today's Web tools generate "sloppy" HTML like many of the early HTML WYSIWYG tools used to do.

For most of its existence, Dreamweaver remained a client-side tool. It didn't provide any help when generating server-side scripting or creating database interaction.

In 2000, when Dreamweaver was at version 3, Macromedia released Dreamweaver UltraDev 1.0. This was a special, extended version of Dreamweaver 3 that supported creation of server-side scripting in ASP, ColdFusion, or JSP. This meant you could now create database-driven sites without ever having to hand code a single line of script.

A few months after Dreamweaver UltraDev version 1.0 was released, Macromedia released Dreamweaver 4.0, and with it, Dreamweaver UltraDev 4.0. This release offered improved database capabilities for the same three server models.

Note

There wasn't an UltraDev version 2 or version 3. Macromedia jumped the version numbering to match UltraDev with its corresponding Dreamweaver version.

In June 2002, Macromedia released Dreamweaver MX. There is no Dreamweaver UltraDev MX. All the features that had previously been available in only the UltraDev release were included as standard in Dreamweaver, with a lot more additional features.

Today, Dreamweaver MX is an extremely capable application for developing visually complex, data-driven Web sites.

DREAMWEAVER MX FEATURES

In this section, you will learn about the new features in Dreamweaver MX, with an emphasis on those parts that apply to building Rich Internet Applications.

While we won't attempt to cover all of Dreamweaver's features in this book, we'll certainly be using many of them. During the process of creating Rich Internet Applications, the Dreamweaver's features you're most likely to use are discussed in the following sections.

Server-Side Scripting

Macromedia has included the capabilities for generating server-side code for ASP (both VBScript and JavaScript), ASP.NET (VB and C#), ColdFusion, JSP, and PHP.

Code libraries are built into Dreamweaver that handle many of the most common requirements when creating data-driven Web sites. Some of these are

- Connecting to databases

- Inserting and updating information

- Authenticating users

- Navigating through databases

Figure 2.1 shows the Server Behaviors panel in Dreamweaver, which is where many of the server-side scripts you will use are specified.

Figure 2.1
The Server Behavior panel in Dreamweaver MX.

Database Integration

Dreamweaver includes full support for connecting to databases, including SQL generation and visual tools for examining database structure.

The Databases panel, shown in **Figure 2.2**, is where any connected database can be examined within Dreamweaver. You can examine both the structure and the data.

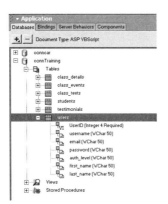

Figure 2.2
The Databases panel in Dreamweaver MX.

A common disadvantage to developing database-driven Web sites is that by using server-side script to construct a page, it's impossible to tell how that page will appear without actually viewing the page in the browser. With Dreamweaver's Live Data View feature, you can preview the page with live data from the database, while staying within the Dreamweaver design environment. You then use Dreamweaver's visual editing tools to apply formatting and layout options, instantly seeing how they will affect the finished page.

XML Web Services

New to Dreamweaver MX are capabilities for communicating with and building XML Web services. Web services are fast becoming the most popular way for computer systems to connect with each other and exchange information. They work from an industry standard and are not tied to any one manufacturer. For our purposes, Web services provide a way to use a dynamic, graphical front-end like Flash, have it connect with a variety of services, and not care about whether those have been programmed in ASP.NET, ColdFusion, or Java.

Web services can be intimidating because of jargon terms such as: XML-RPC, SOAP, WSDL, and UDDI. In later chapters, you will learn how Web services genuinely simplify the development process.

Dreamweaver has great visual tools for introspecting and using (or **consuming**) Web services. The Components panel, shown in **Figure 2.3**, allows you to easily specify a link to any available Web service. You can use Dreamweaver to create your own Web services. In Chapter 5, you'll see how to use many of the publicly accessible services, which range from applications to get weather information or exchange rates, to search engines like Google and commercial sites like Amazon.com.

Figure 2.3
The Components panel .

Note   You will learn more about XML Web Services, including the jargon of SOAP, WSDL, and UDDI in Chapter 5.

Code Editing Features

Dreamweaver MX contains vastly improved hand-coding capabilities, drawing heavily from HomeSite. HomeSite is another Macromedia product with a smaller, but more code-centric, user base. Features now include code hinting, tag editors, and full code coloring support for multiple languages, including Flash Action-Script. Earlier versions of Dreamweaver had fairly minor code editing abilities, but Dreamweaver MX is a highly capable code-editing environment.

Figure 2.4 shows an example of editing code within Dreamweaver MX.

Figure 2.4 Editing code within Dreamweaver MX.

Snippets Panel

This new feature allows snippets of code to be easily saved and reused. Snippets can be anything from sections of HTML representing page layouts or navigation bars, to JavaScript or complex server-side script routines.

Dreamweaver ships with many built-in snippets, and you can easily add your own. These can be reused on other pages in your Web site, on other sites, or saved and sent to other team members.

Components

Dreamweaver MX can build and use ColdFusion components (CFCs), which are reusable Web services that can be used by other Web pages or Flash applications. Dreamweaver aids in creating the .cfc file that makes up a ColdFusion component. As shown in **Figure 2.5**, it supplies menu-driven methods for creating the component.

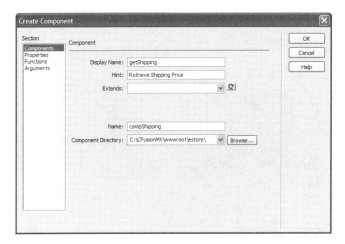

Figure 2.5 Creating a ColdFusion Component (CFC).

Xref

For more information about ColdFusion components, read Chapter 3.

CLIENT-SIDE DEVELOPMENT

Of course, the core of Dreamweaver has always been its HTML design abilities. And while this book mainly uses Flash MX for front-end design, Dreamweaver has at least three obvious places where it often makes more sense to use conventional HTML pages rather than dynamic Flash applications:

- **Administrative screens:** In this book, we use Flash to present users with a graphically intensive, well designed front-end. However, the nitty-gritty of your site administration may well be more practical and down-to-earth than that. Essentially, a common requirement for admin sections of the site is to make them as simple as possible. This is not to say that good information architecture and design don't play a part—they do. But for administrative screens, that part is often simplicity and clarity. Dreamweaver is ideal for this. It can create complex data-driven pages very quickly.

- **Proof-of-concepts:** When connecting to a database or XML Web service, you may want to ensure that you're first getting the data you want, before you start manipulating it in graphical applications created with Flash. Often, it is an easier process to make sure that your logic runs on basic Web pages before creating complex Flash movies to hold the results.

- **Catering to the 4% of people who don't have Flash:** Of course, the purpose of this book is Rich Internet Applications; you're not going to be able to deliver real-time video collaborative applications to someone who still insists on using a text-only browser like Lynx. But chances are that at least some of your rich media site can be adequately presented to users who may be visiting from media-challenged browsers, whether those are on older computers, smart phones, or PDAs.

HTML Page Design

Many Web developers have encountered the requirement to develop two versions of a Web site: one with Flash, one without. Though we have no problems with this scenario, we're not going to do it in this book. We show where Dreamweaver might fit in a rich media situation, but this is not a book about building complex HTML designs.

However, as you saw in the last chapter, Flash MX now contains several components that approximate standard GUI elements for building applications: scrollbars, check boxes, radio buttons and so on. But let's face it, what they're attempting to approximate is built into HTML already. If we're going to build simple pages for data input or output, we're going to use Dreamweaver.

Creating Flash Pages

Flash movies don't run in a vacuum. True, they can be run as a standalone executable (a projector) outside of the browser, but for typical Internet delivery they're contained within an HTML page. Though Flash can generate some basic HTML to hold your SWF files, to have complete control over positioning and page design, you're likely to use Dreamweaver.

Note

More about Dreamweaver and Flash integration can be found later in this chapter.

JavaScript

Dreamweaver MX contains substantial features for adding client-side JavaScript behaviors. Why do we care? Because JavaScript is one of the better ways of detecting whether the visitors to our site can even *see* our rich media. Flash detection is important for proper implementation of a Rich Internet Application, and it's possible to streamline that process with Dreamweaver.

While we can certainly add Flash detection routines by hand coding, the availability of Dreamweaver extensions like the Flash Dispatcher makes the creation of detection schemes much easier.

The Flash Dispatcher is part of Macromedia's Flash Deployment Kit, which can be found at www.macromedia.com/software/flash/download/deployment_kit/.

SERVER-SIDE DEVELOPMENT

That is enough for the basic client-side abilities of Dreamweaver. Let's be honest, that's not where the "juicy stuff" lies. What we are really interested in is the server-side generation abilities of Dreamweaver: the XML Web service abilities and Dreamweaver's integration with scripting languages like ColdFusion and ASP.NET.

Supported Languages

Dreamweaver MX added two new server models to the three (ASP, JSP and ColdFusion) that were previously available in Dreamweaver UltraDev 4. This section briefly covers each of the scripting languages that Dreamweaver MX supports and the reasons you might choose using each.

COLDFUSION

ColdFusion and Dreamweaver work wonderfully together. That's no big surprise because Macromedia makes them both. ColdFusion Markup Language (CFML) is a tag-based language, meaning that its structure is considered intuitive by developers coming from an HTML background. It's a quick and powerful language. ColdFusion MX also integrates well with Flash MX.

Xref

You will learn more about ColdFusion in the next chapter.

ASP

Active Server Pages (ASP) is a Microsoft technology. ASP was probably the most popular choice of server models for users of Dreamweaver UltraDev and had arguably the best resources for support.

ASP is not a language; the term describes the server architecture. ASP pages are typically written in either VBScript or JavaScript (Dreamweaver MX supports both). ASP is available on Microsoft Web servers by default. There is no need to buy extra software.

ASP.NET

ASP.NET is the next version of Microsoft's successful ASP platform. However, the changes in this new version are so substantial that it is considered a completely separate server platform. ASP.NET is part of Microsoft's huge .NET initiative for software integration across every device and system.

Like ASP, ASP.NET is not a language. ASP.NET pages can be written in many languages, but the two most common are VB.NET or C# (pronounced "C sharp").

JSP

Java Server Pages (JSP) is a server model that can be found on many different Web servers, including IBM WebSphere and JRun (also from Macromedia). JSP is more commonly found as a server platform in corporate environments where Java expertise already exists. We won't specifically be covering JSP in this book, though virtually all the methods that we use are applicable to any server platform.

PHP

PHP support was one of the most requested features in UltraDev 4.0 and is a welcome addition to Dreamweaver MX. It's an open source platform and is extremely popular on Linux servers. Typically, PHP is found running in conjunction with the MySQL database. PHP and MySQL talk very easily to each other. Because of this, Macromedia does not include any built-in support for any other databases apart from MySQL when using PHP. Other server models support a variety of databases.

XML Web Services

Earlier in this chapter, we talked a little bit about XML Web services, for their ability in making life easier for the developer and for the popularity that they are rapidly gaining in the Web development world.

XML Web services can be found across a variety of platforms, including ColdFusion, ASP.NET, and JSP. The great thing about using XML Web services is that you don't need to know how they were programmed; they are platform and language agnostic. They're designed to make system-to-system communication fast and easy, without having to know the operations of every computer with which you are trying to talk. Anyone can create a Web service and make it accessible by any other system that understands Web services.

Figure 2.6 shows the XMethods Web site. XMethods is one of several directories of publicly accessible XML Web services.

Note

Web services are covered in more detail in Chapter 5.

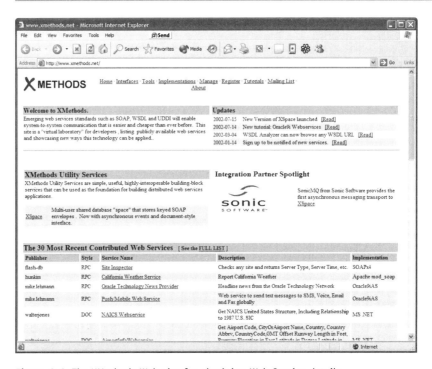

Figure 2.6 The XMethods Web site for obtaining Web Service details.

DREAMWEAVER INTEGRATION

Dreamweaver MX works extremely well with Macromedia's other MX products. They've all been designed to integrate with each other, and the interface for all the MX products has been designed to make switching between the applications as seamless as possible. This section will cover some of the basic features you may wish to know about when working with the MX suite of products.

Dreamweaver and Flash

Because you're likely to be using Flash in conjunction with other HTML and graphical elements, the workflow integration between Dreamweaver MX and Flash MX is extremely helpful. Some of the integration features you're likely to use include:

- **Creating and editing ActionScript files:** Large amounts of ActionScript can be difficult to work with in the small Actions panel within Flash MX. Dreamweaver supports full ActionScript code syntax highlighting and editing, allowing you to create large and complex ActionScript files. These files can be saved externally and imported into your Flash movie when it's published.

- **Launching and editing Flash:** When editing an HTML page in Dreamweaver that contains a Flash .swf, you can click on one button from within Dreamweaver that launches Flash with the corresponding FLA file for the SWF file. You can then edit the Flash movie, and when you're finished editing, Flash will automatically save the FLA document, publish the SWF file and take you back to Dreamweaver MX.

- **Updating links:** Using Dreamweaver's Site Map View, you can change a hyperlink embedded in a Flash movie (SWF file) directly from Dreamweaver without having to use Flash at all.

Dreamweaver and ColdFusion

In previous versions of Dreamweaver, support for ColdFusion was available but marginal. If you were a serious ColdFusion developer, you used ColdFusion Studio instead. With Dreamweaver MX, this is no longer necessary. It contains all the features that were previously only found within ColdFusion Studio, including excellent code editing features, integrated debugging, and reference material.

Note

You will learn more about ColdFusion in the next chapter.

INTERFACE ESSENTIALS

While this chapter does not attempt to teach Dreamweaver MX, you should know some of the main features of the interface. This is particularly important for two groups of developers:

- Those migrating from earlier versions of the product
- Those wanting to know the Dreamweaver features emphasized when developing Rich Internet Applications

Note

If you are a beginner to Dreamweaver, start by exploring the tutorials found in the Help menu.

The new Dreamweaver MX workspace is substantially different from earlier versions of the program. As shown in **Figure 2.7**, it is a single integrated workspace, which allows you to work on multiple documents simultaneously.

Note

The Macintosh version of Dreamweaver MX does not offer the option of the single integrated workspace, instead presenting separate floating windows, similar to Dreamweaver 4.

Document Window

The Document window contains the page on which you're working. Like Word, opening Dreamweaver opens a blank document by default. The Document window has different views available that you use depending on your task. When developing static Web sites, the standard WYSIWYG view suffices, but when developing data-driven sites (and especially when creating ColdFusion components or XML Web services) you need to be able to view the actual code of your page. The different views of the Document window can be selected from the bar at the top of the screen, as shown in **Figure 2.8**

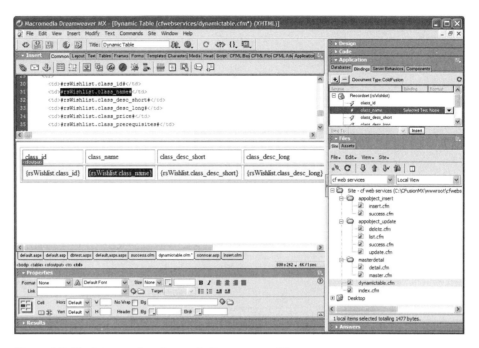

Figure 2.7 The integrated workspace in Dreamweaver MX.

The three views are

- **Design View:** The Design View is a "best guess" of how this page will look in a Web browser. Obviously, different Web browsers represent different things in different ways, but the Design View is a good approximation of how the page will look in a recent (4.0+) version of Internet Explorer or Netscape Navigator.

- **Code View:** The Code View is a way you can see the "behind the scenes" code that comprises the page on which you working. The page could be HTML, ASP, or ColdFusion. As mentioned earlier, in Dreamweaver MX, the code editing abilities are much enhanced from previous versions.

Figure 2.8 The Document window allows selection of different page views.

■ **Design/Code View:** This view, shown in **Figure 2.9,** offers a split view of the code and the design together. Highlighting a page element in the Design View section of the screen will also highlight its corresponding code in the Code View section. This can be very useful for finding elusive problems in your page code.

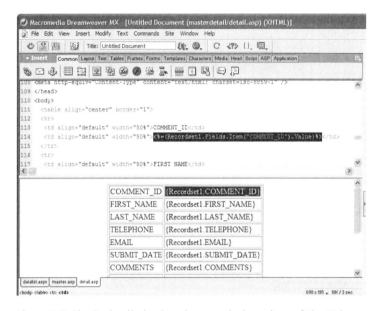

Figure 2.9 The Design/Code view shows equivalent views of the Web page.

Property Inspector

The Property inspector, shown in **Figure 2.10**, is a central part of working with Dreamweaver. It's a context-sensitive panel that has different available options depending on what has been highlighted on the page itself. For example, when text is selected, the Property inspector allows editing of hyperlinks, font, and CSS style. If a Flash movie is selected, the Property inspector shows editable attributes like height, width, filename, and background color.

Figure 2.10 The Property Inspector changes depending on the item selected.

Insert Bar

The Insert Bar, shown in **Figure 2.11,** allows you to visually add elements to the current page. These elements can be anything from images and Flash movies to advanced ColdFusion objects or database navigation bars. Everything that can be added from the Insert Bar can also be added in another way, either through a menu, panel, or keyboard shortcut. The advantage of the Insert Bar is that it groups elements by their type.

Figure 2.11 The Insert Bar is used to visually add elements to the current page.

Panel Groups

The panel groups are located by default on the right-hand side of the screen. Although, the position can be changed if you prefer a layout similar to that found in HomeSite, with the panels on the left. As rich media developers, we're more interested in some panels than in others.

Panel groups are, like almost everything in Dreamweaver, all customizable to suit your preferences. But in this chapter, we'll explore the panels as they appear by default.

- **Code Panel Group:** The Code panel group contains three panels: Tag Inspector, Snippets, and Reference. The Tag Inspector presents a hierarchical and editable view of the selected tag on the page. Snippets allow you to create and reuse sections of code. The Reference panel contains information on all the languages you're likely to use while developing: HTML, JavaScript, ASP, and ColdFusion.

- **Application Panel Group:** This panel group is the core of data-driven site development. It contains four panels: Database, Bindings, Server Behaviors, and Components. The Database panel offers a visual way of connecting to different databases, and once connected, to browse their structure and data. Next, the Bindings panel is where you determine the dynamic data you wish to place on each page. The Server Behaviors panel, shown in

Figure 2.12, allows you to specify what you want to do with that data, and the Components panel is for introspecting and creating Web services.

- **Files Panel Group:** The Files panel group is where you handle the organization and arrangement of your Web site. It contains every file that makes up your site, either viewable in folder order in the Site panel, or grouped into different types (images, Flash movies, or templates) in the Assets panel.

Now, having copies of your files well organized on your own machine is all very good, but you want to be able to ensure that the organization carries over to the Web server.

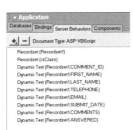

Figure 2.12
The Server Behaviors panel shows the current server behaviors on the page.

SITE MANAGEMENT

The other applications we'll use in this book—Flash, Flash Communication Server, and ColdFusion—have no inherent site management capabilities. Dreamweaver is an ideal choice for the task. It offers many options and abilities for creating a coherent site, not just a collection of stand-alone pages and files without rhyme or reason.

Site Maintenance

To use Dreamweaver effectively, you need to define your site properly before you begin development. Once this has been done, Dreamweaver is very capable at handling any changes you may make inside your site. If you move a Web page from one folder to another, Dreamweaver will ensure that any hyperlinks that refer to that page are updated. This can be an enormous help when working on enterprise-level sites with hundreds of thousands of pages.

Tip

You should always plan your site structure well in advance. Although Dreamweaver MX is very capable of allowing you to reorganize the files and folders within your Web site and still keep the hyperlinks intact, that kind of behavior can lead to link rot (expiring or incorrect URLs) for search engines and other Web sites that link to your pages.

Uploading

Probably still the most common way to upload files from your personal development computer to a Web server is FTP. Once you have defined an FTP connection correctly in your Dreamweaver site definition, both basic and advanced FTP operations are straightforward.

Dreamweaver also offers options for connecting to a Web server over a local area network, or by connecting to versioning systems such as SourceSafe or WebDAV.

Check In/Check Out

When working in a team environment, an important concern is to avoid any conflicts when updating Web pages. For example, one member of the team (Joan) downloads the index page to begin substantial work on it. Then someone else (Fred) downloads the same old version of the page and makes a small change. Joan uploads the page with all the new functionality, and then Fred comes along a moment later and overwrites it with the slightly changed older version effectively deleting all of Joan's hard work.

The Check in/Check out abilities of Dreamweaver are designed to prevent such basic inconsistencies. They are a simple (but certainly not foolproof) way of preventing conflicts when two or more people are editing a site at the same time or even if one developer is working on a site using several different computers.

Check in/Check out is an option that should be set when you are creating the definition for your Web site. It works by creating a small file, ending in .lck, which tells other copies of Dreamweaver that this page is currently being worked on.

Tip

One thing to be aware of is that Check in/Check out does not prevent someone from manually editing a file or overwriting it with an FTP program. Only a copy of Dreamweaver will recognize that a page has been checked out by another copy of Dreamweaver.

Cloaking

A welcome addition to Dreamweaver MX is cloaking, which allows you to exclude certain files from any upload or download file operations. The typical reason for cloaking is to prevent upload of certain source documents to the Web server if they are not needed. Examples of these types of file include:

- **FLA files:** The source files for Flash movies should not be uploaded to the Web server. The visitor to your site only needs to see the SWF file.

- **PNG files:** Even though PNG is a legitimate (though rarely used) Web image format, we're referring to PNG files as the source documents for creating Fireworks images, which typically result in a GIF or JPEG file for use on the Web.

- **AS files:** External Flash ActionScript files are used by Flash when publishing the SWF file. They do not need to exist on the Web server.

Site Synchronization

Site synchronization is a feature of Dreamweaver that allows you to determine if there is a time distinction between files on the Web server and files on the development machine. You use it in a couple of different ways. Most commonly, you use synchronization to make sure that your development machine has the latest versions of the files and more recent ones don't exist on the Web server. You can also use it if you are creating a site definition for a Web site that currently exists. By synchronizing the files you can effectively grab everything from the Web server and bring it down to your own computer.

Before it carries out any file operations, Dreamweaver presents you with a dialog box, shown in **Figure 2.13**, where you confirm all the file operations that will happen in the synchronization of a site. Dreamweaver does not retrieve or upload files without your explicit permission.

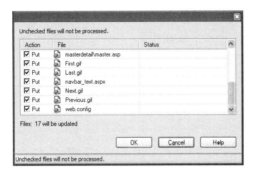

Figure 2.13 Synchronizing sites requires confirmation at each stage.

Site Reports

There are a number of useful reports that Dreamweaver can create for you. These include lists of broken links, reports on files that have been checked out, and untitled documents. These are available through the Site Reports panel or the menu option Site > Reports.

Three other panels in Dreamweaver, the Validation, Link Checker, and Target Browser Check are available through Window > Results. They can generate several reports on a variety of things including accessibility options, validation of HTML to W3C standards, and whether you're using any features that don't exist on your target browser, as shown in **Figure 2.14**.

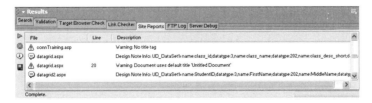

Figure 2.14 The Site Reports panel shows a variety of errors and warnings.

EXTENDING DREAMWEAVER

One of the best features about Dreamweaver is that if it doesn't do everything you want straight out of the box, you can make it do what you want.

Dreamweaver extensions add functionality to the program. This can range from something small, such as a routine for number conversion, to substantial changes to the program, like adding e-commerce shopping cart abilities and several new items to the Dreamweaver menus.

Macromedia Exchange

The Macromedia Exchange, found at `http://www.macromedia.com/exchange`, is a central repository for hundreds of extensions developed by scores of companies and developers. If Dreamweaver doesn't have a particular function that you're looking for, it's always worth checking on the exchange to see if someone else has created that functionality and made it available for others to download.

At the time of this writing, Dreamweaver MX is so recent that there are not many extensions specifically for the MX version of the product. This is likely to change. Macromedia actively sought the support of extension developers during the beta program.

Not all extensions are placed on the Macromedia site. Other sites for finding extensions include:

```
www.yaromat.com
www.basic-ultradev.com
www.massimocorner.com
www.ultradevextensions.com
www.charon.co.uk
www.interakt.ro
```

When you download an extension, it typically comes in the format of an MXP file. Double-clicking on this file opens up the Macromedia Extension Manager, shown in **Figure 2.15**. The process of adding the new behaviors to Dreamweaver is automated.

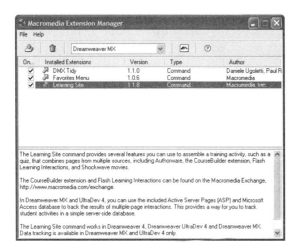

Figure 2.15 The Macromedia Extension Manager.

Commercial Extensions

Dreamweaver exchange, while extensive, does not contain every available option for extending Dreamweaver. There are several commercially available extensions. Some worth mentioning include:

www.ultrasuite.com
www.webassist.com
www.basic-ultradev.com/extensions/
www.magicbeat.com
www.projectseven.com
www.dwmxzone.com
www.webassist.com

Prices range from a few dollars (in US currency) to over a hundred. While this might seem expensive, you should always weigh it against how much it would cost you to personally develop the behavior yourself. For example, the most expensive extensions tend to be those for e-commerce, always a time-consuming task. If an expense of $50 saves you three days of work, why not spend the $50, finish your page, and take the next two days off?

> ### LEARNING MORE ABOUT DREAMWEAVER
>
> As you can tell, Dreamweaver is a wide-ranging subject. Here's where you go and what you do if you need to know more about Dreamweaver.
>
> First, complete the tutorials built into Dreamweaver. Other excellent tutorials are available on the Macromedia Web site.
>
> Books for learning Dreamweaver include:
>
> *Dreamweaver MX: Training From The Source,* by Khristine Page, available from Macromedia Press.
>
> *Developing Database-Driven Sites with Dreamweaver MX,* by Simon Allardice, available from O'Reilly and Associates.
>
> For an up-to-date list of resources, check out this book's Web site at www.mxbook.com.

SUMMARY

- In this chapter, we explored Dreamweaver's basic features and how Dreamweaver fits into the process of developing Rich Internet Applications.

- Our interest in Dreamweaver is not so much for its HTML design abilities, but for its server-side scripting abilities and how we can use it to generate the code to create and consume XML Web services.

- We explored the basic interface elements.

- Dreamweaver can be used for site management in ways that the other programs we're working with cannot.

- Dreamweaver can be extended for additional functionality if it does not do what you want straight out of the box.

In This Chapter:

3 ColdFusion MX: The Application Engine

It's quite possible to create amazing Flash or HTML experiences on the Web that only require client-side development. Meaning, you make Flash movies that have great graphics, interesting sounds, and rich interactivity that captivate a visitor for the duration of the experience. However, if you want to enable a Flash movie or presentation with capabilities that integrate live data, you are heading into territory that requires more than client-side ActionScript or JavaScript. In order to develop a Flash Rich Internet Application that performs a function or operation beyond a one-time use, you need one or more server-side technologies to process and manage data. In this chapter, you will learn about the premiere application server from Macromedia, ColdFusion MX. While there are several application servers available (both proprietary and open-source) from other software companies, ColdFusion's close integration with other MX products such as Macromedia Flash MX and Macromedia Dreamweaver MX makes it an excellent choice for Web application development. This tight integration allows you to easily learn server-side scripting and rapidly development Web applications.

Note   Macromedia ColdFusion MX is part of the Studio MX software package. For more information about each edition of ColdFusion, see the "Fitting ColdFusion MX into Your Workflow" section later in this chapter.

An Overview of ColdFusion MX

For anyone new to Web application development, the concept of an application server may be foreign. What is an application server exactly? In short, an application server (or app server, also known as "middleware") provides the means for a Web resource, such as an HTML document or Flash movie (SWF file), to access various data resources, like databases or media creation utilities. Application servers can also perform calculations or manipulations to data retrieved from these resources. This process is commonly referred to as the "business logic" of a specific application running on an app server.

Note   An application server can run on the same computer that is running a site's Web server. Many hosting packages from ISPs offer integrated application servers, usually as an additional fee to the regular Web hosting cost. Also, most operating systems refer to an application server as a "service." For example, "ColdFusion MX Application Server" is the name of the Windows service for ColdFusion MX.

There are several application servers available for commercial enterprise-level Web sites (see the sidebar at the end of this section for more information). Some app servers are seamlessly integrated with a Web server, such as Microsoft's ASP.NET framework, which is freely available to anyone using a Microsoft IIS Web server. Other middleware applications, like Macromedia ColdFusion MX, are separate software installations that work in tandem with a Web server. Just about every application server processes information by parsing information requested by a template document, as shown in **Figure 3.1**. A user requests a document that is a script written in the language used by the middleware software (step 1). When the Web server receives the request for the script (step 2), the server recognizes that the document should be processed by the middleware (step 3). The middleware processes the script document, fetching data from a database and/or performing other calculations or manipulations within the script (step 4). The middleware creates a new document integrated with the dynamic data (step 5). The document is passed back to the Web server (step 6), which then sends the document to the application on the user's machine that made the initial request (step 7).

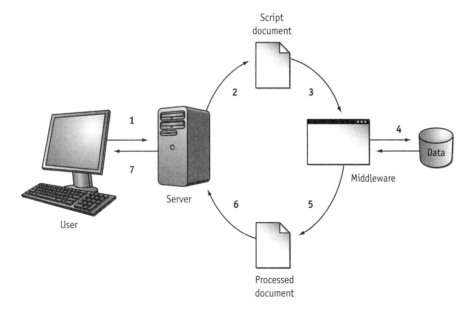

Figure 3.1 An overview of the application server process.

While most application servers share similar features, Macromedia ColdFusion MX was specifically designed to mesh with the powerful capabilities of Flash Player 6. At an authoring level, ColdFusion MX is tightly integrated with Macromedia Dreamweaver MX and Flash MX. In the following sections, you will learn how ColdFusion works together with these programs to build rich media applications.

Connecting Client Interfaces to Remote and Dynamic Resources

ColdFusion MX, like other application servers, gives you the ability to develop Flash movies and HTML documents that integrate dynamic data. Most documents that a user requests from a Web site are static pages, which means that the document doesn't undergo any transformation when the Web server sends it to the user.

 Note
Many Web pages do contain client-side scripting, such as JavaScript, that can add dynamic features to any given page.

JPEG images for a site's home page, for example, are usually just downloaded straight from the Web server. However, static data has a major problem: it stays the same, from one visit to the next. You, as a developer, can keep changing the HTML code, Flash movie contents, and JPEG images to keep the content fresh, but such an approach is a time-consuming task growing exponentially as you add more and more content to a Web site.

Enter ColdFusion MX, an application server that allows you to tap into the resources that a business or organization has in place on a network, such as database, directory, and mail services. ColdFusion MX uses a relatively simple tag-based language to program applications. This tag-based language, called CFML (or **C**old**F**usion **M**arkup **L**anguage), resembles the syntax of other markup languages like HTML. CFML documents are saved with a .cfm (or .cfml) or .cfc file extension. We will take a look at the structure of CFML and the differences among ColdFusion document types later in this chapter.

Note

Examples throughout this book show you how to use CFML for specific purposes related to the functionality of each project. The CFML Reference Guide PDF has over 700 pages of tag names and descriptions, which can be viewed online at: download.macromedia.com/pub/coldfusion/documentation/cfmx_cfml_reference.pdf For more ColdFusion MX resources, see the sidebar at the end of this chapter.

TEXT-BASED DYNAMIC DATA

ColdFusion documents are typically used to request information from a database and return that information in a parsed document to the user. For example, you may want to provide a search field in an HTML document, as shown in **Figure 3.2**. The steps that follow are an analysis of using dynamic data in an HTML document.

1. The user types a term into the form field and submits the request to the site's Web server. In this example, the search term is appended to the URL of the requested ColdFusion document, with the syntax search.cfm?orderID=10012.

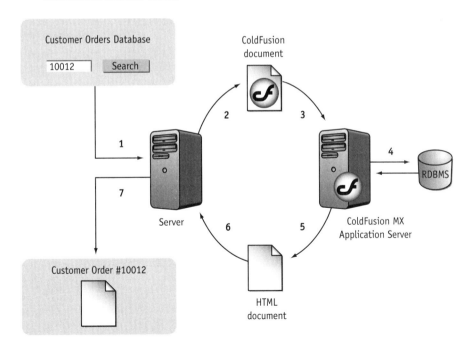

Figure 3.2 Sending and receiving data with HTML documents.

2. The Web server recognizes that the requested document has a .cfm file extension and passes the request along to the ColdFusion MX Application Server.

3. The ColdFusion server reads the CFM document, which contains a query to a data source, pointing to a RDBMS (Relational Database Management System). The query uses the orderID value passed to the CFM document in step 1.

4. The RDBMS receives the query and returns a record (or multiple records) to the application server.

5. The ColdFusion server builds an HTML table from each of the fields within the returned recordset and returns the fully built HTML document to the Web server.

6. The Web server returns the HTML document back to the user's Web browser.

As this process demonstrates, the original CFM document is not actually served to the user. Any scripting you have described in the document is kept safe. The user only sees the requested data in the context of a structure specified by the CFM document.

For Rich Internet Applications that are created with Macromedia Flash MX, you can use the LoadVars object, the loadVariables() method of the MovieClip object, or the XML object in ActionScript to request data through a ColdFusion document. In **Figure 3.3**, the process of a Flash movie (SWF file) requesting data from a CF document is shown. The following steps highlight each stage of the process.

1. The user downloads a Flash movie (SWF file) from the Web server. This Flash movie has an empty Dynamic text field named news_txt and an empty MovieClip object named image_mc on the stage. When the movie loads into the Flash Player, a LoadVars object requests a CFM file, which will return URL-encoded text data to the Flash movie.

2. When the Web server receives the request for the CFM document, the document is passed to the ColdFusion MX Application Server.

3. The server reads the CFM document and retrieves the text and image associated with the current date from the RDBMS.

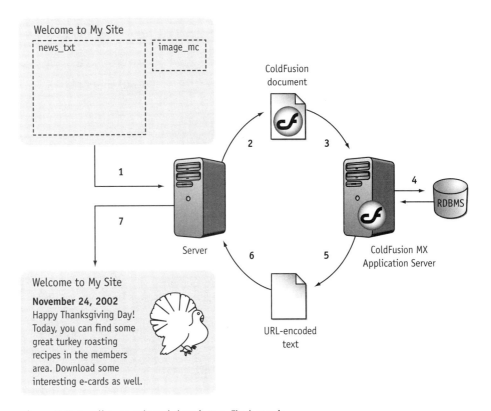

Figure 3.3 Loading text-based data into a Flash movie.

4. The ColdFusion server constructs a URL-encoded text document, specifying the body text and image URL for the Flash movie's empty TextField and MovieClip instances. The following text demonstrates the data shown in **Figure 3.3**.

```
body=%3CB%3ENovember%2024%2C%202002%3C%2FB%3E%3CBR%3EHappy%20Thanksgiving%20D
ay%21%20Today%2C%20you%20can%20find%20some%20great%20turkey%20roasting%20reci
pes%20in%20the%20members%20area%2E%20Download%20some%20interesting%20e%2Dcard
s%20as%20well%2E&imageURL=images%2Fturkey%2Ejpg
```

5. The URL-encoded data is returned to the LoadVars object in the Flash movie. When the data is loaded, the news_txt field displays the text from the body variable, and the image_mc loads the JPEG image specified in the imageURL variable.

Note You can use ColdFusion to generate JPEG, GIF, or SWF files on the fly, for charts or other data-sensitive imagery.

You can also create dynamic XML text data with a ColdFusion document for use in HTML or Flash sites.

FLASH REMOTING DATA

By far the most exciting new development with ColdFusion MX and Flash Player 6 technology is Flash Remoting. Flash Remoting is a method of data transfer from a gateway service on an application server to a Flash movie. Fortunately, if you have ColdFusion MX installed on a computer, then you already have access to the Flash Remoting–it's built into the application server.

Xref Flash Remoting is available for a variety of non-Macromedia application servers. Read Chapter 7 for more information regarding Flash Remoting.

Unlike other data transfer methods available to Flash movies, Flash Remoting is a binary format, called AMF (**A**ction **M**essaging **F**ormat). AMF allows a Flash movie to receive true data objects from an application server like ColdFusion MX. For example, you can create a database query in a ColdFusion document that retrieves a set of records. These records can be returned directly to a Flash movie, where the data can be easily bound to user interface elements like the ComboBox or BarChart component. Because of its streamlined data format, Flash Player 6 can load and integrate Flash Remoting data more quickly and efficiently than equivalent XML or URL-encoded data structures. In **Figure 3.4**, you can see how a Flash movie can use dynamic data from Flash Remoting and ColdFusion MX. The following steps describe the process in more detail.

1. A standard Flash movie (SWF file) from a Web server is loaded into a user's browser. This movie has an empty instance of the ListBox component, named `employeeList_lb`, and an empty Dynamic text field instance, named `personInfo_txt`. As soon as the movie loads, a connection is made to the Flash Remoting service of the ColdFusion server.

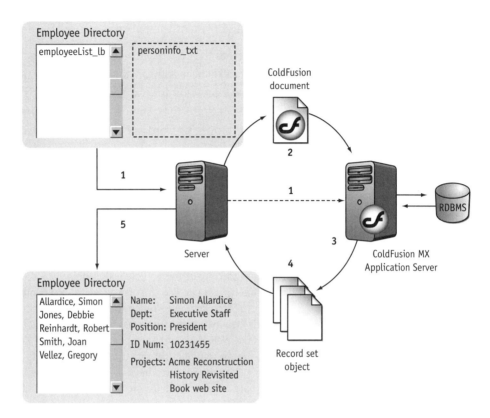

Figure 3.4 Populating Flash UI elements with Flash Remoting data from ColdFusion MX.

2. The Flash movie requests a specific service over the Flash Remoting connection. The service is defined with a ColdFusion document, which is usually a CFC file (ColdFusion Component). You will learn more about CFC files later in this chapter.

3. The Flash movie invokes a method defined within the service, passing parameters from the Flash movie to the service. For example, the method name of the service could be getEmployeeList(), and the parameter passed could be "all". The ColdFusion server executes this method in the CFC document, which sends a query to a RDBMS. The RDBMS returns a series of records (called a recordset) to the ColdFusion service.

4. The service gathers and returns the entire recordset from the RDBMS.

5. The Flash movie receives the recordset as a RecordSet object, which allows the Flash movie to quickly access information from the query. The RecordSet object is used as a data provider for the employeeList_lb instance, which displays each employee's name. When the user selects an employee's name, the details of that employee's record are shown in the personInfo_txt field.

Xref

You will learn how to create Flash Remoting-enabled movies in Chapters 8 and 9.

COLDFUSION AND WDDX

Allaire, the company that created ColdFusion technology before Macromedia's merger, developed a data format called WDDX, which stands for **W**eb **D**istributed **D**ata e**X**change. The CFML tag <cfwddx> allows you to convert native ColdFusion objects and data into the WDDX format, or vice versa. Actually, you can use this tag to perform a number of conversions (see the CFWDDX entry in the CFML Reference Guide for more information). WDDX packages native ColdFusion data into XML data structures. Because XML has fast become a standard of data exchange over the Web, the built-in support of WDDX in ColdFusion (since version 4) allows developers to create Web applications that exchanged data across various systems. Each end of the system, though, needs to have a WDDX module to translate the XML structure back into native data objects. Modules are available for several technologies including ECMAScript/JavaScript, ASP/COM, Perl, PHP, and Java. For more general information on WDDX, review the following FAQ:

www.openwddx.org/faq/

For Rich Internet Applications using Flash movies, Flash Remoting, and application servers such as ColdFusion MX, you might find less use for WDDX than you might in other scenarios. As you will learn in Chapter 7, Flash Remoting enables incredibly fast binary data transfers of entire record sets and other data-typed information between an RDBMS and Flash movie.

Creating Applications with ColdFusion MX

You can make ColdFusion documents in any text editor, from ones as simple as Microsoft Notepad or Apple TextEdit to Macromedia Dreamweaver MX. Dreamweaver MX, however, offers many features specific to ColdFusion MX development. Dreamweaver MX is an IDE, or **I**ntegrated **D**evelopment **E**nvironment, for several application servers, including Microsoft ASP.NET, PHP, and ColdFusion MX. Dreamweaver MX features include:

- **Code syntax highlighting, hinting and tag completion:** CFML tags are recognized by Dreamweaver MX, and displayed as red colored text. As you type a CFML tag in Dreamweaver MX, a code hint menu (shown in **Figure 3.5**) appears, allowing you to quickly add attributes to a tag. Dreamweaver MX also creates the closing tag automatically.

Figure 3.5
Code hinting in
Dreamweaver MX.

- **Easy access to data sources, server behaviors, and components:** The Application panel in Dreamweaver MX (**Figure 3.6**) is the command center for ColdFusion MX development. The Databases tab enables you to view databases that are configured for the ColdFusion MX server. This panel also has a Server Behaviors tab, allowing you to create recordsets and queries with data sources. The Components tab displays the ColdFusion components and Web services available on the server as well. (You will learn more about ColdFusion components (or CFC files) in the next section.)

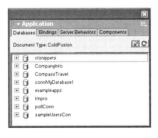

Figure 3.6
The Application panel
in Dreamweaver MX.

- **CFML insertion and reference tools:** The Insert toolbar in Dreamweaver MX (**Figure 3.7**) has several tabs featuring several CFML tags and objects. The

Reference tab of the Code panel (**Figure 3.8**) includes a complete dictionary of CFML tags.

Figure 3.7 The CFML Basic tab of the Insert bar in Dreamweaver MX.

Figure 3.8
The Reference tab of the Code panel in Dreamweaver MX.

ColdFusion Studio is no longer a separate product. Most, if not all, of the features of ColdFusion Studio have been included in Dreamweaver MX. Macromedia includes HomeSite+ on the Dreamweaver MX installation CD as well. HomeSite+ is an updated version of the Homesite application that was included with ColdFusion Studio. You can use HomeSite+ to author ColdFusion and HTML documents.

We will discuss the structure of ColdFusion documents in the next section. You can create ColdFusion documents in Dreamweaver MX for standard HTML-based Web sites or for rich media Flash movies.

This book focuses on using ColdFusion documents employed by Flash Remoting to connect Flash movies to dynamic data sources. See the sidebar at the end of this chapter for other resources pertaining to ColdFusion and HTML development.

You can view Web services, including ColdFusion components, from the Service Browser in Macromedia Flash MX. See Chapter 7 for more information on the Service Browser.

After you have created a ColdFusion document in Dreamweaver MX, the document is saved on a ColdFusion-enabled server. ColdFusion MX has its own built-in standalone Web server. By default, the ColdFusion Web server runs on port 8500, and the default root of the Web server is the wwwroot folder located in the installation directory of ColdFusion MX. If you installed ColdFusion MX on a Windows computer, you can locate the wwwroot folder at the following location:

```
C:\CFusionMX\wwwroot\
```

You can place standard HTML documents or media files in the wwwroot folder, to be served along with ColdFusion documents that are saved here. For example, if you placed a ColdFusion document named search.cfm in the wwwroot folder, you could view it in a Web browser by using the following address:

```
http://localhost:8500/search.cfm
```

The built-in Web server of ColdFusion MX should only be used for development and testing. For live production, use a dedicated Web server such as Microsoft IIS or Apache.

If you have a Windows computer running Microsoft IIS and you choose the IIS option during the installation of ColdFusion MX, your Web sites hosted by IIS should automatically have a connector to the ColdFusion MX Application Server. Therefore, you can place ColdFusion documents into site folders hosted by IIS. You will learn more about the ColdFusion MX installations later in this chapter.

If you installed ColdFusion MX as a stand-alone server, you can reconfigure the setup without reinstalling the software. See the sidebar "IIS Versus Stand-alone Server for ColdFusion MX" later in this chapter.

COMPARING COLDFUSION MX TO OTHER SERVER TECHNOLOGIES

PHP, Microsoft ASP, and ASP.NET are among the popular application scripting languages in use on Web servers today. You can use these technologies to create dynamic HTML pages in Dreamweaver MX. You can also feed text-based data from these environments to Flash movies, using the client-side ActionScript objects LoadVars and XML, as well as the load-Variables() method of the MovieClip object. However, ColdFusion MX and Macromedia JRun 4 are the only application servers that already have the Flash Remoting gateway service preconfigured. While you can purchase and install Flash Remoting MX for a Microsoft .NET server, ColdFusion resources for Flash development are more widely available than other scripting environment. At the time of this writing, Flash Remoting MX was not available for PHP applications.

UNDERSTANDING DYNAMIC PAGES AND COLDFUSION COMPONENTS

When you create applications with ColdFusion MX, one or more ColdFusion documents integrate dynamic data with HTML pages or Flash movies. There are three types of ColdFusion documents: CFM, CFC, and ASR files. In this section, you will learn about the structures of these documents and how each document type is used within a Web application.

CFM Documents

A standard ColdFusion document has a .cfm or .cfml file extension. When a ColdFusion-enabled Web server receives a request for a CFM file, the Web server tells the ColdFusion MX Application Server to process, or parse, the CFM file. The ColdFusion server then looks for CFML tags within the document, executes the operations specified by the tags, and returns a new document to the Web server.

 Note

It's important to remember that the end user never sees the CFML tags that you author in a ColdFusion document. If the user views the source of a ColdFusion-processed document in the Web browser, standard HTML tags and text are displayed.

A CFM file can contain a mixture of regular text or HTML tags combined with CFML tags. It's beyond the scope of this book to cover every tag in CFML; however, you do learn how to program a variety of processes throughout examples in future chapters. Let's take a look at how CFML can be written in a CFM file. The following code shows the current IP address of the user requesting the CFM file:

```
<html>
<head>
<title>Simple ColdFusion document</title>
<meta http-equiv="Content-Type" content="text/html; charset=iso-8859-1">
</head>
<body>
Your IP address is <cfoutput>#CGI.REMOTE_ADDR#</cfoutput>.
</body>
</html>
```

You can find this code in the userIP.cfm file located in the chapter_03 folder of this book's CD-ROM.

The majority of this code is plain HTML, from the <html> tag to the <body> tag. When the ColdFusion MX server parses the CFM document, it looks for any ColdFusion-specific tags. These tags usually begin with the letters cf, such as cfoutput. When a CFML tag is found, ColdFusion goes to work. In this example, the CGI server variable named REMOTE_ADDR is evaluated. When the userIP.cfm document is requested from the Web server, ColdFusion MX returns the following text in the HTML document:

```
Your IP address is 63.192.225.91.
```

The IP address will actually show your computer's address if you load this document into your Web browser. Notice that the CGI.REMOTE_ADDR variable is surrounded by # characters. These characters let ColdFusion know that this text should be evaluated as a variable name. Why is this important? You may have other text within a <cfoutput> tag that doesn't need to be evaluated by ColdFusion. Using the CGI structure once again, the following code displays all of the CGI variables for the ColdFusion document:

```
<html>
<head>
```

```
<title>Simple ColdFusion document</title>
<meta http-equiv="Content-Type" content="text/html; charset=iso-8859-1">
</head>
<body>
Here are all of the properties of the ColdFusion CGI object:<BR>
<HR>
<cfoutput>
  <cfloop collection= "#CGI#" item="varName" >
  Variable: #varName#<br>
  Value: #Evaluate(varName)#<br>
  <HR>
  </cfloop>
</cfoutput>
</body>
</html>
```

 You can find this code in the cgiVariables.cfm file, located in the chapter_03 folder of this book's CD-ROM.

In this code example, <cfoutput> tags surround a <cfloop> tag. CFLOOP has several formats. The one shown here functions similarly to a for in loop in Action-Script or JavaScript. The object (or struct) reference is specified as the value of the collection attribute, and the item attribute is the iterating variable within the loop. This example loops through every variable name in the CGI structure. With regard to the <cfoutput> tag, notice that some text is not surrounded by # characters, such as the Variable:, Value:, and <HR> text. This text simply needs to be repeated "as is" for each iteration of the loop, while varName and Evaluate(var-Name) should be processed by the ColdFusion engine. #varName# returns the variable's actual name, while the #Evaluate(varName)# function returns the value of that variable. When this document is processed by ColdFusion and returned to a Web browser, output similar to that of **Figure 3.9** is displayed.

Tip

If you want to insert the # character in standard text encapsulated by a CFML tag, use two pound symbols: ##. This sequence tells ColdFusion to output the # character in the text.

Figure 3.9 The dynamic output of the `cgiVariables.cfm` document.

ColdFusion Components

ColdFusion MX introduces a new document format, called ColdFusion Component. This type of document has a .cfc file extension. You can author components with the same tools that you use for CFM files, with the same CFML tags. A ColdFusion component is essentially a file describing a Web service (Web services are described in much more detail in Chapter 6).

Caution

Don't confuse ColdFusion components with Flash components. ColdFusion components are server-side scripts that contain functions that are invoked as a Web service from other ColdFusion documents (such as CFM files) or Flash movies via Flash Remoting.

Before we continue to discuss CFC files, let's take another look at CFM files. CFM files are generally written to be processed in a linear fashion. When a CFM file is requested, the ColdFusion MX engine processes the entire document. This doesn't mean that every line of code is necessarily invoked. If a CFM file has several conditionals, then not every condition will be invoked. However, the fact remains that an individual CFM file is generally written to perform one specific function within the greater scope of a Web application. For example, you may have one CFM file that creates a dynamic HTML form, and that form sends its data to yet another CFM file, which passes data to a new record in a RDBMS.

TAG-BASED MARKUP VERSUS THE <CFSCRIPT> TAG

A new feature available for ColdFusion documents processed by a ColdFusion MX server is the ability to write code resembling the dot syntax of JavaScript and ActionScript. If you prefer to code without CFML tags, you can take advantage of ColdFusion features within a <cfscript> tag. For example, here's how you would use traditional CFML tags to create an if/else expression:

```
<!-- Traditional CFML tags -->
From traditional CFML tags:<br><br>
<cfset browser = CGI.HTTP_USER_AGENT>
<cfif Find("MSIE", #browser#) NEQ 0>
   You are using Microsoft Internet Explorer.
<cfelse>
   You are not using Microsoft Internet Explorer.
</cfif>
```

These CFML tags check the user's browser name (CGI.HTTP_USER_AGENT) for the text "MSIE". If you're not familiar with CFML, you probably didn't know that the Find() function could search for text within a string. The NEQ comparison operator is also specific to CFML. If you know JavaScript or ActionScript, the following <cfscript> syntax is easier to interpret:

```
<!-- CFSCRIPT tag usage -->
From a &lt;cfscript&gt; tag:<br><br>
<cfscript>
browserVar = CGI.HTTP_USER_AGENT;
if(browserVar.indexOf("MSIE") NEQ -1){
   writeoutput("You are using Microsoft Internet Explorer.");
} else {
   writeoutput("You are not using Microsoft Internet Explorer.");
}
</cfscript>
```

TAG-BASED MARKUP VERSUS THE `<CFSCRIPT>` TAG *(continued)*

The code within the `<cfscript>` tags declares the `browserVar` variable using JavaScript notation. The `if` and `else` structure uses parentheses around the condition and curly braces, { }, to nest the code. You can utilize basic data types, classes, and their supporting methods in `<cfscript>` tags, such as the `indexOf()` method of the `String` class. There are, however, several operators and functions specific to ColdFusion in the context of a `<cfscript>` tag. For example, you cannot use common comparison operators like `!=` or `==` in a conditional expression; the same operators that are used in standard CFML tags must be used. Also, the `writeoutput()` function works in a similar fashion to the `<cfoutput>` tag, writing the specified string value to the parsed document.

For more information on using code within the `<cfscript>` tag, refer to the following resources:

www.macromedia.com/desdev/mx/coldfusion/extreme/cftags_cfscript.html

bayliss.netbenefit.com/cfdocs/Developing_Web_Applications_with_ColdFusion/
→ contents.htm

www.granularity.com/company/whitepapers/Granularity-CFSCRIPT.pdf

www.michaelbuffington.com/mb/articles.cfm?inc=cf_cfscript.cfm

CFC files, on the other hand, are not processed—or requested—in the same way as a CFM file. While you can load a CFM file directly into a browser (or Flash movie), CFC files are not directly requested by a Web browser or Flash movie. A CFC file contains a series of function declarations. These functions are invoked individually. Collectively, the functions within a CFC file should be related to one another, creating a Web service. If you've written AS files containing several related functions that you reuse from one Flash movie to the next, then you are already familiar this concept. Let's look at a simple example of a CFC file. Open Dreamweaver MX, and perform the following steps.

Note The following example requires that you have Dreamweaver MX and ColdFusion MX installed. The ColdFusion MX installation doesn't necessarily need to be on the same computer, but you will need to define a site that uses ColdFusion technology.

1. In Dreamweaver MX, define a site that uses the wwwroot folder of your ColdFusion MX server as the local root folder, as shown in **Figure 3.10**. This figure shows the Advanced tab of a new site definition.

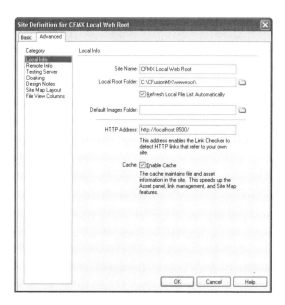

Figure 3.10 The Local Info category of the Site Definition dialog box.

2. In the Testing Server category for the new site definition, make sure Cold-Fusion is selected as the Server Model, and that Access is set to Local/Network (**Figure 3.11**).

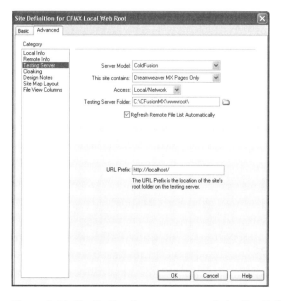

Figure 3.11 The Testing Server category of the Site Definition dialog box.

3. Once the new site is defined, open the Applications panel and click the Components tab. You should see a numbered list of steps, as shown in **Figure 3.12**.

Figure 3.12
The Components tab only displays a live list of ColdFusion MX components when all of the necessary steps to connect to the ColdFusion server have been completed.

4. Steps 1 through 3 of the Components tab should already have check marks next to them. Click the RDS Login link in step 4, and enter your ColdFusion administrator or RDS password into the password dialog box. Once you have successfully authenticated with the ColdFusion MX server, the Components panel updates to show the list of pre-installed example CFC files (**Figure 3.13**).

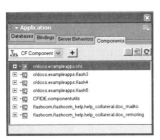

Figure 3.13
ColdFusion MX already has several example components installed for you to test.

5. Click the + indicator to the left of the cfdocs.exampleapps.cfc component. This entry represents the folder named cfdocs/exampleapps/cfc from the wwwroot folder. This folder contains a component file named tempconverter.cfc. Click the + indicator to the left of the tempconverter entry, and you will see the convert() method defined with the component. If you click the + indicator to the left of the convert() entry, you will see the two arguments, scale and temperature, which are used by this method (**Figure 3.14**).

Figure 3.14
You can view the internal methods and arguments of a ColdFusion component in the Components tab.

Let's take a quick look at the internal code of the `tempconverter.cfc` file. In the Components tab of the Application panel, right-click (or Control-click on the Mac) the `tempconverter` entry, and choose Edit the code. The component's code displays in Dreamweaver MX. While you won't make any alterations to this code, we do want to show you how a ColdFusion component is structured. The first CFML tag in the document is a `<cfcomponent>` tag, which declares the name of the component and a label or display name. The display name is shown if you view the details or description of the component from the Components tab in Dreamweaver MX.

```
<cfcomponent name="tempconverter" displayName="Temperature Converter">
```

Between the `<cfcomponent></cfcomponent>` tags, you will find the `<cffunction>` tag, which declares a method of the component. In this simple component, there is only one method available: `convert`.

```
<cffunction name="convert" access="remote" returnType="any">
```

Typically, a component has a series of `<cffunction>` tags, comprising all the functionality necessary to define the service. In later chapters, you create custom components that use several `<cffunction>` tags. Close the `tempconverter.cfc` document in Dreamweaver MX.

Now, you will create a CFM file that invokes the `convert()` method, to convert a Fahrenheit temperature value into a Celsius temperature value. Resume with the following steps:

6. In the Files panel, create a new CFM file by choosing File > New File. Rename the new file `bodyTemp.cfm`.

7. Double-click this file in the Files panel to open it in Dreamweaver MX. Make sure the document is in Code view, and insert an empty line above the starting `<html>` tag. Make sure the cursor is blinking on the first line of the document. Select the `convert()` method in the Components tab of the Applications panel, and drag the item to the top line of the `bodyTemp.cfm` document. The following code appears in the CFM file:

```
<cfinvoke
 component="cfdocs.exampleapps.cfc.tempconverter"
 method="convert"
 returnvariable="convertRet">
</cfinvoke>
```

Here, the `<cfinvoke>` tag calls the `tempconverter` component's `convert()` method, and returns the value of this method to a ColdFusion variable named `convertRet`. Dreamweaver MX automatically names the return variable by appending the suffix `Ret` to the name of the invoked method.

8. As you saw earlier, the `convert()` method takes two arguments, `scale` and `temperature`. Add the following highlighted lines of code before the closing `</cfinvoke>` tag:

```
<cfinvoke
 component="cfdocs.exampleapps.cfc.tempconverter"
 method="convert"
 returnvariable="convertRet">
   <cfinvokeargument name="scale" value="F"/>
   <cfinvokeargument name="temperature" value="98.6"/>
</cfinvoke>
```

The `<cfinvokeargument>` tags allow you to pass values to the `convert()` method of the `tempconverter` component. The `scale` argument tells the convert() method that the temperature argument value is in Fahrenheit (`"F"`); the method has already been written to recognize this value.

9. Once the `convert()` method has a temperature and a scale to convert into Celsius, the `convertRet` value can be inserted into the `<body>` tag of the CFM file. Between the `<body></body>` tags, add the following code:

```
The normal body temperature of a human is
→ <cfoutput>#convertRet#</cfoutput> degrees Celsius.
```

Here, the `<cfoutput>` tag inserts the returned value of the `convert()` method into standard HTML text.

10. Save the CFM file, and choose View > Server Debug. Dreamweaver MX now processes the CFM file on the ColdFusion MX server, and the document window displays the result of the `<cfinvoke>` tag in the HTML:

The normal body temperature of a human is 37 degrees Celsius.

 The `bodyTemp.cfm` document can be found in the `chapter_03` folder of this book's CD-ROM. In this folder, you can also find two additional files, `specifyTemp.htm` and `showTemp.cfm`, that demonstrate how to send data from a form in a standard HTML document to a CFM file.

You now have completed a quick primer on the use of a ColdFusion component. In Chapters 8 and 9, you create custom CFC files that use several component methods to send data back and forth from Flash movies via Flash Remoting.

Tip
There are several example CFC files that are installed with ColdFusion MX. We highly recommend that you read the documentation for these examples. You can find more information about the examples by using the following URL on the machine running ColdFusion MX:

http://localhost/cfdocs/exampleapps/index.cfm

Server-Side ActionScript (or ActionScript Remote) Files

The ColdFusion component isn't the only new file format introduced with ColdFusion MX. You can also script Web services for ColdFusion MX in familiar ActionScript syntax, with ActionScript Remote files. This file format has an .asr file extension and performs the same type of functionality provided by Cold-Fusion components. There's one large difference though: ASR files can only be used by the Flash Remoting service on a ColdFusion MX server. You cannot use ASR files to provide Web services for other CFM files.

Caution
There are two types of server-side ActionScript code, one for ColdFusion MX and one for Flash Communication Server MX (discussed in Chapter 6). Each server's version of server-side ActionScript code employs some unique objects and methods not available in the other.

Why is this the case? Macromedia created the ASR file format with Flash developers in mind. If you're a developer creating Flash movies and you want to take advantage of Flash Remoting capabilities, you may not want to learn a new coding language like CFML to create Web applications. ColdFusion MX can interpret all of the standard classes and data types in ASR files. However, much of the functionality offered by CFML tags does not have an equivalent in server-side ActionScript for ColdFusion MX. For example, there is no direct equivalent of the <cffile> tag in ASR files. This tag can manage file operations on the ColdFusion server. ASR files do give you the opportunity to start learning how to build Flash Remoting-enabled applications with your ColdFusion MX server almost immediately, as you learn how to code more complex operations in CFC files.

There are two ColdFusion-specific functions that you can use in ASR files: CF.query and CF.http. CF.query works much like the <cfquery> tag, allowing you to generate SQL statements that retrieve records from a database. The CF.http works like its <cfhttp> tag counterpart, enabling a script to retrieve data via HTTP operations.

Xref

To learn more about using these functions in ASR files for ColdFusion MX applications, you can read the "Using Server-Side ActionScript in Macromedia ColdFusion MX" PDF available on Macromedia's Web site:

download.macromedia.com/pub/coldfusion/documentation/

→ cfmx_server_side_actions.pdf

If you want to see how the tempconverter.cfc component translates into an ASR file, see the tempconverter.asr file in the chapter_03 folder of this book's CD-ROM. Because ASR files can only be used with Flash Remoting, a Flash project (convert-Temp.fla, .swf, and .html documents) is also included in this folder. For more information on Flash Remoting, read Chapter 7.

FITTING COLDFUSION MX INTO YOUR WORKFLOW

Macromedia ColdFusion MX can be installed on your development machine or a server on your local area network in a matter of minutes. The server software is available for the following operating systems: Windows, HP-UX, Linux, and Solaris. To see a table of the system requirements for each operating system, refer to the following URL on the Macromedia Web site:

www.macromedia.com/software/coldfusion/productinfo/system_reqs/

Tip

For development environments, you can install ColdFusion MX on to any 32-bit version of the Windows operating system, from Windows 98 to Windows XP Professional.

ColdFusion MX is also available as a separate software installation for J2EE application servers. If your organization already has a J2EE application server framework, you can add the rapid development environment of ColdFusion MX to the server. Currently, ColdFusion MX for J2EE Application Servers is available for Macromedia JRun, IBM WebSphere, and Sun ONE. For more information on this product line, see the following URL on Macromedia's Web site:

www.macromedia.com/software/coldfusion/j2ee/

You can install different versions of Macromedia ColdFusion MX on your server. You will need to determine which version is best suited for the needs of your applications.

Trial Version (or Developer Edition)

The trial version of the ColdFusion MX server provides you with the functionality of the Professional Edition (discussed later in this section) for a time period of 30 days. You can find the trial version of the server software on this book's CD-ROM, or download it from Macromedia's Web site at the following URL:

www.macromedia.com/software/trial_download/

Caution

If you install the trial version, you will not have the opportunity to reinstall the trial version again on the same machine. Be sure to install the trial version only when you can take advantage of the time allowed within the trial period.

When the trial period has expired, the ColdFusion MX reverts to a standard Developer edition. The Developer edition only allows ColdFusion documents to be served to two IP addresses: the machine hosting the ColdFusion MX server and one other IP that you can designate in the administrator pages.

All of the examples in this book can be developed and tested with the trial version.

Note

Macromedia Studio MX ships with the Developer edition of ColdFusion MX, which is the same version installed by the trial download.

IIS Versus Stand-alone Server for ColdFusion MX

When you install ColdFusion MX on a Windows machine running Microsoft IIS (Internet Information Services), you have the option of installing ColdFusion MX as a stand-alone server or as a connector to the default Web site configured in IIS. Regardless of which option you choose, you can always use the stand-alone server on port 8500 of your machine's IP address. If you initially configured ColdFusion MX as a stand-alone server and want to reconfigure to work with IIS, read the installation instructions for Windows in the Cold-Fusion MX release notes at the following URL:

www.macromedia.com/support/coldfusion/releasenotes/mx/releasenotes_mx.html

For most of the projects in this book, the wwwroot folder of the ColdFusion MX stand-alone server is used to store documents. If you chose the default location for program files during installation on a Windows machine, this folder is located at C:\CFusionMX\wwwroot.

If you are a running Microsoft Windows 2000 Server or Windows 2000 Advanced Server and have configured several virtual Web sites in IIS, read the following tech note at Macromedia to learn how to configure ColdFusion MX services for each virtual site:

www.macromedia.com/v1/Handlers/index.cfm?ID=23390

For development, it's perfectly fine to use the stand-alone Web server included with Cold-Fusion MX. However, for a live production scenario, be sure to use ColdFusion MX with a robust Web server, such as Microsoft IIS or Apache.

Professional and Enterprise Editions

For production-level servers that host live Web sites, you'll need to purchase the Professional or Enterprise edition of ColdFusion MX. For most advanced Web sites, the Professional edition will be able to meet your needs, allowing you to develop Web applications that serve departmental needs within an organization. The Professional edition can handle the typical traffic of most Internet Web sites. However, if you're developing a ColdFusion MX-driven Web application for Fortune 500 companies, you'll likely need the power of the Enterprise edition. The Enterprise edition of ColdFusion MX allows you to use additional Java interoperability and includes performance, management, and security features that are necessary for high-traffic Web sites hosting thou-sands, if not millions, of documents and data resources. For maximum security and reliability, you'll likely want to use the Enterprise edition.

Xref

For a comprehensive comparison of Professional and Enterprise edition features, refer to the ColdFusion MX Feature Comparison Matrix at the following URL:

www.macromedia.com/software/coldfusion/whitepapers/pdf/
→ ColdFusionMXFeatureGrid_03.pdf

Note

Be sure to download the latest ColdFusion MX updater from the Macromedia site. At the time of this writing, ColdFusion MX Updater Release 1 was available to download. You can find this update (and future updates) at the following URL:

www.macromedia.com/support/coldfusion/
→ downloads_updates.html

ADDITIONAL RESOURCES FOR COLDFUSION MX

You can find the latest developer articles and tutorials for ColdFusion MX at:

www.macromedia.com/desdev/mx/coldfusion/

If you're looking for technical support, downloads, and updates related to ColdFusion MX, check out the following support page at Macromedia:

www.macromedia.com/support/coldfusion

We also recommend the following ColdFusion MX books, published by Macromedia Press:

Reality ColdFusion MX: Macromedia Flash MX Integration

Macromedia ColdFusion MX Web Application Construction Kit, Fifth Edition

Advanced Macromedia ColdFusion MX Application Development, Third Edition

---

SUMMARY

- Macromedia ColdFusion MX is application server software that you can install on the same computer as your Web server.

- ColdFusion MX can create dynamic HTML pages from ColdFusion documents containing CFML tags. CFML, or ColdFusion Markup Language, is the authoring language for ColdFusion documents.

- You can develop ColdFusion documents that create text-based data (as URL-encoded or XML data) or Flash Remoting data for Flash movies.

- Any text editor can be used to write ColdFusion documents. Macromedia Dreamweaver MX and HomeSite+ offer many features that make authoring such documents more efficient and more intuitive.

- CFM documents are typically used to create dynamic output for HTML-based sites. You can insert CFML tags along with ordinary HTML tags and other client-side scripting tags.

- CFC files contain one or more functions that comprise a ColdFusion component. ColdFusion components can be invoked by other ColdFusion documents (such as CFM files) or by Flash movies via Flash Remoting.

- You can also author ColdFusion components with server-side ActionScript code for ColdFusion MX, saved as ASR files. ASR files can only be used by the Flash Remoting service of ColdFusion MX.

- ColdFusion MX is available as a stand-alone product that works in tandem with your Web server, or as an add-on to an existing J2EE application server.

- There are three editions of ColdFusion MX: Developer, Professional, and Enterprise. The Developer version allows you to author and test all aspects of ColdFusion MX applications. However, a live Web server will require the Professional or Enterprise version.

In This Chapter:

4 Databases

Most interesting Web sites are databases. Amazon, eBay, CNN—they're all just databases with HTML front ends. They contain some clever programming, certainly, but at heart, they're all databases.

This chapter is a crash course in modern database systems, covering the concepts behind designing, building, and using databases. It's far beyond the scope of this book to be a definitive text on databases. Database design alone is a huge and thorny topic, never mind the implementations of the different database vendors. We hope to give you a deeper understanding of the reasons behind why databases are an essential part of a modern Web site. We'll also explore the uses of databases within a Rich Internet Application environment.

 Note   If you've been using a Relational Database Management System (RDBMS) for some time, you may already know some of the concepts explored in this chapter.

Databases Overview

Sure, you don't have to store your information in a database. You could use a bunch of text files and save yourself considerable time, trouble, and expense, right? Hack together a couple of simple scripts in your programming language of choice, and you're halfway there in an afternoon.

The trouble is that getting the rest of the way there is going to take an inordinate amount of time. You'd better really enjoy programming. There are many situations that you'll have to consider. These include:

- What happens when two people try to add information at the same time? How about 500 people at the same time?

- How do you back up your data without shutting your site down?

- What stops people from adding corrupt or missing data?

- If your text file is nice and speedy when there're 250 lines in it, what happens when there are 2,000,000 lines?

The point is this: Databases aren't just a place to dump your data. That's the easy part. The power of databases lies in the other stuff: the security, enforced data integrity, indexing and fast access, and data recovery features.

Database Concepts

We're not trying to persuade you one way or the other as to whether you need a database. Chances are if you're reading this, you need one. This chapter is more about getting a proper understanding of database systems beyond considering them a stunningly expensive repository for superfluous information.

Many introductions to databases spend a lot of time comparing them to other things you've previously used:

- "Databases are like spreadsheets..."
- "Databases are like text files..."
- "Databases are like HTML tables..."

While all these analogies are true (to a point), they're also like those science programs that inform you that "the human body is 90 percent water."

Sure, it's true. But it's the other 10 percent that's the really important stuff.

Basic Terminology

If you've had exposure to databases in the past—whether SQL Server, Access, or Oracle—you've probably seen a representation of data similar to that shown in **Figure 4.1**.

While this is a useful representation of how data is stored within a database, it can leave a misconception that a database is essentially some kind of complex version of Excel, only much more expensive and less practical.

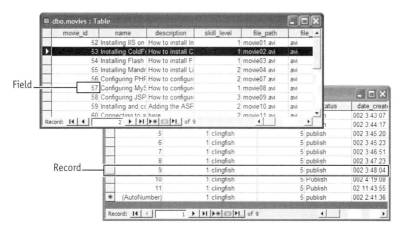

Figure 4.1 A simple representation of database contents.

The fact is that most of the important RDBMS features are invisible: transactions, concurrency, and data integrity. We will explore these invisible elements during this chapter, but for now, let's look at the visible parts.

TABLES

Every database consists of one or more tables. They are the basic building blocks of a database. Each table should represent an entity—an object or "thing" that needs to be represented in your system. Examples of tables would be employees, users, or products.

Tables are typically named in plural, as they contain many occurrences of an entity.

RECORDS

Each table contains multiple records—the details of each individual occurrence of the entity. An employees table contains many records, each representing one employee.

FIELDS

Each record in the table consists of one or more fields. The fields stand for distinct pieces of information about the entity, for example:

- Employee surname
- Product color
- User password
- VIN number

Part of the process of designing and creating a database involves being extremely specific about what separate pieces of information need to be stored in the database, and exactly what type of information that is: a date? A number? A string of text? Not only the type of data but also the length must be specified: if it's text, how long should it be? Do you need 50 characters or 4,000 characters to store that information?

As in spreadsheets, *records* and *fields* are also often referred to as *rows* and *columns*.

KEYS

Each table should have a *Primary key*. This is a method of specifically and uniquely identifying a record in the table, so that there is no possibility of duplicates. Often, the data inherent in the table is not enough to identify a record uniquely. If you have two Bob Smiths in your employees table, you can't identify them just by a name match. Often, a Primary key is achieved by generating an identification number: employee ID, customer ID, and so on.

Tip

Even when uniquely identifying information occurs naturally in the table, a generated ID may be used as a Primary key anyway. For example, a Social Security number may be stored in the database for each employee, but would rarely be used as the sole Primary key, as Primary keys have a habit of being used on reports and paperwork, and most people don't want to see their Social Security number used without restraint.

Database systems can be defined to automatically generate an ID number when adding new information. This is recommended where possible, as it avoids having to add the logic in any programming code.

COMPOUND KEYS

You can also have what's known as a *Compound key*. This is where **two** (or more) fields of the table are treated as the Primary key to make the record uniquely identifiable. Each field by itself may not be enough to make the record unique, but both together are.

For example, in a Movie table, you would commonly store information including the Director and the Title. But neither of these could be used as the Primary key: Many directors make multiple movies, and many movies are remakes. But using the director and the title *together* works as a unique reference: "Scarface" and "Brian De Palma" uniquely identify the 1983 movie, while "Scarface" and "Howard Hawks" uniquely identify the 1932 version.

Tip

Compound keys are also referred to as *Concatenated* or *Composite* keys.

Relationships

Now we start to get into the power and flexibility of relational databases. Tables in RDBMSs have relationships to each other. We've created tables that represent distinct entities—customers, orders, and products. But the relationships between the tables are likely to be what interests us. The relationships allow us to ask questions like these:

- What orders have been placed by Customer ABC?

- How many orders came from a certain zip code or state?

- What products comprise Order no. 123?

The relationships between tables are specified as part of table design. In this case, the orders table would contain a customer ID field. By simply specifying that, we can take any order and link to a unique customer in the customers table, without needing to store any customer information in the orders table. This avoids data redundancy (storing the same data in different places), which is highly discouraged in RDBMS design.

Relationships are part of the incredible power and flexibility that databases possess, and one of the first examples of the "invisible" parts of the database. Correctly specified, they allow data retrieval to encompass a huge area—often more than the original database developers intended—by finding and exploiting the relationships that occur throughout the database.

Relationships are explored in more detail later in this chapter.

Database Lifecycle

Now that we've explored some of the basic concepts of databases—tables, records, fields, and keys—and covered the concepts of relationships implemented in every database, it's time to explore how we actually get to the point of even having a database to design, tables to build, or relationships to specify.

The three stages of the database "lifecycle" can be characterized as follows: *data modeling*, *database implementation*, and *database utilization*, or essentially, design, build, and use.

Database Design

Databases are old. They've been around since the '70s. Virtually every other technology we're going to use is a spring chicken by comparison. RDBMS systems have been tweaked and given pretty graphical interfaces, but their basic nature hasn't changed for a long, long time.

This is a good thing. It means the methodology for designing databases has been tried and battle-tested for years, and all you need to do to make a good one is follow the steps. Designing a database should never be a place to express your inner creativity and find new and unique ways of doing things— quite the opposite. When you want to be creative, be creative in your applications. In your database, be methodical, patient, and by the book.

Data Modeling

Also referred to as "Entity/Relationship Modeling," database modeling is the basic process of designing your database—creating the logical design, detached from any particular DBMS that you intend to use to implement it. This is the stage that should take you the most time. It involves:

- Figuring out what tables should be in your database—what entities need to be represented.

- Determining the fields that need to be in those tables—what information has to be stored for each entity.

- Deciding what kind of data those fields can contain: whether date, text, number, or any other data type. Available data types can differ between the different commercial RDBMSs.

- Choosing if the field can be legitimately empty, and whether it should be restricted to just a certain range of values.

- Specifying the relationships that should exist between the tables.

The design process should always be followed. You should never, ever try to "design" your database by just going ahead and creating it. Modeling is an essential part of creating the database: Everything depends on it.

Most mistakes in databases can be tied to poor or nonexistent design. It's tempting to launch into your RDBMS GUI and start throwing together a few tables, but this tends to be how bad databases get started. The problem is that your database needs to be as static in design as it possibly can be—you need to know that you can rely on your database design not to change. You might be able to hack together a Web application or a Flash movie in short order without spending much time on a formal design. If there's a problem with it, you can always come back and fix it without messing up the other parts of your system too much.

But your database will have roots in every part of your system: If you need to make a major change six months after you built it to cater to something you didn't initially consider, you could break everything else that's been built upon that database in that time.

Building a database is like getting tattooed: You really want it to be correct the first time around.

Let's briefly cover the steps you're likely to take when designing your database.

What Is Your Database For?

Be wary of the answer that leaps first to your mind. Think of Amazon.com as a huge database with some great front-end application development. It's perhaps the archetypal e-commerce site. Now, cast yourself back a few years to when Amazon.com first appeared on the scene—when it was a bookstore rather than a one-stop-shopping bazaar. If you were building Amazon.com, given the task of creating the database from scratch, what would be your answer to the question "What is your database for?"

An easy answer would be: "The database stores information about books."

But that's not it. Amazon's not popular because it's a "big book database." It's popular because it adds a sense of community: the ability for people to communicate to others what they liked or disliked about books, and also to rate both books and various opinions about them. It's a self-moderating community, if you will, with substantial content created by the visitors to the site.

If Amazon.com were just "a searchable list of books," it would have gone the way of so many other dot-com companies.

Thinking of the community aspects of the site, now ask the question again. Your answer might be something like this:

"The database allows customers to find books, to discover what other readers thought about them, to contribute their own opinions, and learn about other books they might like based on people with similar reading habits."

This definition is still not quite to the level of a "mission statement," but it now has a very different focus. Deciding what tables you need with this description is substantially changed from if you just thought, "I'm making a big book database." A couple of sentences can make a world of difference in deciding on the information you need to store.

What Do You Already Have?

The next step is to understand what's already available. Are you building upon a currently existing database? If so, what's wrong with it? Getting a precise understanding of what currently exists will help you determine what requirements are *not* being met by the current system.

Perhaps you're working with a company that isn't computerized. But unless you're working with a brand-new startup, something exists that you need to know about. This might be:

- A filing cabinet
- A stack of paper on someone's desk
- A 70-year-old chain-smoker named Dot, who is the unsung fount-of-all-knowledge in the company, knows what everyone does, and where everything is

Understanding what information you already have is essential before you get to the next step: the table definitions.

Table Definitions

As mentioned earlier, you're typically going to create a separate table for each entity that needs to be represented in your system. A table often mirrors a real-life object: employees, customers, users, and products. However, an entity does not have to have a physical existence: orders, appointments, and flight schedules are also examples of legitimate entities that need to be represented.

After deciding which entities need to have tables, you determine each individual piece of information that needs to be stored in the table for that entity. Be as separate and distinct as possible. Don't just have a "name" field, have separate fields for first name and last name (or possibly even first name, last name, middle initials, honorific, suffix, and so on), as this leads to better separation of data—a good thing.

You also need to decide on the type of data to be stored. You must decide if it is text, a number, a date, and so on. The more exact you can be, the better. Sure, you could declare everything to be a text field—after all, you can store numbers and dates in a text field—but being specific about the type of data leads to vastly improved abilities with searching, sorting, and performing numeric functions (such as "give me the total net price for all orders in the last 90 days"). It also means that your database enforces the correct type of data being entered, and you can be sure that, for example, none of your date fields contain text.

You should consult your database documentation for the exact data types offered. It's one of the areas in which different vendors use different terms. Most RDBMS systems still have the same essential types—text, number, date, and so on—but many are named differently, and the more complex RDBMSs typically have more subtypes, such as several different number types, depending on what is being stored.

Relationships

There are three types of possible relationships between tables in RDBMS design: *One-to-One, One-to-Many,* and *Many-to-Many*. The relationship between tables is also referred to as cardinality.

 Note Some people consider there to be a fourth kind of relationship: **none.** This is just another way of saying that tables do not have to have relationships with other tables—some are independent.

ONE-TO-MANY RELATIONSHIP

The most common relationship between tables is a One-to-Many relationship. One record in one table relates to many records in another table, as shown in

Figure 4.2. The customer "Acme Ltd." appears once in the customers table, but its customer ID ("1") appears multiple times in the orders table.

Some other examples of One-to-Many relationships would be:

- Each customer can have many orders

- Every car can have many parts

- Each department can have many employees

One-to-Many relationships are implemented by including the Primary key of the "one" into the table definition of the "many." In our example, each order record contains not only a Primary key (order ID, to uniquely identify the record) but also a foreign key— a key to another table. In this case, we store the customer ID as a foreign key within the orders table. Within the orders table, the customer ID is not unique; there can be many orders for the same customer.

Note

You often have to be careful that what appears to be a One-to-Many relationship is not in fact a Many-to-Many relationship. For example, you might have a Food database that has two tables: Recipes and Ingredients. It would be very easy to jump to the conclusion that this is a One-to-Many relationship, and that each recipe contains many ingredients. This is true, but if we then implemented a One-to-Many relationship by adding a foreign key to the Ingredients table, we are saying that each ingredient only occurs in one recipe. This is untrue, of course: What we have is a Many-to-Many relationship. Each recipe can contain many ingredients; each ingredient can be in many recipes.

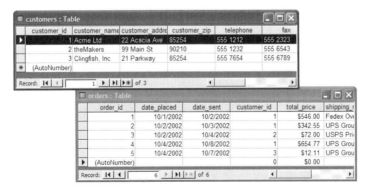

Figure 4.2 A One-to-Many relationship. Each customer ID occurs only once
in the customer table, but can occur many times in the orders table.

One-to-One Relationship

An unusual though possible relationship is *One-to-One*. Perhaps each employee in the company has a company car. As we model tables as separate entities, we build one table for the employees and another for company cars. We then declare a One-to-One relationship: Each employee has one car, each car is owned by only one employee.

One-to-One relationships have a habit of turning into other kinds of relationships. In this example, everything would work fine until someone required a replacement company car. If a One-to-One relationship is enforced, then all details of the previous car have to be wiped from the database before the new car details can be entered. The more likely option is that you would make the relationship a One-to-Many relationship: Each employee could be linked to several cars, but only one car would be active at a given time. You could then still keep records of previous cars, and keeping records is, let's face it, the reason why you're likely to have a database in the first place.

Many-to-Many Relationship

Another very common relationship is Many-to-Many. As an example, we might have an `employees` table and a `projects` table, as shown in **Figure 4.3**.

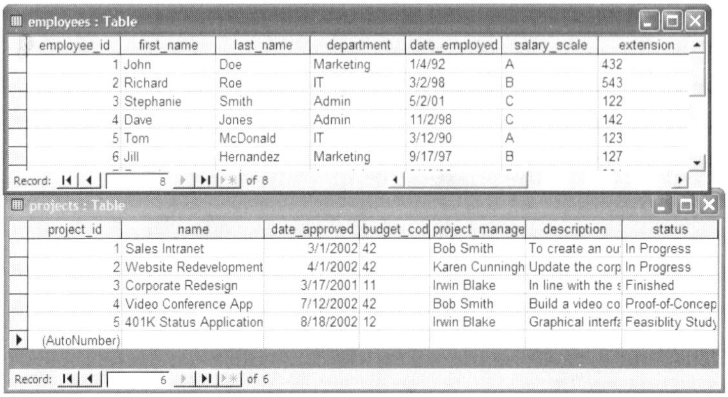

employees : Table

employee_id	first_name	last_name	department	date_employed	salary_scale	extension
1	John	Doe	Marketing	1/4/92	A	432
2	Richard	Roe	IT	3/2/98	B	543
3	Stephanie	Smith	Admin	5/2/01	C	122
4	Dave	Jones	Admin	11/2/98	C	142
5	Tom	McDonald	IT	3/12/90	A	123
6	Jill	Hernandez	Marketing	9/17/97	B	127

Record: 8 of 8

projects : Table

project_id	name	date_approved	budget_cod	project_manage	description	status
1	Sales Intranet	3/1/2002	42	Bob Smith	To create an ou	In Progress
2	Website Redevelopment	4/1/2002	42	Karen Cunningh	Update the corp	In Progress
3	Corporate Redesign	3/17/2001	11	Irwin Blake	In line with the s	Finished
4	Video Conference App	7/12/2002	42	Bob Smith	Build a video co	Proof-of-Concep
5	401K Status Application	8/18/2002	12	Irwin Blake	Graphical interfa	Feasiblity Study
(AutoNumber)						

Record: 6 of 6

Figure 4.3 The `projects` and `employees` tables.

At first glance, it might seem that we have a One-to-Many relationship: that each project (one) can have several employees (many), and we can represent it as shown in **Figure 4.4** by including a project ID field in the `employees` table.

employees : Table

employee_id	first_name	last_name	department	project_id	date_employed	salary_scale	
1	John	Doe	Marketing	1	1/4/92	A	4
2	Richard	Roe	IT	2	3/2/98	B	5
3	Stephanie	Smith	Admin	2	5/2/01	C	1
4	Dave	Jones	Admin	4	11/2/98	C	1
5	Tom	McDonald	IT	1	3/12/90	A	1
6	Jill	Hernandez	Marketing	2	9/17/97	B	1
7	Pamela	Springer	Actuarial	3	3/19/98	D	3

projects : Table

project_id	name	date_approved	budget_cod	project_manage	description	status
1	Sales Intranet	3/1/2002	42	Bob Smith	To create an ou	In Progress
2	Website Redevelopment	4/1/2002	42	Karen Cunningh	Update the corp	In Progress
3	Corporate Redesign	3/17/2001	11	Irwin Blake	In line with the s	Finished
4	Video Conference App	7/12/2002	42	Bob Smith	Build a video co	Proof-of-Concep
5	401K Status Application	8/18/2002	12	Irwin Blake	Graphical interfa	Feasiblity Study
(AutoNumber)						

Record: 1 of 5

Figure 4.4 A One-to-Many relationship between `projects` and `employees`.

But the likelihood is that the situation is more complex than that. What if one of the employees is told that she needs to spend 50 percent of her time on one project and 50 percent on another? We can change the table as shown in **Figure 4.5.**

employees : Table

employee_id	first_name	last_name	department	project_id	project_id_2	date_emplo
1	John	Doe	Marketing	1		1/4/92
2	Richard	Roe	IT	2		3/2/98
3	Stephanie	Smith	Admin	2	4	5/2/01
4	Dave	Jones	Admin	4		11/2/98
5	Tom	McDonald	IT	1	2	3/12/90
6	Jill	Hernandez	Marketing	2	2	9/17/97
7	Pamela	Springer	Actuarial	3		3/19/98
(AutoNumber)				0	0	

Record: 1 of 7

projects : Table

project_id	name	date_approved	budget_cod	project_manage	description	status
1	Sales Intranet	3/1/2002	42	Bob Smith	To create an ou	In Progress
2	Website Redevelopment	4/1/2002	42	Karen Cunningh	Update the corp	In Progress
3	Corporate Redesign	3/17/2001	11	Irwin Blake	In line with the s	Finished
4	Video Conference App	7/12/2002	42	Bob Smith	Build a video co	Proof-of-Concep
5	401K Status Application	8/18/2002	12	Irwin Blake	Graphical interfa	Feasiblity Study
(AutoNumber)						

Record: 1 of 5

Figure 4.5 An incorrect implementation of a Many-to-Many relationship between the `projects` table and the `employees` table.

What happens if yet another project is added to the workload? Do we change the table definition yet again, to have project 1, project 2, project 3, and project 4? When does it stop?

A repeating group, which is any field that seems to occur several times within a table definition, is a sign that your data has been incorrectly structured.

Many-to-Many relationships do not exist directly in a RDBMS. They are typically implemented by creating another table to exist directly between the two tables involved. In this case, we would create a *linking table*, project_employees, to create the correct cardinality between the two tables, as shown in **Figure 4.6**.

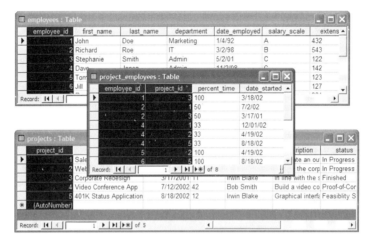

Figure 4.6 A correct implementation of a Many-to-Many relationship between the projects table and the employees table.

Note   Link tables are typically named with both of the surrounding tables; in this case, it could also have been called the employee_projects table.

Both the employees table and the projects table have a One-to-Many relationship with the project_employees table; this in effect creates a Many-to-Many relationship between them.

Note   The project_employees table as illustrated here uses a Compound key: neither project_id nor employee_id is unique in this table, but both fields together are a unique reference to a single row.

> ### GEEK TRIVIA
>
> It's often assumed that RDBMSs are called that because of the relationships between tables. That's not the actual reason. The term "Relational" in RDBMS is a mathematical term originating in set theory and has more to do with the concept of a database table, rather than the concept of the relationships we've just explored.

Normalization

As you've probably noticed, there's a lot of jargon that crops up around databases. Normalization and its flip side, denormalization, are likely to be terms you'll hear a lot when using databases.

Normalization is the process of taking your basic database design through a set of rules called Normal Forms to ensure that it conforms to relational database standards. We're going to briefly take a database through First, Second, and Third Normal Forms.

There are further Normal Forms, such as 4th and 5th Normal Forms and the Boyce-Codd Normal Form, but we're covering the most typical and practical ones here.

WE DON'T NEED NO STINKIN' RULES

Admittedly, the process of normalizing a database can sound a little "ivory tower," especially when most books on the normalization process contain sentences like these:

"A relation schema R is appropriately in Third Normal Form if and when a non-trivial functional dependency X → A holds in R, either X is a superkey of R or A is a prime attribute of R."

Yeah.

Normalization may appear to be a somewhat esoteric and impractical process, but a properly normalized database will contain the minimum of duplicate data, contain data that's easy to find and maintain, and ensure you can perform different operations on your database without creating garbage and messing up subsequent actions. It should be carried out for every database you design.

And it's not that hard, honestly.

FIRST NORMAL FORM (1NF)

The simplest form of normalization, First Normal Form (abbreviated to 1NF), states that in your database:

- There should be no repeating groups
- Each field should contain one—and only one—value

The first point, no repeating groups, was briefly explored in our discussion of relationships. Simply put, it means that if your table design contains multiple occurrences of the same field—such as your `employees` table containing separate fields for `project_1`, `project_2`, `project_3`, `project_4`, and so on—then your database is not in 1NF. Normalizing a table typically entails splitting the repeating group out into its own table and linking it to the first table in a One-to-Many relationship.

The second part of 1NF states that each field should be atomic—that it should contain only one value. In practice, this means that you don't solve the issue of multiple project fields in your `employees` table by simply creating one `project` field that contains multiple values separated by commas (for example, `"1, 94, 18"`).

The classic sign of a repeating group is fields with the same name and different numbers. The classic sign of a nonatomic value is any field contents with commas or any other delimiter.

SECOND NORMAL FORM (2NF)

Second Normal Form requires that all your tables be in First Normal Form. Beyond that, it states:

- Any nonkey field should be dependent on the entire Primary key.

Second Normal Form is only relevant if you have a Compound key—a key consisting of two or more fields.

It means that, if you can take just *part* of the Compound key and use it to ascertain other fields in that row, you're not in Second Normal Form.

That sounds a little abstract, so an example is shown in **Figure 4.7**.

The Primary key here is `order_ID` and `part_number`. Together they are a Compound key. Neither field on its own would make the record unique, but both fields together work as a key.

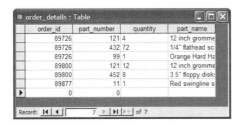

Figure 4.7 The order-details table definition
in 1NF but not 2NF.

In the nonkey fields of the table, quantity is dependent on the Primary key—we
need to know both the order_ID and the part_number to determine the quantity.
But part_name is dependent on the part_ID, which is only half of the Primary key.
It's redundant to store the part_name field here. It belongs in the parts table.

The solution here is to remove the part_name field from the order_details table.
We can link to the parts table to find the part name.

THIRD NORMAL FORM (3NF)

Once your database is in 2NF, you can proceed to Third Normal Form. The formal description of this, turned into as plain English as possible, is:

- No nonkey fields are dependent on another nonkey field.

This is similar to 2NF; it's still saying, "Can I figure out any of these fields from
other fields I have?"

As an example, examine the employees table as shown in **Figure 4.8**.

In this case, we can tell that we can't determine the address from merely
knowing the department.

employee_id	first_name	last_name	department	address	city	zip	date_employed	salary_scale
1	John	Doe	Marketing	47 Main St	Mesa	85212	1/4/92	A
2	Richard	Roe	IT	6633 Park V	Phoenix	85014	3/2/98	B
3	Stephanie	Smith	Admin	11 Grehawk	Tempe	85280	5/2/01	C
4	Dave	Jones	Admin	12 CD Ranc	Scottsdale	85258	11/2/98	C
5	Tom	McDonald	IT	972 Sincuid	Scottsdale	85254	3/12/90	A
6	Jill	Hernandez	Marketing	11 6th St	Phoenix	85013	9/17/97	B
7	Pamela	Springer	Actuarial	42 71st St	Scottsdale	85254	3/19/98	D
(AutoNumber)								

Record: 8 of 8

Figure 4.8 The employees table in 2NF but not 3NF.

But if we know the zip code, we can determine the city regardless of the employee ID. It's not the other way around. We can't necessarily ascertain the zip code from just knowing the city, as most cities have multiple zip codes. But if we have the zip code, we don't need to store the city in the same table.

For proper normalization, there should be a zip code table consisting of zip code and city, and you then remove the city field from the employees table. We wouldn't remove address because we can't determine that from the zip code.

Tip

Many companies sell zip code database information that can be directly imported into your own database. Searching for "zip code database" on Google will return extensive options.

Another example is calculated fields, as shown in **Figure 4.9**.

order_id	part_number	quantity	price	total
89726	99	1	$0.74	$0.74
89726	121	4	$1.55	$6.20
89726	432	72	$2.00	$144.00
89800	121	12	$4.00	$48.00
89800	452	8	$17.00	$136.00
89877	11	1	$432.33	$432.33
89877	99	2	$0.74	$1.48
	0	0	$0.00	$0.00

Figure 4.9 The order_details table definition in 2NF but not 3NF.

If we know the quantity and the price, then we can calculate the total ourselves. It shouldn't be stored in the database.

DENORMALIZATION

Once you've taken your table design through First, Second, and Third Normal Forms, you're ready to implement it in your chosen RDBMS.

At a later stage, you may choose to denormalize your database to purposely introduce redundancy and take it out of the proper Normal Form. This is usually done for reasons of performance. You may have split your tables to properly normalize them and then noticed that the performance of certain operations becomes sluggish. This could possibly occur because instead of retrieving data from one table, you have to retrieve from many tables, each taking its own processor hit.

Denormalization is usually done after strict analysis into why something is running slowly. It should never be taken lightly; introducing redundancy into your database can lead to nightmares with maintenance and increases the chances of incorrect or conflicting data appearing in your tables.

Tools

There are a variety of tools available to help you with the logical design of your database. Unfortunately, many are extremely expensive. The tools range from full-featured database modeling tools such as Allfusion Data Modeler (previously known as ERwin) to multipurpose design tools like Microsoft's Visio, which includes database design tools.

You can, of course, just use paper and pencil.

Xref

For more information on database modeling tools, check the book's Web site at www.mxbook.com.

DATABASE IMPLEMENTATION

Once the logical design has been completed, it's time to implement your database and build it in your RDBMS of choice. In most RDBMSs, there are two main ways of accomplishing this:

- Using a command line interface
- Using a GUI (graphical user interface)

While all database management systems allow building the table definitions using a command line, most also have available graphical tools that help you build the database, allowing you to quickly name and create fields and specify data types and relationships. An example of this, the SQL Server 2000 Enterprise Manager, can be seen in **Figure 4.10**.

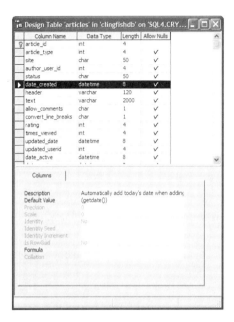

Figure 4.10 Building a database in SQL
Server 2000 Enterprise Manager.

Despite the attraction of using flashy GUIs, it's always useful to be aware of the grungy command line options. Defining tables is done using SQL (Structured Query Language), which is common to virtually all relational databases regardless of manufacturer.

Note

Strictly speaking, the part of SQL used for creating tables is called DDL (Data Definition Language). More about SQL is covered later in this chapter.

Creating a table, for example, requires a few simple keywords and must include the following information:

- The name of the table

- The names of the fields within the table

- The data types for each field

An example for a simple employees database table is as follows:

```
CREATE TABLE employees
 (employee_id INTEGER PRIMARY KEY,
  first_name VARCHAR(30),
  last_name VARCHAR(30),
  date_started DATE,
  extension INTEGER
 )
```

Here you can see the Primary key being specified (employee_id) and examples of fields holding different data types such as INTEGER, DATE, and VARCHAR. VARCHAR is a variable-length text field. This means we can store anything in the first_name and last_name fields up to 30 characters.

However, there are problems with this example. If we were creating our table in SQL Server, we'd have to use DATETIME, not DATE, for the date_started data type. If we used Access, we'd use TEXT not VARCHAR. Data types are one area in which the implementation between database management systems differs, even when the concepts are very similar.

Note

Due to these differences in implementation, it's impossible for this book to cover the different methods in which databases can be defined in the many relational database management systems; please consult your database documentation for full instructions. Some recommended book titles appear at the end of this chapter.

DATABASE UTILIZATION

After the database is designed and built comes the task of using it to its best advantage. There are only four things you do with a database: Read from it, write to it, update information in it, and delete information in it.

There will undoubtedly come a time when you need to return to the design stage again to make alterations, such as when customer demands or new business requirements entail a change to the existing database structure. You should always be overly cautious when doing this and return to a formal design process. Casual changes to your database can have all sorts of drastic side effects.

Database Choices

There are many commercial RDBMSs available, and luckily they're more alike than they are different. There are core similarities with most commercial database systems: the relational database model of tables, records, fields, and keys; the different types of relationships; and SQL (Structured Query Language), which is covered in the next section.

If you know one RDBMS, you know all of them. While there are a few differences in implementation, they're relatively minor. When compared to the level of difference between, for example, scripting languages like ASP and PHP, the differences between database implementations are miniscule.

An understanding of database concepts, database design concepts, and some SQL allows you to be at home with virtually all current RDBMS systems. Let's cover some of the likely contenders that you may be using.

SQL Server 2000

Microsoft's current flagship database, SQL Server 2000 (sometimes pronounced "sequel" and sometimes "S-Q-L") is the RDBMS we use for most of our development. SQL Server is an excellent choice if you are running on a Windows platform. It's a robust and powerful database system with a lot of great graphical tools.

One major plus point is that it is becoming very prevalent as an option on Web hosting packages (the same cannot be said of databases like Oracle) and is arguably easier to implement and administer than other enterprise-level commercial databases.

Xref   SQL Server is an excellent choice for developers with Microsoft Access experience, and Access can even be used as a front end for SQL Server, as explained later in this chapter.

Oracle

The best performing and most expensive of the enterprise RDBMS systems, Oracle, is the database of choice for complex, extreme-traffic Web sites. Oracle is the most powerful and scalable of all databases but can be enormously complex to administer and is not to be taken lightly.

The most essential thing to have on hand when using an Oracle database is a skilled Oracle DBA (**Data**b**ase A**dministrator).

MySQL

MySQL is worth mentioning here, as it is hugely widespread on Linux platforms. For a few dollars a month, you're likely to find it on almost any standard Linux hosting provider.

MySQL is fast and robust. For several years it suffered from not being as fully featured as most commercial RDBMSs and lacked what many considered essential components of an RDBMS (such as transactions). It is available on most platforms. Although MySQL is also available on the Windows platform, it's typically found on Linux boxes in association with the PHP scripting language, with which it works extremely well.

Other Databases

PostGreSQL, DB2, Sybase, and Informix are other RDBMS choices. We have nothing against these databases. The truth is, they'll work just as well and use exactly the same concepts and techniques as those we'll cover. However, we won't explore them specifically due to space limitations of this book. Just going by the numbers of each in use, the chances are that you're going to be using one of the first three databases we mentioned.

WHAT ABOUT ACCESS?

Microsoft Access is a great little database. But it's not a suitable choice for running a high-end Web site and was never intended to be.

MS Access is a file-based database, rather than a client-server database system. This means that all the database definitions, indexes, rules, and data are stored in the same single file. While this makes it easy and convenient to use over a LAN, it is a disadvantage in a more complex environment such as an enterprise-level Web site. It does not have the reliability, scalability, and security options offered by the other databases.

However, Access can be an excellent tool for quickly generating proof-of-concept databases: It's quick, it's easy, and it upgrades very smoothly to SQL Server.

WHAT ABOUT ACCESS? *(continued)*

There's one other feature worth mentioning. Many developers intending to build data-driven Web sites often obtain a high-end Web hosting account with a SQL Server database. However, they're not sure how to start building their database because they don't have their own copy of the SQL Server software and don't have the client tools necessary for building SQL Server databases.

There are two solutions to this problem:

- You can download an evaluation copy of SQL Server from the Microsoft Web site at www.microsoft.com/sql/evaluation/trial/default.asp. This is a 120-day trial, which should be enough time for anyone to determine whether they want to use SQL Server or not.

- Or you can use Microsoft Access to connect to and manipulate SQL Server databases. It's quick and extremely easy. The steps are as follows:

  1. Open MS Access and choose New Project.

  2. Access prompts you to name and save an .adp (Access Data Project) on your machine.

  3. Access then prompts you to create a data link. Here you can specify all necessary connections to your SQL Server database. An example is shown in **Figure 4.11.**

  4. Click OK. That's it! You can now use the familiar Access interface to create tables, add data, and perform most basic database operations.

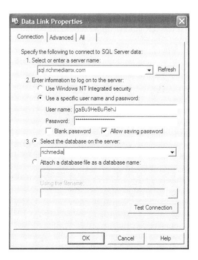

Figure 4.11 Specifying a data link in MS Access.

STRUCTURED QUERY LANGUAGE (SQL)

Structured Query Language (SQL) is the common language of databases. It lies at the core of every RDBMS that you're likely to use. Remove all the fancy GUI interfaces, the query builders, and the wizards, and you can still do anything you need to do to a database, as long as you have a command-line prompt and know a little SQL.

SQL is really two languages. One part deals with manipulating the data inside the database: retrieving information, deleting information, and updating and inserting information. The other part deals with operations on the database structure itself: creating, altering, and deleting tables. In this section, you learn how to use SQL to get information from an existing database. More SQL will be covered in later chapters.

SQL is a declarative language, not a procedural one. What this means is that you use SQL to describe what you want, and you let the RDBMS handle how it's actually done. You don't manually lay out the steps of the procedure as you do in other programming languages.

In practice, this means that if you want to know all the employees whose names begin with "A," you describe what you want:

```
"Give me all the employees with a last name beginning with A."
```

Or write it in SQL syntax:

```
SELECT * FROM employees WHERE last_name LIKE 'A%'
```

This is a different mindset than in most programming languages, where you would have to detail the individual steps, such as in the following pseudocode:

```
FOR EACH employee in employees
   IF last_name BEGINS WITH "A"
      //do some stuff
   ELSE
      //do some other stuff
   END IF
NEXT
```

You can use GUI tools to generate SQL. For example, the Recordset dialog box in Dreamweaver MX can generate SQL for you. However, a modicum of SQL knowledge goes a long way and is essential if you plan to spend any amount of time dealing with databases.

Luckily, SQL is a pretty simple language. Learning how to use a few SQL keywords, perhaps nine or ten, allows you to request virtually anything from a database.

Queries

A piece of SQL that interrogates a database is referred to as a *query*. These can be either extremely complex or very simple. For example, a basic SQL query would be this:

```
SELECT *
FROM customers
```

The asterisk means "bring me all the fields from the table." SELECT and FROM are the SQL keywords, and customers is the table name.

You don't have to always retrieve every field. An important concept when retrieving information from databases is to retrieve only what you need. This saves on both processor time and network traffic.

To retrieve a single field, the syntax is as follows:

```
SELECT fax_number
FROM customers
```

Or you can retrieve multiple fields by separating them with commas:

```
SELECT customer_name, fax_number, phone_number, email
FROM customers
```

The previous example retrieves the contact information for all customers, not necessarily in a particular order. You might want to sort the information by using the ORDER BY keyword, which is easy.

```
SELECT customer_name, fax_number, phone_number, email
FROM customers
ORDER BY customer_name
```

Or you could even restrict information to a single customer by using the keyword WHERE, as follows:

```
SELECT customer_name, fax_number, phone_number, email
FROM customers
WHERE customer_name = "Macromedia"
```

All we've used are four SQL terms: SELECT, FROM, WHERE and ORDER BY. These keywords cover a lot of simple queries.

Joins

Beyond selecting information from one table, you can bring back information from several by performing *joins* within your SQL. We talked earlier about splitting up information into multiple tables in order to decrease data redundancy. The unfortunate flipside to this is that we have to join those tables back up to get the data in a meaningful fashion.

For example, we can create a query that shows us the details for a certain order number:

```
SELECT order_id, customer_id, date_ordered, date_sent
FROM orders
WHERE order_id = 1234
```

This will bring back data like the following:

order_id	customer_id	date_ordered	date_sent
123	5	10/27/02	10/28/02

But what if we want the customer name and not the customer ID? This is easy in theory because we have the unique customer ID. In practice, it takes a little while to get used to, but here's an example:

First, we add the field we want to our example: in this case, **customer_name**

```
SELECT order_id, customer_id, date_ordered, date_sent, customer_name
FROM orders
WHERE order_id = 1234
```

But **customer_name** is not part of the orders table, so we then add the necessary table to the query.

```
SELECT order_id, customer_id, date_ordered, date_sent, customer_name
FROM orders, customers
WHERE order_id = 1234
```

Unfortunately, this is still not specific enough. Now we are selecting from two tables, both of which contain a field called customer_id. The RDBMS is not going to know which customer_id in which table the query is referring to in the first line of the SQL.

We know that it doesn't actually matter because we're talking about the same customer_id in both tables. But we have to be specific, so let's pick a table and qualify the customer_id as follows:

```
SELECT order_id, orders.customer_id, date_ordered, date_sent, customer_name
FROM orders, customers
WHERE order_id = 1234
```

We're nearly there; we have just one more step. We have to tell the database exactly how the two tables are supposed to relate to each other. We need to name the fields on each table that relate to each other as part of our WHERE clause.

```
SELECT order_id, customer_id, date_ordered, date_sent, customer_name
FROM orders, customers
WHERE order_id = 1234
AND orders.customer_id = customers.customer_id
```

If we fail to specify exactly how the tables are joined, the RBDMS brings back the first customer name it finds, which may have nothing to do with the customer ID in our orders table. Running our SQL query should now return:

order_id	customer_id	date_ordered	date_sent	customer_name
123	5	10/27/02	10/28/02	Acme Inc.

For more complex joins, consult a reference on SQL. Some are suggested in the section "Learning More about Database Design and Implementation" at the end of this chapter.

Aggregate Functions

Beyond just retrieving data from tables, whether from a single table or multiple tables, you can also perform numeric functions—averaging, adding, finding minimum and maximum values, and so on— on the data in the tables.

Some examples follow. In later chapters, you will learn how these aggregate functions are used in the context of Rich Internet Application development.

AVG returns the average of a numeric column:

```
SELECT AVG(price)
FROM orders
WHERE zip = 85254
```

COUNT(*) counts the number of records returned from a query:

```
SELECT COUNT(*)
FROM customers
WHERE zip = 85254
```

SUM (*column name*) calculates the total of a specified column:

```
SELECT SUM(price)
FROM orders
WHERE customer_id = 55455
```

MIN determines the lowest value of the specified field in a query:

```
SELECT MIN (price)
FROM orders
```

MAX determines the highest value of the specified field in a query:

```
SELECT MAX(price)
FROM orders
```

These functions are very useful and somewhat underused benefits of SQL. They allow you to request data for graphs and statistics without having to programmatically retrieve all the data and step your way through it, calculating the data you want. You can just request the calculated data directly from the database itself.

LEARNING MORE ABOUT DATABASE DESIGN AND IMPLEMENTATION

As we've mentioned throughout this chapter, we're just attempting to introduce you to the concepts of developing and using relational databases. If you intend to pursue this further, here are some books we recommend on the different areas:

Designing Databases

Database design is an area where you can usually remain agnostic about your choice of database system because it should be completely detached from the actual process of creating your database, once designed. Some books we've found useful include:

Database Design for Mere Mortals, Michael Hernandez, Addison Wesley

Inside Relational Databases, Mark Whitehorn and Bill Markly, Springer Verlag

Building Databases

Building databases is where the database-specific books come in handy, and where you can discover the ins and outs of your chosen RDBMS. Some books we've found useful include:

Step by Step Microsoft SQL Server 2000, Rebecca M. Riordan, Microsoft Press

Oracle in a Nutshell, Rick Greenwald, David C. Kreines, O'Reilly

MySQL: Visual QuickStart Guide, Larry Ullman, Peachpit Press

Using Databases

SQL knowledge is an extremely useful thing to have, and SQL is one of those languages that can take you a weekend to learn and a lifetime to master. We suggest these titles:

SQL in a Nutshell, Kevin Kline and Daniel Kline, O'Reilly and Associates

SQL in 10 Minutes, Ben Forta, Sams

SQL: Visual QuickStart Guide, Chris Fehily, Peachpit Press

For an up-to-date list of resources, check out this book's Web site at www.mxbook.com.

Database Use in Rich Internet Applications

First things first: Your Flash movies can't talk directly to a database. There must be some kind of middleman involved, whether it's a ColdFusion page, an ASP page, a ColdFusion component, or a Web Service accessed by Flash Remoting.

 Note   ColdFusion is explored in Chapter 3, Flash Remoting in Chapter 7.

Beyond that, there aren't any major concerns when you create databases for Rich Internet Application use. The standard concern for building databases is the same, whether the end user will be using HTML, Flash, or a custom-built standalone application.

With the growth of Rich Internet Applications, there really isn't one type of database that can be characterized as the ideal Rich Internet Application database. They're all starting to be used:

- User database—to control user access to Rich Internet Applications

- Content databases—to fuel bulletin boards, articles, and content

- Analytical Databases—to display volatile data in an understandable format using available options like the Flash graphing components

There are some minor concerns when creating, for example, a content database for an HTML site. If you store text data that includes the HTML tags for formatting, you don't need to be restrictive on the type of HTML stored in the database fields. However, if the content database is intended to be used by Flash applications, you need to be aware that Flash is much more picky about what it will and won't represent properly.

Summary

- A Relational Database Management System (RDBMS) is the program that handles the creation and management of your databases. These include Oracle, SQL Server, and MySQL.

- Most commonly available database systems share common core concepts and functionality: If you know one, using another is not a major problem.

- Databases are made up of tables, which represent an entity in your system.

- Tables contain records, which each represent a single occurrence of each entity, such as an employee.

- Each record is defined by a number of fields, which specifically state the information needed to be stored in the database.

- You should be as specific as possible when creating your field definitions, as it increases usability of the database and helps prevent corrupt data from occurring.

- Data modeling is the process of designing your database and should be kept completely separate from the process of implementing your database. Data modeling involves deciding what tables to create, what fields should be in the tables, and what relationships exist between tables.

- There are three types or relationships between tables: One-to-One, One-to-Many, and Many-to-Many. The most common types of relationships are One-to-Many. One-to-One relationships are uncommon.

- Many-to-Many relationships are implemented by creating a linking table between the two tables that need to relate.

- Databases should be taken through the process of normalization, following set rules and guidelines to ensure that the database conforms to relational database concepts.

- SQL is the common language of databases. It can be used to do everything from creating database tables to retrieving, updating, and deleting data. SQL contains aggregate functions that allow you to perform numeric operations on database content without having to do it programmatically within your application.

- Rich Internet Applications, by and large, present no additional complications when creating and implementing databases.

In This Chapter:

5 Web Services

Web Services are a new method of deploying Web applications. They allow Web sites to share functionality and to communicate easily with each other, whether across the room or across the globe.

Web Services are often difficult to understand initially, due to their associated jargon. However, as more and more developers begin to use and build Web Services, they are transforming the way we build dynamic Web sites. This chapter will cover the following:

- What Web Services are

- How Web Services work

- When to use them

- How to use and create them with Macromedia MX tools

- How best to use Web Services in Rich Internet Applications

WHAT ARE WEB SERVICES?

When building Web applications, a substantial amount of time, effort, and expense is put into what can be considered common functionality, such as:

- Figuring out how much it will cost to ship a package from point A to point B

- Getting the current weather in a certain city

- Retrieving a current stock price

- Verifying a credit card

For the most part, you have to write these routines yourself in whatever programming language you've chosen for your Web application. Sometimes it's possible to sign up with a credit card clearance house or EDI (**E**lectronic **D**ata **I**nterchange) bureau that deals in enterprise-level systems integration. After paying their signup fees, you can download substantial documentation so that you can work through your application and change it to meet with their requirements.

Web Services are built to revolutionize that process. By using a combination of different industry standard protocols, Web Services allow integration between computer systems to be substantially automated, and to be cheaper, faster, and easier than ever before.

Why Use Web Services?

In your daily life, you farm out tasks to other people—whether you think of it that way or not—because it's easier, faster, and more economical to do so. Most people rarely bake their own bread, make their own clothes, or build their own cars.

Web Services provide a marketplace of common functionality similar to the services you use from day to day. Some are free; others are available for a price. You decide if the price is worth it. Some Web Services are open to everyone, others to a restricted few. Some of the functionality is minor; some is the result of years of work.

By providing a standardized framework to share and trade functionality, Web Services enable developers to quickly assemble software applications by "plugging in" services, rather than having to custom-develop every part of the application. It also allows applications to make use of services that may be economically unfeasible to include in development. For example, it would take millions of dollars to build a substantial search engine, but you can use Web Services to integrate with Google in a matter of minutes.

Web Services Background

Web Services work because they're built around industry standard methods of exchanging information. They don't tie you to any one company, and they don't rely on proprietary connection methods or protocols, as do many alternative methods of integration. Web Services communicate using HTTP, the basic protocol of the Web, and they pass information back and forth using simple XML for formatting.

Previous attempts at integration were often stymied by differences in hardware platforms or operating systems. By using Web Services, all this is irrelevant. Any platform that understands Web Services—whether on Windows or Unix, using IIS or Apache or WebSphere—can talk to any other Web Service-enabled platform without caring, or even knowing, if there's a difference.

Web Services can be written in virtually any programming language. While some languages (C#, VB.NET, or ColdFusion) are particularly suited, Web Services can be created in anything from Python to COBOL, and once again, it doesn't matter to anyone wanting to use that Web Service.

You only need to know one thing about the Web Service—where it is.

Web Services Requirements

Web Services can be used and created by any of the current generation of application servers, including:

- Microsoft Windows 2000 and XP Professional support Web Services on IIS Web server, as part of the ASP.NET platform. ASP.NET is an additional free download available from www.asp.net.

- XP Home does not come with an option for IIS but can also be used for testing Web Services if the additional WebMatrix tool from Microsoft is installed. This is available from www.asp.net.

- ColdFusion MX includes full support for using and creating Web Services. ColdFusion MX is covered in greater detail in Chapter 3.

- Other application servers include support for Web Services, including IBM WebSphere, Macromedia Jrun, and SunONE.

How Do Web Services Work?

To best explain how Web Services work, let's take a step back and look at an example scenario for using Web Services, illustrated in **Figure 5.1.**

A small business selling widgets builds a Rich Internet Application to allow their customers to use a one-page environment to purchase equipment. They can build the application comfortably, but a sticking point is calculating shipping for their customers' purchases. They've tried building database tables before to cover all the eventualities of shipping, but ran into a lot of issues including:

- They included USPS and FedEx rates, then a customer would complain that they couldn't use their UPS account.

- They weren't always aware when the rates changed, leading to postal discrepancies eating into their profit margin.

- They found it extremely challenging and time consuming to figure out the different rates when shipping to different zip codes.

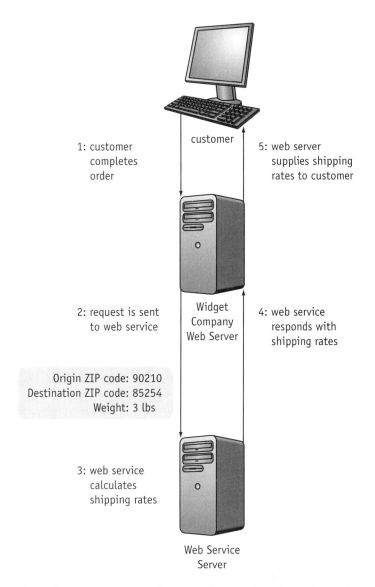

1: customer
completes
order

customer

5: web server
supplies shipping
rates to customer

2: request is sent
to web service

Widget
Company
Web Server

4: web service
responds with
shipping rates

Origin ZIP code: 90210
Destination ZIP code: 85254
Weight: 3 lbs

3: web service
calculates
shipping rates

Web Service
Server

Figure 5.1 An e-commerce site can easily use a Web Service to provide functionality that the site's designers would otherwise find time-consuming or expensive to produce themselves.

The point is this: they want to sell widgets, not build shipping-rate databases. So they find a Web Service provider that has a centralized shipping calculation Web Service. The widget company doesn't know where this Web Service is based, and doesn't care what programming language it's written in. All they know is that they can pass it three things:

- The weight of the package
- Their own zip code
- The destination zip code

And the Web Service will return a long list of different rates for all the options of the major shipping companies. The widget company then presents their customer with a list of all available choices for shipping and allows customers to choose the method they feel is best.

As part of the process of adding this Web Service to their Web site, the developers needed to do three things:

- Find the Web Service—also referred to as *discovery*
- Find out exactly what it does—the process of *description*
- Use—or *consume*—the Web Service

Fortunately, most of this process is automated by the industry standard protocols mentioned earlier.

WEB SERVICE PROTOCOLS

The plethora of abbreviations and jargon is one reason why Web Services seem to have such a steep learning curve. However, it's a little misleading. While it's important to understand what's entailed in the different protocols, it's almost all an automated process. You rarely need to get your hands dirty in the specifics of the protocols themselves.

One could make the analogy that when you use a product like Macromedia Dreamweaver MX to build Web pages, it's vital that you understand that you are, in fact, building HTML, but it's not necessary that you manually do it. This is similar with Web Services. You need to understand the protocols, but you do not manually write them yourself.

In fact, some of the Web Service protocols are specifically designed to be machine-generated.

XML

EXtensible Markup Language (XML) is the foundation of Web Services. Microsoft even refers to Web Services as "XML Web Services." XML is an industry standard for transferring data as structured text files. However, XML by itself can be used for any kind of data exchange; it's too loosely defined to be specific to Web Services. The power of XML comes from its flexibility, but Web Services require a more formal definition in order to be understood by different applications on different platforms.

SOAP

Simple Object Access Protocol (SOAP) is the defined format for using XML as the data exchange language for Web Services. What this means is that although we are using XML to communicate, we are using a particular defined version of it.

 Note If XML were the English language, SOAP would be a more strictly defined usage of it, such as that used in air traffic control. While communication between the tower and the pilot is in English, it's not typical conversation. There are very specific rules and guidelines for correct usage in this circumstance: who speaks first, the order of conversation, even the correct words and terms to use. Anything else leads to miscommunication and misunderstandings with potentially disastrous consequences.

SOAP is what is actually sent back and forth over the Internet when using Web Services, in what are referred to as SOAP envelopes.

Because SOAP is sent over HTTP, it has to follow the Request/Response model like any other Web application. This just means that the requests and responses are structured more formally. The following code example shows a SOAP Request envelope being sent to a simple Web Service to find the current temperature for a given zip code:

```
<SOAP-ENV:Envelope xmlns:SOAP-
➞ENV="http://schemas.xmlsoap.org/soap/envelope/"
➞xmlns:xsi="http://www.w3.org/1999/XMLSchema-instance"
➞xmlns:xsd="http://www.w3.org/1999/XMLSchema">
<SOAP-ENV:Body>
<ns1:getTemp xmlns:ns1="urn:xmethods-Temperature" SOAP-
➞ENV:encodingStyle="http://schemas.xmlsoap.org/soap/encoding/">
<zipcode xsi:type="xsd:string">85254</zipcode>
</ns1:getTemp>
</SOAP-ENV:Body>
</SOAP-ENV:Envelope>
```

The SOAP Response envelope from the Web Service looks like this:

```
<SOAP-ENV:Envelope xmlns:SOAP-
➞ENV="http://schemas.xmlsoap.org/soap/envelope/"
➞xmlns:xsi="http://www.w3.org/1999/XMLSchema-instance"
➞xmlns:xsd="http://www.w3.org/1999/XMLSchema">
<SOAP-ENV:Body>
<ns1:getTempResponse xmlns:ns1="urn:xmethods-Temperature" SOAP-
➞ENV:encodingStyle="http://schemas.xmlsoap.org/soap/encoding/">
<return xsi:type="xsd:float">98.0</return>
</ns1:getTempResponse>
</SOAP-ENV:Body>
</SOAP-ENV:Envelope>
```

In both instances, most of the SOAP content is taken up by the necessary formatting. The two lines that are actually important are the zip code line in the Request envelope:

```
<zipcode xsi:type="xsd:string">85254</zipcode>
```

and the returned temperature in the Response envelope:

```
<return xsi:type="xsd:float">98.0</return>
```

You don't normally have to worry about formatting the SOAP messages yourself. When you use the tools within Dreamweaver MX, SOAP formatting is automatically generated by the created Web Service.

WSDL

Web **S**ervices **D**escription Language (WSDL) is another way that the Web Service process is automated. Typically, when you develop a Web Service using a tool like Dreamweaver or Microsoft's Visual Studio.NET, a WSDL file is automatically generated that describes in a specific format exactly what the Web Service does and what it needs to run correctly. In turn, when you use a Web Service on one of your pages, the WSDL that was generated by the developer is interpreted by Dreamweaver and used to create the code necessary to talk to the Web Service with the minimum of difficulty on the part of the developer. So, in that sense, even though WSDL is readable, as shown in the next code example, it's essentially *by* machines, *for* machines. Human intervention is rarely needed.

The following is a WSDL file for the simple Weather Temperature Web Service used in the SOAP examples:

```
<?xml version="1.0" ?>
<definitions name="TemperatureService"
→ targetNamespace="http://www.xmethods.net/sd/TemperatureService.wsdl"
→ xmlns:tns="http://www.xmethods.net/sd/TemperatureService.wsdl"
→ xmlns:xsd="http://www.w3.org/2001/XMLSchema"
→ xmlns:soap="http://schemas.xmlsoap.org/wsdl/soap/"
→ xmlns="http://schemas.xmlsoap.org/wsdl/">
<message name="getTempRequest">
  <part name="zipcode" type="xsd:string" />
  </message>
<message name="getTempResponse">
  <part name="return" type="xsd:float" />
  </message>
<portType name="TemperaturePortType">
<operation name="getTemp">
  <input message="tns:getTempRequest" />
  <output message="tns:getTempResponse" />
  </operation>
  </portType>
<binding name="TemperatureBinding" type="tns:TemperaturePortType">
  <soap:binding style="rpc"
→ transport="http://schemas.xmlsoap.org/soap/http" />
<operation name="getTemp">
  <soap:operation soapAction="" />
<input>
```

```
  <soap:body use="encoded" namespace="urn:xmethods-Temperature"
→ encodingStyle="http://schemas.xmlsoap.org/soap/encoding/" />
  </input>
<output>
  <soap:body use="encoded" namespace="urn:xmethods-Temperature"
→ encodingStyle="http://schemas.xmlsoap.org/soap/encoding/" />
  </output>
  </operation>
  </binding>
<service name="TemperatureService">
  <documentation>Returns current temperature in a given U.S.
→ zipcode</documentation>
<port name="TemperaturePort" binding="tns:TemperatureBinding">
  <soap:address
→ location="http://services.xmethods.net:80/soap/servlet/rpcrouter" />
  </port>
  </service>
  </definitions>
```

While most of the WSDL content is the formalities of the structure, you can see useful content, such as a description, by browsing the following code:

```
<documentation>Returns current temperature in a given U.S.
→ zipcode</documentation>
```

and the following lines, which determine the request and response from the Web Service:

```
- <message name="getTempRequest">
  <part name="zipcode" type="xsd:string" />
  </message>
- <message name="getTempResponse">
  <part name="return" type="xsd:float" />
  </message>
```

These lines of code directly tie to the SOAP Request and Response envelopes shown previously.

UDDI

Another term you'll come across when exploring the world of Web Services is **U**niversal **D**iscovery **D**escription and **I**ntegration (UDDI). UDDI is gaining headway as the protocol used to create Web Service directories.

At this point, Web Services can be hard to find. Although it's easy to explore the world of Web Services with big-name examples like Amazon.com and Google, it's not so easy to find a specific and less-general Web Service. So how do you know if they exist? An obvious step is the creation of Web Service directories— essentially, phone books for Web Services. These directories are how you can find out if Web Services for a particular task exist, whether commonplace or esoteric.

While the most important thing to know about a Web Service is its WSDL location, directories should contain more information about the Web Service, such as descriptions, example code, and links to the developer's site.

When adding a Web Service in Dreamweaver MX, if you don't know the WSDL location, Dreamweaver can provide you with quick links to UDDI directories, as seen in **Figure 5.2.**

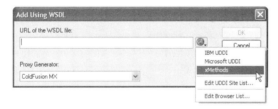

Figure 5.2 When adding Web Services, Dreamweaver MX provides links to Web Service directories on the Web.

These options simply take you to the respective Web sites for the Web Service directories; they don't do anything beyond opening a browser window. You can then explore the directory to find the Web Service that meets your needs. All the major UDDI directories are supposed to exchange information with each other and so should contain identical information; only the interfaces should differ.

As yet, none of the Web Service directories contain rating information; this is a sorely missed feature, as users cannot determine anything about the Web Service's ease of use or reliability.

WHEN TO USE WEB SERVICES

The more obscure your Rich Internet Application functionality, the less likely you are to use Web Services, and the more likely you'll have to develop the functionality yourself. Web Services aren't for everything and you shouldn't feel the need to use them just to fulfill some imaginary need. The main reasons for using Web Services are the following:

- **Common functionality:** Web Services are used to avoid redundant code for functions that are required in many places and that have already had substantial time and effort expended into solving the problem. Don't reinvent the wheel if you don't have to.

- **Time and effort savings:** Many Web Services can be implemented in minutes or hours rather than weeks or months of custom development.

- **Increased functionality:** When you have to develop your own system, such as a shopping cart, it's possible that you only have time and/or expense to implement the core functionality. Web Services could allow you to use an external service, which supplies extra abilities, such as wish lists or collaborative filtering.

HOW TO USE WEB SERVICES

You can make use of Web Services in both regular HTML pages and in Flash-based Rich Internet Applications. You use Dreamweaver to build HTML pages that use—or more correctly, consume—Web Services. Dreamweaver MX contains substantial support for using Web Services in the ASP.NET, ColdFusion, and JSP server models.

 Dreamweaver MX does not include Web Services support for the PHP or "classic" ASP server models.

You also use Dreamweaver MX to create Web Services that are accessible by other Web applications. This is particularly straightforward in ColdFusion MX, as **C**oldFusion **C**omponents (CFCs) can be easily turned into publicly accessible Web Services. You can find more detailed information about CFCs in Chapter 3.

Flash MX, along with Flash Remoting, is used to connect Flash applications to Web Services. More about Flash Remoting is covered in Chapter 7.

Note — Flash Remoting must be installed on the Web server to enable Flash MX applications to connect to Web Services. Only Flash Player 6 movies can use Flash Remoting.

CONSUMING WEB SERVICES IN DREAMWEAVER MX

To use, or *consume*, Web Services in Dreamweaver MX is a straightforward process, although it is essential that you have a few prerequisites in place. The most important aspect is the WSDL location of the Web Service you wish to use. If you don't have one in mind, you can go to any of the Web Service directories and find one for testing.

You copy the URL of the WSDL file and paste it into a dialog box accessed from Dreamweaver's Components panel. Dreamweaver then examines the WSDL, essentially finding out everything there is to know about the Web Service by looking at the WSDL file that was generated when the Web Service was written. Dreamweaver uses this information to create a *proxy*. This is a file of machine-generated code that acts as a middleman (or proxy), making it simple for your page to connect to the Web Service without knowing the specifics of how it was implemented.

Note — The proxy is generated in the language you have chosen for your Web site: C#, VB.NET, ColdFusion MX, or JSP.

Dreamweaver also populates the Components panel with a visual representation of the Web Service, showing its properties and methods and allowing you to drag and drop elements onto your page.

You add all the necessary code to your page to use the Web Service. This is often a small amount of code, as most of the coding necessary to use the Web Service has been created in the proxy.

Because your page makes use of the proxy class files that Dreamweaver generates, you must first make sure that those files are copied to your server, and then test your page.

Consuming a Web Service in ColdFusion MX

This section reconstructs an example of creating a ColdFusion MX page that consumes the simple Web Service used in the earlier examples—to find the weather in a certain U.S. zip code.

 Note

Before adding a Web Service, you must have a ColdFusion site correctly defined in Dreamweaver. Consult the Dreamweaver Help files if you need assistance.

TO CREATE A PAGE TO CONSUME OUR WEB SERVICE:

1. Create a new ColdFusion MX page in your Web site.

2. In the Components panel, select Web Services and click the plus (+) button, as shown in **Figure 5.3**. The Add Using WSDL dialog box appears.

Figure 5.3 The Components panel in Dreamweaver MX allows you to add Web Services.

3. Click the Globe icon and select the xMethods entry. This will open a browser to the xMethods Web site at www.xmethods.net.

4. Find the Weather Temperature Web Service and click the link. This will open a page to show greater details about the Weather Temperature Web Service, including what we're most interested in: the location of the WSDL. This is shown in **Figure 5.4**.

5. Select the entire URL of the WSDL entry, including the http:// portion, and copy it.

6. Switch back to Dreamweaver. The Add Using WSDL dialog box should still be open. Paste the entire WSDL URL into the dialog box and click OK.

7. At this point, Dreamweaver connects to the WSDL file and *introspects* it: It figures out exactly what it does, and the information it needs to work, and generates any proxy classes that need to sit between your page and the Web Service.

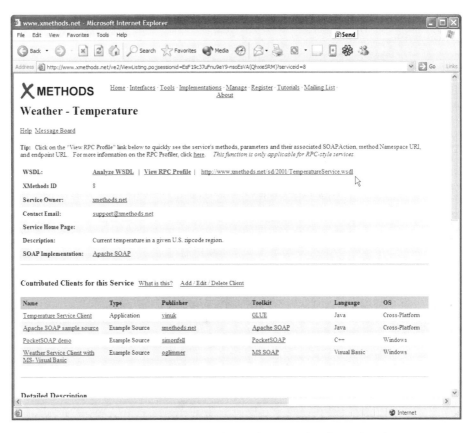

Figure 5.4 The xMethods Web site is one of several Web Service directories where you can find details on available Web Services.

Dreamweaver populates the Components panel with a visual representation of the Web Service, as shown in **Figure 5.5.** You can expand the Web Service details by clicking the Plus (+) button beside it.

8. On your ColdFusion page, switch into Code View.

Figure 5.5 After a Web Service has been added, the Components panel provides a visual breakdown of its methods and properties (ColdFusion MX).

Note You can't work with Web Services completely in design view; they all require at least a small amount of hand-coding.

9. In Code View, highlight the `float getTemp` line in the Components panel and drag it into page code between the `<body>` tags. Your code should now look like this:

```
<html>
<head>
<title>Weather Temperature Page</title>
<meta http-equiv="Content-Type" content="text/html; charset=iso-8859-1">
</head>

<body>
<cfinvoke
 webservice="http://www.xmethods.net/sd/2001/TemperatureService.wsdl"
 method="getTemp"
 returnvariable="aTemp">
   <cfinvokeargument name="zipcode" value="enter_value_here"/>
</cfinvoke>

</body>
</html>
```

10. As you can see, Dreamweaver creates a `CFINVOKE` tag that calls the Weather Web Service. Dreamweaver even shows you where you need to make changes, in the line:

```
<cfinvokeargument name="zipcode" value="enter_value_here"/>
```

11. Change the value to use a valid ZIP code. The example uses 85254.

What's missing is any output of information onto the page itself; what you've done so far will correctly consume the Web Service but won't yet show it on your page.

Looking at the ColdFusion code that Dreamweaver generated, you can see the line that shows us what is returned from the Web Service invocation:

```
returnvariable="aTemp"
```

12. Enter a new line in your page to output aTemp when the page is used. Add the following code after the last line of the CFINVOKE tag. This example text uses Scottsdale, which matches the 85254 ZIP code.

```
The Temperature in Scottsdale is now: <cfoutput> #aTemp#</cfoutput>
```

13. Your code should now look like this:

```
<html>
<head>
<title>Weather Temperature Check</title>
<meta http-equiv="Content-Type" content="text/html; charset=iso-8859-1">
</head>

<body>
<cfinvoke
 webservice="http://www.xmethods.net/sd/2001/TemperatureService.wsdl"
 method="getTemp"
 returnvariable="aTemp">
 <cfinvokeargument name="zipcode" value="85254"/>
</cfinvoke>
The Temperature in Scottsdale is: <cfoutput>#aTemp#</cfoutput>
</body>
</html>
```

14. Save and test your page. When viewed through a browser, you should see the correct temperature for the zip code you entered.

Consuming a Web Service in ASP.NET

When developing ASP.NET pages that consume Web Services, you need to have the ASP.NET **S**oftware **D**evelopment **K**it (SDK) installed on your authoring machine. This is because Dreamweaver MX makes use of the tools in the ASP.NET SDK to generate the proxy classes that interface between your page and the Web Service.

Note   The ASP.NET Software Development Kit is available as a free download from www.asp.net. Make sure you choose the full install (currently 130Mb+) rather than the smaller ASP.NET framework, as Dreamweaver requires some tools that are not included in the smaller download.

This section will reconstruct an example of an ASP.NET page that consumes the simple Web Service used in the previous example and illustrates the similarities and differences when developing pages that consume Web Services.

Before adding a Web Service, you must have your ASP.NET site correctly defined in Dreamweaver. Consult the Dreamweaver documentation for further details.

TO CREATE AN ASP.NET PAGE TO CONSUME OUR WEB SERVICE:

1. Create a new ASP.NET page in your Web site. This can be either C# or VB.NET.

2. In the Components panel, select Web Services and click the Plus (+) button. The Add Using WSDL dialog box appears.

3. Click the Globe icon and select the xMethods entry. This will open a browser to the xMethods Web site at www.xmethods.net.

4. Find the Weather Temperature Web Service and click the link. This will open a page to show greater details about the Weather Temperature Web Service, including what we're most interested in: the location of the WSDL.

5. Select the entire URL of the WSDL entry, including the http:// portion, and copy it.

6. Switch back to Dreamweaver. The Add Using WSDL dialog box should still be open. Paste the entire WSDL URL into the dialog box and click OK.

7. At this point, Dreamweaver connects to the WSDL file and *introspects* it: figuring out exactly what it does, and the information it needs to work, and generating any proxies that need to sit between your page and the Web Service.

In ASP.NET, these proxy classes will be generated in either C# or VB.NET and compiled into a DLL. This DLL must then be deployed to the remote Web server in order for the page to work. Luckily, Dreamweaver makes this very easy, as we'll see in a moment.

Dreamweaver populates the Components panel with a visual representation of the Web Service, as shown in **Figure 5.6.** As you can see, this is different from the ColdFusion version, as shown in the previous exercise.

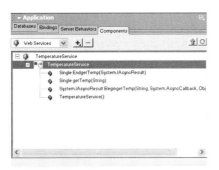

Figure 5.6 After a Web Service has been added, the Components panel provides a visual breakdown of its methods and properties (ASP.NET).

8. On your ASP.NET page, switch into Code View.

9. In Code View, highlight the last TemperatureService() entry in the Components panel and drag it into the page code between the <body> tags.

10. Select the Single getTemp(String) entry and drop it after the line you just inserted.

Your code should now look something like this:

```
<%@ Page Language="VB" ContentType="text/html" ResponseEncoding="iso-8859-1" %>
<html>
<head>
<title>ASP.NET Weather Temperature Page</title>
<meta http-equiv="Content-Type" content="text/html; charset=iso-8859-1">
</head>
<body>

dim aTemperatureService as new TemperatureService()
dim aTemp as Single = aTemperatureService.getTemp(String)

</body>
</html>
```

You've added two lines of code to call the Weather Web Service. This is substantially different in format than the ColdFusion version. The first line declares a new TemperatureService object, and the second line calls the get-Temp() method of that object.

However, this code still needs to be surrounded with <% … %> tags to denote that it is server-side code, so add those next.

11. Change the word "String" in the following line in the code to point to a valid zip code.

```
dim aTemp as Single = aTemperatureService.getTemp(String)
```

The method expects a string and not a number, which Dreamweaver has told us by introspecting the WSDL. Surround the zip code with double quotes, as in:

```
dim aTemp as Single = aTemperatureService.getTemp("85254")
```

12. What's missing is any output of information onto the page. What you've done so far will correctly consume the Web Service, but it won't yet show it on your page.

13. Enter a new line in your page to output aTemp when the page is used by adding the following code in the body of the page:

```
The Temperature is: <% =aTemp %>
```

14. Your code should now look like this:

```
<%@ Page Language="VB" ContentType="text/html" ResponseEncoding="iso-8859-1"%>
<html>
<head>
<title>ASP.NET Weather Temperature Page</title>
<meta http-equiv="Content-Type" content="text/html; charset=iso-8859-1">
</head>
<body>
<%
dim aTemperatureService as new TemperatureService()
dim aTemp as Single = aTemperatureService.getTemp("85254")
%>

The Temperature is: <% =aTemp %>
```

```
</body>
</html>
```

15. Save your page.

16. Before testing your page, you must make sure that the DLL proxy files created by Dreamweaver have been uploaded to your remote Web server.

Note Your remote Web server must be a valid ASP.NET server to make use of ASP.NET Web Services.

From the Site menu, choose Deploy Supporting Files.

The Deploy Supporting Files dialog box appears, as shown in **Figure 5.7.**

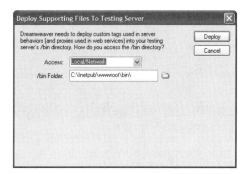

Figure 5.7 The Deploy Supporting Files dialog box ensures that you upload your proxy class files to the correct area on your Web Server.

Make sure the **/bin Folder** entry in the dialog box is pointing to the correct /bin directory for your Web server and click OK. You should see a message that confirms the correct proxy DLL files have been uploaded, as shown in **Figure 5.8.**

Figure 5.8 Proxy components must be uploaded successfully for Web Service consumer pages to work correctly.

17. Save and test your page. When viewed through a browser you should see the correct temperature for the ZIP code you entered.

CONSUMING WEB SERVICES IN FLASH

Flash MX can communicate with Web Services using Flash Remoting, which is included with ColdFusion MX and available as an add-on for ASP.NET and J2EE servers.

Flash Remoting makes it easy for Flash to connect to Web Services and to other server-side components and databases.

An additional add-on, the Flash Remoting Components, installs several components and panels into the Flash MX authoring environment to make it easier to use and debug Flash Remoting applications.

Xref

Flash Remoting is covered in more detail in Chapter 7.

SUMMARY

- Web Services are a new method that Web applications can use to communicate with each other more effectively.

- There is a growing marketplace of Web Services available, removing the need for every Web application to develop functionality that's been developed many times before.

- Web Services use standard industry protocols and do not tie you to a particular software or hardware manufacturer.

- Web Services are available on virtually all current-generation application servers, including Microsoft's ASP.NET and Macromedia's ColdFusion MX.

- Web Services are based on XML. More specifically, they use a defined version of XML known as **S**imple **O**bject **A**ccess **P**rotocol (SOAP).

- **W**eb **S**ervices **D**escription **L**anguage (WSDL) is generated automatically by most Web Service programming tools and also interpreted by the tools when you decide to use a particular service. This makes it easy for the tool to determine exactly what the Web Service does, and what it needs to work.

- Dreamweaver can be used to both create pages that consume Web Services and to create the Web Services themselves.

- Dreamweaver has support for Web Services in the ASP.NET, ColdFusion MX, and JSP server models.

- Although the concepts are similar, using Dreamweaver to create Web Service consumer pages differs from platform to platform and requires at least some knowledge of the code for the server model you use.

- Web services can be used by Flash movies when Flash Remoting is available on the server.

In This Chapter:

6 Flash Communication Server MX: The Switchboard

Just when you thought you'd seen (or learned) everything there is to know about Flash MX, Macromedia unleashed an incredibly potent server specifically designed to work with Flash MX movies. Enter Macromedia Flash Communication Server MX, also known as FlashCom or FCS. As you will learn in this chapter, a FlashCom server is the backbone for multi-user applications designed in Flash MX. But read on! FlashCom can do much more than simultaneously connect several users to one another.

REVEALING A NEW MX TECHNOLOGY

While most products in the Macromedia MX product family have been publicly available in various versions for the last few years, Flash Communication Server MX is a brand-new product that enables an entire new breed of Rich Internet Applications for Flash developers. In this section, you will learn about the capabilities of a FlashCom server.

 Note Macromedia Flash Communication Server MX is not part of the Studio MX software package. You must purchase FlashCom separately. If you don't want to purchase a full version of FlashCom, you can find shared hosting from third-party ISPs. See the book's Web site at www.richmediamx.com for more information on FlashCom hosting.

Like Macromedia ColdFusion MX, FlashCom is a server application. In order to provide a public Web site (or private corporate intranet site) with FlashCom functionality, you must have a FlashCom server to which a Flash movie (also known as a client) connects, as shown in **Figure 6.1**.

 Note Flash Communication Server is a software product, not a piece of computer or network hardware. FCS is a server application that only runs on Windows servers. Future releases of FCS will be available for other operating systems.

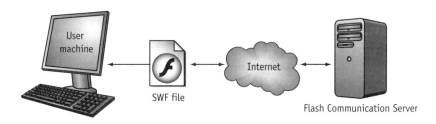

Figure 6.1 A SWF file can make a connection to a Flash Communication Server.

You develop a FlashCom-enabled Flash movie (SWF file) in the same way you make any Flash movie in the Macromedia Flash MX authoring tool. As you will learn in the "Framing Applications and Clients" section later in this chapter, there are two aspects to application development with FlashCom: client-side ActionScript and server-side ActionScript. You can develop fully functional FlashCom clients and applications by dragging and dropping FlashCom components onto the Flash document's stage, setting a few parameters, and creating a simple server-side script that connects all of the FlashCom components automatically. You can also build FlashCom clients and applications from scratch, without the use of FlashCom components. Before you start to use FlashCom, you should know what type of functionality the server can add to your Flash content.

Note   Unlike ColdFusion MX or other application servers, FlashCom works exclusively with Macromedia Flash Player 6. You cannot tap into the functionality of FlashCom with HTML pages or any other media player.

Streaming Media

By far, the most popular of FlashCom's capabilities is streaming video and audio. You can create Flash movies that broadcast video from a user's webcam and/or audio from a user's microphone to one or more users. The process of a user broadcasting video and audio through a FlashCom server is called publishing. Anyone who views or receives a published stream is called a subscriber. A Flash application can send and receive multiple simultaneous streams. The only limiting factors are the bandwidth available to the server and each client and the license of the FlashCom server. **Figure 6.2** illustrates how FlashCom acts as a stream manager for published and subscribed content.

Tip   Refer to Appendix A, "Typical Bandwidth Consumption for Streams," for more information on bandwidth consumption by various stream qualities. As you will learn later in this chapter, the number and total bandwidth of all streams allowed by a FlashCom server is determined by the license of the software.

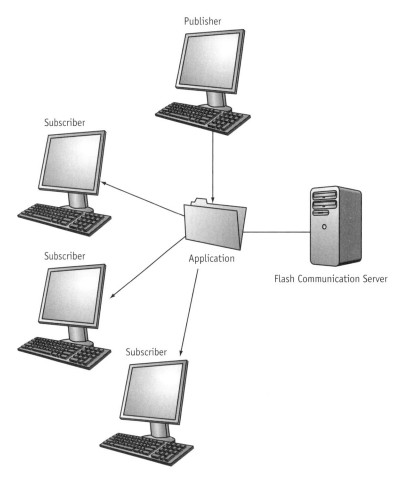

Figure 6.2 When a user publishes a stream to a FlashCom server, other users can subscribe to the stream.

Both video and audio content can be bound to one stream, or you can selectively add either video or audio to a published stream. More importantly, FlashCom applications can play stored streams as well. FlashCom has the ability to serve precompressed FLV files (discussed in Chapter 1) or FLV files that have been directly recorded from published or subscribed streams. That's right! A FlashCom server can record and archive video that a user broadcasts from Flash Player 6.

Xref

You will learn how to play and record streams in Chapter 10.

FLASHCOM AND STREAM MANAGEMENT

All compression or decompression for audio and video in the published or subscribed streams, respectively, takes place within Flash Player 6. As we'll discuss later in this chapter, FlashCom does not recompress any streaming content. Therefore, when you plan a FlashCom-enabled application, you need to make sure that published and subscribed content is designed to work with the target bitrate of your audience. For example, if one user publishes a live video and audio stream over a 384 Kbps DSL modem, a 56 Kbps modem user will not be able to handle the bitrate of the subscribing stream. The server cannot recompress the higher bitrate stream into a lower bitrate stream for the 56 Kbps user. As a result, the 56 Kbps subscriber will experience choppy playback of the stream. A FlashCom server, however, can change the frame rate of the video stream delivered to each client.

For stored streams, you can enable higher bitrate content for slower connections by enabling a longer buffer time for the streaming content. Using either client-side or server-side ActionScript, you can determine how much of a stream should buffer into the Flash Player's cache before playback begins.

A wide variety of webcams or microphones can be used with Flash Player 6 to broadcast content to a FlashCom server. For a list of known compatible camera devices, refer to the following Macromedia tech note:

www.macromedia.com/support/flashcom/ts/documents/cam_matrix.htm

If you don't see a specific device listed, that doesn't necessarily mean it isn't supported. If you can capture audio and video from your device in a video-editing application and/or use your device with other conferencing applications, chances are that the device is compatible with Flash Player 6. You can test your devices in the Settings dialog box of Flash Player 6, in the Microphone and Camera tabs (as discussed in Chapter 1).

Currently, Flash Player 6 on Windows operating systems cannot use the DV audio connection from a Firewire (aka IEEE 1394) device, such as a miniDV camcorder, as a microphone. Flash Player 6 on the Macintosh, however, can access DV audio as an active microphone. Windows users can use a separate microphone (attached to the computer's sound card) in conjunction with a Firewire camera.

STREAMING FLV FILES VERSUS "STREAMING" SWF FILES

When a Flash Communication Server streams an FLV file to a connected user, the audio and video content is not cached within the Web browser. The Flash Player has an internal buffer to hold the video and audio content as it loads and plays. You cannot stream an FLV file into a Flash movie (SWF file) without a FlashCom server connection.

Oftentimes, you will see references to SWF files as "streaming" content. While you can embed video content into a SWF file, any user who wants to watch the video will have to download the SWF file. Playback of embedded video can begin without waiting for the entire file to download, but the user cannot jump to later parts of the video that have yet to download. This is one of the primary advantages of streaming FLV content with a Flash Communication Server. You can start playing an audio/video stream at specific points within the FLV, without waiting for the rest of the file to download. You can also seek (or jump to) other areas of the FLV file instantaneously!

Real-time Message Protocol (RTMP)

The FlashCom server technology and Flash Player 6 use a proprietary protocol for transmitting streams and shared data to an application's connected users. A protocol is the means by which data is transmitted and regulated between two computers over the Internet. Most Web traffic uses HTTP, or **H**yper**T**ext **T**ransfer **P**rotocol, to send and receive requests for Web documents between a user's Web browser and a public Web server. A FlashCom server and Flash Player 6, however, use RTMP, or **R**eal **T**ime **M**essaging **P**rotocol, to relay information between a connected user's Flash movie (SWF file) and the server.

 Note

Multiuser connections with FlashCom are not peer-to-peer. This means that individual users never connect directly to one another, as do some messaging or conferencing applications (such as Windows Messenger or Microsoft NetMeeting).

RTMP is used exclusively with the new NetConnection object in Flash MX ActionScript. Once an RTMP connection is established between a Flash movie (SWF file) and a FlashCom server, the user can send and receive data from the server. No other data transfers with a Flash movie require RTMP. For example, a Flash movie (SWF file) is loaded into a Web browser with standard HTTP, but any communication between the SWF file and a FlashCom server is conducted over RTMP.

Caution

A FlashCom server is not a stand-alone Web server. You can integrate a FlashCom installation with another Web server such as Microsoft IIS or Apache, but FlashCom itself does not respond to HTTP requests. At the time of this writing, FlashCom is only available for the Windows operating system.

RTMP is not a secure protocol. For more information on RTMP and security concerns, see the information at the following URLs:

```
www.macromedia.com/desdev/mx/flashcom/articles/security_overview.html
www.macromedia.com/desdev/mx/flashcom/articles/securityreview_flashcom.pdf
```

Remote SharedObjects

FlashCom applications can do more than stream multimedia content. You can send and receive text-based messages among connected users as well. As indicated earlier, RTMP also transmits shared data that is separate from published and subscribed streams. The Flash Communication Server MX has a unique server-side SharedObject object, called remote SharedObjects. Like local SharedObject data (discussed in Chapter 1), remote SharedObject data can store any of the basic data types available in Flash MX ActionScript. Using client-side or server-side ActionScript code, you can create an application that connects to a remote SharedObject and synchronizes the data stored within the object with other connected users. In this way, you can develop live text chat applications or share properties of objects within the Flash movie among users.

One of the examples that ships with the default FlashCom installation is a shared ball demonstration. When one user moves the ball on the stage, everyone else who is connected to the application on the server can see the ball move to the new position as well. How does each user's Flash movie know that a change has occurred? When each Flash movie connects to a remote SharedObject, the FlashCom server registers the user's Flash movie with the application. When a change to the data within the remote SharedObject occurs (initiated by another user or the server), all of the Flash movies that are connected to the server are notified (**Figure 6.3**).

Remote SharedObject data can be temporary (that is, it only exists while users are connected to an application in progress) or persistent. Persistent remote SharedObject data is stored within an FSO file on the FlashCom server. Each persistent remote SharedObject has its own FSO file as well.

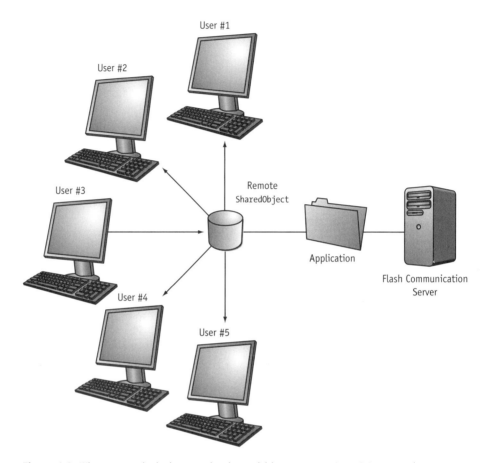

Figure 6.3 When a user (#3) changes the data within a remote SharedObject, other users who are connected to the same remote SharedObject can automatically receive the updated information.

Connectivity to Other Servers

Not only can FlashCom connect several users together, but it can also connect FlashCom applications to other remote servers, like a Macromedia ColdFusion MX server or another FlashCom server. Connections from one FlashCom server to another are possible by creating a new server-side NetConnection object that specifies the other FlashCom server. By connecting two or more FlashCom servers together, you can balance stream loads, or share data and streams from one application with another application (**Figure 6.4**).

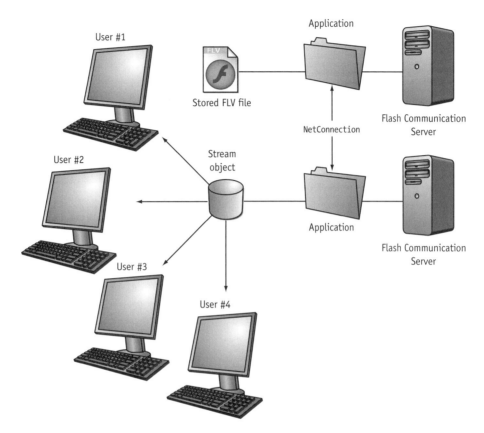

Figure 6.4 A Flash Communication Server can access content (such as a stored FLV file) on
another FlashCom server and broadcast it to connected users.

In order to connect a FlashCom application to a ColdFusion MX server or other
middleware server, you need to include the server-side Flash Remoting files (such
as netservices.asc) that are installed into the scriptlib folder of your root Flash-
Com directory. You can tap into the same power of Flash Remoting that client-side
ActionScript has at its disposal. You learn more about Flash Remoting in the next
chapter. Flash Remoting allows a FlashCom application to connect to Web services
provided by a variety of application servers, including Macromedia ColdFusion
MX, Macromedia JRun 4, Microsoft ASP.NET, and EJB (Enterprise JavaBeans). Once a
FlashCom application has connected to a remote service via Flash Remoting, data
such as record sets can be retrieved and loaded into the FlashCom application. You
can then disperse the information simultaneously to connected users of the
application, through the use of a remote SharedObject (**Figure 6.5**).

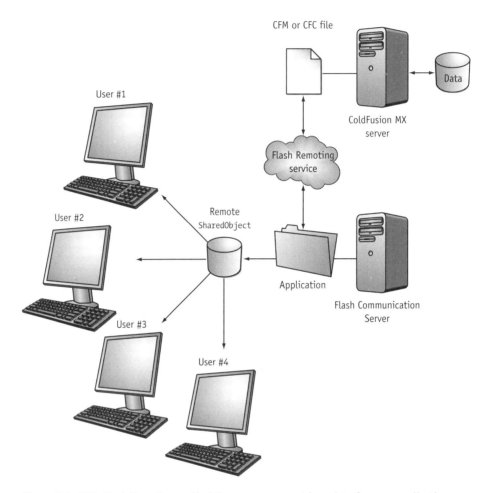

Figure 6.5 With Flash Remoting, a FlashCom server can retrieve data from an application server such as ColdFusion MX. Once the data has been retrieved, it can be distributed to connected users via a remote SharedObject.

FRAMING APPLICATIONS AND CLIENTS

When you create a FlashCom-enabled Rich Internet Application, there can be a number of files that are required for the application to function properly. In this section, you will learn the difference between application and client files that are used in conjunction with a Flash Communication Server.

COMPARING FLASHCOM TO OTHER SERVER TECHNOLOGIES

You may wonder if and how FlashCom's capabilities compare to existing server applications. Most streaming content today is delivered with industry-standard media servers such as Apple QuickTime Streaming Server, RealNetwork's Helix Universal Server, and Microsoft Windows Media Services. Most, if not all, of these media servers can take a high-quality media source file and recompress the source file on the fly to cater to a wide range of target bitrates. FlashCom, however, cannot recompress FLV files in this fashion. A FlashCom server can alter the frame rate of a published video stream to accommodate the speed of a connection, but it cannot adjust the quality (or degree) of compression applied to the content. The onus is upon you, as the developer, to create a range of source files for published streams.

As you have already learned, though, a FlashCom server does more than simply provide streaming content to a Flash movie. It can connect and share script-based objects and data among multiple users as well. Prior to the release of Macromedia's MX products, XML socket servers were the primary means of providing this type of multi-user interactivity with Flash 5 movies. Products such as Xadra Fortress and MOOCK.ORG's Unity Socket Server enable Flash clients to connect to one another via the XMLSocket object in client-side Flash ActionScript. While these products are perfectly viable for several forms of multi-user interactivity, Flash-Com provides an integrated solution with a fully documented API (Application Programming Interface) already built into Flash MX ActionScript. Currently, no third-party socket server has the audio and video capabilities of Flash Communication Server. However, most other socket servers have lower price points than the Professional edition of Macromedia Flash Communication Server MX.

Tip

Jump to the next section, "Fitting FlashCom into Your Workflow," for more information on the location of application and client files.

Defining a FlashCom Application

The first step to making a FlashCom-enabled Flash movie is to create an application on the Flash Communication Server. An application is a unique identifier that lets a FlashCom Server know which files (and directories) it should process when a connection is made to the server. It couldn't be easier to create this identifier. Simply make a new folder in the applications directory of your FlashCom installation. The name of this folder is the name of your FlashCom application. For example, if you wanted to make an application named radioshow, you would make a new folder named radioshow in the default applications directory of your FlashCom installation.

When you install the FlashCom Server software into a system, several demo applications can be put into use right away. Everything from a sample text chat to a sample videoconference is ready to go (**Figure 6.6**). Of course, you wouldn't be reading this book unless you wanted to do something more than use these examples, but the samples provide an excellent introduction to the capabilities of a FlashCom Server.

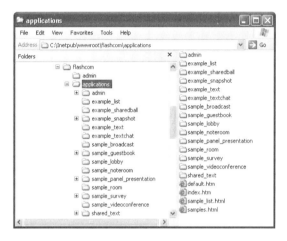

Figure 6.6 The applications folder contains the names (as folders) of all available FlashCom applications.

Tip

You can read an overview of the sample applications included with a FlashCom Server installation by viewing the samples.html document (located at the root of the applications directory) in a Web browser.

APPLICATION NAMES AND CONNECTIONS

Once you have an application folder created, the application name is refer-enced in a URI (**U**niform **R**esource **I**ndicator) within a NetConnection.connect() method. You can write the connect() method in a Flash movie (SWF file) client-side ActionScript or another FlashCom application's server-side ActionScript.

For example, if you created a new folder named pokerGame in your default applications directory, you would use the following ActionScript within your Flash document (FLA file) to connect to the FlashCom server:

```
myConnection_nc = new NetConnection();
myConnection.connect("rtmp://flashcomserver.com/pokerGame");
```

All connections to a FlashCom Server use the rtmp:// protocol reference. Flash Player 6 will automatically try to access the IP assigned to the hostname specified in the URI on port 1935. In a default installation, FlashCom services are bound to this port number. You do not need to specify this port number in your connection URI, unless you are using a port other than 1935, 80, or 443. Because a Flash Communication Server is listening for rtmp requests on port 1935 (or whatever ports it has been assigned), any Web server on the same machine will not process the request (**Figure 6.7**).

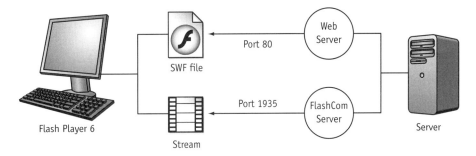

Figure 6.7 You can enable both a Flash Communication Server and a Web server on the same physical machine. Flash movies (SWF files) are served over port 80 via http requests, while FlashCom content is served over port 1935 via rtmp requests.

Note To learn more about the rtmp protocol and port numbers, refer to the "Protocol and Port Concerns" section later in this chapter.

If the FlashCom application exists on the same machine as the Flash movie (SWF file), then you can specify the application name in a shortened URI:

```
myConnection_nc = new NetConnection();
myConnection.connect("rtmp:/pokerGame");
```

In this syntax, you simply specify the rtmp reference followed by a single slash (/) and the application name.

APPLICATION INSTANCES

Just as symbols in Flash movies can have several instances, FlashCom applications can have several occurrences running simultaneously. For example, if you create a chat application, you can enable chat rooms as instances of the chat application. Each room's chat operates independently of other chats, even though each chat inherits its functionality from the default application.

The process of creating an instance of an application is nearly as simple as creating an application folder on the server. Once you create an application, you can invoke instances of it. An application instance name follows the name of the application in the URI of a NetConnection.connect() method, as in the following example:

```
myConnection_nc = new NetConnection();
myConnection.connect("rtmp://flashcomserver.com/chat/room_01");
```

This client-side ActionScript would connect the Flash movie to an application named chat, and create an instance of it named room_01. Other connected users could participate in the same chat, as long as they connected to the room_01 instance.

Most applications that use instances will require functionality that is defined in one or more server-side ActionScript files.

Note Even if you don't specify named instances in your client-side or server-side Action-Script code, a FlashCom application creates a _definst_ instance name. You will find this instance name associated with streams or SharedObject data that is saved by the primary application.

SERVER-SIDE ACTIONSCRIPT

Just as you add logic and interactivity to a Flash movie (SWF file) by adding ActionScript code to keyframes and symbol instances, the functionality of a Flash Communication Server application is described within a server-side ActionScript document (ASC file). Server-side ActionScript code is not necessarily required for an application to work. It all depends on the type of functionality that you wish to accomplish with your application. For example, you can broadcast streams to which other users can subscribe without creating any server-side ActionScript code. However, if the FlashCom application needs to send specific messages to connected users or manage unique streams for specific users, then you need to create one or more server-side ActionScript files. These files are stored within the specific named application folder within the default `applications` directory.

The syntax of server-side ActionScript is nearly identical to client-side Action-Script. Client-side ActionScript is the term used to describe ActionScript code that you create within a Flash MX document (FLA file). Not all client-side Action-Script objects (or classes) exist within server-side ActionScript. For example, you cannot create `MovieClip` or `Sound` objects in server-side ActionScript. However, you can create `Object` and `Array` objects in server-side ActionScript, just as you can with client-side ActionScript. There are even some classes and event handlers specific to server-side ActionScript, such as the `Application` and `Client` objects. In many examples throughout this book, you will learn how to use these objects to add logic to your FlashCom applications.

The primary server-side ActionScript document (ASC file) for an application is named `main.asc`. Whenever the first user of a FlashCom application connects to the application, FlashCom will automatically look for and load the `main.asc` file that resides in the application's folder.

Tip

Macromedia has pre-built a powerhouse of server-side functionality for all of the Communication components that are installed into the Flash MX authoring environment by the FlashCom Server installation. By loading the `components.asc` file into the `main.asc` file for any given application, you can easily integrate the capabilities of a Communication component. You learn more about Communication components later in this chapter.

Defining a FlashCom Client

As you learned at the start of this chapter, all of FlashCom's power relies upon Flash Player 6. In order to tap into the features of a Flash Communication Server, a Flash MX movie (SWF file) provides the interface and client-side ActionScript code to connect the FlashCom application. For most FlashCom applications, every user that connects to the Flash Communication Server will download the same Flash movie (SWF file) residing on your Web server. For example, if you want to stream a recorded FLV file to a connected user, you can create a

Flash movie (SWF file) that plays that specific recording. Any user who loads the Flash movie will be able to watch the FLV file. This process is illustrated in **Figure 6.8**. In step 1, each user requests the SWF file from the Web server. Once the Flash movie begins playback on each user's machine, the movie makes a connection to an application residing on the FlashCom server (step 2). In step 3, a recorded FLV file is streamed to each user.

If necessary, you can assign unique user IDs to each connection so that the Flash Communication Server "sees" each movie independently from the others, as a chat room would require. In **Figure 6.9**, when each user receives the Flash movie (SWF file) in step 1, a connection is made to the FlashCom application (step 2). Then the server-side ActionScript code for the application assigns a unique ID to each client (step 3).

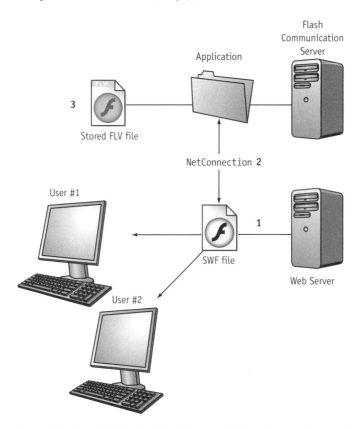

Figure 6.8 The SWF file for a FlashCom-enabled application is served by a Web server, while FlashCom-specific data, such as a FLV file, is delivered by the FlashCom server.

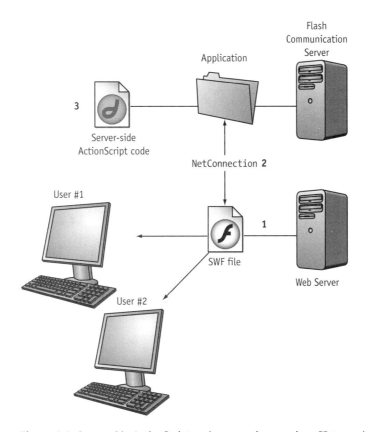

Figure 6.9 Server-side ActionScript code can assign a unique ID to each connected user.

Some applications may use two or more SWF files, each providing a specific function. For example, as shown in **Figure 6.10**, if you want to broadcast your camera to other connected users, the presenter can view a SWF file (step 1) that accesses his camera and microphone and publishes the retrieved video and audio to a stream on the Flash Communication Server (step 2). The users who want to watch the presentation can view another SWF file (step 3), which subscribes to the publishing video and audio stream (step 4).

Note

In a live production environment, the FlashCom Server should be a separate physical computer from the Web server. The Web server delivers SWF files to a user (via http), while the dedicated FlashCom server responds to connection requests (via rtmp).

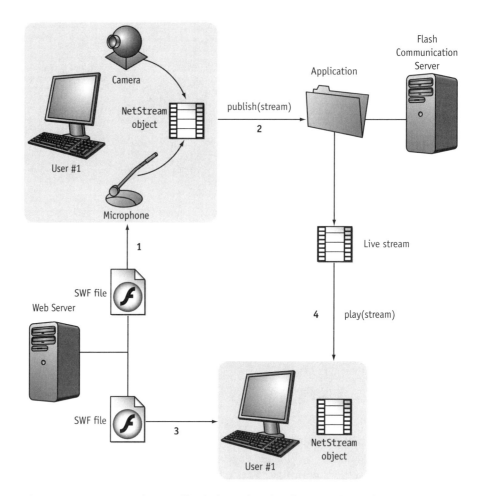

Figure 6.10 You can assign specific FlashCom functionality to each SWF file delivered by the Web server.

CLIENT-SIDE DEVELOPMENT

Once you have defined a unique application directory on the Flash Communication Server, you create a Flash document (FLA file) in Flash MX. The Flash movie (SWF file) that you publish from the FLA file should have an interface that allows the user to login to the application and use its features. The majority of this book shows you how to create Flash MX documents that interact with custom applications on a Flash Communication Server.

The process of developing FlashCom-enabled Flash movies is similar to other Flash movies that you may have built for your Web sites. As a developer or a designer, you have the choice of creating everything from scratch—anything from buttons to artwork to ActionScript code. Alternatively, you can take advantage of the new component architecture introduced with Macromedia Flash MX. As you learned in Chapter 1, components allow you to quickly add user-friendly interface elements or interactive behaviors to your Flash movies. Most components have "skins" that control their appearance. You can modify the look of these skins to conform to the identity and branding required for your Rich Internet Application. The examples in this book use a combination of custom elements, scripting, and a variety of components in order to create practical solutions.

CLIENT-SIDE ACTIONSCRIPT

As you learned at the start of this section, a Flash MX movie connects to a Flash-Com Server with a `NetConnection` object. Once a connection is established between the Flash movie (SWF file) and an application on the FlashCom Server, you can exchange or synchronize data with other connected users, or send and receive streams. Later in this chapter, you will learn more about specific objects in the ActionScript language that allow you to tap into this connectivity.

FITTING FLASHCOM INTO YOUR WORKFLOW

You can set up a development server with Macromedia Flash Communication Server MX software within a few minutes. Currently, the server software is available only for Microsoft Windows operating systems, but future support for Unix and Linux servers is anticipated. For PC-based systems, Macromedia lists the following requirements for FlashCom production-level installation:

- Pentium III 500 MHz processor (Dual Pentium IV or better recommended)
- Windows 2000 Advanced Server or Windows NT 4.0 Server (SP6 or later)
- 256 MB of available RAM (512 MB recommended)
- 50 MB of available disk space
- CD-ROM drive

Note

You can install FlashCom onto Windows XP Home, Windows XP Pro, Windows 2000 Professional, or Windows NT 4.0 Workstation SP6 or later. However, we recommend that you only use such machines for development environments, not for final production servers.

If you plan to create your own production server for FlashCom applications, make sure you also have a suitable Internet connection for your server, to accommodate the number of users (and bandwidth) that your applications will require. You can quickly eat up any high-speed Internet connection with video and audio streaming.

Xref

See Appendix A, "Typical Bandwidth Consumption for Streams," for a list of stream qualities and their corresponding bitrates. Also, refer to the book's Web site, www.richmediamx.com, for the latest news about FlashCom availability on other operating systems.

Product Editions

You can install different editions of Macromedia Flash Communication Server MX on your server. You will need to determine which version is best suited for the needs of your applications.

Tip

While you will find references to the FlashCom servers located at this book's domain, richmediamx.com, you will need to install a version of Flash Communication Server MX on your computer or Web server to test your specific files and applications.

TRIAL VERSION

The trial version of the FlashCom server provides you with the functionality of the Professional Edition (discussed later in this section) for a time period of 30 days. You can find the trial version of the server software on this book's CD-ROM, or download it from Macromedia's Web site at the following URL:

    www.macromedia.com/software/trial_download/

Note

If you install the trial version, you will not have the opportunity to reinstall the trial version again on the same machine. Be sure to install the trial version only when you can take advantage of the time allowed within the trial period. Unlike the Macromedia ColdFusion MX trial version, you cannot continue to use the Flash Communication Server trial version in any capacity beyond the trial period.

All of the examples in this book can be developed and tested with the trial version.

PERSONAL EDITION

The Personal Edition of FlashCom Server provides all of the functionality previously described in this chapter. However, this edition will only allow a maximum of 10 simultaneous connections to applications hosted by the server. Many entry-level developers mistake this to mean that only 10 users in total can ever access the server. You can easily serve content to hundreds of users each day with the Personal Edition—you just cannot serve content with more than 10 active connections at a time.

The Personal Edition also restricts the maximum data bandwidth to 1 Mbps. For example, if you created an FLV file that broadcasted a 128 Kbps audio and video stream, only 8 users could subscribe to the stream.

8 users × 128 Kbps = 1024 Kbps = 1 Mbps

We recommend that you only use the Personal Edition of FlashCom for development purposes. It is possible, though, to use the Personal Edition for small-scale production purposes, where the goals of the intended application are not hampered by the user or bandwidth limitations.

Caution

You cannot purchase an upgrade license from a Personal Edition installation to a Professional Edition (discussed next), nor can you purchase Capacity Pack licenses for the Personal Edition.

PROFESSIONAL EDITION

The Professional Edition of the Flash Communication Server is intended for a live production environment. The Professional Edition can serve content with a maximum of 500 simultaneous connections and serve a maximum of 10 Mbps in data bandwidth. Using the previous streaming 128Kbps content example, 80 users can connect (Internet bandwidth permitting) to the server and subscribe to the stream.

$$80 \times 128 \text{ Kbps} = 10{,}240 \text{ Kbps} = 10 \text{ Mbps}$$

If your application(s) requires more bandwidth or users, you can purchase additional Capacity Packs. Each pack adds another 500 simultaneous connections and 10 Mbps in data bandwidth to your FlashCom server's functionality. A Capacity Pack is simply an additional license key that you add to your existing Professional Edition installation of FlashCom.

Tip

You can upgrade or replace your FlashCom license key(s) by using the `admin.html` (and `admin.swf`) files that are installed into FlashCom's application `admin` directory.

Development and Production Installations

When you install any edition of the Flash Communication Server, the setup application asks you if you prefer a Developer Install or a Production Install, as shown in **Figure 6.11**. Each option handles client and application files differently.

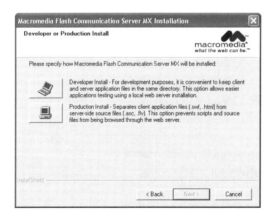

Figure 6.11 You can keep your application and client files together with a Developer Install, or you can keep them separated with a Production Install.

DEVELOPER INSTALL

This option installs both the client and application files (including the samples created by Macromedia) into the default wwwroot directory of your machine's Web server if IIS (Internet Information Services) or PWS (Personal Web Server) is detected. If you have a default installation of IIS or PWS, you will find the FlashCom client and application files in the following location:

```
C:\Inetpub\wwwroot\flashcom\applications
```

If you prefer, you can choose to install the client and application files to a different directory.

The Flash Communication Server software (that is, the actual server executable file and configuration files) has the following default installation path:

```
C:\Program Files\Macromedia\Flash Communication Server MX
```

As the install option's name implies, you may want to use this option when you install FlashCom on your own personal machine or on a development server connected to your LAN (Local Area Network).

You would not want to choose this installation for a final live FlashCom server because users could potentially download your server-side ActionScript documents (ASC files), FLA files, and recorded streams. For a live production server, you should use the Production Install, discussed in the next section.

PRODUCTION INSTALL

When several users connect to publicly accessible FlashCom-enabled Flash movies (SWF files) on a Web site, you will want to restrict users from viewing the source files of your FlashCom application, such as server-side ActionScript files, stored SharedObject data, and recorded streams. The Production Install option of the FlashCom Server setup allows you to install application files in a location different than the client files. By separating the FlashCom application files from the client files (SWF files), your Web server will have access only to the client files, while the Flash Communication Server will have access to the application files. Remember, the FlashCom Server is not a Web server; it cannot serve SWF files over an http connection. The FlashCom Server will only respond to rtmp connections, in order to send and receive streams and data from connected users.

Tip

You can edit the location of application files by editing the `<AppsDir>` location tag located with the `Vhost.xml` configuration file for Flash Communication Server. On a Windows machine, the default location of this file is `C:\Program Files\Macromedia\Flash Communication Server MX\conf\_defaultRoot_\_defaultVHost_`.

CLIENT AND APPLICATION FILE LOCATIONS

It is not necessary or recommended to serve your client files (SWF files) from the same physical machine as your application files (FlashCom ASC files, stored FLV files, and so on). For example, your Web server (such as Microsoft IIS or Apache) can host your Flash movie (SWF files) at www.yourdomain.com. Your FlashCom application files can be hosted on a machine running Flash Communication Server MX, at a different domain such as fcs.yourdomain.com or apps.yourdomain.com. In order for a Flash movie (SWF file) on one Web server to connect to a FlashCom Server, the host name of the Web server must be allowed by the `Vhost.xml` configuration file of the FlashCom server. By default, the `Vhost.xml` document has an `<Allow>` value of all, which means that any Flash movie (SWF file) located on any server (or that is running from a stand-alone player) can access the applications on your FlashCom server. In a live production installation of FlashCom, you should change the `<Allow>` value to indicate only the host names of your Web server(s) to prevent unauthorized access to your FlashCom applications.

Protocol and Port Concerns

Macromedia Flash Communication Server MX responds only to `rtmp` requests on ports that are specified in the `Adaptor.xml` configuration file. If you installed FlashCom to the default installation directory, you can find this file at the following location on Windows systems:

```
C:\Program Files\Macromedia\Flash Communication Server MX\conf\defaultRoot\
Adaptor.xml
```

Because most Microsoft Windows servers (or Windows 2000/XP Pro) have IIS 5.0 or greater installed, FlashCom responds to `rtmp` requests on port 1935. Most Web servers respond to `http` requests on port 80. As such, it is feasible to have a FlashCom Server and a Web server running on the same machine. However, many people connect to the Internet behind firewalls, which restrict a browser's (or plug-in's) access to obscure ports, such as port 1935. As such, it's quite possible that some users will not be able to connect to your FlashCom Server if it's running on port 1935.

To resolve this problem, you can configure FlashCom Server to listen on port 80. Most firewalls allow any Internet traffic on port 80. However, you cannot have a Web server and FlashCom Server both listening to port 80 on the same machine. Unless you have multiple static IPs that can be assigned to one machine running both a Web server and a FlashCom Server, we recommend that you install FlashCom Server on a separate server with its own static IP address. This server should not have any Web server running on port 80. In the Adaptor.xml configuration file for FlashCom Server, you can specify ports 1935, 80, and 443 in the default <HostPort> tag. This is the exact order that Flash Player 6 will try to access a URI specified in a NetConnection.connect() method within a Flash movie. You do not need to append these port numbers to the URI in the connect() method. For more information on protocol and port issues with Flash Communication Server, see the following tech note at Macromedia's Web site:

www.macromedia.com/support/flashcom/ts/documents/firewall.htm

UNDERSTANDING FLASHCOM FILE FORMATS

Throughout this chapter, you have learned about various file types that are associated with Flash Communication Server application development. In this section, each of these file types is described in more detail.

SWF

Every Flash Communication Server application requires a connection from a Flash movie (SWF file). The Flash movie must use a NetConnection object and connect() method in order to establish a link between the movie and the Flash-Com Server application. The SWF file can contain other Flash components and client-side ActionScript that support the functionality of the application.

FLV

A FlashCom Server can play (or publish) and record Flash Video files. Flash Video files have a .flv extension. Whenever a FlashCom Server application records a stream, a FLV file is stored in a directory named after the application's instance name, within a streams folder of the application's main directory. For example, if you made a FlashCom application named broadcast and recorded a stream named announcement, the FLV file would have the following path:

```
...\applications\broadcast\streams\_definst_\announcement.flv
```

If you installed FlashCom with a Developer Install within Microsoft IIS, you would find the file in the following location:

```
C:\inetpub\wwwroot\flashcom\applications\broadcast\streams\_definst_
⤳ \announcement.flv
```

FlashCom will automatically create the streams directory and application instance sub-directories if they do not exist. Notice that the application instance name for this example is _definst_. Remember, this stands for "default instance" and is the reference name that a FlashCom Server uses whenever an application is called without a named instance.

Note

FLV files can store audio, video, and/or synchronized data. For example, you can record an audio-only stream to an FLV file.

You can also place your own FLV files created from third-party utilities such as Sorenson Squeeze and Wildform Flix. For example, if you recorded a 30-minute lecture on DV (Digital Video) tape, you could transfer the footage to your computer, compress the footage with a third-party utility or Flash MX, and output an FLV file. This file would then be placed within the appropriate streams/applicationInstance folder on your FlashCom Server, where the FLV file can be published to connected users.

In addition to the Flash Video file, FlashCom creates an accompanying index document (IDX file) in the same directory as the FLV file. The IDX file indexes the FLV file and allows the server to find the FLV file faster for subsequent publishing and seeking within the stream. If you accidentally delete the IDX file associated with a FLV file, FlashCom creates a new IDX file the next time the FLV is accessed.

Caution

Do not delete IDX files, as they provide information to the FlashCom Server about the length and time intervals of the recorded stream. If you create your own FLV file in Sorenson Squeeze or Wildform Flix for a FlashCom application, the FlashCom Server creates an IDX file for the FLV file the first time the FLV file is published.

> ### USING COMMON DIRECTORIES FOR RECORDED STREAMS
>
> You can also map common directories for recorded streams in the Vhost.xml configuration file for your FlashCom Server. The <Streams> node of the <VirtualDirectory> node allows you to specify shared locations for recorded streams that can be used by several applications. For more information, read the HTML document installed at the following path:
>
>   C:\Program Files\Macromedia\Flash MX\flashcom_help\admin_help\admin\html
>   \03_Configuring9.html
>
> In Chapter 13, you will learn how to use a common directory with a conference recorder and retrieval application.

FSO

A Flash Communication Server creates an FSO file whenever a remote SharedObject is referenced in client-side or server-side ActionScript, with SharedObject.getRemote() or SharedObject.get(), respectively. **FSO** stands for "Flash Shared Object." A remote SharedObject can store data that is shared among connected users and can be saved for later reuse as well. For example, a remote SharedObject can keep track of the names of users participating in a chat. If necessary, you can create or use several remote SharedObjects for a single application.

Currently, only Macromedia Flash Communication Server MX can create FSO files that are stored within the server's application folders. Remote SharedObject data is only saved as an actual FSO file when you create a persistent SharedObject (discussed later in this chapter). SharedObject data is saved in the same manner as recorded streams. By default, FlashCom stores FSO files in a sharedobjects folder for each application. Inside an application's sharedobjects folder, you will find folder instances names that contain the actual FSO files. If you do not use named instance for your FlashCom application, FSO files for an application are created in the _definst_ folder of the sharedobjects folder. For example, if a Flash movie (SWF file) connects to an application named chat and creates (or retrieves) a persistent remote SharedObject named chatHistory, you will find a chatHistory.fso file in the following directory:

    .../applications/chat/sharedobjects/_definst_/chatHistory.fso

You can also enable client-side or server-side ActionScript to connect to a remote SharedObject from another FlashCom application as well.

ASC

 Server-side ActionScript code is saved within a text file with a .asc file extension. ASC files are loaded when a FlashCom application starts. Usually, an application is started when the first user connects to the FlashCom application. By default, a FlashCom application will look for a file named main.asc when an application (or application instance) loads. You can use other names and extensions for server-side ActionScript code. For more information on the load order and search path of ASC files, read the following Macromedia tech note:

> www.macromedia.com/support/flashcom/ts/documents/serverside_names.htm

Using the server-side ActionScript load() method, you can load other Action-Script code files (ASC files) that are located in the scriptlib folder of your Flash-Com installation. Applications that use the Communication components, for example, require the components.asc file, which is located in the scriptlib folder. You can also place your own custom ASC files into this folder, so that they are accessible by all of your FlashCom applications.

XML

 You can manage and administer the configuration of a Flash Communication Server by editing the XML documents found in the conf folder of the FlashCom program folder. If you installed FlashCom on a Windows machine, the default location of the conf folder is the following path:

> C:\Program Files\Macromedia\Flash Communication Server MX\conf

Within the conf folder, you can find various XML documents that control everything from host IP addresses and port numbers to administrator user names and passwords.

 For more information on the settings within these XML documents, refer to the Managing Flash Communication Server PDF (available on the Flash Communication Server MX install CD) or the Managing the Server HTML help accessible from Flash MX.

DEVELOPING CLIENT-SIDE AND SERVER-SIDE COMMUNICATION

In previous sections, you have learned that there are two aspects to developing logic and interactivity for FlashCom-enabled Rich Internet Applications: client-side and server-side ActionScript code. In this section, we qill provide an overview of new ActionScript objects and MX components that are specifically used for FlashCom applications.

Knowing ActionScript for Flash Communication Applications

In order to successfully deploy your own custom Rich Internet Applications that integrate Flash Communication Server services, you need to learn how to create ActionScript objects that connect a SWF file to a FlashCom application or publish a user's webcam video and microphone output to a new stream. It is beyond the scope of this book to provide a comprehensive reference for every ActionScript object and method that is new to Flash MX and Flash Communication Server. We will, however, highlight the fundamental ActionScript objects in this section. You will learn more about these objects as you create the projects throughout this book.

APPLICATION AND CLIENT OBJECTS

The Application and Client objects are strictly used with server-side Action-Script code within ASC files residing in a FlashCom application directory. The Application object allows you to execute specific ActionScript with application events, such as onAppStart() and onConnect(). For example, you can initialize server-side SharedObjects and Stream objects when a user connects to a chat application. The Client object allows you to access information regarding each user that connects to the application, such as IP address and the URL of the SWF file used to make the connection. The Client object's call() method allows you to execute functions defined within a client-side NetConnection object.

Camera AND Microphone OBJECTS

These exciting objects allow you to capture the output from a user's webcam and microphone, respectively. The Camera and Microphone objects can only be used in client-side ActionScript. Each of these objects has several methods and properties that allow you to control the quality and bitrate of these sources. Whenever a Flash movie (SWF file) tries to access a user's camera or microphone, Flash Player 6 opens a security dialog box that asks for the user's permission. Once you have access to a user's camera or microphone, you attach the Camera or Microphone object to a NetStream object to publish the output to a FlashCom application. You can also attach these objects to local objects, like Video objects and MovieClip objects.

Tip

Flash Player 6 can access just about any USB or Firewire (IEEE 1394) digital video device. If you can use your camera and microphone in other conferencing applications such as Microsoft NetMeeting, chances are they will work in Flash Player 6.

NetConnection OBJECT

This ActionScript object can be used in both client and server-side ActionScript code. As its name implies, this object allows a Flash movie (SWF file) or a Flash-Com application to connect to another FlashCom application. The NetConnection object is used specifically for rtmp connections. You cannot use a NetConnection object to connect to a different type of application server such as Macromedia ColdFusion or a Microsoft .NET server.

A NetConnection object must have a successful connect to a FlashCom Server application in order for NetStream and remote SharedObject objects to function properly. The onStatus() handler for NetConnection objects can determine the state of a FlashCom application connection, allowing your code to detect if a connection was successful, or if a FlashCom application has disconnected a user.

NetStream AND Stream OBJECTS

The NetStream or Stream objects allow a Flash movie (SWF file) or FlashCom application (via code within an ASC file), respectively, to publish or subscribe to streaming content to and from a FlashCom Server. With the client-side Net-Stream object, you can attach Camera and Microphone objects to publish content, or you can attach a NetStream object to a Video object in order to play subscribed content. With the server-side Stream object, you can initiate streams from other FlashCom Servers or record published streams from other connected users.

SharedObject.getRemote() AND SharedObject.get()

To create or access a remote SharedObject within a FlashCom application, you can use the SharedObject.getRemote() method within client-side ActionScript code or the SharedObject.get() method within server-side ActionScript code. If you are accessing a remote SharedObject within client-side ActionScript, you must make a successful connection to the FlashCom application with a NetConnection object before you attempt to read and write data to the Shared-Object. The onSync() handler for a remote SharedObject in both client-side and server-side ActionScript allows your code to detect changes to properties of the remote SharedObject.

Video OBJECT

A Video object displays the video output from either a Camera object or a Net-Stream object. To create a Video object, click the options menu in the upper right corner of the Library panel in Flash MX, and choose New Video. The new video container will appear in the Library as an Embedded Video symbol. Once you have placed an instance of the Embedded Video symbol on the stage of a Flash MX document, you can assign an instance name to it in the Property inspector. This instance name is targeted with the attachVideo() method, specifying a NetStream or Camera object as the argument.

Tip

You cannot create a Video object strictly with ActionScript code. You must physically place a Video object on the Flash MX document's stage or within a MovieClip symbol.

Simplifying Connections with Communication Components

Macromedia Flash MX has introduced a new way of quickly adding user interface elements and behaviors to Flash MX documents—components. As described in Chapter 1, components let you focus your attention on the interactive goals of a project, without worrying about developing the code and logic for simple interface elements like scrollbars and combo boxes. Macromedia has released several component "sets," some of which are additional interface elements that take advantage of other MX products such as Flash Communication Server.

In order to complete the FlashCom projects discussed in this book, you need to download and install the Communication components for Flash MX. You can find the installation files at the following URL:

www.macromedia.com/software/flashcom/download/components/

If you downloaded and installed the Communication components from the Macromedia Web site **before** November 13, 2002, make sure you download the latest installer. Macromedia has improved the client- and server-side code base for many of the components and added two new components, VideoRecord and VideoPlayback. The exercises in this book use the latest versions of the Communication components.

The rest of this section provides a quick overview of these Communication components. You will use several of these components throughout examples in this book. In order to utilize any of these components in your FlashCom applications, the following line of code must be added to the main.asc document for the application:

load("components.asc");

The components.asc file is provided with the Communication component installation files and should be copied to the scriptlib folder of your FlashCom Server.

You may want to check the Flash Communication Server support page at Macromedia's Web site for updates to the Communication Components. The support page is located at www.macromedia.com/support/flashcom. You can also find new updates and articles about FlashCom Server at www.macromedia.com/desdev/mx/flashcom.

All of the following components require the SimpleConnect component in order to connect to a FlashCom application without any additional ActionScript code. If you do not use the SimpleConnect component, you need to add further client-side ActionScript code to your Flash MX document to provide a connection to the components.

Several of the exercises in Part III of this book show you how to implement the SimpleConnect component with other Communication Components.

AudioConference

This component adds a multiplexed audio conference to your Flash movie and FlashCom application. Multiple connected users can talk to each other simultaneously, and each user's login name is shown in a list box. When a user speaks, a green light appears next to his/her login name.

AVPresence

By far one of the most powerful and versatile Communication components, the AVPresence component provides an interface to publish or subscribe to live audio and video streams. You can broadcast the output of your camera and microphone to other users, or you can view the stream of another user. You can add multiple instances of the AVPresence component to a Flash MX document so that several users can be broadcasting simultaneously. This component has several parameters that allow you to control the size of the video window and the bandwidth consumed by the stream, as well as settings for other controls. When this component is used in conjunction with the SetBandwidth component, the video quality, size, bandwidth, and frame rate settings of the AVPresence instance are ignored.

Use extreme care with your decisions to use the AVPresence component. As we will discuss in later projects of this book, an application can easily expend an inordinate amount of bandwidth on your server's Internet connection with multiple simultaneous audio and video broadcasts and subscriptions.

Chat

The Chat component adds a display and input area for text-based chats in your FlashCom-enabled applications. This component can work in conjunction with the PeopleList, SimpleConnect, and UserColor components to create a fully functional chat room.

ConnectionLight

This component provides a visual cue about the current connection state of a FlashCom client and application. If an application is successfully connected, then the light turns green. When an application disconnects, the light turns red.

The ConnectionLight component also monitors the network latency between the client and the FlashCom Server. Latency is the amount of time required for network packets to be sent from the client (that is, the SWF file) and the Flash-Com Server. If the latency is too high, indicating that there may be significant delays in audio and video transmission among connected users, the connection light turns yellow. A user can also click the connection light to access more detailed information about the latency time as well as the upload and download rates of the connection.

Cursor

This component displays a custom mouse cursor (or pointer) and the name of each user that is connected to the application. Each user's mouse movement is reflected in the other user's SWF file. If this component is used in conjunction with the UserColor component, the mouse cursor displays the user's chosen color as well.

PeopleList

This component shows a list of connected users within the application. Most multiuser applications have this type of functionality, so that users can see who is online and using the application. The name of each user is retrieved from the login field of the SimpleConnect component.

PresentationSWF

This advanced component allows you to create a presentation environment for viewing and sharing a SWF file with an audience. This component can be configured as a speaker client or an audience client. As a speaker client, the PresentationSWF component synchronizes audience clients with the current frame of the SWF file that the speaker is presenting. As an audience client, this component can navigate the frames of a SWF file that the speaker has already presented.

PresentationText

This component works in a similar fashion to the PresentationSWF component, providing a functional interface for viewing, editing and deleting text-based slides that are presented to a connected audience in real time. This component has a speaker mode that can be set to either true or false.

Audience members can navigate text slides with forward and back buttons as well. The login names of all connected users are displayed to the left of the presentation area.

RoomList

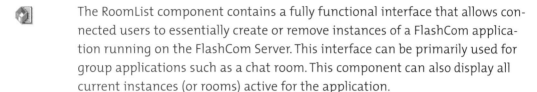

The RoomList component contains a fully functional interface that allows connected users to essentially create or remove instances of a FlashCom application running on the FlashCom Server. This interface can be primarily used for group applications such as a chat room. This component can also display all current instances (or rooms) active for the application.

SetBandwidth

This component provides a drop-down list displaying bandwidth speeds. The user can choose a bandwidth speed from the menu in order to optimally transmit audio and video with other Communication components, such as the AudioConference, AVPresence, and VideoConference components. In the component parameters area of the Property inspector, you can specify the maximum bytes per second of each bandwidth speed displayed in the menu.

SimpleConnect

This integral component makes the initial connection to your FlashCom application. The component contains an input text field where the user can type his preferred login name, and a login button to make the connection to the Flash-Com application. In the component parameters area of the Property inspector, you can specify the `rtmp` URI for the FlashCom application and the instance names of all of the Communication components and/or custom objects that require a connection to the FlashCom application.

UserColor

This component allows a connected user to choose a preferred color for text-based elements in other Communication components. A list of predefined colors is already created in the combo box interface of this component. For example, this color will be applied to the text that a user sends to other users in the Chat component.

VideoConference

This component integrates the AVPresence component to provide an auto-mated system for connecting several users into a live videoconference. When-ever a user connects to the application, a new instance of the AVPresence component representing the user is added to the stage.

VideoPlayback

This component, introduced in a later revision of the Communication com-ponents installer, allows you to access a prerecorded stream (such as a FLV file) from a FlashCom application. When this component is used in conjunc-tion with the SimpleConnect component, you can simply specify the name of the stream to play from the application URI specified in the SimpleConnect instance's parameters. By default, the VideoPlayback component is designed to display video in a 320×240 window. You can also adjust the buffer time for the stream in the component parameters. The component's user interface includes a play/pause button, a draggable slider to scrub the video, and a pop-up volume control slider.

VideoRecord

This component, also introduced in a later revision of the Communication compo-nents, can record and play back output from a webcam and microphone. The component can work in conjunction with the SetBandwidth component. Depend-ing on the speed selected by the user, the VideoRecord component records the live stream with varying degrees of quality. You can control the buffer time and qual-ity settings (for each respective bitrate setting in the SetBandwidth component) in the instance parameters of the VideoRecord component. The user interface for the component includes a record/stop button to start and stop the recording of the stream, as well as a play/stop button to watch the stream when you have fin-ished the recording. An indicator light flashes during the recording operation.

Whiteboard

As its name implies, this component contains a drawing area and tools to let multiple users collaborate with text, box shapes, and lines in a live environ-ment. You can see other users draw shapes or edit text in real time.

> ### MACROMEDIA ONLINE RESOURCES FOR FLASH COMMUNICATION SERVER
>
> You can find the latest developer articles and tutorials for Flash Communication Server at
>
> www.macromedia.com/desdev/mx/flashcom/
>
> If you're looking for downloads and updates related to FlashCom, check out the following support page at Macromedia:
>
> www.macromedia.com/support/flashcom

SUMMARY

- Macromedia Flash Communication Server MX (also known as FlashCom or FCS) is a server product that extends the capabilities of the Flash Player. A Flash movie that has access to a FlashCom server can take advantage of real-time audio/video streaming and synchronized shared data with connected users.

- Using the new Camera and Microphone objects in client-side ActionScript code, you can create Flash movies that broadcast the video from a user's webcam and/or the audio from a user's microphone. When a FlashCom server receives a broadcast (or published) stream from another user, multiple users can simultaneously subscribe to the stream.

- A Flash Communication Server and a Flash MX movie communicate with the Real Time Messaging Protocol, or RTMP. Macromedia developed this protocol exclusively for Flash Player 6.

- Remote SharedObject data can be stored for each application (and instance) on a Flash Communication Server. When any data within a SharedObject changes, all users that are connected to the SharedObject can receive the updated data.

- An application is a unique identifier that lets a FlashCom server know which files and directories to process when a connection is made to the server from a Flash movie.

■ An application can have several instances running simultaneously. Each instance of an application can connect different sets of users, such as a chat application with multiple rooms.

■ Many FlashCom applications will require server-side ActionScript code for enhanced multi-user interactivity. Server-side ActionScript is written within ASC files that are stored within an application's folder on the Flash Communication Server. The primary server-side ActionScript file for an application should be named `main.asc`.

■ Flash Communication Server MX is available in two editions, Personal and Professional. You can download and install a trial version of the Professional Edition for 30 days. Unlike the Macromedia ColdFusion MX trial version, you cannot continue to use the trial after the time period has expired.

■ By default, a FlashCom server is set up to respond to `rtmp` requests on port 1935. You can reconfigure the `adaptor.xml` file to bind the server to one or more ports.

■ In order to develop FlashCom-enabled Rich Internet Applications, you need to utilize a series of new Flash MX ActionScript objects, both in client-side and server-side ActionScript code.

■ Communication components allow you to quickly add multi-user interactivity to your Flash movies.

In This Chapter:

7 Flash Remoting MX

Flash Remoting vastly simplifies the process of connecting your Flash movies with ColdFusion MX, .NET, Java, and XML Web Services. It allows for integration with complex external programs and databases much more easily than was possible in previous versions of Flash.

Using Flash Remoting MX can be a slippery concept to grasp at first, as there are two distinctly different parts to Flash Remoting. What's more, neither part stands alone; they both integrate into other applications—there is no actual "Flash Remoting" application that you open and use.

The two parts to Flash Remoting are

- **The Flash Remoting server gateway**: Installing this adds the necessary features to your application server. It is included as standard in ColdFusion MX and JRun 4 and is available for an additional fee for .NET and J2EE Web servers.

- **The Flash Remoting authoring tools**: Installing these adds new features to the Flash MX application itself. These are free to download from Macromedia's Web site.

Flash Remoting support is built into the standard Flash Player 6, so your Web site users don't need anything additional to use the Flash movies you create, although it is recommended that users have Flash Player 6 release 47 or above.

In this chapter, we will explore both the client- and server-side elements of Flash Remoting MX, and how to develop Flash movies that make the most of it.

BACKGROUND

If you've been developing with previous versions of Flash, the new capabilities of Flash Remoting might not seem all that impressive at first. After all, Flash movies talk to databases and server-side pages already, right?

Well, yes and no. While it is certainly possible for Flash movies to utilize server-side scripting to interface with databases, it is typically a long and convoluted process. On the Flash side, you might use `loadVariables` and require your data to be passed from the server in long text strings of name/value pairs separated by ampersands. To allow this on the server side, you must create specific routines just for use by the Flash application. They aren't elegant, and they typically aren't reusable.

More advanced solutions format the data in XML or even connect Flash to XML socket servers, but these too have their drawbacks in practicality and flexibility.

And while it could be relatively simple to exchange information with straight-forward data structures, a whole level of difficulty arises when attempting to exchange complex data types such as arrays or objects. These would need to be *serialized* (split up into their separate constituent elements) on one side, transmitted, and then *deserialized* (constructed back into an object definition) on the other. This can be a time-consuming and inefficient process.

With Flash Remoting, instead of programmatically parsing out information into XML structures or long strings of name/value pairs, we can now directly pass complex data types like objects, arrays, and recordsets between the Flash movie and the server-side function.

How It Works

Flash Remoting uses its own message format to send data: **A**ction **M**essage **F**ormat (AMF). AMF is a binary format delivered over regular HTTP. It's based on SOAP (**S**imple **O**bject **A**ccess **P**rotocol—see Chapter 5), though it is a more streamlined and lightweight version of it.

The implementation of AMF should be essentially transparent to you, as the conversion to and from AMF is done automatically by Flash Remoting. It allows you to use multiple data types, from primitives like integers and strings to complex data types like dates, arrays, objects, and recordsets.

Note

There is a problem transmitting Boolean data types over Flash Remoting when using ColdFusion. The Boolean values `true` and `false` are both converted to zero during the process, and zero will always evaluate as false. Instead, use numeric values of 1 for true and 0 for false. Please check the Macromedia Flash Remoting release notes at www.macromedia.com/support/flash/flashremoting/releasenotes/releasenotes.html

Flash Remoting in ActionScript

Using Flash Remoting in ActionScript is similar to the way you use other ActionScript objects, such as Date objects, arrays, or movieclips. However, Flash MX doesn't automatically understand the Flash Remoting objects; extra capabilities have to be added to the Flash MX application before it will understand the ActionScript that deals with Flash Remoting.

Installation Process

During the installation process of Flash Remoting (either when installing ColdFusion, JRun, or the separate Flash Remoting product for .NET or J2EE), the install procedure attempts to detect a copy of the Flash MX application on the machine. If one is found, additional components are added to Flash MX. These are the **Flash Remoting Components** and must be installed if you are to create Flash movies that use Flash Remoting.

There are a few reasons why you might not have the Flash Remoting Components in your copy of Flash MX:

- If you installed ColdFusion MX before Flash MX

- If your Flash development machine is completely separate from any machine you use as a Web server

In either case, the Flash Remoting Components need to be installed manually. They are free and can be downloaded from:

www.macromedia.com/software/flashremoting/downloads/components/

Installing the Flash Remoting Components adds several supporting files to your Flash configuration and also adds some new features to the application itself: a NetConnection Debugger panel and a Service Browser panel. More about these new features is covered later in this chapter.

Necessary Files

The installation of the Flash Remoting Components places several ActionScript .as files into your Flash MX Configuration/Include directory. Three of these files are of particular interest.

To use these files, they need to be included in your Flash movie with the #include directive. As you develop Flash Remoting movies, you're going to become very accustomed to beginning the first frame of your movies with these lines of ActionScript:

```
#include "NetServices.as"
#include "NetDebug.as"
```

Note As a reminder, the #include directive brings in the content of an external Action-Script file at publish time—when the Flash document (FLA file) is turned into a Flash movie (SWF file). This means you do not have to worry about making the .as files available on your Web server; they're only needed on your development machine.

NetServices.as

The most essential file is NetServices.as, which will be included in every Flash movie you create that uses Flash Remoting. It contains the core ActionScript used to make connections to server-side services. Including the NetServices.as file in your movie allows you to create and use three new objects that are essential to Flash Remoting: NetServices, NetConnection, and Recordset.

The NetServices object aids in creating the connection to the Flash Remoting gateway service on the server side. It contains only two methods:

- **setDefaultGatewayURL**: Use this method to specify the location of the Flash Remoting gateway on the server.

- **createGatewayConnection**: Use this method to connect to Flash Remoting and create a NetConnection object.

Note In truth, only a pseudo connection is made to the gateway when the createGateway-Connection method is used. Nothing is actually transmitted over the wire until the first service method is called. This is for all intents and purposes transparent to the developer. However, it is worth bearing in mind when debugging because this line could be completely wrong but won't itself cause an error.

The NetConnection object is created when connecting to the Flash Remoting gateway and is used to call the remote service on the server side. Its main methods are:

- **trace:** Use this method to output messages when testing and debugging. This works differently than the normal ActionScript trace() method and outputs to the NetConnection Debugger panel, not the Output window.

- **setCredentials**: Use this method to pass user information. It's only relevant when using ColdFusion user security using the <cflogin> tags.

- **getService**: Use this method to connect to a remote service. It returns a service object that allows you to directly call the methods of that service.

The NetConnection object also contains several methods specifically for debugging purposes.

Note

NetConnection objects can also be created directly, but the way we're describing—creating them as a result of using the NetServices createGatewayConnection method—is the normal way to create them.

Finally, including NetServices.as also allows you to use the Recordset object to manipulate recordsets. The classic example of this is, of course, a recordset returned from a database query. Some of the most useful Recordset object methods include:

- **addItem:** Adds a record into the Recordset object.

- **addView:** Defines an object that will receive notifications when the Recordset object changes. The object must include a modeChanged() function that can accept a parameter detailing the changes that have taken place (rows changed, rows deleted, recordset sorted, and so on).

- **filter:** Uses a filter to create a new Recordset object containing only certain records from the original object.

- **getColumnNames:** Returns all column names in a recordset.

- **getLength:** Returns the number of records in a Recordset object.

- **removeAll:** Removes all records from the Recordset object.

- **removeItemAt**: Removes one specified record from the Recordset object.

- **replaceItemAt**: Replaces a record in the recordset using an index.

- **sortItemsBy**: Sorts all records in the Recordset object without making a new copy. (There is also a sort method, but the sortItemsBy method is quicker.)

For a full description of all possible Recordset methods, consult the Flash Remoting documentation.

NetDebug.as

Including the NetDebug.as file allows much more detailed debugging and testing abilities when using Flash Remoting than would otherwise be possible.

We mentioned earlier that installing the Flash Remoting Components added a couple of new panels to your Flash MX authoring application. The most important panel, the NetConnection Debugger, allows you to view the details of Flash Remoting interaction between client and server as the Debugger is running and spot any bugs or difficulties. However, the NetConnection Debugger relies on the NetDebug.as file being included in the Flash movie in order to work properly.

To use these capabilities, you must import the NetDebug.as file in the first frame of the Flash application, using the include directive as follows:

```
#include "NetDebug.as"
```

Caution

Once your Flash movie is debugged and ready for production, you should always remove or comment out any reference to NetDebug.as. It adds unneeded file size and functionality to a completed movie and should only be used for testing.

DataGlue.as

The DataGlue.as file should be included when you wish to use recordset data to fuel Flash UI components, such as ListBoxes and ComboBoxes. It includes two methods: bindFormatStrings() and bindFormatFunction(). These methods simplify the process of populating both the label and value sections of UI components by removing the necessity of writing ActionScript functions to map the values in UI elements across from recordset columns.

The DataGlue object and its methods are explored in an exercise in Chapter 9.

Making and Using a Connection

Now we've covered the essential files that need to be included to perform various tasks within Flash Remoting. Let's go step by step through the process of making a connection.

To summarize the process before getting into the code, there are several things we need to do:

- Specify the Flash Remoting gateway on the server.
- Connect to the gateway—connecting creates a `NetConnection` object.
- Use the `NetConnection` object to link to a remote service.
- Use the service to call a remote method.
- Handle the data returned from that method.

When writing the necessary ActionScript , we start off with the `#include` tags for the needed Flash Remoting ActionScript files:

```
#include "NetServices.as"
#include "NetDebug.as"
```

If you were intending to use Flash UI components, which pull their data from a Recordset, you'd also add the line:

```
#include "DataGlue.as"
```

Next, The location of the Flash Remoting Gateway must be specified. To do this, use the `NetServices.setDefaultGatewayURL` method. This should point to the Flash Remoting gateway, which is a virtual directory created when Flash Remoting is installed. For a typical installation using a ColdFusion standalone server, this would be:

```
NetServices.setDefaultGatewayURL("http://localhost:8500/flashservices/
➝ gateway");
```

Or, for an ASP.NET server running locally:

```
NetServices.setDefaultGatewayURL("http://localhost/flashremoting/
➝ gateway.aspx");
```

These examples tell the Flash movie where the gateway is located, nothing more. The next step is to use the `NetServices.createGatewayConnection` method:

```
gatewayConnection = NetServices.createGatewayConnection();
```

This creates a `NetConnection` object we've called `gatewayConnection`. This can be used to call a remote service, such as a ColdFusion Component (CFC).

To know exactly how to call the service, we need to know where it is located, so we can give Flash the correct path to it. This is very similar to creating links in a normal Web site. If we want to link from the home page to another page, we need to know the page's relative location.

So if we've created the connection to the gateway by specifying the `http://localhost:8500/flashservices/gateway` in the `setDefaultGatewayURL` statement, where does that actually take us? Well, it effectively takes us to the Web root. The gateway URL is a virtual location that is equivalent to the Web server root folder. We don't need to look for hidden `flashservices` or `gateway` folders. Once connected to the gateway URL, every reference from this point is taken by default as originating from the Web root folder.

SPECIFYING COMPONENT PATHS IN FLASH REMOTING

When a Flash movie connects to components using Flash Remoting, we need to be aware of the folder path, but we use dots rather than slashes. As an example, if you created a CFC file called `foobar.cfc` and placed it in your Web root folder at

```
\\CFusionMX\wwwroot\foobar.cfc
```

you could then use Flash Remoting to refer to that CFC directly by its name, without the file extension foobar.

If the .cfc file is one level down inside a `mxbook` folder in the Web root, at:

```
\\CFusionMX\wwwroot\mxbook\foobar.cfc
```

You would then use a dot to separate the folder and the component:

```
mxbook.foobar
```

So we can now use our `NetConnection` object to link to a service on the Web server:

```
myService = gatewayConnection.getService("mxbook.myCFC", this);
```

This creates a service object called `myService` that can be used to directly call methods of that service.

Calling Remote Service Functions

To call the functions of a service object, use the service object name followed by the service functionality name. Parameters are optional and depend on the definition of the service function. The following are examples:

```
myService.myMethod();
stockSVC.getHistory("MACR");
shipSvc.trackItem("ZYXW123", 85254, 90210);
```

In these examples, it can be seen that parameters of different types—string, numeric, and so on—can be passed.

 Note

Although there are many different types of services that you can connect to with Flash Remoting (ColdFusion Components, ASP.NET pages, Enterprise JavaBeans, and so on), you obviously need to have some idea about what they do and the parameters they expect before you begin to use them. However, there are various ways in which many of these remote services can be interrogated or introspected to determine their exact requirements. One of these options is the Service Browser panel, explained later in this chapter.

Dealing with Server Responses

There are two main problems when attempting to do complex data exchange with previous versions of Flash. First, there is the difficulty of coding individualized routines to call server-side scripts written in different languages running on various platforms. But a more insidious problem is that, due to the vagaries of the Internet, you're never quite sure just how long it's going to take to get a response from the remote site.

For example, many Flash 4 and 5 movies might issue a call to a server-side script on frame 1, then loop around continually, asking, "Have I heard back yet? Have I heard back yet?" to attempt to determine exactly when a response arrived. This is an inefficient and clunky way of doing things.

Using Flash Remoting, we avoid all that. True, we still don't know exactly how long it's going to take to get a response from the remote server, but that very eventuality is fully dealt with in Flash Remoting. Whenever you use Flash Remoting to call a remote method on the server, Flash Remoting will automatically "call you back" as soon as a response has occurred.

It does this by looking for a function in your ActionScript with the same name as the remote method, but with _result attached to it.

For example, say you connect to the Flash Remoting gateway, then call a method of the remote service called findEmployee:

```
myService.findEmployee("123-1234-123");
```

When anything is returned from that method, Flash will automatically look for and try to execute a function with that name and a suffix of _result:

```
function findEmployee_Result ( resultData )
{
// code goes here
}
```

So for every method you may end up calling, you simply declare callback functions in your ActionScript to deal with the returned information. Refer to exercises in Chapters 8 and 9 for an exercise based on an example of this.

Flash Template for Flash Remoting

There is a useful template in Flash MX when you want to quickly develop a Flash Remoting app. Create a new Flash document by selecting the File > New from Template. Then select the Web category and choose Basic. Click OK.

A movie will be created without artwork, but with the following ActionScript on frame 1. This ActionScript creates a basic framework for a connection and a callback function:

```
i#include "NetServices.as"

// uncomment this line when you want to use the NetConnect debugger
//#include "NetDebug.as"

// -------------------------------------------------
// Handlers for user interaction events
// -------------------------------------------------

// This gets called when the "aaaa" button is clicked
function aaaa_Clicked ()
{
// ... put code here
```

```
// For example, you could call the "bbbb" function of "my.service" by
// doing:
// myService.bbbb(123, "abc");
}

// ---------------------------------------------------
// Handlers for data coming in from server
// ---------------------------------------------------

// This gets called with the results of calls to the server function //"bbbb".
function bbbb_Result ( result )
{
// ... put code here

// For example, if the result is a RecordSet, you could display it in a
//  ListBox by doing:
// myListBox.setDataProvider(result);
}

// ---------------------------------------------------
// Application initialization
// ---------------------------------------------------

if (inited == null)
{
// do this code only once
      inited = true;

// set the default gateway URL (this is used only in authoring)

NetServices.setDefaultGatewayUrl("http://localhost:8100/flashservices/gate
→ way");

// connect to the gateway
gateway_conn = NetServices.createGatewayConnection();

// get a reference to a service
myService = gateway_conn.getService("my.service", this);
}

stop();
```

You'll notice that the actual connection code is executed at the end of the ActionScript. This is done so that the functions can be declared and recognized before any of the connection code is run.

Putting It All Together

To summarize the process, the Flash movie must first create a connection to the Flash Remoting gateway, such as:

```
NetServices.setDefaultGatewayUrl("http://localhost:8100/flashservices/gate
→ way");
gateway_conn = NetServices.createGatewayConnection();
```

The next step is to connect to the service on the application server. This could be a CFC or a SOAP-based Web Service. For example, with a CFC called testCFC, we could use the following:

```
myService = gateway_conn.getService("testCFC", this);
```

Any available function within that CFC can then be called. If the testCFC CFC includes a simple Hello() function that accepts a single parameter of a user name, we can then call it easily in ActionScript:

```
myService.Hello("Joe");
```

The Flash movie takes that parameter, constructs the AMF, and passes the information to the Flash Remoting gateway. The Flash Remoting gateway, in turn, calls the CFC function and passes it the parameter.

When the CFC function executes, the flow is reversed, and any parameters are passed back from the application server to the Flash movie.

Once a result has been returned to the Flash movie, Flash will then search for a function with the same name as the CFC function, but with _result as a suffix. (In this case, the function would need to be called Hello_result.) This is where the code can be written that handles any parameters sent back from the CFC, such as:

```
function Hello_Result ( result )
{
   trace(result);
}
```

Of course, there is likely to be substantially more complex functionality in both the component and also in what should be done with the returned result. But the basic concept and flow of information is the same.

Xref

ColdFusion Components (CFCs) are discussed in Chapter 3 and used in Chapters 8 and 9.

SERVER-SIDE ACTIONSCRIPT

When using ColdFusion MX, you can create server-side ActionScript files (saved as .asr files) in your Web site folders under the ColdFusion Web root. These allow developers experienced in ActionScript to start creating server-side scripting files that can be called using Flash Remoting.

Note

Server-side ActionScript files are only used with Flash Remoting. They cannot be called from other ColdFusion documents.

Using the CF.query and CF.http functions in server-side ActionScript files allows you to directly run SQL queries and issue HTTP operations (such as sending information with GET and POST, or creating cookies).

As a basic example, the following server-side ActionScript file returns a Record-Set object when called by a Flash movie:

```
function myFunction()
{
rsQuestions = CF.query({datasource:"PollDB", sql:"SELECT * FROM questions"});

return rsQuestions;
}
```

This example obviously assumes the existence of a ColdFusion data source called PollDB that contains a table called questions.

Saving this code in a file called test.asr under the ColdFusion Web root folder would allow you to then call it in Flash by using code such as the following:

```
#include "NetServices.as"
#include "NetDebug.as"
```

```
if (inited == null) {
    inited = true;
    gConn = NetServices.createGatewayConnection("http://localhost:8500/
    ➝ flashservices/gateway");
// the next line creates the service object myService that
// points to the test.asr file - you don't use the .asr suffix
    myService = gConn.getService("test", this);
}
//this line calls the function in test.asr
myService.myFunction();
// and this function is the callback function, automatically
// run when data is returned from the function. All this does is
// display all the table column names to the output window.
function myfunction_Result(result_rs) {
    colNames = result_rs.getColumnNames();
    for (name in colNames) {
        trace(colNames[name]);
    }
}
```

Xref

ASR files are also discussed in Chapter 3.

NETCONNECTION DEBUGGER

The NetConnection Debugger, installed as part of the Flash Remoting Components, is a customizable tool that allows you as a developer to inspect the
communication that occurs between the Flash movie, the Flash Remoting
gateway, and the application server. The NetConnection Debugger requires the
NetDebug.as file and uses its functions to allow you to watch every step of the
communication. As mentioned previously, you need to include the NetDebug.as
file in the first frame of your Flash movie in order to use it.

Note

You should only include the NetDebug.as file while testing your movie. When it
comes time to deploy your Flash movie in a production environment, either remove
or comment out that line.

To use the NetConnection Debugger, open it (Window > NetConnection Debugger) before you test your movie using Ctrl+Enter. The NetConnection Debugger contains several areas. The main section (the Debug Events panel) contains a clickable list of events on the left side, with further details about each selected event on the right. Furthermore, information about each individual event is available in two levels: summary and detail.

Each event is displayed in a color-coded format:

- Red represents property names.

- Black represents the property values.

- Blue represents objects that may contain properties and/or other objects.

By default, the NetConnection Debugger does not show every single event that occurs when using Flash Remoting, as showing every single possible piece of network traffic might seem overwhelming if you don't know exactly what you're looking for. The events shown can be edited using the Filters drop-down option.

Filters Menu

The Filters menu allows you to determine which events are reported in the NetConnection Debugger. These are separated into three areas: `client`, `app_server,` and `flashcom_server.`

The `client` section includes four possible events that can be selected or deselected as desired:

- **HTTP**: Shows client communication using the HTTP protocol

- **Recordset**: Shows events connected with Recordset transmission.

- **RTMP**: Turns on **R**eal-**T**ime **M**essaging **P**rotocol. This is used by Flash Communication Server and will be explored in later chapters.

- **Trace**: Shows the `NetConnection.trace` methods.

The `app_server` section contains several options for event monitoring:

- **HTTPHeaders**: Shows client communication using the HTTP protocol

- **Recordset**: Shows events connected with Recordset transmission

- **Trace**: Not used at this point

- **ColdFusion**: Shows ColdFusion debugging information

- **Error**: Shows errors that may occur on the server-side during Flash Remoting operations

- **AMF and AMFheaders**: By default unselected, these may be turned on if you wish to see the real behind-the-scenes communication dealing with the serialization and deserialization of data.

The `flashcom_server` section also shows traces issued from Flash Communication Server.

Figure 7.1 shows the NetConnection Debugger with all options expanded for editing.

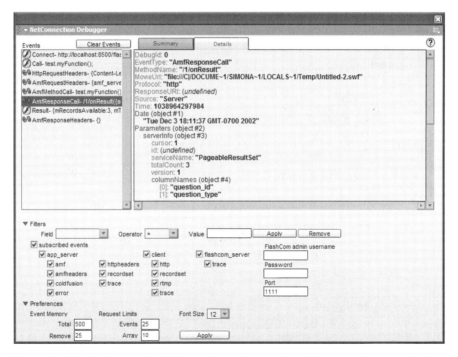

Figure 7.1 The NetConnection Debugger is used to monitor all aspects of communication between the Flash client, Flash Remoting, and the application server.

You can also create rules to display only certain filtered events by entering comparison details for particular fields. This can be useful if the Flash movie is creating a great deal of network traffic, but you are only looking for a certain type of event or are only interested in (for example) events occurring over RTMP but not HTTP.

To create a filtering rule, select the relevant field from the Field menu, then select an Operator (equal to, greater than, contains, and so on) and enter a Value. The value is case-sensitive, so make sure to use the correct case. Then click Apply to apply the rule to the displayed events. Click Remove to reset the event display.

Preferences Menu

The Preferences menu allows you to set basic parameters for the NetConnection Debugger.

EVENT MEMORY

This is where you can control the number of event details stored.

- **Total** is the maximum number of events to be stored.
- **Remove** specifies the size of a block of events that will be removed whenever the total number is reached.

REQUEST LIMITS

These parameters allow you to specify the maximum number of events that are stored *per transaction,* and also to set the maximum number of elements in an array that can be returned from the application server.

FONT SIZE

Finally, you can alter the font size displayed for event details in the summary or details pane. The default font size is 12.

SERVICE BROWSER

Macromedia Flash MX features a new Service Browser panel, which can be opened by choosing Window > Service Browser. The Service Browser is similar in concept to Dreamweaver MX's Components tab in the Application panel: It allows visual browsing of ColdFusion services.

However, there is no "autodiscovery" of ColdFusion services from Flash MX like there is in Dreamweaver MX. All services must be manually added.

If you are using a Windows computer with ColdFusion MX installed, follow these steps to see one of the built-in example services in ColdFusion MX.

TO ADD A SERVICE TO THE SERVICE BROWSER:

1. Open the Service Browser in Flash MX by choosing Window > Service Browser.

2. In the top-left corner of the panel, click the blue-and-white arrow button, and choose Add gateway. Specify the following gateway if you installed ColdFusion MX to work with IIS: `http://localhost/flashservices/gateway`.

   If you are running ColdFusion as a stand-alone server, type **http://localhost:8500/flashservices/gateway.**

3. Click the Add Gateway button when you are finished.

   The Service Browser shows the new gateway on your ColdFusion MX server. Now, you need to specify a service that is running on the ColdFusion MX server.

4. Select the gateway address in the browser, and choose Add service from the top-left menu options.

5. Type **cfdocs.exampleapps.cfc.tempconverter** into the service address field, and click the Add Service button. The Service Browser shows you the service name, the methods and arguments of the service, and a short description, as shown in **Figure 7.2**.

Figure 7.2 The Service Browser is a basic method of viewing information about ColdFusion MX components and services.

The Service Browser interrogates the CFC and displays the following details:

- Function name and description, if any

- Function argument name and required data type

- The data type returned by the function

The description is obtained by using the description attribute of the cffunction tag. For example, we could add a description for the example component by opening the tempconverter.cfc file in the ColdFusion Web root exampleapps/cfc folder and finding this line:

```
<cffunction name="convert" access="remote" returnType="any">
```

Add a description attribute, as in:

```
<cffunction name="convert" description="This is a temperature converter. I'm
pretty sure you got that already." access="remote" returnType="any">
```

Save this, then in the Service Browser, click the blue arrow button and select Refresh All Service Descriptions. Then select the convert() function again. The result should look similar to **Figure 7.3**.

Figure 7.3 Adding descriptions to your CFCs can make it easier for other developers to understand the component requirements.

FLASH REMOTING AND JAVA

Although we've mainly discussed Flash Remoting in the context of ColdFusion, it is included as part of JRun 4 and is also available for other J2EE-compliant servers. For exact requirements, consult this URL:

www.macromedia.com/support/flash_remoting/installation.html

If you're an enterprise-level Java developer, Flash Remoting has many options of interest for you. It supports calling methods in several types of Java objects, including:

- Java classes
- JavaBeans and Enterprise JavaBeans
- Java servlets
- JavaServer pages

The connection details are essentially the same as when creating a Flash Remoting connection in ColdFusion MX.

More details on the specifics of using Flash Remoting in a Java environment are beyond the scope of this chapter. For more about Flash and Java, consult the "Using Flash Remoting" document available from Macromedia at `www.macromedia.com/support/flash_remoting/documentation.html`.

FLASH REMOTING AND .NET

Written in C#, Flash Remoting on the .NET platform is a pure .NET implementation, running as managed code. It uses a .NET assembly (`flashgateway.dll`), which is placed in the `bin` directory as part of the installation process.

Connecting to the Flash Remoting gateway is slightly different on .NET than on ColdFusion because by default the gateway address—although still a virtual directory—uses an .aspx page, such as:

```
NetServices.setDefaultGatewayUrl("http://localhost/flashremoting/gateway/
→ default.aspx");
```

The page itself is actually meaningless; the default `gateway.aspx` page, installed by Flash Remoting as part of the install process, is actually empty. It's just that you need to use a physical page location when connecting to Flash Remoting in ASP.NET. The page isn't importantæit's just important that there *is* one.

Because Flash Remoting for .NET uses the `flashgateway.dll` assembly, you must register it in all .aspx pages that you wish to use with Flash Remoting. This is done like any custom server control:

```
<%@ Register TagPrefix="Macromedia" Namespace="FlashGateway"
Assembly="flashgateway" %>
```

Beyond that, you call the functions in .aspx pages just like calling the functions in .cfc pages: Drop the file extension and use dot syntax. The function `myFunc` in `myPage.aspx` is called by using `myPage.myFunc()`.

Flash Remoting MX is available as a free 30-day trial from `www.macromedia.com/software/trial_download/` and is also available on the CD-ROM for this book.

Note   If you are a .NET developer, be aware that Flash Remoting doesn't support the cookie-less state-management capabilities of ASP.NET.

For more about Flash and .NET in Flash Remoting, consult the "Using Flash Remoting" document available from Macromedia at www.macromedia.com/support/flash_remoting/documentation.html. This document contains details on using Flash Remoting with specialized ASP.NET features, such as code-behind, ADO.NET, and state management options—all of which are outside the scope of this chapter.

LEARNING MORE ABOUT FLASH REMOTING.

Substantial documentation is available from the Macromedia Web site at www.macromedia.com/support/flash_remoting/documentation.html and also from the Macromedia Designer/Developer center at www.macromedia.com/desdev/

Books for learning Flash Remoting include:

Complete Flash Remoting, by Joey Lott, available from Wiley & Sons.

For an up-to-date list of resources, check out this book's Web site at www.mxbook.com.\

SUMMARY

- Flash Remoting means two things: a server-side gateway and client-side tools, both of which are integrated into other products. It doesn't have any life of its own.

- The server-side element is installed as standard in ColdFusion MX and JRun 4, and is available at an additional price for ASP.NET and J2EE servers.

- The client-side tools, called the Flash Remoting Components, are installed automatically if flash is detected during the server gateway install process. Otherwise, they can be downloaded for free from the Macromedia Web site. They are essential for developing Flash movies that use Flash Remoting.

- The Flash Remoting Components install several ActionScript files in the Flash configuration directory, some of which are used in development.

- The `NetServices.as` file should be included in every .fla that uses Flash Remoting because it handles the core functionality of client-side Flash Remoting.

- The `NetDebug.as` file should be included in your movie while testing, as it is invaluable for debugging Flash Remoting.

- The `DataGlue.as` file is used to simplify the process of binding Recordset data to Flash UI components.

- A connection is made to the Flash Remoting gateway before any remote services can be used.

- Once a connection is made, the remote service functions can be called using dot syntax from within Flash.

- Responses from remote functions are automatically handled. Flash Remoting will look for and execute an ActionScript function with the same name as the remote function, suffixed with `_result`, whenever data is returned from the remote function.

- In ColdFusion MX and JRun, you can create server-side ActionScript (.asr) files to perform server-side functionality if you don't wish to use ColdFusion or ASP.NET.

- The NetConnection Debugger is a new panel in Flash MX, added by the Flash Remoting Components install. It is used to monitor the communications between the client, Flash Remoting, and the application server.

- The Service Browser window allows basic inspection of server-side components in ColdFusion MX.

- Flash Remoting is available on the Java platform and allows you to use such objects as Java classes, JavaBeans, and JavaServer pages.

- Flash Remoting for Microsoft ASP.NET can be used to implement the same methods with ASP.NET pages.

- Your users don't need additional software in their browsers to use Flash Remoting, although it's highly recommended that they use Macromedia Flash Player 6.0, version 47 or later. You should also consider a detection method to ensure this.

II
Establishing Links to Data

In This Chapter:

8 Gathering and Saving Data

In this chapter, you will learn how many of the components described in previous chapters fit together to build a complete Rich Internet Application. You're going to begin with a simple poll (survey) application, by creating a Flash movie that uses Flash Remoting to call a ColdFusion MX component (CFC) on the server. The ColdFusion component returns information from the database into the Flash movie, presenting questions to the user. As the user moves through the application, the Flash movie will continually use Flash Remoting to save responses to the database and request new questions.

Although the functionality of a Poll application isn't particularly complex, for our purposes it's ideal to explore as an introductory but realistic example of how different components are used together. In this chapter, you will use:

- Macromedia Dreamweaver MX

- ColdFusion MX

- Flash MX

- Flash Remoting

- SQL Server or Microsoft Access to create the database

 Note

This example does not use Macromedia Flash Communication Server MX.

An Overview of the Application and Production Process

Before you launch into the planning and design of the Poll application, you can familiarize yourself with the finished example by going to the book's Web site at:

www.mxbook.com/v1/ch08/

On the Web page at the book's Web site, click the Poll link. A Flash client movie loads into the Web browser.

The Flash movie connects to a database and retrieves and formats the first question using standard Flash UI components—PushButton, CheckBox and RadioButton.

Select a response and click the Next button. Proceed through the poll until it's completed.

Planning and Prerequisites

Even for small projects such as this, it's necessary to have a planning step to determine exactly which elements need to be constructed and in what order. Before proceeding, our basic assumptions are that we will use Flash for the front-end application and require Flash to interface with a database. As Flash can't talk directly to a database, ColdFusion MX will be used to do that. The choice of database isn't going to matter much. For this exercise, we'll demonstrate with SQL Server and Microsoft Access, but it could just as well be Oracle, PostGreSQL or DB2. Any of the modern relational SQL-based databases fit the bill.

The basic steps that we need to take to get up and running are as follows:

- Setting up the development environment
- Creating the data model
- Designing the database
- Writing the ColdFusion components to manipulate the database
- Creating the Flash application to act as the front-end
- Debugging and testing the application

You have the following programs installed and available on your development machine:

- Flash MX
- ColdFusion MX
- Flash Remoting Components

Flash Remoting Components, as described in the Flash Remoting chapter, are add-ons to Flash MX that are essential when building and testing Flash Remoting applications. If you installed ColdFusion MX after you installed Flash MX, the add-ons will be installed automatically. Otherwise, download them from

```
www.macromedia.com/software/flashremoting/downloads/components/
```

Dreamweaver MX will also be used in this chapter to create the ColdFusion Component (CFC) code. Although preferred, Dreamweaver isn't essential. You can use HomeSite+ or even Notepad to write this chapter's simple ColdFusion code.

If you use a Macintosh computer to author Flash and Dreamweaver documents, refer to the online information described in Appendix B of this book.

This chapter assumes a ColdFusion MX installation within IIS and refers to the web root folder at

```
C:\Inetpub\wwwroot\
```

The path to the web root folder may vary depending on the location you chose during the installation of ColdFusion or IIS. If you specified the web root folder in a different location, or if you installed ColdFusion as a standalone Web server, please take that into account when executing procedures for the poll application.

Requirements

So we're building a poll application—a survey of public opinion. But what does that mean in practical terms? We need to know exactly what it is our application needs to do: what is essential, what is preferable, what is irrelevant. We need to determine the requirements for our system.

Even a poll application can vary widely, depending on the type of questions the poll is likely to ask. For example, the question "What's your favorite book?" has many more potential answers than "What Macromedia product do you use most often?" You would build the interface for these questions differently: a fill-in-the-blank for the former and a series of predefined options for the latter. Your focus on building this application is likely to change depending on the types of questions you're going to ask and the level to which you want a reply. For small surveys, constraining responses to predefined options is usually the way to go, as these can be collated and organized simply.

In this planning stage, questions should arise such as:

- What kind of questions is the poll going to ask?

- How many questions will there be?

- Can questions expire?

- Do we need to save comments from the user?

- Is it going to open in its own window, or is it a Flash movie that fits in part of another page?

- Can the poll be completed anonymously, or does the user need to be logged on to our Web site before completing it?

- Do we keep track of the user's details, such as IP address, etc?

- Do we limit the number of times a user can complete the poll?

Many of these questions won't have a dramatic impact on development time, but we need to know the answers in order to proceed. The point is to make the application as flexible as possible, without trying to be all things to all people.

The poll in this chapter is intended to be a short, easy survey as opposed to an exhaustive analysis. As such, we can decide to ignore user authentication and concentrate on a small, flexible, easy to use application.

Xref

You will learn how to add user authentication functionality in Chapter 14.

CREATING SURVEYS

Creating a basic survey can seem straightforward, but there's both art and science in creating a successful online survey. At more complex levels, the design, usability, and presentation can affect the results greatly. There are several professional areas related to this including Statistics, Human Factors, Ergonomics, and **H**uman-**C**omputer **I**nteraction (HCI). To summarize, you must make sure you capture the needed information, that your questions are not unwittingly skewed to favor certain responses, and that the responses are clear and not open to misinterpretation.

For more information about surveys and statistical analysis, visit:

customer-satisfaction-surveys.custominsight.com/collecting-data.html
davidmlane.com/hyperstat/
www.ubmail.ubalt.edu/~harsham/stat-data/opre330.htm

For understanding visual presentation of statistical results, the classic books from Edward Tufte are the masterworks in the field:

The Visual Display of Quantitative Information

Envisioning Information

Visual Explanations: Images and Quantities, Evidence and Narrative

More information can be found at this book's web site at www.mxbook.com

The following are the requirements we will use to determine how the application is built:

- Questions are stored in the database. Nothing is stored in the Flash movie itself.

- New questions should be able to be added without making any changes to the Flash movie.

- Responses shall be constrained to pre-defined options, either multiple-choice or single-choice. There are no open-ended "fill-in-the-blank" responses.

- Some questions may only be relevant between set dates.

- The poll application is to fit in a small screen area as part of another page, so the application will use a small movie size and present one question at a time.

- There are several types of questions, requiring different UI elements. The standard Flash UI components will be used.

- Responses are stored in the database for later retrieval and reporting (this will be explored in the next chapter).

- The user's IP address is tracked, but at this point the user should not be prevented from filling in the survey multiple times.

We might also choose to mock up an example user interface. This could be done in Flash, but it's preferable to use a drawing tool like Freehand, or even a program with built-in interface elements such as Visio, which allows you to mock up a standard Windows-style interface as in **Figure 8.1**. Doing this can often be a surprisingly good choice even if you don't intend it to resemble a Windows application, as it allows you to concentrate on standard interface elements without getting distracted by how cool you can make it look.

Figure 8.1 Programs like Microsoft Visio can be used to mock up interface screens without being distracted by code.

If you do use Flash, be careful at this point not to be tempted to start writing ActionScript. This stage of the process allows you to play around with the design without attempting to code any functionality and see if it affects your requirement decisions.

Using these requirements as a basis for our design, we can proceed to the first step: that of designing and building the database.

CREATING THE DATABASE AND DATA SOURCE

As discussed in Chapter 4, a formal procedure for designing a database should always be followed; it's not the kind of thing you should just attempt to "knock out." You might think that a small database doesn't need a formal procedure, but unfortunately, small databases have an unerring tendency to turn into very large ones.

Xref

Many of the database-related terms and concepts used in this chapter are more fully explained in Chapter 4.

Modeling the Database

Although the information we need to store is somewhat more abstract than, for example, storing employee information, we can begin to concretize it into several fields as in **Table 8.1**. This table is a list of the different fields (or columns) that we need in the database *before* attempting to split them up into their constituent tables.

TABLE 8.1 FIELD LISTING FOR POLL APPLICATION

FIELD NAME	DESCRIPTION
Question ID	An identifying Primary key for each question.
Question Text	The question itself.
Choice Text	Multiple choices for each question, even if only "true" or "false".
Question Type	True / False, Select One, Select All That Apply.
Question Component	The associated Flash UI component for this type of question.
Question Start Date	Optional field that can be used if a question should not be asked until a certain date. If no value is entered, the question is taken as immediately being active.

TABLE 8.1 FIELD LISTING FOR POLL APPLICATION *(CONTINUED)*

FIELD NAME	DESCRIPTION
Question Expiry Date	Optional field that can be used if a question should not be asked after a certain date. If no value is entered, the question will be taken as having no end date.
Response Value	To measure a meaningful response, we need to know both which question it refers to and the chosen option or value.
Response Date / Time	Date and time, automatically stored when each question is answered.
Response IP Address	IP address of the responder, automatically stored when each question is answered.

 Note

If storing specific user information is something you ever intend to do, you should of course include that from the very beginnings of your database design.

This initial field listing suggests at least two database tables: questions and responses. However, a little further thought makes it clear that won't be enough. If we only have one questions table, how do we represent the fact that there may be zero, one or multiple choices? A quick and dirty solution might look something like the table described in **Table 8.2**.

TABLE 8.2 DATA MODEL FOR QUESTIONS TABLE, VERSION 1

FIELD NAME	SAMPLE VALUE
Question ID	1
Question Text	What is your favorite operating system?
Question Type	Select One
Question Component	RadioButton
Question Start Date	Null (always active)
Question Expiry Date	Null (no end date)
Choice 1	Windows XP
Choice 2	Mac OS X
Choice 3	Windows 2000
Choice 4	Linux
Choice 5	Mac OS 9
...Choice 99?	Et cetera, et cetera.

But this breaks first normal form (1NF) of relational database design: that there are **no multiple value fields or repeating groups**. Furthermore, it begs the question: how many choices are enough? If you define this table with five choices, and later have a six-option question, you'd have to redefine the database.

The solution is to split them into two tables, which we shall call questions and choices. All the fields referring to choice data are split out into their own table, linked back to the questions table using the question_id field. There can be several choice records for each question, or there can be none.

That leaves us with our questions table looking similar to **Table 8.3**.

TABLE 8.3 DATA MODEL FOR QUESTIONS TABLE, VERSION 2

FIELD NAME	SAMPLE VALUE
Question ID	1
Question Text	What is your favorite operating system?
Question Type	Select One
Question Component	RadioButton
Question Start Date	Null
Question Expiry Date	Null

However, we're not quite out of the woods yet; there's still an issue with the question_type and question_component fields. Because if you've decided what type of question it is, the UI component is automatically dependent upon that choice—all "Select all that apply" questions should use checkboxes, all "Select one option" questions should use radio buttons, as should "True or False" questions. You shouldn't have to continually specify both the question type and its associated component.

Note

In normalization jargon, this means that one non-key field (question_component) is dependent on another non-key field (question_type) and breaks Third Normal Form (3NF).

While a distinction definitely needs to be made about which Flash UI components are used for which questions, it's arguable whether this information should be stored in the database. After all, it is an implementation detail. If we recap our potential question types as:

- Multiple choices (select one answer)

- Multiple choices (select all that apply)

- True or False

We realize that "True or False" *is* actually a "Multiple Choice (select one answer)" question. So we really only have two types of questions: those with one possible answer and those with several. If we redefine the question_type column in our questions table to always have a value of "single" or "multiple", then we can use that in our Flash movie and rely on it to use the correct component.

The final version of the questions table is detailed in **Table 8.4**.

TABLE 8.4 DATA MODEL FOR QUESTIONS TABLE, FINAL VERSION

FIELD NAME	DESCRIPTION
Question ID	An automatically generated Primary key. In Access, this would be an AutoNumber. In SQL Server this is an Identity field.
Question Text	The question text itself.
Question Type	Constrained to be either "single" or "multiple". See **Figure 8.2** for an example of placing this constraint on a table design in Microsoft Access. The Validation Rule field shows this constraint specified.
Start Date	Optional field that can be used if a question should not be asked until a certain date. If no value is entered, the question is taken as immediately being active.
Expiry Date	Optional field that can be used if a question should not be asked after a certain date. If no value is entered, the question will be taken as having no end date.

TABLE 8.5 DATA MODEL FOR CHOICES TABLE

FIELD NAME	DESCRIPTION
Choice ID	An automatically generated Primary key. In Access, this would be an AutoNumber. In SQL Server, this is an Identity field.
Question ID	This is a foreign key to the questions table. All choices must be linked to a specific question.
Choice Text	The text for each option.

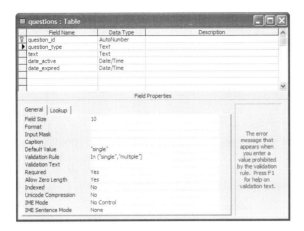

Figure 8.2 When designing and building a database, you can enforce set values in a field.

For every question in the questions table, there will be multiple associated records in the choices table, which is described in **Table 8.5.**

Now the questions side of the database is covered, we turn to the responses. This is an easier table, as we just need to store a few pieces of information:

- What was the choice selected?

- What question did it refer to?

- What IP address did this come from?

- When was the response made?

However, because of the way the questions and choices tables are defined, we don't need to store both a question ID and a choice ID. Just by knowing what choice was selected, we inherently know the question it was for—the choice ID on the choices table is unique, and each unique choice can refer to one question only.

The data model for the responses table is detailed in **Table 8.6**.

Once you have built the tables, you can begin to add some example questions and question choices, or you can use the questions in the Microsoft Access .MDB file found in the chapter_08 folder of this book's CD-ROM.

TABLE 8.6 DATA MODEL FOR RESPONSES TABLE

FIELD NAME	DESCRIPTION
Response ID	An automatically generated Primary Key field.
Choice ID	Foreign Key to the Choices table.
Response Date / Time	This field should be defined to automatically enter default value of the current date and time whenever a new record is added to the table. This is expressed differently in the various RDBMSs. For example, a default date and time in Microsoft Access is expressed in the table definition by using the Now() function, whereas in SQL Server, you'd use GETDATE().
Response IP Address	IP address of the responder, automatically stored when each question is answered.

Determining the Data Relationships

We've built the tables, and referred to some foreign keys, but in all good database definitions, the relationships should be explicitly defined and referential integrity enforced.

Referential integrity, when properly set up, will prevent you from entering choices for questions that don't exist, and prevent your Flash movie from trying to save responses for choices that don't exist. True, your Flash movie shouldn't do that anyway, but without implementing referential integrity correctly, you might not be alerted to the fact that your Flash movie isn't doing what you'd expect.

Figure 8.3 shows the Relationship properties dialog box in SQL Server 2000. It allows you to choose whether to enforce referential integrity and also whether or not to enforce cascading updates and deletes.

 Note

Be careful with these options. Turning cascade deleting on means that if you delete a question, all choices attached to that question will immediately be deleted, then, as cascading implies, all responses relating to any of the just-deleted choices will also be deleted. Leaving cascading delete off—often the smarter choice—will simply not allow you to delete a parent record until all related records have been manually deleted.

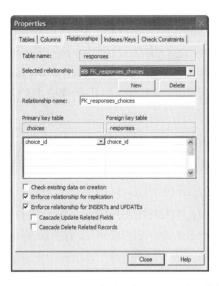

Figure 8.3 The Relationship properties dialog of SQL Server 2000 is where you specify many details about relationships between tables.

A one-to-many relationship exists between questions and choices. For every question there can be many choices. This relationship is on question_id.

A one-to-many relationship exists between choices and responses. Each choice can be used as a response many times. This relationship is on choice_id.

Most database systems have visual diagrams of the relationships. The SQL Server 2000 database diagram for this database is in **Figure 8.4.**

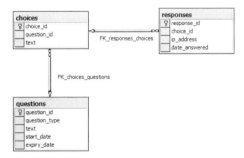

Figure 8.4 Most RDBMS programs have visual diagrams of table relationships. This example is from SQL Server 2000.

Enabling a Data Source in ColdFusion MX

With our database in place, we can proceed to the next step, that of making the databases known to ColdFusion. Until we create a *Data Source*, ColdFusion is unaware of the existence of our database. Fortunately, creating one is a fairly easy process.

Note

To enable a data source in ColdFusion MX, you have access to the ColdFusion Administrator. If you do not, speak to your system administrator or ISP about getting a Data Source set up.

You can use the sample Microsoft Access database, `poll.mdb`, included in the `chapter_08` folder on the accompanying CD-ROM. Copy it to a location on your hard drive and make sure it isn't read-only.

Although all your HTML pages, ColdFusion pages and Flash SWF files, must be placed in a folder under your web root to be publicly accessible, the database file doesn't need to be under the web root. It can be anywhere on your machine. In fact, it's better if it *isn't* under your web root folder.

That may seem odd, but the reason is this: for a database-driven site, you don't actually want visitors to your site to access the database. You want them to access *Web pages* that access your database. There's a big difference.

Note

One good location for a file-based database is `C:\CFusionMX\db`. This keeps the database file within the ColdFusion file structure, but is not directly accessible by regular visitors to the Web site.

To create an Access data source in ColdFusion MX:

1. Open the ColdFusion MX Administrator. For a Windows installation of ColdFusion MX, you can access the Administrator page by choosing Start > Programs > Macromedia ColdFusion MX > Administrator.

2. Select the Data Sources section under the Data & Services category.

3. In the Add New Data Source section, type a name for your new data source, such as **pollDB** and select the Microsoft Access driver. Click Add.

4. In the Microsoft Access Data Source dialog, select the Browse Server button for the Database File entry.

5. Navigate through the dialog box to the location of the poll.mdb file. Click Apply.

6. You can enter a description or change advanced settings, but it's not necessary. Click Submit to create the data source.

ColdFusion will take you back to the Data Source page. Your new data source should appear in the list, with a status of OK, as in **Figure 8.5**.

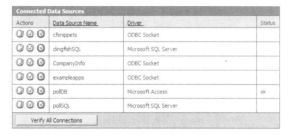

Actions	Data Source Name	Driver	Status
	cfsnippets	ODBC Socket	
	dingfishSQL	Microsoft SQL Server	
	CompanyInfo	ODBC Socket	
	exampleapps	ODBC Socket	
	pollDB	Microsoft Access	ok
	pollSQL	Microsoft SQL Server	

Figure 8.5 ColdFusion MX allows you to easily and quickly
specify and test Data Sources.

Alternatively, the procedure for creating a SQL Server data source is as follows:

To create an **SQL server data source in ColdFusion MX**:

1. Open the ColdFusion MX Administrator. For a Windows installation of ColdFusion MX, you can access the Administrator page by choosing Start > Programs > Macromedia ColdFusion MX > Administrator.

2. Select the Data Sources section under the Data & Services category.

3. In the Add New Data Source section, type a name for your new data source, such as **pollDB** and select the Microsoft SQL Server driver. Click Add.

4. In the Microsoft SQL Server Data Source, specify the details for connecting to your SQL Server database. You should be able to determine these from your ISP or System Administrator. This information should include the database name, server name, port (by default, 1433) and username/password.

5. Add an optional description for this data source.

6. Click Submit to create the data source.

ColdFusion will take you back to the Data Source page. Your new data source should appear in the list, with a status of OK.

Now that you have created the data source, we can move on to interrogating it to get some information.

DEVELOPING THE SERVER-SIDE FUNCTIONALITY

The Flash movie doesn't talk directly to a database. It can't. There is no built-in database connectivity within Flash, just as there's none within an HTML page. You always need a "middleman" to broker the information between your Flash movie and your database. These days, it's smoother than ever, but the same concept still stands.

Understanding ColdFusion Components and Flash Remoting

ColdFusion Components (CFCs) are a new feature of ColdFusion MX, which is particularly relevant for our purposes. They're easy-to-write, reusable chunks of code that can be called from other ColdFusion pages, or from within Flash using Flash Remoting. There are two elements to Flash Remoting: the server-side elements, which are automatically installed when you install ColdFusion MX, and the client-side elements (Flash Remoting Components) to allow creation of Flash movies that use Flash Remoting.

Xref

For more about Flash Remoting, see Chapter 7. For more about ColdFusion and ColdFusion components, see Chapter 3.

As a developer, it's easy to draw the distinction between working in Flash and working in ColdFusion or even HTML. But there's not really much of a distinction between Flash and Flash Remoting. It's necessary to install the Flash Remoting Components, which add a few extra doodads to Flash, but after a while, they just feel like they've been part of the application forever. You don't think of Flash Remoting as an entity separate from Flash itself.

To create a ColdFusion Component:

1. If you haven't already, create a folder under your ColdFusion MX web root to handle files from this chapter. This example uses the default installation web root created at `C:\Inetpub\wwwroot`, but yours may be different. We've created an `mxbook` folder and under that, a `ch08` folder for this chapter. So, `C:\Inetpub\wwwroot\mxbook\ch08\` is the folder where we'll keep all the files for this chapter.

2. If you're going to use Dreamweaver MX to create your ColdFusion MX code, open Dreamweaver MX and define a ColdFusion site for this chapter, using the folder created in step 1 as your root folder.

3. In Dreamweaver, select File > New. The New Document dialog box appears.

4. Select the Dynamic Page category, and choose ColdFusion Component. Click Create. Dreamweaver creates a CFC shell. If you select Code View, an outline for a ColdFusion Component code is automatically created:

```
<cfcomponent>
   <cffunction name="myFunction" access="public" returntype="string">
      <cfargument name="myArgument" type="string" required="true">
      <cfset myResult="foo">
      <cfreturn myResult>
   </cffunction>
</cfcomponent>
```

5. Save this CFC file in the `mxbook\ch08` folder with a name of **poll.cfc**.

So what does this do? The `.cfc` tells ColdFusion it's a ColdFusion Component file (rather than a normal ColdFusion page, which ends in .cfm). The `access="public"` attribute makes it available to other locally-running ColdFusion pages, although we will have to changed this attribute to make this CFC available to external elements such as Flash movies.

In fact, after saving this shell file you can immediately point your browser to its location (`http://localhost/mxbook/ch08/poll.cfc`). Then ColdFusion will inspect it and list the public methods (functions) within it, as in **Figure 8.6**.

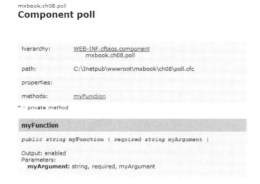

```
mxbook.ch08.poll
Component poll

hierarchy:       WEB-INF.cftags.component
                 mxbook.ch08.poll

path:            C:\Inetpub\wwwroot\mxbook\ch08\poll.cfc

properties:

methods:         myFunction
* - private method

myFunction

public string myFunction ( required string myArgument )

Output: enabled
Parameters:
   myArgument: string, required, myArgument
```

Figure 8.6 Even a basic ColdFusion MX Component definition can be inspected.

Note You may have to change the URL in this example based on your setup. This is for a local installation using ColdFusion installed within IIS, not as a standalone server.

Each ColdFusion Component can have several methods or functions within it. We're going to need to create several functions to handle the different database operations that we need to do:

- Retrieve the questions from the questions table.
- Get the choices for a particular question.
- Save the responses.

Let's take these one by one.

Retrieving the Poll's Questions

The first method we need interrogates the database for the questions. This is a simple component. We just want to be able to call it from our Flash movie to retrieve every question.

As we're accessing the database, we need to think about the necessary SQL code to retrieve the information we want. Fortunately, that's very easy.

```
SELECT * FROM questions
```

That's it. This SQL code will bring back a recordset containing everything from the questions table. We don't care about ordering or sorting the information; we just want all the questions. Change the existing CFC code you just created to the following:

```
<cfcomponent>

    <cffunction name="getQuestions" access="remote" returntype="query">
      <cfquery name="pollRecords" datasource="pollDB">
      SELECT * FROM questions
      </cfquery>
      <cfreturn pollRecords>
    </cffunction>

</cfcomponent>
```

Let's go through the important lines. First, the `<cfcomponent>` tags should be left as the first and last lines of the page. Within those, we can create multiple functions by using the `<cffunction>` tags. Next, the line:

```
<cffunction name="getQuestions" access="remote" returntype="query">
```

This line specifies the function name, getQuestions. This is how we call the method from within our Flash movie.

Access="remote" (which should be changed from public) tells ColdFusion that this function can be called externally, as opposed to some functions which can only be used from within the CFC itself.

The returntype="query" tells ColdFusion to return a recordset from this function.

The `<cfquery name="pollRecords" datasource="pollDB">` line specifies the data source pollDB that we created using the ColdFusion administrator.

Retrieving the Choices

When retrieving the response choices for the questions, there are a few options open to us. We could just retrieve every single choice, then programmatically work through them in Flash to determine which choice goes with which question. We could even use some more complex SQL to bring back both the questions and choices as joined data. However, the easiest route is just to create a function that can fetch the choices for a particular question. As we decided earlier that the Flash movie only shows one question at a time, we can use Flash to take each question in turn, and find out the choices for that question alone.

Add the following code after the closing `</cffunction>` tag of the `getQuestions()` function but before the closing `</cfcomponent>` tag:

```
<cffunction name="getChoices" access="remote" returntype="query">
  <cfargument name="questionID" type="numeric" required="true">
    <cfquery name="choiceRecords" datasource="pollDB">
    SELECT * FROM choices WHERE question_id = #questionID#
    </cfquery>
    <cfreturn choiceRecords>
</cffunction>
```

There are a couple of new lines that weren't in the `getQuestions()` function. First, the `<cfargument name="questionID" type="numeric" required="true">` line tells ColdFusion that this function must be called with an argument of `questionID`. This is because we only want this function to fetch the choices for a specific question, so we must say which one we want.

The SQL itself is slightly different:

```
SELECT * FROM choices WHERE question_id = #questionID#
```

The `#questionID#` refers to the argument passed to this function. In Flash, we could call this function using literals or variables, such as:

```
getChoices(7);
```

or

```
getChoices(currentQuestion);
```

Adding Poll Responses to the Database

There are a couple of additional challenges when inserting information back into our database. First, let's generate a basic insert function.

If we were writing plain SQL to insert information into the `responses` table, we'd use something like this:

```
INSERT INTO responses (choice_id, ip_address) VALUES (17, '127.0.0.1')
```

Even though the `responses` table contains four columns (`response_id`, `choice_id`, `date_entered` and `ip_address`) we only need to specify the `choice_id` and `ip_address`, as the `response_id` is an automatically generated number, and the `date_entered` column has a default value of the current date and time.

So far, so good. However, of course, we aren't going to be inserting literal values. The choice ID will need to be an argument passed from the Flash movie, and the user's IP address can be determined using a ColdFusion function.

Add the following code within the `<cfcomponent>` tags:

```
<cffunction name="addResponse" access="remote" returntype="query">
   <cfargument name="choiceID" type="numeric" required="true">
   <cfquery name="responseRecord" datasource="pollDB">
   INSERT INTO responses (choice_id, ip_address)
   VALUES ('#choiceID#', '#CGI.REMOTE_ADDR#')
   </cfquery>
   <cfreturn responseRecord>
</cffunction>
```

The `<cfargument name="choiceID" type="numeric" required="true">` tells ColdFusion that this function must be called with a numeric `choiceID` parameter. It will cause an error if called without a parameter or if called with the wrong data type (an array or string, for example).

The `#CGI.REMOTE_ADDR#` is a convenient way to determine the user's IP address within ColdFusion.

But there's a problem. This function will successfully allow us to insert one response at a time. However, in some circumstances we may need to add more than one record at a time. For example, a question that asks "Which Macromedia products do you use?" needs to insert a separate response record for each selected choice.

There are two ways of doing this. Our Flash movie could call the `addRecord()` function several times, or we could create a new method that allows Flash to call our CFC once but pass several values to be inserted. Our CFC can then handle the job of inserting each record into the `responses` table.

To build a CFC that handles several values, we first have to decide how Flash will pass the information. Remembering that there are two essential options—a single response or a multiple response—we can determine that Flash should pass the information in one of two ways: a numeric value for a single response, or an array for a multiple response.

We already have a completed addResponse() function to add each record, so we need to add another function to accept the information from Flash. In pseudocode, this would be:

```
Function (requires argument)
If the argument is an array
   Loop through the array
      Call the addResponse function with each array entry
   Next loop
Else it's a single value
   Call the addResponse function
End if
End function
```

In ColdFusion, we add the following code to our ColdFusion component:

```
<cffunction name="checkResponse" access="remote" returntype="query">
   <cfargument name="choiceID" type="any" required="true">
   <CFSCRIPT>
   if(IsArray(choiceID)){
      for(i = 1; i LTE ArrayLen(choiceID); i = i + 1){
         returnObj = addResponse(choiceID[i]);
         }
   } else {
      returnObj = addResponse(choiceID);
   }
   return returnObj;
   </CFSCRIPT>
</cffunction>
```

For security, we could now change the addResponse() function to be a private function. This means it could not be called from Flash. It must be called from another function within the CFC, in this case, the checkResponse() function. We change the function to private by altering the cffunction tag for the addResponse() function, as in:

```
<cffunction name="addResponse" access="private" returntype="query">
```

The final CFC code should look like Listing 8.1:

Listing 8.1 CFC code

```
<cfcomponent>
   <cffunction name="getQuestions" access="remote" returntype="query">
      <cfquery name="pollRecords" datasource="pollDB">
      SELECT * FROM questions
      </cfquery>
      <cfreturn pollRecords>
   </cffunction>

   <cffunction name="getChoices" access="remote" returntype="query">
   <cfargument name="questionID" type="numeric" required="true">
      <cfquery name="choiceRecords" datasource="pollDB">
      SELECT * FROM choices WHERE question_id = #questionID#
      </cfquery>
      <cfreturn choiceRecords>
   </cffunction>

<cffunction name="addResponse" access="private" returntype="query">
      <cfargument name="choiceID" type="numeric" required="true">
      <cfquery name="responseRecord" datasource="pollDB">
      INSERT INTO responses (choice_id, ip_address)
      VALUES ('#choiceID#', '#CGI.REMOTE_ADDR#')
      </cfquery>
      <cfreturn responseRecord>
</cffunction>

<cffunction name="checkResponse" access="remote" returntype="query">
   <cfargument name="choiceID" type="any" required="true">
   <CFSCRIPT>
   if(IsArray(choiceID)){
      for(i = 1; i LTE ArrayLen(choiceID); i = i + 1){
         returnObj = addResponse(choiceID[i]);
      }
   } else {
      returnObj = addResponse(choiceID);
   }
   return returnObj;
   </CFSCRIPT>
</cffunction>


</cfcomponent>
```

Save the file. We can use the ColdFusion component inspector again by pointing the browser at the CFC at `http://localhost/mxbook/ch08/poll.cfc`. You should see a screen similar to that in **Figure 8.7.**

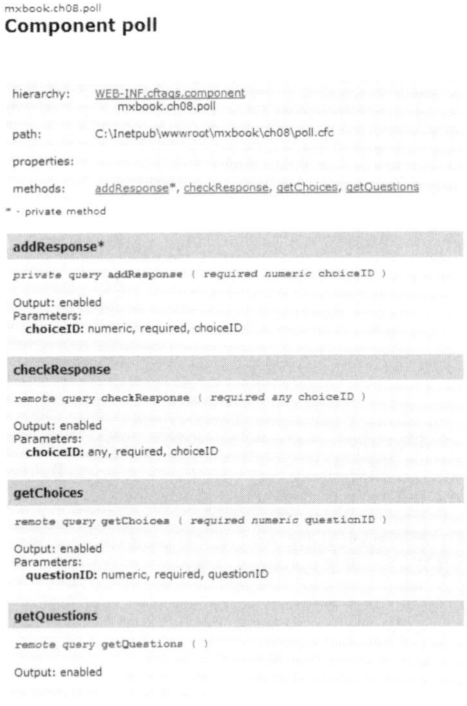

Figure 8.7 ColdFusion components can be inspected to list available methods and arguments.

PRODUCING THE FLASH CLIENT

With the database created, the data source specified, and the ColdFusion component methods all coded, the final step is to create the Flash movie front end for the application.

First, it's worth sketching out the different steps and procedures that the Flash movie will need to do. These include:

- Connect to the ColdFusion component using Flash Remoting

- Retrieve the questions from the ColdFusion component

- Retrieve the choices for each question
- Format the information into user interface elements
- Allow the user to submit a response
- Move to the next question

A basic flowchart of operation can be useful, as seen in **Figure 8.8.**

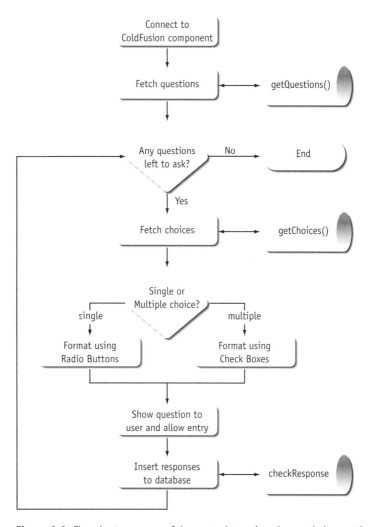

Figure 8.8 Flowcharts are a useful way to determine the needed operations of your application before you begin to build.

Creating the Interface

We're going to create most of the positioning of the UI elements using Action-Script, but the one element we can be sure of having on the stage is a button.

To create the interface:

1. Make a new Flash movie and save it in your ch08 folder as **poll.fla**.

2. Rename Layer 1 to a**ctions** and add a new layer, **nextButton**. From the Flash UI Components section of the Components panel, drag out a PushButton component on to frame 1 of the nextButton layer.

3. Give the PushButton component an instance name of **nextButton**, and in the Property inspector set its Label value to **Next Question** and its Click Handler to **submitAnswer**. **Figure 8.9** shows how the Property inspector should look for this component.

Figure 8.9 The Property inspector is used to specify options for Flash UI components.

Making a Connection to the Service

Before any of the CFC methods can be called, we must connect to the CFC itself. This is one of the first things to do in our Flash movie.

To connect to the service:

Open the Actions panel for the first frame of the actions layer. Add the code in Listing 8.2. Do not add the line numbers.

Listing 8.2 Connecting to the ColdFusion Component using Flash Remoting

```
1. #include "NetServices.as"
2. #include "NetDebug.as"
3. if (inited == null) {
```

Listing 8.2 Connecting to the ColdFusion Component using Flash Remoting *(continued)*

```
4.   inited = true;
5.   nextButton.setEnabled(false);
6.   NetServices.setDefaultGatewayURL("http://localhost/
     ➝ flashservices/gateway");
7.   gatewayConnection = NetServices.createGatewayConnection();
8.   pollService = gatewayConnection.getService("mxbook.ch08.poll",
     ➝ this);
9.   pollService.getQuestions();
10. }
```

Let's examine this code line by line:

The first two lines tell Flash to include the ActionScript libraries necessary for using and debugging Flash Remoting. These are preprocessor instructions, so unlike normal ActionScript, make sure there are no semicolons at the end of these lines.

Note These ActionScript libraries are installed when you install Flash Remoting components on your machine and are located in the Configuration\Include folder in your Flash MX program directory.

The next lines 3 and 4 are just a simple test to make sure that the connection code we're adding is only run once when the Flash movie is first run.

We're not going to allow the user to proceed until they've made a selection, so line 5 disables the button so it can't be clicked on.

Line 6 is our first Flash Remoting line. It specifies the gateway that Flash needs to connect to. Flash must connect to the designated gateway in order to use Flash Remoting. Our example uses the default gateway location for a ColdFusion installation within IIS; yours may be different.

After specifying the gateway, we then connect to it in line 7.

However, connecting to the gateway still hasn't actually connected us to the ColdFusion Component that we want to use. Connecting to the gateway effectively takes us to the ColdFusion web root folder. We can then connect to any ColdFusion component (CFC files) stored within the web root folder, as long as we know the folder path.

COMPONENT PATHS IN FLASH REMOTING

When a Flash movie connects to components using Flash Remoting, we need to be aware of the folder path. This path uses dots rather than slashes.

As an example, if you created a ColdFusion component file called `foobar.cfc` and placed it in your web root folder at:

`\\Inetpub\wwwroot\mxbook\foobar.cfc`

You could then use Flash Remoting to refer to that ColdFusion component directly by its name, without the file extension:

`foobar`

If the CFC file is one level down inside an `mxbook` folder in the web root, at

`\\Inetpub\wwwroot\mxbook\foobar.cfc`

You would then use a dot to separate the folder and the component:

`mxbook.foobar`

And in this chapter example, our folder is one level further down so the absolute path would be:

`\\Inetpub\wwwroot\mxbook\ch08\foobar.cfc`

And we would refer to it as:

`mxbook.ch08.foobar`

Line 8 is responsible for actually connecting to the component and sets up `pollService` as the name by which we refer to this connection. The reference to `this` in line 8 tells Flash Remoting to return any responses to the main timeline of the movie.

And finally, line 9 calls the `getQuestions()` function of our ColdFusion component to retrieve the questions from the database.

As an interim trial, you can save and run this code. It's not going to visually do anything, but if you open the NetConnection Debugger (Window > NetConnection Debugger) and test the movie, you should see some activity listed in the Debugger window, as shown in **Figure 8.10**.

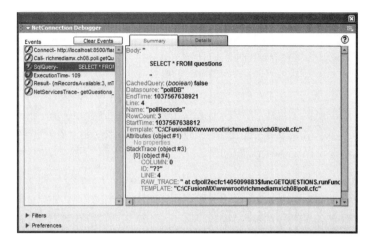

Figure 8.10 The NetConnection debugger is essential when creating and testing Flash Remoting applications.

Retrieving Questions

In earlier versions of Flash, it was often a logistical nightmare to integrate with a database. While it's easy to issue a call to a database, the unreliable speed of the Internet makes it hard to know if and when you'll get a response. Early methods of doing this involved creating timelines that looped around many times, continually checking whether a response had been received.

Fortunately, we don't need to do that anymore. With Flash Remoting, a mechanism is built in to ensure we can perform exactly the right operations when a response is received from the database.

This is how it works. In the last piece of code, we issued a call to the getQuestions() function of our ColdFusion component. When this function executes, it will attempt to return a recordset to the Flash movie. To handle this, Flash will first look for a callback function with the same name as the CFC function, but ending in "_result".

This means that when a result is returned from the getQuestions() function in the CFC, Flash will look for a getQuestions_result() function in the Flash movie. When we call the getChoices() function in the CFC, Flash will automatically look for the getChoices_result() function in the Flash movie when it returns data.

Even a simple piece of code added to frame 1 would let you test this out. Add this code after the #include statements, but *before* the if(inited==null) line. This is because the ActionScript to connect to the Flash Remoting gateway should only be executed after all the functions have been declared.

```
function getQuestions_Result(result) {
    trace("questions received! ");
}
```

Now, test the movie. The output window should show you the trace message. If not, examine the NetConnection Debugger to see if there are any errors being returned by ColdFusion.

An initial idea might be to have the getQuestions_result() function set up the user interface and start asking the questions, but this is a bad place for that. We only call the getQuestions() function in the ColdFusion component once, so this getQuestions_Result() function in our Flash movie is also only called once. A better idea is to initialize a few items and move on.

Change the code to the following:

```
function getQuestions_Result(result) {
    rsQuestions = result;
    question_index = 0;
    nextQuestion(rsQuestions);
}
```

This code will do three things:

- It saves the recordset to a persistent variable. If we don't do this, the question information returned from the ColdFusion component will disappear, as it's only in a local variable and scoped to this function.

- Set a question_index variable to zero, so Flash can keep track of where it is in the questions Recordset.

- Finally, call the nextQuestion() function, passing it the questions Recordset.

Let's add the nextQuestion() function. Add this code after the getQuestions_result() function.

```
function nextQuestion() {
    if (question_index<rsQuestions.getLength()) {
        showQuestion();
    } else {
        question_txt.text = "Poll completed.";
    }
}
```

THE onRESULT EVENT

You saw how responses from remote services will cause the Flash movie to look for a callback function with the same name as the remote function, but ending in _result. This happens because when we created the connection to the service, we passed it a reference to this as a responder object:

```
pollService = gatewayConnection.getService("mxbook.ch08.poll", this);
```

Any response from the service is passed to the root timeline and a function with a suffix of _result is searched for on the root timeline.

There is a different and more object-oriented method of handling service responses. Rather than specifying a general responder object when the service connection is made, we connect without using a responder object and then name each individual responder object in the service function calls.

We then tie the individual responder objects together with their own responder functions, rather than declaring many callback functions on the root timeline.

For example, the example in this chapter calls the service functions as follows:

```
pollService.getQuestions();
```

Which entails that a callback function ending in _result is created for each remote service method:

```
function getQuestions_Result(result) {
   // code to handle the result from the CFC function getQuestions()
}
```

However, to use the onResult event in a more formal object-oriented manner, we would first connect without naming a general responder object (not using this).
```
pollService = gatewayConnection.getService("mxbook.ch08.poll");
```

And each call to the remote service would pass a responder object as its first parameter, for example:

```
pollService.getQuestions(new questionsResult());
```

This object (questionsResult) can then declare its onResult() function to handle the event:
```
function questionsResult() {

   this.onResult = function(result) {
      // code to handle the result from the CFC function getQuestions()
   };
}
```

It's more object-oriented to code this way, although there is an argument that the _result method can be easier to read.

The exercise detailed in this chapter uses the _result method. An alternate version of this exercise that uses the onResult event can be found in the chapter_08 folder on the book's CD-ROM under the name poll_onResult.fla.

This function, which will be called several times, basically asks: are there any more questions left? If not, it will set message text to display, "poll completed." The movie would then be over. But if there are still questions available, the nextQuestion() function will call the showQuestion() function.

Building the UI with ActionScript

This next step in producing our application is to add elements of user interface to prepare to present the question to the user. The showQuestion() function starts to add the elements.

Add the following code after the nextQuestion() function:

```
function showQuestion() {
    _root.createTextField("question_txt", 1, 25, 25, 400, 20);
    _root.question_txt.text = rsQuestions.items[question_index].text;

    if (rsQuestions.items[question_index].question_type == "single") {
        componentName = "FRadioButtonSymbol";
    } else {
        componentName = "FCheckBoxSymbol";
    }

    pollService.getChoices(rsQuestions.items[question_index].question_id);
}
```

The showQuestion() function does the following:

- Creates a text field on the stage and loads the current question text.

- Determines if the question is a single choice question (which should use radio buttons) or a multiple-choice question, which will use check boxes. It uses the official Flash UI component names, FRadioButtonSymbol and FcheckBoxSymbol.

- Calls the ColdFusion component function named getChoices(), passing the current question number.

The getChoices() ColdFusion component function will attempt to retrieve a recordset containing all the choices for the stated question. When this is passed back to Flash, the movie will look for a getChoices_result() callback function, which is an ideal location for most of the user interface code. Listing 8.3 shows the getChoices_Result() function, which should be added after the showQuestion() function.

Make sure the CheckBox and RadioButton UI components have been added to your movie library. You can just drag them to the stage and then delete them from the stage, as they will stay in the library.

Listing 8.3 getChoices_Result() **function**

```
1.function getChoices_Result(rsChoices) {
2    for (var i = 0; i<rsChoices.getLength(); i++) {
3.      _root.attachMovie(componentName, "choice_"+i, i+10,
        → {_x:question_txt._x, _y:(i*25)+question_txt._y+30});
4.      var currentItem = _root["choice_"+i];
5.      if (componentName == "FRadioButtonSymbol") {
6.        currentItem.setGroupName("radioGroup_1");
7.        currentItem.setData(rsChoices.items[i].choice_id);
8.      } else if (componentName == "FCheckBoxSymbol") {
9.        currentItem.data = rsChoices.items[i].choice_id;
10.     }
11.     currentItem.setLabel(rsChoices.items[i].choice_description);
12.     currentItem.setChangeHandler("enableSubmit");
13.     currentItem.setSize(200);
14.   }
15.}
```

In line 1 we declare that this function will be passed a recordset rsChoices by the ColdFusion component; it's up to us to name the returned object, but we have to call it something in order to refer to it later. rsChoices is as good a name as any. The prefix rs lets us know what kind of data it is, so when we're looking at this code in a year's time we can have a clue as to what it's doing.

Line 2 tells Flash to loop around as long as there are choices left in the recordset.

For each loop, line 3 attaches a MovieClip symbol from the library to the root timeline. The name of the MovieClip symbol is stored in the variable component-Name, which was set to either FRadioButtonSymbol or FCheckBoxSymbol in a previous function. We'll use the loop index i to ensure that all the instance names are different, and we'll spread each one slightly apart on the Y axis.

Lines 5 through 7 handle adding radio buttons. If radio buttons are used, they must all have the same group name. This ensures that if one radio button is clicked on, all the others are clicked off In line 7 the `choice_id` number is loaded as the data for each option.

If we're using checkboxes, they don't need to be grouped. Line 8 just loads the `choice_id` number as the data for each option.

Line 11 sets the text label for each option with the correct description.

Finally, line 12 sets the changeHandler for each option so that every time any option is clicked, it calls the `enableSubmit()` function. Line 13 widens the available width for the label so that the text is not cut off.

PREPARING THE ANSWERS FOR SUBMISSION

Every time an option is clicked (either on or off), the `enableSubmit()` function is called. This function is responsible for keeping track of which options are selected and allowing the next button to be pressed after a selection has been made.

Part of the challenge is keeping track of multiple selections when several checkboxes are selected and also making sure that choices are removed when checkboxes are deselected. The pseudo code to prepare answers for submission follows:

```
If item is a checkbox
   If checkbox has just been selected
      Add the choice number to the array
   Else (checkbox has been deselected)
      Remove the choice number from the array
      If the array is empty
         Set the "next button" to disabled
   End if
Else (it's a radio button)
   Save choice number
End if
Set "next button" to enabled (clickable)
```

Listing 8.4 shows the ActionScript code to prepare the answers for submission. Add this code after the `getChoices_result()` function.

Listing 8.4 enableSubmit() **function**

```
function enableSubmit(obj) {
  nextButton.setEnabled(true);
  if (obj instanceof FCheckBoxClass) {
    if (obj.getValue()) {
      choiceSelected = (choiceSelected) ? choiceSelected :
      → new Array();
      choiceSelected.push(obj.data);
    } else {
      var itemCount = choiceSelected.length;
      for (var i = 0; i<itemCount; i++) {
        if (choiceSelected[i] == obj.data) {
          choiceSelected.splice(i, 1);
          if (choiceSelected.length == 0) {
            nextButton.setEnabled(false);
          }
          break;
        }
      }
    }
  } else if (obj.radioInstances[obj.getInstance()] instanceof
  → FRadioButtonClass) {
    choiceSelected = obj.getValue();
  }

}
```

This gets us to the point of being able to make our selections and click the next question button, which will submit the answers to the database and take us to the next question.

Submitting Responses to the Service

The nextButton instance was placed on the stage with a Click Handler of submitAnswer, meaning that whenever it's clicked, the submitAnswer() function, shown in Listing 8.5, will be called. The submitAnswer() function should call the checkResponse ColdFusion component function to insert the responses into the database. Add the following code after the enableSubmit() function.

Listing 8.5 submitAnswer() **function**

```
 1. function submitAnswer() {
 2.    nextButton.setEnabled(false);
 3.    question_index++;
 4.    question_txt.text = "Submitting answer...";
 5.
 6.    for (var i in _root) {
 7.        if (i.indexOf("choice_") != -1) {
 8.            _root[i].removeMovieClip();
 9.        }
10.    }
11.    pollService.checkResponse(choiceSelected);
12. }
```

Line 2 disables the button so it can't be pressed. Line 3 increments the questions index.

Line 4 changes what was the question text to a more descriptive message

The loop beginning in line 6 removes all the choices (radio buttons and check boxes) for the previous question.

And finally, line 11 calls the ColdFusion component function checkResponse(), passing the choiceSelected variable. The checkResponse() CFC function will handle the insertion of response records, whether single or multiple.

The final function to be added is the callback function that will be called when the checkResponse() ColdFusion component function returns. All this needs to do it delete the saved choiceSelected array and call the nextQuestion() component.

Add the following code after the submitAnswer() function.

```
function checkResponse_result(result) {
  delete choiceSelected;
  nextQuestion();
}
```

And that's all the code necessary. Save and test the movie.

Final ActionScript

The final ActionScript is shown in Listing 8.6. The order of the functions is mainly immaterial, as long as they are all declared before the ActionScript that connects to the Flash Remoting gateway. This is because we don't want to call any server-side functions before we have created the related callback functions in the Flash client.

Listing 8.6 Completed ActionScript for Poll Application

```
#include "NetServices.as"
#include "NetDebug.as"

function getQuestions_Result(result) {
    rsQuestions = result;
    question_index = 0;
    nextQuestion(rsQuestions);
}

function nextQuestion() {
    if (question_index<rsQuestions.getLength()) {
        showQuestion();
    } else {
        question_txt.text = "Poll completed.";
    }
}


function showQuestion() {
    _root.createTextField("question_txt", 1, 25, 25, 400, 20);
    _root.question_txt.text = rsQuestions.items[question_index].text;
    if (rsQuestions.items[question_index].question_type == "single") {
        componentName = "FRadioButtonSymbol";
    } else {
        componentName = "FCheckBoxSymbol";
    }
    // call the getChoices function in the CFC, passing the current
    → question_id
    pollService.getChoices(rsQuestions.items[question_index].question_id);
}

function getChoices_Result(rsChoices) {
    for (var i = 0; i<rsChoices.getLength(); i++) {
        _root.attachMovie(componentName, "choice_"+i, i+10,
        →{_x:question_txt._x, _y:(i*25)+question_txt._y+30});
        var currentItem = _root["choice_"+i];
```

Listing 8.6 Completed ActionScript for Poll Application *(continued)*

```
        if (componentName == "FRadioButtonSymbol") {
          currentItem.setGroupName("radioGroup_1");
          currentItem.setData(rsChoices.items[i].choice_id);
        } else if (componentName == "FCheckBoxSymbol") {
          currentItem.data = rsChoices.items[i].choice_id;
        }
        currentItem.setLabel(rsChoices.items[i].choice_description);
        currentItem.setChangeHandler("enableSubmit");
        currentItem.setSize(200);
    }
}


function enableSubmit(obj) {
  nextButton.setEnabled(true);
  if (obj instanceof FCheckBoxClass) {
    if (obj.getValue()) {
      choiceSelected = (choiceSelected) ? choiceSelected : new Array();
      choiceSelected.push(obj.data);
    } else {
      var itemCount = choiceSelected.length;
      for (var i = 0; i<itemCount; i++) {
        if (choiceSelected[i] == obj.data) {
          choiceSelected.splice(i, 1);
          if (choiceSelected.length == 0) {
            nextButton.setEnabled(false);
          }
          break;
        }
      }
    }
  } else if (obj.radioInstances[obj.getInstance()] instanceof
  ➞ FRadioButtonClass) {
    choiceSelected = obj.getValue();
  }

}

function submitAnswer() {
  //turn off the button
  nextButton.setEnabled(false);
```

Listing 8.6 Completed ActionScript for Poll Application *(continued)*

```
      question_index++;
      // change the page text
      question_txt.text = "Submitting answer...";
      //remove all the options
      for (var i in _root) {
         if (i.indexOf("choice_") != -1) {
            _root[i].removeMovieClip();
         }
      }
      // call the insert method, passing the selected choice(s)
      pollService.checkResponse(choiceSelected);
   }

   function checkResponse_result(result) {
      delete choiceSelected;
      nextQuestion();
   }

   if (inited == null) {
      inited = true;
      nextButton.setEnabled(false);
      NetServices.setDefaultGatewayURL("http://localhost/
      → flashservices/gateway");
      gatewayConnection = NetServices.createGatewayConnection();
      // needs to use the path to the component
      pollService = gatewayConnection.getService("mxbook.ch08.poll", this);
      // call the first method
      pollService.getQuestions();
   }
```

NetConnection Debugger

One of the elements installed by the Flash Remoting Components is the Net-Connection Debugger. It's an essential tool when building and testing your applications, as it offers you behind-the-scenes inspection of the communication going on between your Flash movie, ColdFusion, and the database.

The NetConnection Debugger (Window > NetConnection Debugger) needs to be turned on before you test your movie. When testing, it shows the different requests and responses carried out between the elements of your application.

The items shown in the debugger include viewing the SQL that's being issued to the database, seeing the contents of recordsets being returned, and the guts of the AMF (**A**ctionScript **M**essage **F**ormat) messages being exchanged.

Which events you view are up to you; they are customizable in the Filters section, as shown in **Figure 8.11.**

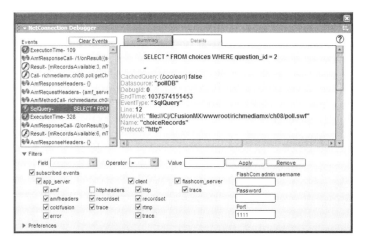

Figure 8.11 The NetConnection debugger allows you to filter exactly which events are reported.

For more detailed ColdFusion error messages, make sure debugging is turned on in your ColdFusion Administrator.

Wrapping Up

When you're happy with your application, you should remove (or comment out) the `#include "NetDebug.as"` line in your ActionScript. This file is only necessary for debugging purposes and adds extra file size to your SWF.

The completed document, `poll_100.fla`, can be found in the `chapter_08` folder of this book's CD-ROM. You can look for further enhancements to this exercise on the book's Web site at www.mxbook.com.

In the next chapter, you will learn how to build upon this application to present the results graphically.

SUMMARY

- Always carry out a planning process, even for the smallest projects. It will help you focus your application.

- Always follow a formal design process to ensure the correct normalization of your tables.

- When building your database, you should enforce referential integrity on your relationships. This will help prevent your database filling up with garbage. Unfortunately, enforcing referential integrity can have a performance impact on a database.

- Before a ColdFusion page or ColdFusion component can connect to a database, you must create a Data Source in the ColdFusion administrator. This can be created for virtually all current DBMS systems.

- ColdFusion components are reusable code that can be used by other Flash movies or ColdFusion pages. They can also be turned into full-blown Web Services.

- If you want the functions in your ColdFusion component to be accessible by external elements, they must be marked as `public`.

- After calling a function in a ColdFusion component, Flash automatically attempts to return values to a callback function, which has the same name as the CFC function but ends in "`_result`".

- To construct Flash user interfaces using ActionScript, make sure that the UI components you need have been added to the library of your movie.

- Make sure that you do not add more UI components than you need, as they add to your file size even if not used.

- The NetConnection Debugger is an invaluable tool in creating and testing flash movies that use Flash Remoting.

- When your movies are complete and tested, you should remove the included `netDebug.as` file, as it is not needed for production movies.

In This Chapter:

9 Displaying Data

In the previous chapter's poll application, you learned how Flash Remoting is used to connect Flash movies to server-side components. You explored straightforward methods for both retrieving and inserting data into the database using ColdFusion components (CFCs).

This chapter is concerned more with techniques than full applications. It covers several methods for retrieving data from databases, including an example to display the data created by the poll application in the previous chapter. We're also going to show several ways of using the data to fuel

GUI components, and more importantly, how to display dynamic data using graphical methods, such as charts and diagrams.

In this chapter, you will use:

- Dreamweaver MX

- ColdFusion MX

- Flash MX

- Flash Remoting

- Flash Charting Components

- A relational DBMS such as SQL Server or Microsoft Access

 Note

This chapter does not use Flash Communication Server MX.

THE FLASH ADVANTAGE

A great deal of attention is focused on Flash's ability to develop interfaces for Rich Internet Applications. The primary focus is on its ability to develop an application that is not constrained by the page model as an HTML-based application is. Relevant sections of the Flash movie can be loaded in and out as needed, and it's not necessary to interrupt the user's experience by traipsing from page to page to page.

However, in this chapter we're interested in another of Flash's strengths. Flash offers us a much better way to represent data visually. If we just wanted to compile a huge list of numbers and show it on a page, we could do that in HTML. Using Flash, we have all sorts of options available to us that aren't possible in HTML:

- Dynamic charts and graphs using scalable vector graphics

- Interactivity

- Motion over time

And it's these aspects—using Flash to display visual information, rather than lists of numbers—that we'll concentrate on in this chapter.

 Note   Sure, there are ways to accomplish some of these dynamic options in an HTML-based site. For example, there are commercial server components (depending on your chosen server platform) that can generate dynamic JPEG charts, but they can't touch Flash's interactive potential.

THE SQL ADVANTAGE

In this chapter, we want to visually display data that is retrieved from a database. It might be tempting to ignore the mundane aspects of data retrieval and concentrate on how Flash must programmatically handle the data. This would be a mistake. An *enormous* amount of development time in any application can be saved by getting the RDBMS to do a lot of work for us. SQL is an extremely powerful and much underused language, and this chapter covers some complex queries to show just how much programming can be avoided by simply making the database queries a little smarter.

SQL AND THE DESIRE FOR INNOVATION

You should always have a slightly different mindset when thinking about your database development than when thinking about Flash development.

Flash, ActionScript, Flash Remoting, Flash Communications Server—these are all innovative, recent advances, and we're trying to find the most efficient, interesting and coolest ways of developing with them.

SQL on the other hand, is old, old tech. It's been around since the 1970's. Attempting to find a cool and innovative way to use SQL reminds me of this quote:

Never try to teach a pig to sing. It wastes your time and annoys the pig.

SQL is very good at what it does. There are many ways to be creative with it, but they're not new. If there's something you want to do with SQL, trust me, someone has already accomplished it—twenty years ago, on punch card driven mainframes.

There's a huge body of knowledge available to tap into, and you should make the most of it.

Unfortunately, one of the problems with database development becoming commonplace on the Web is that there's a large contingent of developers who make do with a few introductory SQL keywords. They learned something like:

```
SELECT * FROM employees WHERE department = "marketing"
```

Every SQL statement they write from that point on looks fairly similar. "If all you have is a hammer, everything looks like a nail." For example, we created a database in the last chapter that consisted of three tables: questions, choices and responses. This database layout was normalized to attempt to store the minimum amount of redundant data. Now, we want to show this stored data in a meaningful way, which can be expressed as follows:

"Show me how many people answered each question."

We know that the answers are stored in the responses table, so we could create a ColdFusion component function with some basic SQL, such as:

```
SELECT * FROM responses
```

This would return the data:

```
response_id   choice_id   ip_address      date_answered
-----------------------------------------------------------------
56            3           127.0.0.1       11/17/2002 9:52:02 AM
57            7           127.0.0.1       11/17/2002 9:52:09 AM
58            11          127.0.0.1       11/17/2002 9:52:09 AM
59            17          127.0.0.1       11/17/2002 9:52:23 AM
60            3           127.0.0.1       11/17/2002 9:53:04 AM
61            7           127.0.0.1       11/17/2002 9:53:20 AM
62            10          127.0.0.1       11/17/2002 9:53:20 AM
63            9           127.0.0.1       11/17/2002 9:53:20 AM
(etc.)
```

The problem with this, of course, is that we can't tell from looking at this what each of the responses mean. A Bar chart or a Pie chart with numbers on it is not meaningful. We need to know to what these responses refer. So, we can create another function that contains yet more SQL:

```
SELECT * FROM choices
```

This would return the data:

```
choice_id    question_id    choice_description
-------------------------------------------------
1            2              Windows 98
2            2              Windows 2000
3            2              Windows XP
4            2              Mac OS 9
5            2              Mac OS X
6            2              Linux
7            3              Windows 98
8            3              Windows 2000
9            3              Windows XP
10           3              Mac OS 9
11           3              Mac OS X
12           3              Linux
(etc.)
```

However, we still have a problem. We might be able to take these two recordsets and using some ActionScript, match up the choice_id fields, and calculate that "75 people said Linux was the answer." However, that's fairly useless when we don't know what the question was. So we use some more SQL to find the questions:

```
SELECT question_id, text FROM questions
```

```
question_id    text
----------------------------------------------------------------
2              What's your Favorite OS?
3              Which Operating Systems do you use?
4              Which Macromedia MX product do you use the most?
```

So, we have three separate database queries to return the information we need. Unfortunately, the work has barely begun. If we use such basic SQL as this, we need to rely on substantial ActionScript to organize the data:

- First, loop through the responses—of which there may be hundreds or thousands—to determine how many people picked each choice.

- Take each totaled response and loop through the choices data to find the description for each choice.

- Then take each choice to find the question description

- And last but not least, now that we know the questions to which each response relates, we have to sort through the totaled responses to group them under the correct question for presentation.

As you can imagine, the resulting amount of ActionScript code would be substantial. But using ActionScript code ignores the best aspect of SQL. SQL is a declarative language and can pretty much give you anything you want, if you ask it nicely. You don't have to tell it the programmatic steps, as you have to do in ActionScript. Instead, you just tell it specifically what you want:

"I want to know each question, what the possible answers were for that question, and how many people chose each answer."

The best way to fetch this is a detailed SQL query that combines the relevant database tables:

```
SELECT questions.text, choices.choice_description, Count(*) AS how_many
FROM questions INNER JOIN
(responses INNER JOIN choices ON responses.choice_id = choices.choice_id) ON
questions.question_id = choices.question_id
GROUP BY responses.choice_id, questions.text, choices.choice_description;
```

At this point, don't be too concerned about each part of the syntax here. Yes, it's a complex SQL query. Yes, it might take a while to write and debug. But these few lines of SQL will return meaningful, useful data that's *exactly* what we need to know:

```
text                                          choice_description   how_many
--------------------------------------------------------------------------
What's your Favorite OS?                       Windows 2000          3
What's your Favorite OS?                       Windows XP            12
What's your Favorite OS?                       Mac OS 9              1
What's your Favorite OS?                       Mac OS X              1
What's your Favorite OS?                       Linux                 2
Which Operating Systems do you use?            Windows 98            4
Which Operating Systems do you use?            Windows 2000          5
Which Operating Systems do you use?            Windows XP            3
Which Operating Systems do you use?            Mac OS 9              3
Which Operating Systems do you use?            Mac OS X              4
Which Operating Systems do you use?            Linux                 2
Which Operating Systems do you use?            Other                 2
Which Macromedia MX product do you use the most?  Fireworks MX      1
Which Macromedia MX product do you use the most?  FreeHand MX       4
Which Macromedia MX product do you use the most?  FlashCom          2
```

More importantly, by using a few lines of SQL, we no longer need scores or even hundreds of lines of ActionScript code. We can use a single line of Action-Script to fuel a Flash component with this recordset.

AN OVERVIEW OF THE PRODUCTION PROCESS

Before launching into any planning and design, you might want to familiarize yourself with the finished examples by going to the book's Web site at:

www.mxbook.com/v1/ch09/

At the site, there are several examples:

- Bar charts
- Pie charts
- Line charts
- Flash UI components

Rather than build an application, this chapter is concerned with examining these techniques for displaying data visually and the methods for how and why each option should be used.

Prerequisites

Our basic assumptions are that we will use Flash for the front-end application, ColdFusion components for the database queries, and Flash Remoting to join the two together. Any modern relational SQL-based database is practical.

The basic steps that we need to take to get up and running is as follows:

- Writing the ColdFusion components to manipulate the database
- Creating the Flash application to act as the front-end
- Debugging and testing

We're making the assumption that you have the following programs installed and available on your development machine:

- Flash MX

- ColdFusion MX

- Flash Remoting Components

- Flash Charting Components (see "Flash Charting Components" section of this chapter)

Flash Remoting Components, as described in Chapter 7, are add-ons to Flash MX that are essential when building and testing Flash Remoting applications. If you installed ColdFusion MX after installing Flash MX, they will be installed automatically. Otherwise, download them from

```
www.macromedia.com/software/flashremoting/downloads/components/
```

This chapter uses a ColdFusion MX installation under Internet Information Services (IIS) and refers to the web root folder at

```
C:\Inetpub\wwwroot\
```

This may vary depending on your configuration. If your web root folder is in a different location, or if you installed ColdFusion as a standalone Web server, please take that into account when following the steps.

Planning

Because the examples in this chapter are about techniques rather than full applications, we can afford to be a little less stringent about a full planning process and more focused on the techniques themselves. However, we still need to precisely detail the expected results. There are many different aspects to displaying data visually, and these need to be considered before launching into any part of the application construction.

In the last chapter, we touched upon very basic aspects of GUI design, namely that the choice between checkboxes and radio buttons is not arbitrary and should depend upon the question being asked:

- A section with two radio buttons means one *or* the other, but never both, and never neither.

- A section with two checkboxes can represent one or the other, both, or neither.

There are similar concerns when generating charts. The kind of data that's best to show in a Pie chart is markedly different from the kind of data that should be shown in a Line chart. Your focus on building these examples is likely to change depending on the types of data you're going to show and the level of detail you need to display.

In this planning stage, questions should arise such as:

WHAT KIND OF DATA IS TO BE SHOWN?

The effective presentation of statistical information differs widely depending on the nature of the data to be displayed. For example, a typical Line chart might depict the growth of company sales (see **Figure 9.1**) over the period of a year. Line charts are ideal for showing growth over time.

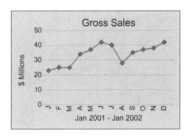

Figure 9.1 A Line chart is an ideal way to show numeric growth or decline over a period of time.

To display a comparison, you're likely to use a Bar or Pie chart, as in **Figure 9.2**.

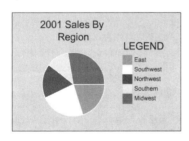

Figure 9.2 A Pie chart is a good way to quickly show comparisons between a small number of options, but is difficult to show the differences when values are close.

HOW MANY OPTIONS WILL BE SHOWN ON THE SAME PAGE?

The amount of options to be displayed also affects your choices. For example, if you have forty points of data to show, it's highly unlikely you'll generate a Pie chart divided into forty segments; it would be unreadable. This kind of information might be better shown in a Bar chart or Scatter Graph.

What Is the Variance Between Points Likely to Be?

This will affect the scale of your diagram. In our poll application, we ask people to choose their favorite OS. Simple enough, yet what's also important is how many people are likely to answer and what the spread of data is likely to be. Generating a Bar chart that shows the differences between 20 people picking one option and 25 people picking another is very different from a Bar chart where 20 people pick one option and 10,000 pick another. You would need to alter the scale of your bars, lest you end up with some meaningless diagram such as is shown in **Figure 9.3**.

Think about the information you need and how you're likely to display it. Not only will this analysis affect your decisions on what to use for visuals, it will also help you when constructing the most efficient SQL.

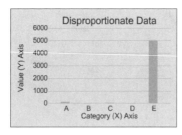

Figure 9.3 Disproportionate data can unduly affect your diagrams if you don't take this into account.

Flash Charting Components

New to this chapter are the Flash Charting Components, a free extension available from Macromedia. They can be downloaded from the Macromedia exchange at:

> `www.macromedia.com/exchange/flash/`

It is a free extension, but as is usual with the Macromedia Exchange, you will need to be logged in to download the extension, which can be found in the "User Interface" section. Download the `.mxp` file and install it using the Macromedia Extension Manager. After restarting Flash, you should see the Charting Components available in your Components panel, as shown in **Figure 9.4**.

The Flash Charting Components consist of three different components:

- Pie chart

- Bar chart

- Line chart

These each have their best uses, as we will explain in the following examples.

Figure 9.4 The Flash Charting Components are a free extension from Macromedia that cover the most commonly used chart types.

Note

Obviously, there are many more available options for chart display than the three we've listed. Scatter graphs, High/Low charts and Stacked Columns are just a few of the other options. However, the three included in the Flash Charting Components are undoubtedly the most common.

The three charting components all come with their own methods to use to programmatically alter the properties of the chart.

PieChart Component

Pie charts are ideal for conveying proportional relationships at a given time. They're not great when you need to convey exact amounts. For example, it can be harder to determine a small relative difference between two segments of a Pie chart than two points in a Line chart.

Pie charts have a few limitations. They can't show very small percentages well, cannot represent total values beyond 100%, and aren't useful for showing linear growth. Each Pie chart should only be used to represent a single point in time. Pie charts should also only be used to represent a small amount of values.

In this exercise, we use a Pie chart to present the data created by the poll application from the previous chapter. Each question in the poll can be represented by a different Pie chart showing the frequency of responses for each choice.

The Pie chart Flash component, part of the Flash Charting Components extension, doesn't have to be used with dynamic data. You can simply drag it out to a Flash page and set the parameters manually, as in **Figure 9.5**.

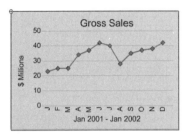

Figure 9.5 The Flash Charting Components can be populated manually if necessary but have many methods built-in specifically for dynamic data.

However, the component itself has been written in such a way that it's an easy task to assign dynamic data, rather than typing it all in. All the charting components contain the setDataProvider method, which allows you to directly assign a recordset to the component.

To show this in action, there are two steps: first, to build the ColdFusion component (CFC) to retrieve the data, and second, to create the Flash application itself.

To create the ColdFusion Component:

1. If you haven't already, create a folder under your web root to handle files from this chapter. We have the default web root at C:\Inetpub\wwwroot, but yours may be different. We've then created an mxbook folder, and under that, a ch09 folder for this chapter. So, C:\Inetpub\wwwroot\mxbook\ch09\ is the folder where we'll keep all the files for this chapter.

2. If you're going to use Dreamweaver MX to create your ColdFusion MX code, open Dreamweaver MX and define a ColdFusion site for this chapter.

3. In Dreamweaver, select File > New. The New Document dialog box appears.

4. Select the Dynamic Page category and choose ColdFusion Component. Click Create. Dreamweaver creates a CFC shell. If you select Code View, an outline for a ColdFusion Component code is automatically created:

```
<cfcomponent>
  <cffunction name="myFunction" access="public" returntype="string">
```

```
        <cfargument name="myArgument" type="string" required="true">
        <cfset myResult="foo">
        <cfreturn myResult>
    </cffunction>
</cfcomponent>
```

5. Save this CFC file in the mxbook\ch09 folder with a name of **pieChart.cfc**.

We're going to need to create two functions to handle the different database operations that we need to do.

- The first function should retrieve a recordset containing all question IDs in the database.

- The second function should take a question ID number and retrieve the choices and number of responses for each question.

Let's take these one by one.

Retrieving the Questions

The first method—let's call it getQuestions—interrogates the database for the questions. This is a simple component. We just want to know how many questions there are, and use the Primary key for these questions to find the related choices and responses.

The SQL is easy for this:

```
SELECT question_id FROM questions
```

We don't care about ordering or sorting the information, we just want all the questions. Change the existing CFC code to the following:

```
<cfcomponent>

    <cffunction name="getQuestions" access="remote" returntype="query">
        <cfquery name="pollRecords" datasource="pollDB">
        SELECT question_id FROM questions
        </cfquery>
        <cfreturn pollRecords>
    </cffunction>
</cfcomponent>
```

The `<cfquery name="pollRecords" datasource="pollDB">` line specifies the data source pollDB that we created in the previous chapter.

RETRIEVING THE RESPONSES

The second function—let's call it getAnswers—should accept a parameter of question_id and then find all the relevant information.

This means we need to:

- Retrieve the question text, from the questions table

- Retrieve the choice text, from the choices table

- Calculate the number of times a choice has been picked from the responses table

Let's take the SQL step by step. First, the basic SQL that contains the fields that we need is:

```
SELECT text, choice_description, responses.choice_id
FROM questions, choices, responses
```

 Note

As choice_id exists in both the choices table and the responses table, we have to stipulate which one we're trying to select. We do this by prefixing it with the table name. That's why the first line uses responses.choice_id rather than just choice_id.

However, running only this SQL will just give us a mass of unrelated data. We haven't indicated how the tables are related to each other. For each question, we're only interested in the choices that are tied to that question_id. For each choice, we're only interested in the responses that are tied to that choice_id.

There are two ways to join these tables together. The first uses the WHERE clause to effectively say "only where these fields match each other", as in this example:

```
SELECT text, choice_description, responses.choice_id
FROM questions, choices, responses
WHERE choices.question_id = questions.question_id
AND choices.choice_id =  responses.choice_id
```

An alternative is to use the SQL term INNER JOIN, as follows:

```
SELECT text, choice_description, responses.choice_id
FROM questions INNER JOIN (choices INNER JOIN responses
ON choices.choice_id =  responses.choice_id)
ON choices.question_id = questions.question_id
```

If this is your first exposure to inner joins, it might look a little confusing, because we're joining three tables together. But essentially, these two previous SQL examples do exactly the same thing: join the tables together, and for each response, show the associated choice and its parent question.

Running this SQL right now would return something like this:

```
Text                      choice_description   choice_id
---------------------------------------------------------
What's your Favorite OS?  Windows 2000         2
What's your Favorite OS?  Windows 2000         2
What's your Favorite OS?  Windows 2000         2
What's your Favorite OS?  Windows XP           3
What's your Favorite OS?  Windows XP           3
What's your Favorite OS?  Windows XP           3
What's your Favorite OS?  Windows XP           3
What's your Favorite OS?  Windows XP           3
What's your Favorite OS?  Windows XP           3
(etc.)
```

This still isn't quite finished. We now have one row for each time the option was chosen. We could certainly use ActionScript code to start totaling the rows, but why waste time in ActionScript when SQL can do it for us?

Using the SQL terms COUNT and GROUP BY, we can total the number of responses (COUNT) where the question and choice are the same (GROUP BY). For example:

```
SELECT text, choice_description, count(responses.choice_id)
FROM questions INNER JOIN (choices INNER JOIN responses
ON choices.choice_id = responses.choice_id)
ON choices.question_id = questions.question_id
GROUP BY text, choice_description
```

Running this query will give us the totaled amounts for each choice:

```
Text                                              choice_description   Expr1002
--------------------------------------------------------------------------------
What's your Favorite OS?                          Linux                2
What's your Favorite OS?                          Mac OS 9             1
What's your Favorite OS?                          Mac OS X             1
What's your Favorite OS?                          Windows 2000         3
What's your Favorite OS?                          Windows XP           12
Which Macromedia MX product do you use the most?  Fireworks MX         1
Which Macromedia MX product do you use the most?  FlashCom MX          2
(etc.)
```

However, we still have an unsightly column name (Expr1002) for the amount column. This is due to being a calculated column without an inherent name, and may differ depending on your RDBMS. Let's give it a little more presentable and more appropriate column name:

```
SELECT text, choice_description, count(responses.choice_id) AS how_many
FROM questions INNER JOIN (choices INNER JOIN responses
ON choices.choice_id =  responses.choice_id)
ON choices.question_id = questions.question_id
GROUP BY text, choice_description
```

Running this query will give us the totaled amounts for each choice, with a more descriptive name for the total.

```
Text                          choice_description   how_many
--------------------------------------------------------
What's your Favorite OS?      Linux                2
What's your Favorite OS?      Mac OS 9             1
What's your Favorite OS?      Mac OS X             1
What's your Favorite OS?      Windows 2000         3
What's your Favorite OS?      Windows XP           12
(etc.)
```

Two small matters are left. We can see that there is no ordering of the counts, and it might be useful to have the largest value first, presenting them in descending order by the number of responses.

The first thing that leaps to mind is to order by our new column how_many, but unfortunately many SQL interpreters are too lame to allow us to order by a calculated field, so we have to use COUNT again:

```
SELECT text, choice_description, count(responses.choice_id) AS how_many
FROM questions INNER JOIN (choices INNER JOIN responses
ON choices.choice_id =  responses.choice_id)
ON choices.question_id = questions.question_id
GROUP BY text, choice_description
ORDER BY count(responses.choice_id) DESC
```

Finally, the only thing left is to add a WHERE clause to limit this recordset to one question at a time. We mentioned earlier that we were going to split up the recordsets one by one. This is because we're going to use the recordsets to directly fuel the charting components, and we only want to show one question at a time.

```
SELECT text, choice_description, count(responses.choice_id) AS how_many
FROM questions INNER JOIN (choices INNER JOIN responses
ON choices.choice_id =  responses.choice_id)
ON choices.question_id = questions.question_id
WHERE questions.question_id  = #questionID#
GROUP BY text, choice_description
ORDER BY count(responses.choice_id) DESC
```

So, including the parameter in the ColdFusion, our finished CFC file should look like this:

```
<cfcomponent>

  <cffunction name="getQuestions" access="remote" returntype="query">
  <cfquery name="pollRecords" datasource="pollDB">
    SELECT question_id FROM questions
  </cfquery>
  <cfreturn pollRecords>
  </cffunction>

  <cffunction name="getAnswers" access="remote" returntype="query">
    <cfargument name="questionID" type="numeric" required="true">
    <cfquery name="rsAnswers" datasource="pollDB">
      SELECT text, choice_description, count(responses.choice_id)
      AS how_many
      FROM questions INNER JOIN (choices INNER JOIN responses
      ON choices.choice_id =  responses.choice_id)
      ON choices.question_id = questions.question_id
      WHERE questions.question_id  = #questionID#
      GROUP BY text, choice_description
      ORDER BY count(responses.choice_id) DESC
    </cfquery>
    <cfreturn rsAnswers>
  </cffunction>

</cfcomponent>
```

Save this file. We're now ready to build the Flash part of the scenario.

To build the Flash Application:

1. Create a new Flash document in the ch09 directory. Save it as **pieChart.fla**.

2. In the Components panel (Window > Components), select the Flash Charting Components from the drop-down menu.

3. Drag an instance of the PieChart component to the stage. Use the Property inspector to give it an instance name of **pieResults**.

4. Select the Flash UI components from the Components panel drop-down menu and drag an instance of a PushButton component to the stage. Use the Property inspector to give it an instance name of **btnNext**, a label of **Next** and a Click Handler of **nextQuestion**, as shown in **Figure 9-6**.

Figure 9.6 Setting the Click Handler, Instance name and Label of a PushButton component.

5. Add a new layer and name it **actions**.

6. On the first frame of the actions layer, add the following ActionScript code:

```
#include "NetServices.as"
#include "NetDebug.as"
```

This includes the external ActionScript files necessary for Flash Remoting and debugging.

Note

The #include "NetDebug.as" line should be commented out once you have finished testing. It adds unnecessary file size to a production Flash movie.

We have two functions in the CFC: getQuestions() and getAnswers(). As soon as we run this program, we will call getQuestions() to retrieve the first recordset. When this happens, the responder function getQuestions_result() will be triggered. This would be a good place to set up any indexing variables we need in the movie.

7. Beneath the code you just added, add the following function:

```
function getQuestions_Result(result) {
    rsQuestions = result;
```

```
   question_index = 0;
   nextQuestion(rsQuestions);
   nextButton.setEnabled(true);
}
```

The first line copies the temporary recordset result into the rsQuestions variable to make it available to other code outside this function. We then set an index to zero, call the nextQuestion() function and enable the Push-Button component on the stage.

8. Next, add the code for the nextQuestion() function. This is called by the getQuestions_result() function and also when the user presses the Next button.

```
function nextQuestion() {
   pollService.getAnswers(rsQuestions.items[question_index].question_id);
   question_index++;
   if (question_index>=rsQuestions.getLength()) {
      nextButton.setEnabled(false);
      nextButton.setLabel("Completed");
   }
}
```

It calls the getAnswers() function in the CFC, passing it the current question_id from the rsQuestions recordset. It also checks to see if we're now at the final question and if so, disables the button and shows a Completed message.

9. Next, we create the getAnswers_Result() function. This will be called when the getAnswers() function has pulled all the information from the database for a particular question. Add the following code after the existing Action-Script. Don't add the line numbers.

```
1. function getAnswers_Result(rsChoices) {
2.    pieResults.setChartTitle(rsChoices.items[0].text);
3.    pieResults.setDataProvider(rsChoices);
4.    pieResults.setLabelSource("choice_description");
5.    pieResults.setValueSource("how_many");
6. }
```

This function uses four methods built into the PieChart component:

Line 2 uses the `setChartTitle` method to set the title for the chart; in this case, we're pulling the `text` field from the `rsChoices` recordset to use as the title. This field contains the question text.

Line 3's `setDataProvider` method attaches a recordset to the component.

The `setLabelSource` method on line 4 sets the labels of each Pie segment. In this case, we will show a different segment for each possible option for the question.

Line 5 uses the `setValueSource` to set the values for each Pie segment to the corresponding value in the `how_many` column created by the SQL statement.

Note More information about the methods of the PieChart component is available from the Reference panel of Flash MX.

10. Finally, we add the code to set up the Flash Remoting connection and initialize the first function call in the CFC. Add the following code after the existing ActionScript.

```
if (inited == null) {
   inited = true;
   pieResults.setSize(500, 200);
   nextButton.setEnabled(false);
   NetServices.setDefaultGatewayURL("http://localhost/
   ➞ flashservices/gateway");
   gatewayConnection = NetServices.createGatewayConnection();
   pollService = gatewayConnection.getService("mxbook.ch09.pieChart",
   ➞ this);
   pollService.getQuestions();
}
```

This final section of code first checks to see if the code has been run. Then it uses the `setSize` method of the PieChart component to alter the Pie chart height and width. Next, it disables and grays out the Next button, so it can't be clicked until an example has loaded.

The `setDefaultGatewayURL` line assigns the address of the virtual Flash services gateway. Again, if your installation is different this will need to change accordingly. The next line actually creates the connection itself.

Next, we link to the `pieChart` CFC using the dot syntax explained in the previous chapter.

Finally, we use `pollService.getQuestions()` to call the first method of the CFC. The callback functions will handle everything from here.

11. Save and test your movie. You should see the information loaded into the PieChart component (**Figure 9.7**)

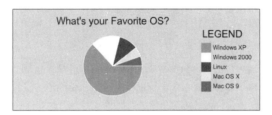

Figure 9.7 If you spend time on the SQL code, the ActionScript needed to generate Dynamic Pie charts is minimal.

When you hover the mouse over each segment, you can see pop-up information about each segment (number of responses, percentage of total). By clicking the Next button, you can navigate through each question and its responses.

The completed file for this exercise is `PieChart_500.fla` and can be found in the `chapter_09` folder.

LineChart Component

Line charts are ideally used for displaying growth over time. Users automatically associate a left-to-right axis with time movement. They're best when you have several data points—at least five or six. If the data you're displaying can be described with words like growth, escalation or trend, it's probably ideal for a Line chart.

In this example, we're going to use the sample database from the poll application to show the amount of responses per month in a calendar year. The example Access database, `poll.mdb`, which can be found in the `chapter_09` folder, contains data that simulates responses as occurring through all the months of 2002.

To show this in action, there are two steps: first, to build the ColdFusion component (CFC) to retrieve the data, and second, to create the Flash application itself.

To create the ColdFusion Component:

Create a new CFC file in the mxbook\ch09 folder with a name of **lineChart.cfc**.

We're going to create a single function that takes an argument of the year and totals all responses for each month of that year. This is another example of something that could be done with ActionScript, but splitting the logic off to the database query allows us to do a couple of things:

■ Removes the burden of processing from the Flash client. Users with slow machines don't have to wait while their Flash client loops and collates all the data.

■ Reduces network traffic if you have a large database. You don't have to transmit large amounts of data from the database into the Flash movie for parsing. All the totaling is done on the server side, and only the results are transmitted to the client.

Retrieving the Totals

The function—let's call it getMonthTotals—should accept a parameter of year and then find all the relevant information. We need to know two things: The month being totaled (January, February, etc.) and the total number of responses for that month.

Let's take the SQL step by step. You might expect to do a COUNT and a GROUP BY, something like:

```
SELECT date_answered, count(*)
FROM responses
GROUP BY date_answered
```

However, running this SQL will soon reveal a problem. When we store a date in an SQL database, it typically stores the date and time down to the second or even millisecond. Performing a GROUP BY won't help much if we're grouping down to the millisecond, rather than the month.

Luckily, most databases include functions by which we can use different parts of our data. Using Access or SQL Server, this is the DATEPART() function, which takes two arguments: the date to manipulate and what you want instead of the full date—i.e., the month, the day of the week, etc.

```
SELECT datepart('m',date_answered), count(*)FROM responses
GROUP BY datepart('m',date_answered)
```

This will return something along the lines of:

```
Expr1000        Expr1001
-------------------------
1               4
2               8
3               10
4               9
5               6
6               3
7               4
8               4
9               22
10              7
11              20
```

This is actually all the data we need, though it could be a bit more presentable with regards to its column names. Using the AS keyword, we can assign our own names to these columns.

Note

In case you're wondering why the date_answered column name doesn't show up, that's because we're performing a function to split out just the month, so showing the month alone is a constructed column.

```
SELECT datepart('m',date_answered) AS month,
count(*) AS how_many
FROM responses
GROUP BY datepart('m',date_answered)
```

Finally, we should add an ORDER BY clause to make sure we're always getting the months in order and add a WHERE clause to restrict the months to a specific year. Again, we'll use the DATEPART() function to name a specific year:

```
SELECT datepart('m',date_answered) AS month,
count(*) AS how_many FROM responses
WHERE datepart('yyyy',date_answered) = #yearParam#
GROUP BY datepart('m',date_answered)
ORDER BY datepart('m',date_answered) ASC
```

So, including the parameter in the ColdFusion, our finished CFC file should look like this:

```
<cfcomponent>
  <cffunction name="getMonthTotals" access="remote" returntype="query">
    <cfargument name="yearParam" type="numeric" required="true">
    <cfquery name="rsMonths" datasource="pollDB">
      SELECT datepart('m',date_answered) AS month,
      count(*) AS how_many FROM responses
      WHERE datepart('yyyy',date_answered) = #yearParam#
      GROUP BY datepart('m',date_answered)
      ORDER BY datepart('m',date_answered) ASC
    </cfquery>
    <cfreturn rsMonths>
  </cffunction>
</cfcomponent>
```

Save this file (as lineChart.cfc). We're now ready to build the Flash part of the scenario.

To build the Flash Application:

1. Create a new Flash movie in the ch09 directory. Save it as **lineChart.fla**.

2. In the Components panel (Window > Components), select the Flash Charting Components from the drop-down menu.

3. Drag an instance of the LineChart component to the stage. Use the Property inspector to give it an instance name of **lineResults**.

4. Add a new layer and name it **actions**.

5. On the first frame of the actions layer, add the ActionScript from Listing 9.1:

Listing 9.1 ActionScript for Line chart example

```
1. #include "NetServices.as"
2. #include "NetDebug.as"
3.
4. function getMonthTotals_Result(rsMonths) {
5.   lineResults.setChartTitle("Response Levels in 2002");
6.   lineResults.setDataProvider(rsMonths);
7.   lineResults.setLabelSource("month");
8.   lineResults.setValueSource("how_many");
```

```
9.  lineResults.setXAxisTitle("Months");
10. lineResults.setYAxisTitle("Responses");
11. }
12.
13. if (inited == null) {
14.    inited = true;
15.    NetServices.setDefaultGatewayURL("http://localhost/
       ➝ flashservices/gateway");
16.    gatewayConnection = NetServices.createGatewayConnection();
17.    pollService =gatewayConnection.getService("mxbook.ch09.lineChart",
       ➝ this);
18.    pollService.getMonthTotals(2002);
19. }
```

This is the complete code needed for this example. Line 4's function declaration for getMonthsTotals_result() simply accepts the returned recordset from the CFC and fills the LineChart component with any needed data.

Almost identically to the PieChart component, the setDataProvider method in line 6 assigns the recordset to the components, then the setLabelSource and setValueSource methods in lines 7 and 8 specify the columns in the recordset to use to fuel the points on the LineChart component.

Line 17 connects to the lineChart.cfc component, and line 18 calls the remote service getMonthTotals.

Note More information about the methods of the LineChart component is available from the Reference panel in Flash MX.

---

6. Save and test your movie. You should see the information loaded into the LineChart component (**Figure 9.8**)

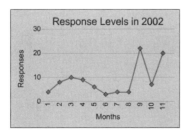

Figure 9.8 Line charts should not be used if you only have a few data points.

BarChart Component

Bar charts should be used to present a few points of data. They are very useful for comparisons. For example, when the numbers being displayed are close in value to each other, it's easier to figure out the tallest bar on a Bar chart than the widest slice of a Pie chart. Unlike a Line chart, Bar charts don't usually indicate motion over time.

In this example, we're going to use the sample database from the poll application to show a Bar chart that displays responses by the day of the week. Although this is date and time related, it isn't, strictly speaking, motion over time. We're going to display a comparison of the totaled number of responses to find the busiest day of the week. We're not displaying data for any particular Monday-to-Sunday period.

To show this in action, there are two steps: first, to build the ColdFusion component (CFC) to retrieve the data, and second, to create the Flash application itself.

To create the ColdFusion Component:

Create a new CFC file in the mxbook\ch09 folder with a name of **barChart.cfc**.

The function—let's call it getDays—doesn't need any parameters.

We need to know two things: The day being totaled and the total number of responses for that day.

Similarly to the Line chart example, we'll use DATEPART() function to manipulate the date so that, this time, we're only working with the day of the week. The SQL looks like this:

```
SELECT COUNT(*) AS how_many, DATEPART('W',date_answered) AS day
FROM responses
GROUP BY DATEPART('W',date_answered)
ORDER BY DATEPART ('W',date_answered)
```

Finally, we're using the GROUP BY clause to make sure we're always getting the days of the week grouped together and an ORDER BY clause to make sure they're always returned in the order we want.

So, including the parameter in the ColdFusion, our finished CFC file should look like this:

```
<cfcomponent>
 <cffunction name="getDays" access="remote" returntype="query">
```

```
<cfquery name="rsDays" datasource="pollDB">
  SELECT COUNT(*) AS how_many,
  DATEPART('W',date_answered) AS day
  FROM responses
  GROUP BY DATEPART('W',date_answered)
  ORDER BY DATEPART ('W',date_answered)
</cfquery>
<cfreturn rsDays>
</cffunction>
</cfcomponent>
```

Save this file as barChart.cfc. We're now ready to build the Flash part of the scenario.

TO BUILD THE FLASH APPLICATION:

1. Create a new Flash movie in the ch09 directory. Save it as **barChart.fla**.

2. In the Components panel (Window > Components), select the Flash Charting Components from the drop-down menu.

3. Drag an instance of the BarChart component to the stage. Use the Property inspector to give it an instance name of **barResults**.

4. Add a new layer and name it **actions**.

5. On the first frame of the actions layer, add the ActionScript from Listing 9.2:

Listing 9.2 ActionScript for Bar chart example

```
1. #include "NetServices.as"
2. #include "NetDebug.as"
3.
4. function getDays_Result(rsChoices) {
5.    barResults.setChartTitle("Responses by Day of Week");
6.    barResults.setDataProvider(rsChoices);
7.    barResults.setLabelSource("day");
8.    barResults.setValueSource("how_many");
9.    barResults.setXAxisTitle("");
10.    barResults.setYAxisTitle("Responses");
11. }
12.
13. if (inited == null) {
14.    inited = true;
```

Listing 9.2 ActionScript for Bar chart example *(continued)*

```
15.   NetServices.setDefaultGatewayURL("http://localhost/
      → flashservices/gateway");
16.   gatewayConnection = NetServices.createGatewayConnection();
17.   pollService = gatewayConnection.getService("mxbook.ch09.barChart",
      → this);
18.   pollService.getDays();
19. }
```

This is the complete code needed for this example. The function declaration for getDays_result() in line 4 simply accepts the returned recordset from the CFC and fills the BarChart component with any needed data.

Almost identically to the PieChart component, the setDataProvider method in line 6 assigns the recordset to the components, then the setLabelSource and setValueSource methods in lines 7 and 8 specify the columns in the recordset to use to fuel the points on the BarChart component. The setXAxisTitle method in line 9 is blank, as the title of the chart set in line 5 says it all.

More information about the methods of the BarChart component is available from the Reference panel of Flash MX.

6. Save and test your movie. You should see the information loaded into the BarChart component (**Figure 9.9**)

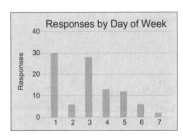

Figure 9.9 Bar charts are useful for displaying comparisons that don't necessarily need to display growth over time.

EXTRA CREDIT

Unfortunately in our example, we end up looking at a number, rather than the name of the day. And, in fact, this might be misleading, as some might imagine 1 represents Monday, when in fact it represents Sunday.

What would be better is to have the names of the days, rather than numbers. Unfortunately, DATEPART doesn't do that. But luckily, we can use another SQL function, FORMAT(), which will. Change the SQL in the lineChart.cfc ColdFusion component to the following (the changes are highlighted):

```
SELECT COUNT(*) AS how_many,
DATEPART('W',date_answered),
FORMAT(date_answered, 'ddd') AS day
FROM responses
GROUP BY DATEPART('W',date_answered),
FORMAT(date_answered, 'ddd')
ORDER BY DATEPART ('W',date_answered)
```

We're using 'ddd' in the FORMAT() function, which returns the abbreviated name of the day (Mon, Tue, etc.). We're now creating the constructed day column from the FORMAT() function rather than the DATEPART() function. You might wonder why we still need the DATEPART() function. The reason is that we need to be able to use the ORDER BY clause to ensure our days are ordered correctly, and if we order on the *names* of the days, it will sort alphabetically. Our days would appear sorted nonsensically: Fri, Mon, Sat, Sun, Thu, Tue, Wed. This is not the most useful way. So we keep the numbered days of the week in order to sort them meaningfully.

The wonderful touch is that because we've changed the SQL, we don't need to touch the Flash movie at all! It will draw the x-axis labels from whatever is in the day column, which now contains the name of the day.

Save and test your movie. You should see the information correctly loaded into the BarChart component (**Figure 9.10**)

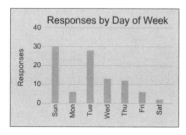

Figure 9.10 Using more advanced SQL to retrieve more information can pay huge dividends in the usability of your diagrams.

LINKING TO COMPONENTS WITH DATAGLUE

Although creating graphs and charts is obviously an important part of representing dynamic data, there's perhaps an ever more down-to-earth, but essential, side to the story. You can use dynamic data to fuel Flash UI (user interface) components, such as ListBoxes and ComboBoxes.

The `DataGlue.as` file, which is part of the Flash Remoting installation (like `NetServices.as` and `NetDebug.as`), provides a simple method of assigning your recordset data to UI components. It contains two methods: `bindFormatStrings` and `bindFormatFunction`.

bindFormatStrings()

There are four parameters to the `bindFormatStrings()` method:

- The instance name of the UI component object

- The recordset name

- The recordset field, which is used to define the UI component labels

- The recordset field, which is used to define the UI component values

In the last two parameters listed, the recordset field names are placed between pound signs (#) to evaluate them correctly. An example of using this method follows.

TO IMPLEMENT A BINDFORMATSTRINGS() METHOD:

1. Create a simple CFC and save it in the ch09 folder as **dataglue.cfc**. Add the following code to create two simple functions:

```
<cfcomponent>

<cffunction name="getQuestions" access="remote" returntype="query">
  <cfquery name="pollRecords" datasource="pollDB">
  SELECT * FROM questions
  </cfquery>
  <cfreturn pollRecords>
</cffunction>
```

```
<cffunction name="getChoices" access="remote" returntype="query">
  <cfargument name="questionID" type="numeric" required="true">
  <cfquery name="choiceRecords" datasource="pollDB">
  SELECT * FROM choices WHERE question_id = #questionID#
  </cfquery>
  <cfreturn choiceRecords>
</cffunction>

</cfcomponent>
```

2. Create a new Flash movie and save it as **dataGlue.fla**. From the Flash UI Components in the Components panel, drag a ComboBox and a ListBox onto the stage. Using the Property inspector, give the ComboBox an instance name of **cboQuestions**, and give the ListBox an instance name of **listChoices**.

3. Add a new **actions** layer. On the first frame of the actions layer, add the code from Listing 9.3. Make sure you include the #include statement for the DataGlue.as file.

Listing 9.3 ActionScript for bindFormatStrings() **example**

```
1. #include "NetServices.as"
2. #include "DataGlue.as"
3.
4. function getQuestions_Result(rsQuestions) {
5.   cboQuestions.setSize(230);
6.   DataGlue.BindFormatStrings(cboQuestions, rsQuestions, "#text#",
   → "#question_id#");
7. }
8.
9.
10. if (inited == null) {
11. inited = true;
12. NetServices.setDefaultGatewayURL("http://localhost/flashservices/
    → gateway");
13. gatewayConnection = NetServices.createGatewayConnection();
14. pollService = gatewayConnection.getService("mxbook.ch09.dataGlue",
    → this);
15. pollService.getQuestions();
16. }
```

Lines 4 through 7 detail one callback function for the `getQuestions()` function of the CFC, and it only has two lines. Line 5 resizes the ComboBox a little wider and line 6 uses the `DataGlue.BindFormatStrings` method to tie the recordset details to the ComboBox.

Save and test this movie. The ComboBox should be populated with the data from the CFC function.

bindFormatFunction()

The other method in `DataGlue` is the `bindFormatFunction()` method, which takes three parameters. The first two are the same as in the `bindFormatString()` method: UI instance name and recordset name.

The third parameter is a reference to a function, which needs to return an object with two properties: `label` and `data`. This function is automatically called once for each record in the recordset.

To show an example, we'll use the `bindFormatFunction()` method to populate the ListBox whenever an item is clicked in the ComboBox.

TO IMPLEMENT A BINDFORMATFUNCTION() METHOD:

1. In the `dataGlue.fla` file created in the previous section, select the ComboBox and use the Property inspector to give it a Click Handler of **cboClick**. This function will be called whenever the ComboBox is clicked on.

2. Add the following function to the ActionScript on frame 1, after the existing `getQuestions_Result()` function but before the `if(inited == null)` line:

```
function cboClick(obj) {
    pollService.getChoices(obj.getValue());
}
```

This will call the `getChoices()` CFC function, passing the value of the currently selected item in the ComboBox.

3. Next, add the callback function for `getChoices()`:

```
function getChoices_Result(rsChoices) {
    DataGlue.BindFormatFunction(listChoices, rsChoices, fnFormat);
}
```

So, instead of using `bindFormatStrings()`, we use `bindFormatFunction()` and give it a function name of **fnFormat**. This function is automatically called once for each record in the recordset and is passed the record as a parameter.

Add the following code after the `getChoicesResult()` function:

```
function fnFormat(rec) {
    obj = new Object();
    obj.label = rec.choice_description;
    obj.data = rec.choice_id;
    return obj;
}
```

This function must return an object with `label` and `data` properties. The example code shown does essentially the same thing as a `bindFormatStrings` method, but it should be apparent that if you needed complex formatting options for each record in the recordset, you could add the relevant ActionScript to your formatting function.

 The finished file `dataGlue.fla` can be found in the `chapter_09` directory of the CD-ROM.

SUMMARY

- Flash offers many advantages over HTML when designing Rich Internet Applications. Aside from not having to follow a locked-in page model like HTML sites, Flash presents many options for representing data visually.

- SQL is a much underused aspect of many Web sites, but when used properly, can negate the need for a lot of complex programming.

- When planning Flash pages that represent data visually, several concerns should be raised. These include knowing the type of data to be shown, how many data points are needed, and the variance between high and low points.

- The Flash Charting Components are a free extension by Macromedia and are available on the Macromedia exchange.

- The Pie chart component is a good way to show small groupings of data at a single point in time, but should not be used when exact comparisons are necessary.

- The Line chart component is an excellent way of showing numeric growth over time, such as increased sales in a given year.

- Bar charts are excellent for comparison when given a small amount of options to deal with, and in respect to their appropriate use, lie somewhere between Pie and Line charts.

- When using the Flash Charting Components, the `setDataProvider` method assigns a recordset to fuel the component, and the `setLabelSource` and `setValueSource` specify the data to be used for the chart.

- The `DataGlue.as` file is installed as part of the Flash Remoting install, and makes it easy to assign dynamic data to UI components, with the `bindFormatStrings` and `bindFormatFunction` methods.

- When your movies are complete and tested, you should remove the included `NetDebug.as` file, as it is not needed for production movies. It adds unnecessary file size and functionality to the movie.

III
Communicating Between Clients

In This Chapter:

10 Publishing, Playing, and Recording Streams

One of the most popular features of Macromedia Flash Communication Server MX is its ability to send and receive live audio and video content from one connected user to another. As you learned in Chapter 6, FlashCom can also record and archive live streams, as well as play pre-recorded streams "on demand" to a connected user. In this chapter, you will learn how to build Flash movies that broadcast (or publish) a stream to a FlashCom server and enable other users to receive (or subscribe to) that stream.

Note   The examples in this chapter require an installed version of Macromedia Flash Communication Server MX on your computer or another computer accessible to you over your network or the Internet.

Developing a Plan

When you want to build a Rich Internet Application that requires Flash Communication Server capabilities, you should devise a production plan that affords you the time to solve the problems of the project and addresses the needs of potential users of the application. While it is beyond the scope of this book to provide detailed information about multimedia project planning, you will learn how to prepare an architecture for a FlashCom-enabled application in this chapter.

Limitations of Streaming Content with Flash Communication Server

Unlike other multimedia streaming servers such as Apple QuickTime Streaming Server, Flash Communication Server does not perform any recompression on a stream that is sent to a connected user. For example, in a two-way conference call, if one connected user uploads a high bitrate stream (such as 120 Kbps) and the other user only has a 56 Kbps connection, FlashCom cannot recompress or change the quality of the outgoing stream to the 56 Kbps user. The server can change the frame rate of the stream, but the sampling rate of the audio stream and the quality and keyframe interval of the video stream cannot be altered. As such, the onus is upon you, as the developer, to make sure that you tailor the data transfer rates of streams according to the intended audience of your application. If a connected user attempts to subscribe to a stream with an overly demanding bitrate, the audio and video will "cut out" at regular intervals, leaving disturbing gaps in conversations and content.

Another limitation, albeit a minor one, of Flash Communication Server is that live audio streams from a Flash movie can only be delivered in mono, or single channel, audio. If you want to send stereo audio (such as music tracks) to a connected user, you will need to convert the digital audio file into a stereo FLV file using a third-party application like Sorenson Squeeze or Wildform Flix.

Future releases of FlashCom will likely address some if not all these issues. If you would like to send your suggestions for improving FlashCom to Macromedia, use the form at www.macromedia.com/support/email/wishform/.

Note For more information on project planning, see the sidebar "More Resources on Project Planning" at the end of this section.

Before you begin to build the Flash MX documents in this chapter, let's review an important tenet of the Flash Communication Server. In Chapter 6, you learned that FlashCom provides a means of connecting one or more users to an application that resides on the server. In order to send live audio and video streams to another user, one user (or application) must publish content on the FlashCom server. The Flash movie (SWF file) must connect to a Flash Communication Server to send and receive multimedia streams (**Figure 10.1**).

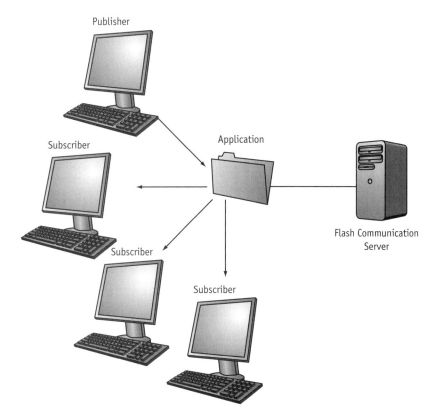

Figure 10.1 When one user publishes a stream to a FlashCom application, other connected users can play or subscribe to the stream.

Other videoconferencing applications that use the Internet (such as Microsoft Windows Messenger on Windows XP), however, utilize peer-to-peer connections, which means that the video and audio streams between two users are directly exchanged without the necessity of a go-between server (**Figure 10.2**). Flash Player 6 does not allow this type of peer-to-peer connectivity.

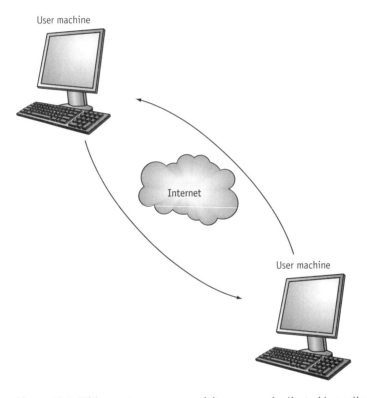

Figure 10.2 With peer-to-peer connectivity, one user's client-side application directly connects to another user's client-side application.

While it may seem ideal to allow connections directly between two users, potential bandwidth limitations can quickly impede the effectiveness of peer-to-peer connections. For example, if you wanted to have a four-way conference call, each connected user would be required to send three streams, while receiving three other streams (**Figure 10.3**).

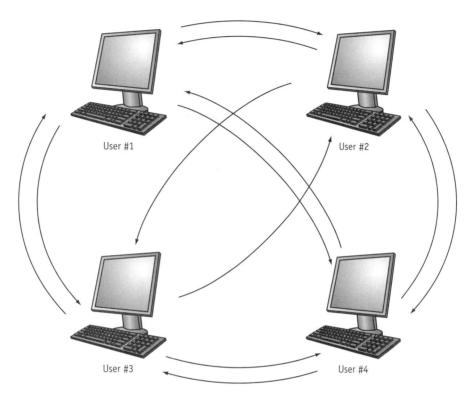

Figure 10.3 Peer-to-peer connectivity can place inordinate demands upon a user's bandwidth if several users are involved.

However, using Flash Communication Server and Flash Player 6, the same four-way conference call would require much less bandwidth from each partici-pant. Each connected user would send only one stream to the server, and the server, in turn, would broadcast each user's stream to the other participants (**Figure 10.4**). This scenario places the burden of bandwidth consumption upon the server, not the connected client.

Now that you understand how a FlashCom server handles streaming content and connections among several connected users, you're ready to set up a new application on your FlashCom server.

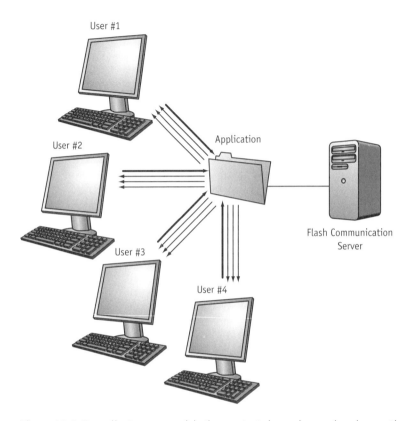

Figure 10.4 In a client-server model, the greatest demands are placed upon the server, not the connected user.

Setting up the Application on the Server

In order for a Flash Communication Server to connect one or more client SWF files together, the server must have an application name defined in the applications directory. You can name your applications whatever you want, as long as the name conforms to the naming conventions of your operating system, just as any other file or directory name does. The application name is referenced in the URI (**U**niform **R**esource Indicator) within the NetConnection.connect() client-side ActionScript code of the Flash movie (SWF file).

Perform the following steps with your installed version of Macromedia Flash Communication Server MX.

To create the application on the server:

1. Locate the `applications` directory on your FlashCom server. In a default Developer Install, the path to this directory is `C:\Inetpub\wwwroot\flashcom\applications\`

You will see other sample application folders installed by the FlashCom setup in the `applications` directory. If you don't know where your `applications` directory is located, you can search for the `Vhost.xml` configuration file. In this file, the path to the `applications` directory is specified in the `<AppsDir>` node.

2. In the `applications` directory, create a new directory (or folder) named **broadcast** (**Figure 10.5**).

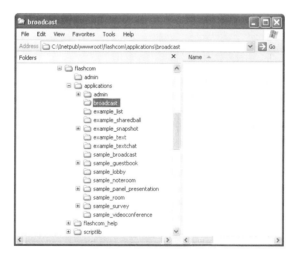

Figure 10.5 The applications directory of your FlashCom server holds individual named applications, such as separate folders.

That's all there is to it! This basic FlashCom application will not require any server-side ActionScript code (that is, ASC files). You can specify `broadcast` in the URI of a `NetConnection.connect()` method, such as:

```
app_nc = new NetConnection();
app_nc.connect("rtmp:/broadcast");
```

Don't insert this code into any Flash MX document just yet. In the next section, you will learn how each Flash movie communicates with the `broadcast` application.

Planning the Client Architecture

In order to publish and receive streams by way of a Flash Communication Server, you begin with two separate Flash documents (FLA files): one that publishes the stream to the server, and another that receives the stream from the server. In this scenario, the broadcaster's camera and microphone output is attached to a NetStream object on the FlashCom server, and the other users watch (or subscribe to) the stream name published to the FlashCom server (**Figure 10.6**).

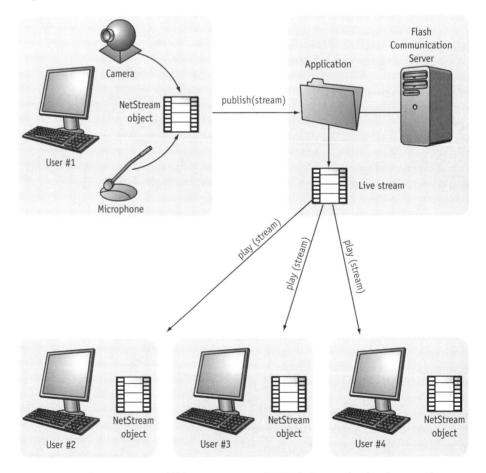

Figure 10.6 When one user publishes a stream to the Flash Communication Server, other users can access that stream from the same application on the server.

Later in the chapter, you will combine both the publish and subscribe capabilities into one Flash document. If a stream has already been initiated, the Flash movie shows the publishing stream. Otherwise, the user is free to broadcast his/her image and voice files to other connected users. Later in the book, you will also learn how the AVPresence automatically provides this type of functionality along with other playback controls.

While the examples in this chapter have already been developed for you, you should consider the following points when you are planning the interface and functionality of your Flash movie front end:

- **Application access:** Who will be able to access the application? Will you allow any public user to use the Flash movie and stream functionality?

- **Number of streams:** How many streams can your server support? Does your FlashCom Server license allow this number of connections?

- **Stream permission:** Can every user publish and receive a stream? Or will you allow only a certain group of administrators to publish streams?

- **Status indicators:** Does the interface indicate the current activity of the stream? Will the user know if he is successfully publishing or receiving a stream? Do button graphics and/or text change to indicate their current functionality?

- **Usability:** Will your target audience know how to use the Flash movie? Do you provide instructions for users new to Flash Player 6's camera and microphone features?

- **Device support:** As Flash Player 6 becomes available for more devices (such as Pocket PCs, digital phones, and so on), can your Flash movie's interface and functionality be easily reconfigured to accommodate non-desktop Flash Players?

Determining Your Audience

Whenever you use the streaming capabilities of Flash Communication Server, you must carefully determine the bandwidth requirements for the application, from both the server's point of view and that of each connected user. Streaming audio and video content isn't for the faint of heart, or those with severely limited connection speeds. For example, to simultaneously connect audio-only streams (at 5 kHz) from four users would require 160 Kbps of bandwidth from your server, and demand 40 Kbps of bandwidth from each user (**Figure 10.7**).

Note   10 Kbps per user is an average speed. If continuous sound is transmitted over a stream, the stream's bitrate could be as high as 11.2 Kbps for a 5 kHz audio stream. See Appendix A for more information on common bitrates associated with FlashCom streams.

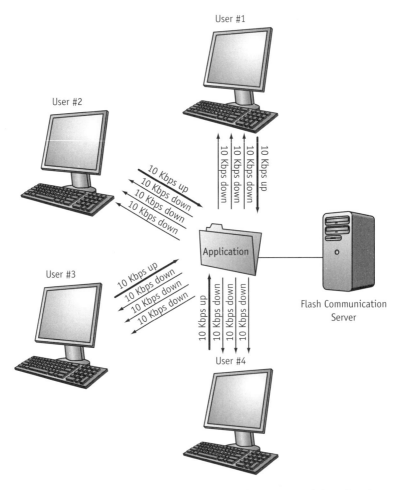

Figure 10.7 If an application seeks to connect four users, each broadcasting a 5 kHz audio-only stream, then each user's bandwidth consumption is approximately 40 Kbps.

As with any Web site or application, knowing who is using the information or functionality that you are creating is paramount to the success of your work. The following questions should be answered well before you begin any development with Flash MX documents or server-side ActionScript:

- **User bitrate:** What connection speeds will be required from a user? What do you anticipate as the average (or median) speed, as well as the slowest and highest speeds? Once you have determined the target bitrate for the average user, you can determine the maximum quality for audio and video content for that bitrate.

- **Server bitrate:** How many users will be able to connect to the application simultaneously? Can your server's connection (and processing power) handle the anticipated demand? Will you need to limit the number of users that can access each application? These questions will also help you decide how access to the application is controlled—will you need to consider authentication for each user? Because most hosting providers or Internet connections have transfer rate limits, you may need to make sure that you have the financial ability to sustain large groups of users (and their streaming content).

- **User input devices:** Will your application completely rely on camera and microphone feedback from a connected user? Will you offer an alternative method for communication for bandwidth- or device-impaired users, such as a text chat?

- **Playback support:** What types of Flash Players will your application support? Will the interface be designed for a large browser window or a stand-alone player? When future support for Pocket PCs and other devices is available for Flash Player 6, how easily can you accommodate the limited screen size, bandwidth, and functionality of these devices?

For the examples in this chapter, you will create applications that are targeted at an average bitrate of 128-144 Kbps. Dialup users with 56 Kbps connection speeds can use the applications, but the quality will suffer as a result. The intended delivery platform is a desktop Web browser with Flash Player 6 installed. Any user who wants to publish a live stream should have a Webcam and a microphone accessible by the Flash Player. Subscribers do not need a Webcam or microphone. The maximum number of simultaneous users for this application will be 10. The average bitrate of a single stream for the application is estimated to be 144 Kbps, using the calculation below. These calculations use the default values for the Camera and Microphone objects.

```
Audio:              8 kHz = 16 Kbps
Video:              16,384 bytes/sec = 16 KB/sec = 128 Kbps
Total bandwidth: 128 Kbps + 16 Kbps = 144 Kbps
```

Note

The Microphone object uses a default sampling rate of 8 kHz, which is 16 Kbps with the Speech codec, used by Flash Player 6 to stream live audio. The Camera object uses a default bandwidth limit of 16,384 bytes per second with the Sorenson Spark Basic codec built into Flash Player 6. For more information on bandwidth rates, see Appendix A.

As discussed in the next section, the Flash movie will also search for a valid camera. Flash Player 6 recognizes optical cameras in addition to screen capture drivers such as TechSmith's Camtasia. This screen capture driver can send live video output of your desktop to other applications, including Flash Player 6. The application you develop in this chapter requires a physical camera device and checks if the user's camera is a screen capture driver.

MORE RESOURCES ON PROJECT PLANNING

The details of properly planning any multimedia projects should not be overlooked. You can learn more about project planning from these books:

Interactive Design for New Media and the Web, by Nicholas V. Iuppa, Focal Press.

Collaborative Web Development: Strategies and Best Practices for Web Teams, by Jessica Burdman, Addison-Wesley.

Software Project Survival Guide, by Steve McConnell, Microsoft Press.

PUBLISHING A LIVE STREAM

The first Flash document that you create for the application allows the user to publish a live stream to the FlashCom server. In order to send audio and video content to a Flash Communication Server, you need to know how to access the Camera and Microphone objects, their properties, and methods in client-side ActionScript code.

Detecting a User's Camera and Microphone

In order for a user to send a live audio and video stream to a FlashCom server, he/she must have a compatible microphone and Webcam, respectively, connected to the computer. Luckily, Flash MX ActionScript gives you direct access to properties of a user's camera and microphone. In this section, you will create a Flash document (FLA file) that determines if the user has a valid camera and microphone. As we discussed briefly in the last section, this Flash document also checks the camera device to see if it is a capture driver—this specific application is designed for optical cameras. Here's a quick overview of what the client-side ActionScript in this Flash document will do.

1. The movie will make a list of all the camera devices connected to the user's computer.

2. Then, it will create a list of all the microphone devices connected to the user's computer.

3. If the user has only one camera attached to the computer, the movie should check the camera's name for the word camtasia. If that word is found in the name, the camera device is actually a software driver for screen captures and is not acceptable for use in this particular application. If the user has at least one camera attached (which doesn't contain the word camtasia in its name), then a valid camera has been found.

Note   Camtasia is currently the only screen capture driver compatible with Flash Player 6. The code within this movie may need to be altered if additional drivers from other manufacturers become available.

4. Otherwise, if no camera names exist, the movie should know that a camera device is not available.

5. If there is one or more microphone names, the movie should know that there is a valid microphone device. Otherwise, the user does not have a valid microphone.

6. If the user has a valid camera and microphone, he can publish audio and video streams to the Flash Communication Server. The movie should direct these users to a frame label in the movie named start.

7. If the user does not have a valid camera or microphone, the movie should direct the user to a frame label named no_input.

Before you begin, make sure you have installed the latest version of Flash Player 6 in your preferred Web browser. You should also update your Flash Player files for the authoring environment of Flash MX. For more information on this procedure, read the release notes at the following URL:

www.macromedia.com/support/flash/ts/documents/flashplayer_r40.htm

You must also install the Flash UI Components Set 2 for the following exercise. You can download this free extension from the Macromedia Exchange for Flash Web site at www.macromedia.com/exchange/flash.

Perform the following steps in Macromedia Flash MX on your preferred development platform.

TO DETECT A VALID CAMERA AND MICROPHONE:

1. Create a new document (Ctrl+N or Command+N).

2. Rename Layer 1 to **labels**. On the labels layer, select frame 1 and assign a frame label of **check** in the Property inspector.

3. Select frame 30 on the labels layer, and press the F5 key to insert a blank frame. Create keyframes on frames 10 and 20, and label them **no_input** and **start**, respectively, in the Property inspector (**Figure 10.8**).

Figure 10.8 The Timeline window should show three separate frame labels.

4. Make a new layer named **actions**, and place this layer beneath the labels layer. Select frame 1 of this layer, and open the Actions panel (F9). In the Script pane of the panel, type the following actions in Expert mode (**Listing 10.1**). The comment lines starting with // are optional and explain each line of code.

Tip

To use Expert mode, click the options menu at the top-right corner of the Actions panel and choose Expert Mode.

Listing 10.1 The checkInput() **function**

```
function checkInput() {
   //set installedCams to list of user's camera devices
   installedCams = Camera.names;

   //set installedCams to list of user's microphone devices
   installedMics = Microphone.names;

   //if user has only one camera device
   if (installedCams.length == 1) {
      // if it's a screen capture driver
      if (installedCams[0].toLowerCase().indexOf("camtasia") != -1){
         //set validCam_optical to false
         validCam_optical = false;
      } else {
         //otherwise set validCam_optical to true
         validCam_optical = true;
      }
   // if user has no cameras available
   } else if (installedCams.length == 0){
      // set validCam_optical to false
      validCam_optical = false;
   } else {
   // otherwise, user has valid camera device
      validCam_optical = true;
   }
   trace("validCam_optical = " + validCam_optical);

   validMic = (installedMics.length >= 1) ? true: false;
   trace("validMic = " + validMic);
}

// Run the checkInput() function to look
// for camera and microphone devices
checkInput();

// if the user has a camera and a mic
if(validCam_optical && validMic){
   // jump to the start label
   _root.gotoAndStop("start");
} else {
   // otherwise go to the no_input label
   _root.gotoAndStop("no_input");
}
```

5. Select frame 1 of the actions layer. In the Property inspector, type **//check-Input** in the Frame Label field. This comment identifies the function that is on this frame.

Note

Frame comments are not necessary for the proper functionality of a Flash movie. A frame comment is simply a note that you can insert on a frame as a reminder to yourself and others on your development team.

6. Create a new layer, and name it **alert_mc**. Place this layer beneath the other two layers. Make a new keyframe (F6) on frame 10. On this keyframe, place an instance of the MessageBox component. (To find this component in the Component panel, choose Flash UI Components Set 2 in the panel's top menu. If you haven't installed this component set, see the note earlier in this chapter.) The MessageBox component is essentially a dialog box that you can script with dynamic text and buttons, which can be presented to the user at any point in the movie.

7. Select the new instance on the stage, and name this instance alert_mc in the Property inspector. For the Title parameter, type **Devices Not Present**. For the Message parameter, type **This application requires a camera and a microphone. No compatible devices were found on your computer. Click OK to watch an existing stream.** (You can change or replace this text later.) For the Icon parameter, choose **warning**. For the Close Handler, type **watchStream**. (You define the watchStream() function in the next step.) Leave all other settings with the default values. When you are finished, your Message-Box instance on the stage should resemble **Figure 10.9**.

Figure 10.9
After you have entered the parameter values into the Property inspector, the live preview of the MessageBox instance should resemble this figure.

8. Create a new keyframe on frame 10 of the actions layer. Select this frame and open the Actions panel (F9). Here, you define the watchStream() function called by the alert_mc MessageBox component. This function loads the

playStream.swf file that you create in a later section of this chapter. Type the following code in the Script pane of the Actions panel:

```
function watchStream(){

   loadMovieNum("playStream.swf", 0);
}
```

9. Assign a comment of **//watchStream** to frame 10 of the actions layer, to identify the function on this frame. (Refer back to step 5 for more information about inserting frame comments.)

10. Make a new layer named **heading**, and place this layer at the bottom of the layer stack. Add a new keyframe on frame 20 of this layer. On this keyframe, use the Text tool to add a heading to the upper left area of the stage. Type **Send Audio and Video to Server** as the heading.

11. Save your document as `checkInput_100.fla` and test it using Control > Test Movie (Ctrl+Enter or Command+Enter). If your computer has a valid camera and microphone, the Flash movie jumps to the start label. Otherwise, the movie goes to the no_input label.

Note
If you have not changed the <Allow> tags within the Vhost.xml configuration document of your FlashCom server, you should be able to save and test your Flash documents and movies anywhere on your local machine. For an accurate testing environment, though, you may want to save and test your Flash movies in a folder that is accessible by a Web server installed on your machine.

You can find the completed file, `checkInput_100.fla`, in the `chapter_10` folder of this book's CD-ROM.

In the next section, you will create the objects and code necessary to display the user's camera locally.

Viewing Local Camera Output

Using client-side ActionScript and an empty **embedded video** object, you can create a Flash movie that displays the live output of a user's camera. No Flash Communication Server connection is necessary to view your own camera. Of course, no one but the user will be able to see the output because it's not being transmitted to other users via FlashCom. In this section, you will learn how to add an embedded video object to a Flash movie, and use it to display the live image from a camera.

 For this section, continue to use the Flash document (FLA file) that you created in the last section. You can also use the `checkInput_100.fla` found in the `chapter_10` folder of this book's CD-ROM to start this section.

To view local camera output:

1. In the Flash document (FLA file) you created in the last section, create a new layer named **videoWin**. Place this layer at the bottom of the layer stack.

2. On frame 20 of the videoWin layer, create a new keyframe.

3. Open the Library panel (F11). Click the options menu in the top right corner of the panel, and choose New Video. A new embedded video symbol appears in the Library panel.

4. With frame 20 of the videoWin layer selected, drag the new embedded video symbol from the Library panel to the left-hand side of the stage, under the heading. In the Property inspector, name this symbol videoWin. By default, a Video object is sized at 160×120 pixels. If you prefer, you can adjust the width and height of the object in the Property inspector to accommodate your needs.

5. Now, you're ready to add the client-side ActionScript code to frame 20 of the actions layer. This code retrieves the output from the user's camera, and attaches it to the videoWin object. The last line of code also gets the output from the user's microphone, but this object won't be used until later in this chapter. Select frame 20 of the actions layer, and open the Actions panel (F9). In Expert mode, type the following code into the Script pane:

```
userCam = Camera.get();
videoWin.attachVideo(userCam);
userMic = Microphone.get();
```

6. Assign a frame comment of **//attach camera** to frame 20 of the actions layer.

7. Save your document as **localCamera_100.fla**, and test it by choosing Control > Test (Ctrl+Enter or Command+Enter). If a camera and microphone are detected on your system, the Flash movie jumps to the start frame. As soon as the Camera.get() method is invoked, the Flash Player asks you for permission to access your camera and microphone. After you choose Allow in the Security Settings dialog box, you will see the live image from your camera displayed in the videoWin object.

Again, the output that you see in the videoWin object (even if the SWF file is uploaded to your Web server) is only viewable by the individual user loading the SWF file. If several people view the same SWF file, each user will only see himself or herself. In order to send the video from one SWF file to other SWF files, a stream must be initiated with a Flash Communication Server. In the next section, you will learn how make such a connection.

Making a Connection to the Application

Once you have access to a user's camera and microphone, you can initiate a connection to the named application on your Flash Communication Server. Earlier in this chapter, you created a new application folder named broadcast. This name is used in the URI (**U**niform **R**esource **I**dentifier) for the connect() method of a NetConnection object in ActionScript code. There are four steps to creating and implementing a complete NetConnection object. Use the following guidelines to help you create connections for FlashCom applications.

1. A NetConnection object is created with the new NetConnection() constructor. Each object should have a unique name.

2. A NetConnection object should always have an onStatus() handler. This handler is called whenever an event occurs involving the connection. For example, onStatus() is invoked whenever a connection succeeds or fails.

3. A NetConnection object should connect to a specific rtmp URI. This URI is an absolute or relative path to the named application on your Flash Communication Server.

4. A NetConnection object can be passed to other FlashCom-enabled objects, such as NetStream and SharedObject instances.

In the next procedure, you will continue to build upon the Flash document (FLA file) you created in the previous section. In this section, you add to the functionality defined in guidelines 1 through 3, creating a new NetConnection object that will be used for later builds of the Flash document.

TO ESTABLISH A CONNECTION TO THE APPLICATION:

1. Open the Flash document you created from the previous section, or open the localCamera_100.fla file located in the chapter_10 folder of this book's CD-ROM.

2. Select frame 20 of the actions layer, and open the Actions panel (F9). Beneath the existing lines of code, add the following line of code:

```
app_nc = new NetConnection();
```

This code creates a NetConnection object named app_nc. For most FlashCom-enabled applications, you don't need more than one NetConnection object per Flash movie in client-side ActionScript code.

3. Now add the following lines of ActionScript code underneath the code you inserted in step 2:

```
app_nc.onStatus = function(info){
   if(info.code == "NetConnection.Connect.Success"){
      trace("---Connected to FlashCom server.");
   } else if (info.code == "NetConnection.Connect.Failed" || info.code
   → == "NetConnection.Connect.Closed"){
      trace("---No connection to FlashCom server.");
   }
};
```

This code creates an onStatus() handler for the app_nc object. When an event occurs with the connection, this handler is invoked. Flash Player 6 passes an information object to the onStatus() handler, indicating the nature of the event. In this code, you check the code property of the information object (represented by info). There are several code values for NetConnection information objects. For this example, you check for either a successful connection or a failed/closed connection. In the next section, you will add more code within the if statement to set up an actual stream to the server.

Tip

To see a list of the NetConnection information objects, see page 109 of the Client-Side Communication ActionScript Dictionary PDF (included with a purchased copy of Flash Communication Server MX), or search for "NetConnection information objects" in the HTML help from Flash MX (Help > Welcome to FlashCom, and choose General, then Client-Side Communication ActionScript Dictionary).

4. Connect to the broadcast application on your FlashCom server. Depending on where your FlashCom server resides, you will need to choose an appropriate URI to the application. If you have installed FlashCom on the same machine you are developing and testing your Flash movies (SWF files) on, then type the following code after the last line of code you inserted from step 3:

```
app_nc.connect("rtmp:/broadcast");
```

If you installed FlashCom on a separate server, indicate the domain name of that server, such as:

```
app_nc.connect("rtmp://myflashcomserver.com/broadcast");
```

Note that you do not need to specify any parent folder names of the application directory in an rtmp URI.

5. Save your Flash document as **netConnection_100.fla**, and test the movie (Control > Test Movie). If you have properly created the broadcast folder on your FlashCom server and specified the correct URI, the trace() action from the onStatus() handler should display in the Output window:

```
---Connected to FlashCom server.
```

You can find the completed netConnection_100.fla file in the chapter_10 folder of this book's CD-ROM.

Now that you have a NetConnection object that establishes a link between the Flash movie (SWF file) and the broadcast application on your FlashCom server, you're ready to publish audio and video content to the server.

Creating a Stream on the Server

After you have determined that the user has a valid camera and microphone and has made a successful connection to the broadcast application, the Flash movie is ready to publish the audio and video from the user's devices to the

FlashCom server. The server can then send the stream to other connected users who subscribe to the same stream name. Here's an overview of the processes you will add to the Flash document in this section:

1. Enable a PushButton component instance to start or stop a published stream to the FlashCom server.

2. Create a NetStream object to carry the audio and video output from a user to the FlashCom server.

While these goals sound simple enough, you begin to learn how client-side ActionScript objects handle events. One of the most common errors that developers make with FlashCom applications is failing to wait for connections with the FlashCom server. In a standard application, you should always wait for a successful connection to the FlashCom server before you try to initiate NetStream or remote SharedObject objects. onStatus() handlers act as an invaluable ally in the management of events initiated with (or by) FlashCom-related objects.

In this section, you will learn how to process events with onStatus() handlers for NetConnection and NetStream objects.

Tip

If you didn't complete the steps in the last section, you can use the netConnection_100.fla file located in the chapter_10 folder of this book's CD-ROM.

To process events with an onStatus() handler:

1. Open the Flash document (FLA file) that you created from the last section, or use the one located on the book's CD-ROM.

2. Create a new layer, and name it **sendButton**. Select frame 20 of this layer, and make a new keyframe (F6).

3. With frame 20 of the sendButton layer selected, drag an instance of the PushButton component from the Component panel to the stage. Place the instance just below the videoWin object. In the Property inspector, name the component instance **sendButton**. In the Label parameter, type **Publish Stream**. In the Click Handler parameter, type **initStream** as shown in **Figure 10.10**. initStream refers to a function named initStream(), which you will create in a later step.

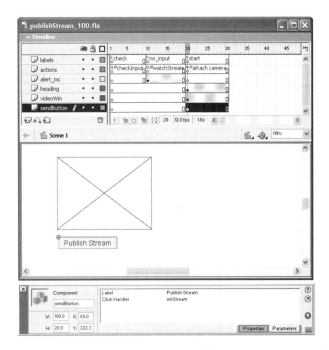

Figure 10.10 The sendButton instance's parameters are entered
in the Property inspector.

4. When the user first loads the Flash movie (SWF file), the sendButton instance
   should not be enabled—why would you want to allow the user to publish if
   there isn't a successful connection to the server? To disable the sendButton
   instance, insert the following code after the userMic = Microphone.get(); line
   of code on frame 20 of the actions layer:

```
sendButton.setEnabled(false);
```

5. Now, adjust the code for the app_nc object, which handles the connection
   to the broadcast application on the Flash Communication Server. Select
   frame 20 of the actions layer, and add the three highlighted lines of code
   shown in the following code block. You should already have the remaining
   code on this keyframe.

```
app_nc = new NetConnection();
app_nc.setUpStream = setupStream;
app_nc.onStatus = function(info) {
    if (info.code == "NetConnection.Connect.Success") {
```

```
        trace("---Connected to FlashCom server.");
        this.setupStream(true);
    } else if (info.code == "NetConnection.Connect.Failed" ||
        ⇥ info.code == "NetConnection.Connect.Closed") {
        trace("---No connection to FlashCom server.");
        this.setupStream(false);
    }
};
app_nc.connect("rtmp:/broadcast");
```

Here, you declare a method named setupStream for the app_nc object. This method will refer to a setupStream() function that you will create later in this section. When the app_nc successfully connects to the server, the setUp-Stream() method of app_nc is invoked and passed a true argument value. If the connection fails or is closed, the same method is invoked with a false argument. In this way, you create a toggle switch for the application.

6. The setupStream() function referenced in the app_nc.setupStream = setup-Stream; line of code needs to be defined. When a connection is made to the broadcast application, this function is called as a method of the app_nc object. Therefore, any this references in the setupStream() function point back to the object itself—in this case, app_nc. On frame 20 of the actions layer, add the following lines of code before the userCam = Camera.get(); line of code. The setupStream() function should be declared before other code is executed on the frame (**Listing 10.2**).

Note

The line numbers shown in the following code are only for analytical purposes. Do not type these numbers into your actual code. The line numbers are relative to this block of code, and are not meant to match the actual line number(s) in the Actions panel.

Listing 10.2 The setupStream() **function for the publisher**

```
1. function setupStream(init) {
2.     sendButton.isPublishing = false;
3.     sendButton.setEnabled(init);
4.     if (init) {
5.         pubStream_ns = new NetStream(this);
6.         pubStream_ns.onStatus = function(info) {
7.             trace("---"+info.code);
8.             if (info.code == "NetStream.Publish.Start") {
9.                 sendButton.setLabel("Stop Publishing");
```

Listing 10.2 The setupStream() **function for the publisher** *(continued)*

```
10.                 sendButton.isPublishing = true;
11.             } else if (info.code == "NetStream.Unpublish.Success") {
12.                 sendButton.setLabel("Publish Stream");
13.                 sendButton.isPublishing = false;
14.             }
15.         };
16.     } else {
17.         sendButton.setLabel("Publish Stream");
18.     }
19. }
```

In this code block, a number of tasks are performed. In lines 2 and 3, the sendButton instance you created in an earlier step is prepared for the application. Line 2 sets an isPublishing variable to false, indicating that the user has yet to click the sendButton instance. Line 3 controls the button's enabled state, using the init argument (passed by the app_nc.onStatus() handler). When the app_nc object connects to the broadcast application instance, the init argument is set to true, which enables the sendButton instance. When the app_nc disconnects, the init argument is set to false and the sendButton instance is disabled.

Lines 4 through 15 are executed when init is set to true (that is, when the app_nc object successfully connects to the broadcast application). Line 5 creates a NetStream object named pubStream_ns. The new NetStream() constructor requires a valid NetConnection object as a parameter. In this example, the this reference points back to the app_nc object, which is a NetConnection object. The pubStream_ns object, like the app_nc object, can also have an onStatus() handler. For a NetStream object, the onStatus() handler is invoked whenever an event occurs with the stream. In lines 8 and 11, you check the code property of the info object. When a stream is initiated with a publish() method (performed in a later step), a NetStream.Publish.Start event is sent to the onStatus() handler. When this event is detected (line 8), the sendButton instance's label is changed to Stop Publishing (line 9) and its isPublishing variable is set to true. When a NetStream.Unpublish.Success event is detected (line 11), the label is changed to Publish Stream (line 12) and isPublishing is set to false. The NetStream.Unpublish.Success event is sent to the onStatus() handler when a publish(false) method is invoked on the NetStream object. This action occurs in a later step.

Lines 16 through 18 are invoked when the app_nc object's connection to the application is closed or unexpectedly disconnected. Here, once again, the sendButton instance's label is switched back to Publish Stream.

7. The initStream() function that the sendButton instance uses as a Click Handler needs to be defined. The initStream() function controls the publish() method of the NetStream object, pubStream_ns, that you declared in the last step's code. After the code you inserted in step 6, add the following lines of code. Again, this code should be inserted before the userCam = Camera.get(); line of code.

```
1. function initStream(obj) {
2.    if (!obj.isPublishing) {
3.        pubStream_ns.publish("hostStream", "live");
4.        pubStream_ns.attachVideo(userCam);
5.        pubStream_ns.attachAudio(userMic);
6.    } else {
7.        pubStream_ns.publish(false);
8.    }
9. }
```

The obj argument of the initStream() function refers to the sendButton instance. When a PushButton component's Click Handler is invoked, a reference to that instance is passed as the sole argument of the function called. If the isPublishing variable for sendButton is equal to false (as declared in lines 2 and 13 of the step 6's code), the publish() method of the NetStream object is invoked for the pubStream_ns object. The first argument, "hostStream", is the name of the actual stream published on the FlashCom server. The second argument, "live", determines how the server handles the stream. When a stream is "live", the server does not save a copy of the stream as a FLV file. Any user who connects and subscribes to the hostStream stream sees the live output from this user's SWF file. Remember, in the last step, you created an onStatus() handler for the pubStream_ns object. When the publish() method in line 3 is executed, the sendButton instance's label and isPublishing values are changed.

When you publish a stream to a FlashCom server, you usually attach the output from the Camera and Microphone objects. Lines 4 and 5 of this function uses the attachVideo() and attachAudio() methods of the NetStream object to do just that.

If the `isPublishing` variable is equal to true (indicating that a stream is currently publishing), lines 6 through 8 are executed. Here, the `publish()` method is invoked with a false argument, indicating that the stream should stop publishing to the server. When publishing stops, the `onStatus()` handler of the `pubStream_ns` object is called with an `info.code` value of "NetStream.Unpublish.Success". As such, the `sendButton`'s label and `isPublishing` values are changed.

8. Save your Flash document as **publishStream_100.fla**, and test it (Control > Test Movie). When the SWF file loads, a user with a valid camera, microphone, and connection to the application can press the `sendButton` instance and publish his/her audio and video to the FlashCom Server.

You can find the completed `publishStream_100.fla` file in the `chapter_10` folder of this book's CD-ROM.

Tip

To monitor the `hostStream` stream to the FlashCom application while you are testing the Flash movie in Flash MX, you can use the Communication App Inspector (Window > Communication App Inspector). You will learn more about this panel later in Chapter 11.

In the next section, you will create the Flash document (FLA file) for a Flash movie that subscribes to the `hostStream` stream.

Subscribing to a Stream

Whenever a stream is publishing within a FlashCom application instance (such as the `broadcast` application used throughout this chapter), you can enable another Flash movie (SWF file) to receive, or subscribe to, that stream. In this section, you will learn how to play streams within a FlashCom application instance.

Retrieving the Live Stream from the Server

Most of the code and elements from the previous `publishStream_100.fla` document can also be used for the playback Flash movie. Instead of publishing a stream to the FlashCom server, the playback movie uses the play() method of the NetStream object. To play a stream from a specific FlashCom application, use the following guidelines.

1. The movie should connect to the application instance on your Flash Communication Server.

2. After a successful connection is made, a NetStream object should be created for each video item you wish to play.

3. The play() method of the new NetStream object is invoked, specifying the name of the stream as the method's argument.

4. The NetStream object is attached to a Video object on the stage. (A Video object is the same as an empty Embedded Video instance.)

5. Optionally, the audio of a NetStream object can be attached to a MovieClip object, in order to control the volume of the audio via a Sound object.

Playing a stream, in some ways, is the exact opposite of publishing a stream. Instead of using the publish("streamName", "live") method, you use the play("streamName") method. Also, instead of attaching the user's camera and microphone output to a NetStream object, you attach the NetStream object to a Video object. Because the user is simply watching another stream, the user's input devices do not need to be accessed, nor are they required.

Note

There are several other parameters for the publish() and play() methods for Net-Stream objects, some of which you will use throughout other examples in this book.

In the following steps, you build a playback Flash movie interface for the stream published from last section's Flash movie.

To subscribe the movie to a stream:

1. Create a new Flash document (FLA file) in Flash MX.

2. Save the document as **playStream100.fla**.

3. Rename Layer 1 to **header**. On frame 1 of this layer, use the Text tool to add the text **Receive Audio and Video from Server** to the upper left corner of the document's stage.

4. Make a new layer, and name it **videoWin**. On this layer, place an empty Embedded Video instance on the stage, just beneath the header. Remember, to create an Embedded Video symbol, open the Library panel (F11) and choose New Video from the options menu.

5. Name the Embedded Video instance **videoWin** in the Property inspector. In a later step, you will attach a stream to this object.

6. Create a new layer, and name it **receiveButton**. On this layer, place an instance of the PushButton component. Assign the name **receiveButton** to this instance in the Property inspector. In the Label parameter, type **Receive Stream**. In the Click Handler, type **initStream** (**Figure 10.11**).

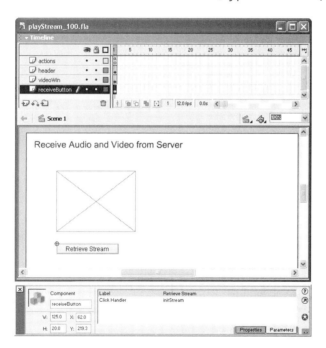

Figure 10.11 The receiveButton instance's parameters are entered in the Property inspector.

7. Make a new layer named **actions**, and place it at the top of the layer stack. Select frame 1 of this layer, and open the Actions panel (F9). Type the following code into the panel (**Listing 10.3**):

Listing 10.3 The checkInput() **function for the subscriber**

```
1. function setupStream(init) {
2.    receiveButton.isSubscribing = false;
3.    receiveButton.setEnabled(init);
4.    if (init) {
5.       subStream_ns = new NetStream(this);
6.       subStream_ns.onStatus = function(info) {
7.          trace("---"+info.code);
8.          if (info.code == "NetStream.Play.Start") {
9.             receiveButton.setLabel("Stop Subscribing");
10.            receiveButton.isSubscribing = true;
11.         } else if (info.code == "NetStream.Play.Stop") {
12.            receiveButton.setLabel("Retrieve Stream");
13.            receiveButton.isSubscribing = false;
14.         }
15.      };
16.   } else {
17.      receiveButton.setLabel("Retrieve Stream");
18.   }
19. }
20. function initStream(obj) {
21.    if (!obj.isSubscribing) {
22.       subStream_ns.play("hostStream");
23.       videoWin.attachVideo(subStream_ns);
24.    } else {
25.       subStream_ns.play(false);
26.    }
27. }
28. receiveButton.setEnabled(false);
29. app_nc = new NetConnection();
30. app_nc.setupStream = setupStream;
31. app_nc.onStatus = function(info) {
32.    if (info.code == "NetConnection.Connect.Success") {
33.       trace("---Connected to FlashCom server.");
34.       this.setupStream(true);
35.    } else if (info.code == "NetConnection.Connect.Failed" ||
           → info.code == "NetConnection.Connect.Closed") {
36.       trace("---No connection to FlashCom server.");
37.       this.setupStream(false);
38.    }
39. };
40. app_nc.connect("rtmp:/broadcast");
```

While this code block may seem overwhelming, the code uses the same structure as the publish SWF file that you created in the previous section. The `setupStream()` function prepares the new `NetStream` object once a successful connection to the `broadcast` instance is made (line 34). The `isPublishing` variable name is changed to `isSubscribing` (lines 2, 10, 13, and 21), and the `NetStream` object's name is `subStream_ns` instead of `pubStream_ns` (lines 5, 6, 22, and 25).

Other minor changes include different `info.code` events, such as `"NetStream.Play.Start"` (line 8) and `"NetStream.Play.Stop"` (line 11). Because this movie subscribes to a stream, the events sent to the `onStatus()` handler for the `subStream_ns` object are different from those sent to the publisher of the stream (`pubStream_ns` in the SWF file from the last section).

The most important changes in this code occur in lines 20-27. Here, the `initStream()` function (called by the `receiveButton` instance) invokes the `play()` method of the `subStream_ns` object, specifying `"hostStream"` as the stream to play (line 22). The `subStream_ns` is then attached to the `videoWin` object, using the `attachVideo()` method of the `Video` object (line 23).

Finally, the connection to the FlashCom server must specify the same application name that the published stream uses, as shown in line 40. If the `hostStream` stream was published to an application named `broadcast`, then any other Flash movie that wants to access the `hostStream` stream must also connect to the `broadcast` application.

8. Save your Flash document again. You're now ready to test both SWF files at the same time. Open the `publishStream_100.fla` document and preview the HTML and SWF files (File > Publish Preview > Default - HTML). With the `publishStream_100.html` document open in your Web browser, click the Publish Stream button to begin publishing the `hostStream` stream. Keep the browser window open, and go back to Flash MX. Select the `playStream_100.fla` document window, and choose Control > Test Movie. When the Flash movie opens in a new window, click the Receive Stream button. You should now see the live video in both SWF files (**Figure 10.12**).

Tip

If you are using a relative URI for the `NetConnection` object, remember to save your Flash documents (and test your Flash movies) on the same machine where you installed the FlashCom server.

Figure 10.12 When one user is publishing to the stream named hostStream, other users can watch it.

 You can find the completed playStream100.fla in the chapter_10 folder of this book's CD-ROM.

In order to use the playStream_100.swf with the loadMovie() action that you created on the no_input frame of the publishStream_100.fla document, rename the playStream_100.swf file to playStream.swf. The loadMovie() action refers to a file named playStream.swf; therefore, if you don't rename your tested movie, the publish movie will be unable to locate the subscriber movie.

Limiting the Number of Connections to the Application

For a publicly available FlashCom application, you may want to consider limiting the number of users that can connect to your server at any given point. Oftentimes, you may be creating bandwidth-intensive applications, and you will want to ensure that each user who connects has an optimal experience. You can limit the number of users in the following ways:

■ Adjust the Vhost.xml configuration file for your Flash Communication Server. By editing the <MaxConnections> node value in this configuration file, you can limit the total number of connections available with a specific virtual host (that is, a domain name to which your Flash Communication Server responds). This method limits the total number of connections that all applications running within the virtual host can use.

- Track the number of connections within server-side ActionScript code per application. With this method, you limit the number of connections by only allowing a user to connect to the application if the current number of connected users is less than a specified value. The value can be set with a variable in server-side ActionScript.

To be clear, these methods won't allow a connection only if the maximum number of connections is reached. These methods should not be confused with authentication. Authentication is the process of checking for a valid username and password against a secure database.

Xref

User authentication with Rich Internet Applications is discussed in Chapter 14.

TO LIMIT SERVER CONNECTIONS BY MODIFYING THE VHOST.XML DOCUMENT:

1. Locate the Vhost.xml configuration file for your default virtual host on the Flash Communication Server. If you have only one virtual host on a Windows-based FlashCom server, the file should have the following path:
   ```
   C:\Program Files\Macromedia\Flash Communication Server
   MX\conf\_defaultRoot_\_defaultVHost_\Vhost.xml
   ```

2. Open the Vhost.xml file in Macromedia Dreamweaver MX or your preferred text editor.

3. Find the <ResourceLimits> node within the document. Within this node, you should see the <MaxConnections> node. By default, this node has a value of -1, which means that the connections to the FlashCom server are only limited by the license key. For example, if you have the Personal Edition of Flash-Com, the maximum number of connections is 10, regardless of what value you enter into this node. At this point, change the node value to your preferred limit for the broadcast application you built in previous sections. In the following text, the number of connections is limited to 5:
   ```
   <MaxConnections>5</MaxConnections>
   ```

4. Save the Vhost.xml file when you are finished editing. Then, restart the Flash Communication Server service. You can restart the server by opening the Services console on your Windows server. Click the Start button, choose Run, and type **services.msc**. In the Services console, find the Flash Communication Server service, right-click it, and choose Restart.

Once the Flash Communication Server has restarted, only four users will be able to connect to and view the publishing stream. Why four? Remember, the <MaxConnections> value controls the total number of connections, not users. One connection is required to send the stream to the server, which leaves four connections available to receive the stream.

Note

Check out this book's Web site, www.mxbook.com, to stay up to date with other techniques you can use to limit the number of users for a FlashCom application.

INTEGRATING PUBLISHER AND SUBSCRIBER CAPABILITIES

Using information objects for NetStream objects, you can create one Flash movie that can publish or play the same stream. In this section, you will deconstruct a Flash movie that combines the functionality of the previous exercises. The Flash movie has the following primary features:

- If a stream is available for publishing, and the user has a valid camera and microphone, the movie presents two options to the user: Publish or Receive.

- If a stream is available, but the user doesn't have a valid camera and microphone, the movie presents only a Receive option to the user.

- If another user is publishing a stream, the movie informs the user that the stream is occupied and presents a Receive option that enables the user to view the stream.

The movie has other features that are examined throughout this section.

Before you continue to the next section, open a copy of the pubPlay_100.fla document from the chapter_10 folder of the book's CD-ROM.

Examining the Main Timeline and Interface

Let's start examining the main timeline by opening the pubPlay_100.fla document in Macromedia Flash MX. **Figure 10.13** shows the Timeline window, which
illustrates the overall construction of the Flash document.

 The term "main timeline" is often used to refer to the first scene (or Scene 1) of a
Flash document.

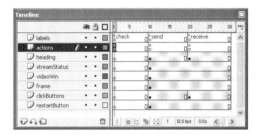

Figure 10.13 The timeline of the pubPlay_100.fla
document shows sections dedicated to
sending and receiving a live stream.

You have created similar content in previous exercises of this chapter. This
movie uses the same basic object types, such as the Video object and the Push-
Button component. Let's review each layer's contribution to the functionality
of the movie.

LABELS AND HEADING

There are three essential sections for the pubPlay_100.fla document, which are
marked as frame labels on the labels layer: check, send, and receive. When the user
first loads the Flash movie, the movie stops on the check frame and presents a
MessageBox component instance to the user (this component is discussed in the
sidebar following this section). The user clicks a Publish or Receive button in the
message box. If the Publish button is clicked, the timeline jumps to the send
frame. If the Receive button is pressed, the timeline jumps to the receive frame.

The heading layer serves the same purpose as it did in earlier sections. When a
user is sent to the send or receive frame, the Static text in the heading layer
indicates the current functionality of the application.

ACTIONS

As its name implies, this layer contains all the ActionScript code used by the movie. If you choose frame 1 of the actions layer and open the Actions panel (F9), you will see that a substantial amount of code is loaded from ActionScript (AS or .as) files. You will learn more about the actual code in the "Breaking Down the Code" section, later in this chapter. If you quickly peruse the code for each section of the timeline, you'll notice that the code is rather sparse. The send and receive sections only have the code necessary to invoke the functions and event handlers contained within the AS files included on frame 1.

STREAMSTATUS, VIDEOWIN, AND FRAME

These layers enhance the overall appearance of the videoWin object, which presents the video from the published or subscribed stream to the connected user.

The streamStatus layer contains a TextField object named streamStatus. This text field is positioned near the top-right corner of the videoWin object. This field displays the current activity of the stream to the user. When the user publishes the stream, the text field displays LIVE. If the user stops publishing (by clicking the PushButton instance on the send frame), the text field displays STANDBY. When the user is using the Receive mode of the application (that is, the timeline is on the receive label), the field displays WAITING FOR STREAM if no stream is currently publishing. When a stream starts to publish, the field is empty.

The frame layer adds a filled black rectangle to the background of the videoWin object. In previous sections, the user was presented with a blank area for the video stream until the remote stream or local camera was attached to the videoWin object. Now, the user sees a defined area before streaming starts.

CLICKBUTTONS AND RESTARTBUTTON

These layers contain the instances of the PushButton component. In previous exercises, you used this component to add the same functionality you see in the pubPlay_100.fla document. The sendButton and receiveButton (appearing on their respective frames) are collectively referenced as the clickButtons. (In our discussion of the ActionScript code for this example later in this chapter, you see a clickButton object reference, which is set to refer to either one of these buttons.) As with the previous exercises, the `sendButton` and the `receiveButton` both refer to the `initStream()` function as the Click Handler (in the Parameters area of the Property inspector).

The `restartButton` instance (on the same named layer) invokes a `restartMovie()` function when clicked. As its name implies, this button reinitializes the movie, taking the user back to the `check` frame of the timeline.

A Note about the MessageBox Component

One essential element of the Flash document is not visible in the Timeline window or the stage: the `MessageBox` component. This component is part of Flash UI Components Set 2, available as a free extension download from www.macromedia.com/exchange/flash. Open the Library panel (F11), and in the Flash UI Components folder, you will find the `MessageBox` component symbol. If you expand the width of the Library panel, you can read the linkage identifier of this component: `FMessageBoxSymbol` (**Figure 10.14**). This name is referenced within an `attachMovie()` method in order to dynamically insert an instance of the Message-Box component onto the stage. You can access the Linkage Properties by right-clicking (or Control-clicking on the Mac) a symbol's name and choosing Linkage.

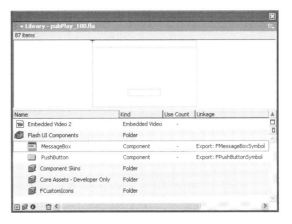

Figure 10.14 The Library panel displays the linkage identifier for exported assets.

The `MessageBox` component allows you to quickly add a dialog box to your Flash movie. You can configure just about every attribute of the box with ActionScript, from the title of the message to the number of buttons presented to the user. In the next section, you will learn how the `MessageBox` component is used within ActionScript code.

Breaking Down the Code

Admittedly, the code used in the pubPlay_100.fla file is much more comprehensive than any previous example in this chapter. Most of the ActionScript code is contained within AS files, which are included on frame 1 of the actions layer. In this section, you will learn how the process of the application interoperates with the code within these files and the actions assigned to keyframes of the actions layer on the Main Timeline of the Flash MX document. Instead of dissecting each line of code in a linear fashion, the following six sections will deconstruct the process flow of the ActionScript code. While several functions and methods are declared within the AS files on frame 1 of the movie, most of this code is only utilized in later frames of the movie.

Tip

Usually, it's a good idea to initialize functions early in your Flash document. While you do not have to declare functions until you need to utilize them, declaring your functions at the beginning of your movie makes them available throughout the entire duration of the movie.

STAGE 1: MAKING A CONNECTION AND CHECKING THE STREAM

When the user loads the Flash movie, the movie attempts to connect to the broadcast application on the FlashCom server (just as you have done in previous exercises). On the check frame, the Flash movie verifies a successful connection to the FlashCom server and checks the availability of a stream named hostStream. **Figure 10.15** illustrates the processes that occur on the check frame. The following numbered list analyzes the pubPlay_100.fla file and corresponds to the steps shown in the figure:

1. When the check frame plays, the app_nc object (line 60 of frame 1 on the actions layer) connects to the broadcast application.

2. The Flash movie receives a status event from the FlashCom server. In lines 30 through 56 of frame 1, the onStatus() handler checks this result.

3. If the connection fails (lines 41 through 56), the showMessageBox() function is invoked with the parameters specified.

4. If the connection succeeds, the checkStream() method of the app_nc object is invoked (lines 35 through 38).

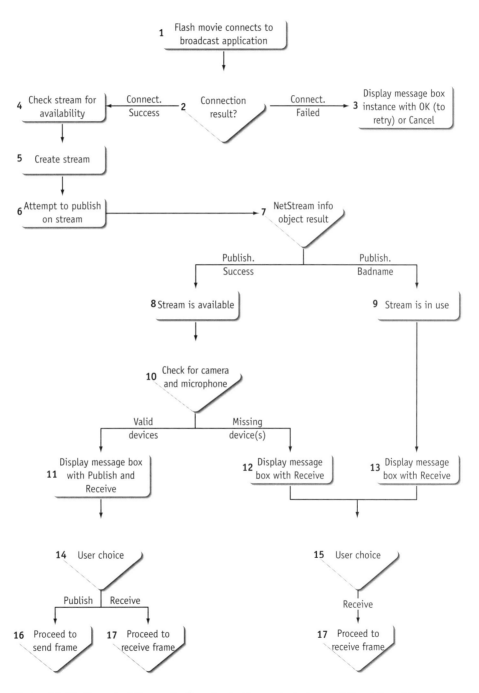

Figure 10.15 Stage 1 of the application checks the user's devices and the status of the stream.

5. In the checkStream() function (found in the checkStream.as file), a new Net-Stream object named stream_ns is created (line 14 of checkStream.as).

6. A publish() method is issued on the stream_ns object, which specifies the "hostStream" name (line 53 of checkStream.as).

7. The result of the publish() method is checked, and the result is returned as an info object to the onStatus() handler defined in lines 17 through 50 of checkStream.as.

Note

The onStatus() handler is also used for detection of a separate condition (line 21, and lines 36-49 of checkStream.as) not shown in **Figure 10.15**. This condition is discussed after the last step of this section.

8. If the info.code property of the stream_ns object is equal to "NetStream.Publish.Success", no other user is publishing on hostStream, and the stream is available (lines 27-29). The displayFirstOptions() function is invoked with a true argument (line 33), and the movie proceeds to the code discussed in step 10.

9. If the info.code property of the stream_ns object is equal to "NetStream.Publish.Badname", another user is publishing on hostStream, and the stream is unavailable (lines 23-25). The displayFirstOptions() function is invoked with a false argument (line 33), and the movie processes the code discussed in step 13.

10. In the displayFirstOptions.as file, you find the displayFirstOptions() function defined. On lines 10-13, the test publish on hostStream is stopped, and the movie begins to monitor activity on hostStream. On line 30, the checkDevices() function (found in the checkDevices.as file) checks for a valid optical camera and microphone.

11. If the checkDevices() function returns a true value, then lines 30-34 execute, setting up the buttons and message parameters for the showMessageBox() function on line 59. Other message box properties are also defined on lines 51-56. The movie moves to the code outlined in step 14.

Note

The showMessageBox() function is defined in the showMessageBox.as file.

12. If the checkDevices() function returns a false value, then lines 36-41 of the displayFirstOptions() function execute, setting up the Receive button and the message value for the showMessageBox() function on line 59. Other message box properties are also defined on lines 51-56. The code in step 15 is then processed.

13. If the stream is unavailable (from step 9), lines 43-48 of the displayFirstOptions() function execute, setting up the Receive button and the message value for the showMessageBox() function on line 59. Again, the same message box properties are defined on lines 51-56, and the movie invokes the code discussed in step 15.

Note — One of the shared properties of the MessageBox instance is the close handler, pickFirstOption(). This function is described in the pickFirstOption.as file.

14. At this point, a MessageBox instance is presented to the user (via the showMessageBox() function), with Publish and Receive options. The user must choose one of these options.

15. A MessageBox instance with a Receive only option is presented to the user. The user must click the Receive button to proceed.

16. If the user presses the Publish option (from step 14), the pickFirstOption() function (described in the pickFirstOption.as file) is invoked. This close handler knows which button was clicked by the user and directs the user to the send frame (line 21 of the pickFirstOption.as file). The movie processes the code discussed in "Stage 2: Preparing the Send Frame."

17. If the user presses the Receive option (from step 14 or 15), the pickFirstOption() function directs the user to the receive frame (line 25 of the pickFirstOption.as file). The movie then proceeds to process the code explained in "Stage 3: Preparing the Receive Frame."

In step 7, you learned that the onStatus() handler detected events occurring on hostStream via the stream_ns object. This handler also checks to see if it's the first time the stream_ns has attempted a test publish (lines 21 and 36 of checkStream.as). When the displayFirstOptions() function is invoked for the first time, a variable named inited is declared and set to true on the stream_ns object. This variable tells the onStatus() handler for the stream_ns object if the user has attempted a test publish, and subsequently if a MessageBox instance has been displayed to the user. This condition was created in the event that a user connected to the application while another user was just about to publish the stream, or if another user who was publishing suddenly stops. With the inited variable, the onStatus() handler can reinitialize the MessageBox instance whenever activity along the stream changes.

STAGE 2: PREPARING THE SEND FRAME

If the hostStream is available and the user has a valid optical camera and micro-phone, the option to Publish is available in the MessageBox component instance in Stage 1, on the check frame. When the user clicks the Publish button, the timeline goes to the send frame and attempts to access the user's camera and microphone. If the user allows access to these devices, the movie starts to pub-lish the stream to the FlashCom server. At that point, other connected users can begin to play the stream as well. This process is illustrated in **Figure 10.16** and analyzed in the following steps:

1. Once the user presses the Publish button in the MessageBox component instance on the check frame, the Flash movie jumps to the send frame of the pubPlay_100.fla document. On frame 10 of the actions layer (just beneath the send frame label), you will find all the code referenced in **Figure 10.16**.

2. On lines 2 and 4 of this frame, the camera and microphone output is assigned to the userCam and userMic objects, respectively.

3. On line 25, the userCam object is attached to the videoWin object.

4. Whenever a Flash movie attempts to use the attachVideo() or attachMic() methods, the Flash Player checks its stored settings for the domain from which the Flash movie (SWF file) was downloaded.

5. If the Flash Player does not find any saved (or remembered) Privacy set-tings, the Flash Player Settings dialog box opens.

Xref

For more information on the Flash Player Settings, see Chapter 1.

6. The user makes a decision to allow or deny access to his/her camera and microphone. (If the user enabled the Remember option from a previous experience with this Flash movie, that setting is invoked.)

7. In line 29, the setupStream() function is invoked with a type argument of "send". If the user allowed access in step 6, the muted property of the userCam Camera object is equal to false. If the user denied access, this property is equal to true. In order for the setupStream() function to operate properly, the opposite Boolean value of the muted property is used as the init argument of the setupStream() function. Jump to "Stage 4: Setting Up the NetStream Object" to see how this function works.

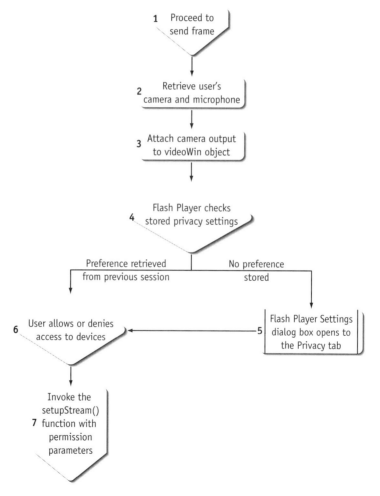

Figure 10.16 Stage 2 of the application directs the user to the send frame, where the Flash Player asks the user for permission to access his/her devices.

In lines 10-22, an onStatus() handler is defined for the userCam object. This handler is invoked whenever a *change* occurs with the Privacy options in the Flash Player Settings dialog box. You may be wondering why the setupStream() function is repeated so often in the actions list for frame 10. Because a user can enable the Flash Player to remember Privacy options for each site, the Flash Player Settings dialog box may not automatically pop open for the user. Therefore, the code needs to retrieve the Privacy options (via the userCam.muted property) for both active changes to these options during the movie's duration (in the onStatus() handler), and for remembered values (in line 29).

STAGE 3: PREPARING THE RECEIVE FRAME

At the end of stage 1, if the user chooses the Receive option in the MessageBox component instance, the pickFirstOption() function directs the timeline to the receive frame. This frame has the same primary elements as the send frame: a videoWin object to display the stream and a PushButton component to control the activity of the stream. **Figure 10.17** shows the process of interaction on the receive frame, and the following steps analyze the interaction:

1. During stage 1, the user chooses the Receive option. The pickFirstOption() function moves the playhead to the receive frame.

2. On frame 20 of the actions layer (beneath the receive frame label), the setupStream() function in invoked with a type parameter of "receive", and an init parameter of true.

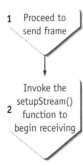

1   Proceed to
    send frame

2   Invoke the
    setupStream()
    function to
    begin receiving

Figure 10.17 Stage 3 of the application directs the user to the receive frame, where the movie plays, or subscribes to, the stream.

STAGE 4: SETTING UP THE NETSTREAM OBJECT

When the timeline executes the actions on the send or receive frame, a call to the setupStream() function is made. This function has been constructed to allow the creation of a NetStream object that can either publish or play a stream on the Flash-Com server. As **Figure 10.18** shows and the following steps analyze, the onStatus() handler of the stream_ns object is defined for specific publish or play tasks:

1. If the setupStream() function is invoked from the send frame, and the user's devices are accessible, the setupStream() function receives the arguments "send" and true. If the user denied access to his/her devices, the setupStream() function receives the arguments "send" and false.

2. If the setupStream() function is invoked from the receive frame, the function accepts "receive" and true as its arguments.

3. The setupStream() function is defined in lines 9-116 of the setupStream.as file. Lines 10-22 prepare either the sendButton or the receiveButton instance. A clickButton reference is created on the stream_ns object in line 15, and the button is given an initial isActive value of false. If init is equal to true, the button is enabled (line 21). Otherwise, the button is disabled.

4. The init argument passed to the function is checked (line 24).

5. If the init value is true, then the type argument passed to the function is checked (line 27). The movie jumps to the code discussed in step 7.

6. If the init value is false, then the type argument passed to the function is checked (line 112). The movie jumps to the code in step 9.

7. If the type argument is equal to "send", the movie establishes the info.code events and button labels that detect activity along a published stream (lines 29-49). In lines 84-104, these values are referenced in the onStatus() handler of the stream_ns object. The movie processes the code in step 10.

8. If the type argument is equal to "receive", the movie declares the info.code events and button labels that detect activity along a subscribed stream (lines 55-80). In lines 84-104, these values are referenced in the onStatus() handler of the stream_ns object. Jump to step 10.

9. If the init value is false and the type value is "send", the text property of the streamStatus field is set to "Devices Inaccessible" (line 113).

10. Once the onStatus() handler is established on the stream_ns object, the init-Stream() function is invoked, passing the current clickButton value as the argument (line 107). This function is described in "Stage 5: Controlling the Stream."

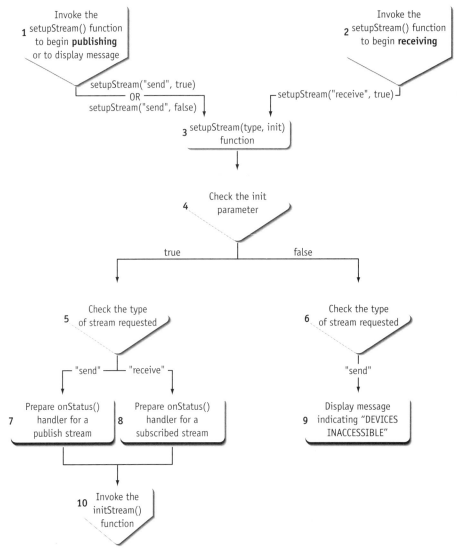

Figure 10.18 Stage 4 of the application sets up the stream_ns object's onStatus() handlers to provide the proper interactions with the user and the stream.

STAGE 5: CONTROLLING THE STREAM

The final stage of the Flash movie is the initStream() function, which issues a publish() or play() method on the stream_ns object. **Figure 10.19** shows the steps involved with this function. The initStream() function is defined in lines 122-174 of the setupStream.as file and is analyzed in the following steps:

1. The initStream() function is invoked from the setupStream() function or by the user clicking the sendButton or receiveButton instance.

2. The initStream() function uses an argument named obj.obj, which represents the current PushButton instance on the stage.

3. The isActive variable of the button is checked (line 124). isActive for either button is initially set to false in the setupStream() function.

4. If isActive is false (meaning, no publishing or subscribing is currently happening with the stream), and the _name property of the button is checked (line 126), then jumps to step 6.

5. If isActive is true (meaning, the stream is currently publishing or playing), the _name property of the button is checked (line 156). The movie then processes the code in step 14.

6. The standby variable on the stream_ns object is checked (line 129). The standby variable is equal to true whenever a user who had started to publish clicks the sendButton to halt publishing.

7. If standby is equal to false, the movie begins publishing on a stream named "hostStream" (line 131).

8. In lines 134 and 135, the video and microphone output are attached to the stream. At this point, the initStream() function completes.

9. If standby is equal to true (line 138), the onStatus() handler on the stream_ns object is cleared (line 140). This condition occurs when a user who stopped publishing clicks the sendButton again to resume publishing.

10. Once standby status is detected, the standby variable is reset to false (line 143).

11. To re-establish the onStatus() handler of the stream_ns, the setupStream() function is invoked (line 146). At this point, the initStream() function no longer executes any other code.

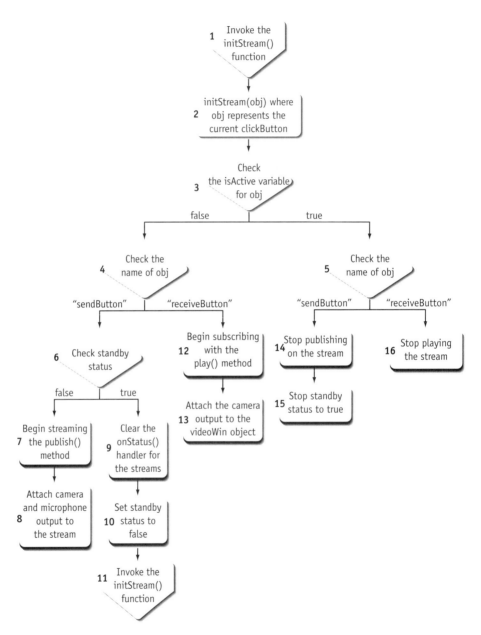

Figure 10.19 Stage 5 of the application determines whether the publish() or play() method is invoked on the stream_ns object.

12. If the button's name is receiveButton (line 149), the movie starts playing the stream named "hostStream" (line 151).

13. Once the play() method has been issued, the stream's video output is attached to the videoWin object (line 153). At this point, no other code within the initStream() function is executed.

14. If the init value is false, and the name of the button is sendButton (line 158), the movie stops publishing on the stream (line 161).

15. The standby variable on the stream_ns object is set to true. This variable is detected within subsequent invocations of the initStream() object.

16. If the init value is false, and the name of the button is receiveButton (line 169), the movie stops playing the stream from the FlashCom server (line 171). At this point, no other code within the initStream() is executed.

Figure 10.19 does not show the events that occur when the standby variable on the stream_ns object is set to true. The onStatus() handler of the stream_ns object invokes the detectPublish() function. This function overwrites the onStatus() handler to detect if another user wants to publish on the stream. If another user begins to publish while the user is in standby, then the original user is sent back to the check frame.

Note

In this implementation, if any user connects to the application while a user is in standby mode, the standby user's movie jumps to the first frame of the movie. Why? When any user connects to the application, a test stream is initiated. The standby user detects this publishing event, and, as a result the application believes that a stream is publishing. If remote SharedObject data was implemented (which you will learn about in later chapters), you could detect if a user was simply testing a stream or actually trying to publish to it continuously.

ADDITIONAL METHODS AND FUNCTIONS

While the primary functions of the Flash movie have been discussed within the scope of five stages, frame 1 of the actions layer refers to other AS files. In this section, a brief description of each of these AS files is given.

The getMovieSize.as file contains a function named getMovieSize(). This function establishes two global variables, movieWidth and movieHeight, which indicate the pixel width and height of a movie as reported by the Document Properties dialog box. Because the `Stage` object's `width` and `height` values are relative to the `scaleMode` property, these global variables are created for a consistent reference. For example, if `Stage.scaleMode` is set to `"noScale"`, then `Stage.width` and `Stage.height` report the width and height, respectively, of the Flash Player area, not necessarily the movie's stage area itself.

The `movieclip_center.as` file creates a `center()` method for the `MovieClip` class. The `center()` method aligns a `MovieClip` object to the center of the stage. The method can use an argument describing where the object's registration point is set. In this Flash movie, the `center()` method is used by the `showMessageBox()` function to center the `MessageBox` component instance on the stage.

RECORDING STREAMS

One of the most amazing features of Flash Communication Server MX is its ability to record live video and/or audio streams on the fly. When the server records a stream, the output is saved as an FLV file in a streams folder nested within the application's folder. Each application saves its own streams, and unless you create common stream folders (discussed in Chapter 13), a Flash movie must connect to the specific application in order to access its streams. The `publish()` method of the `NetStream` object allows three unique string values for its second argument, *howToPublish*:

- **"live":** If you specify this parameter, the Flash movie publishes the live data to the FlashCom server, and the server does not record or store the stream. If another user plays the same stream, FlashCom sends the same data that is publishing live. The following syntax publishes a live stream named `hostStream`.

  `stream_ns.publish("hostStream", "live");`

- **"record":** This parameter instructs the server to begin storing the live stream data as a new FLV file in the streams folder of the application instance. If an FLV file already exists in the application's stream folder, the file is overwritten. The following syntax publishes a live stream named "hostStream", which is recorded as an FLV file named `hostStream.flv`.

```
stream_ns.publish("hostStream", "record");
```

The playback of this `hostStream` stream depends upon the parameters passed to the `play()` method of the `NetStream` object inside of another user's Flash movie. If -2 is passed as the *start* argument of the `play()` method, such as:

```
stream_ns.play("hostStream", -2);
```

then the Flash movie will try to play the live stream named "hostStream". If no live data is being streamed on hostStream, the Flash movie will play the recorded stream named "hostStream" (as in `hostStream.flv`). If there is no live or recorded stream by that name, then the Flash movie opens a stream by the name of "hostStream" and waits for data to be published on that stream.

```
If -1 is passed as the start argument of the play() method, such as:
```

```
stream_ns.play("hostStream", -1);
```

then the Flash movie plays the live data currently published on the stream named "hostStream".

If 0 (or any positive number) is passed as the start argument of the `play()` method, such as:

```
stream_ns.play("hostStream", 0);
```

then the Flash movie plays only a recorded stream named "hostStream". Even if live data is being streamed over `hostStream`, the Flash movie plays data from the recorded stream (or file) named "hostStream".

(If you do not specify a start argument for the `play()` method, the Flash movie interprets the `play()` method with a -2 start argument.)

- **"append":** This parameter of the `publish()` method tells the Flash Communication Server to record the live stream. If a stream by the same name has already been recorded, then the FlashCom server appends the new live data to the existing stream file. If there is not a stream already recorded, the server creates a new FLV file for the stream. The following syntax publishes a live stream named "hostStream", which is recorded or appended to an FLV file named hostStream.flv:

```
stream_ns.publish("hostStream", "append");
```

Tip

If you do not specify a howToPublish value, the stream defaults to a "live" value.

In the remaining two sections of this chapter, you will learn how to record a stream and how to play a recorded stream.

Creating a Movie that Records a Stream

The Flash document (FLA file) that you create in this section follows the basic architecture of previous examples: If a user has a valid camera and microphone, then he/she is permitted to publish a stream to the FlashCom server. You will revise one of the earlier examples in order to record this stream to the server, with the added capability of specifying a stream name.

Tip

Before you begin the steps in this exercise, make a copy of the publishStream_100.fla that you created earlier in this chapter, or locate the file within the chapter_10 folder of this book's CD-ROM.

TO RECORD THE LIVE STREAM FROM THE MOVIE:

1. Open the publishStream_100.fla document in Macromedia Flash MX, and resave the document as **recordStream_100.fla** using the File > Save As command.

Note

For an accurate testing environment, though, you may want to save and test your Flash movies in a folder that is accessible by a Web server installed on your machine.

2. Create a new layer named **streamName_txt**. On this layer, add an empty keyframe on frame 20. Here, use the Text tool to create an Input text field named **streamName_txt**. Place this text below the sendButton instance. You can

also add the Static text **Stream name:** above the Input text field, as shown in **Figure 10.20**.

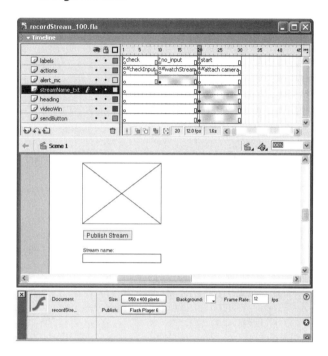

Figure 10.20 The streamName_txt field allows the user to specify the name of the recorded stream.

Tip

You may want to limit the characters that can be specified in the stream's name. The naming restrictions of your FlashCom server's operating system apply to named streams as well. Therefore, you should prevent illegal filename characters such as : and * in the text field. You can use the new restrict property of TextField objects to address such concerns. Note that you can specify virtual paths in a stream name. As such, forward-slash characters (/) can be permitted. The use of virtual paths for streams is discussed in Chapter 13.

3. Select frame 20 of the actions layer, and open the Actions panel (F9). Add the highlighted code shown in **Listing 10.4** to the initStream() function.

Listing 10.4 Adding record functionality to the publisher movie

```
function initStream(obj) {
  if(streamName_txt.text != ""){
    if (!obj.isPublishing) {
      pubStream_ns.publish(streamName_txt.text, "append");
      pubStream_ns.attachVideo(userCam);
      pubStream_ns.attachAudio(userMic);
    } else {
      pubStream_ns.publish(false);
    }
  } else {
    _root.attachMovie("FMessageBoxSymbol", "messageBox", 1);
    with(messageBox){
      _x = 275 - (_width/2);
      _y = 200 - (_height/2);
      setTitle("No Stream Name Specified");
      setMessage("Please specify a name for the stream.");
      setIcon("warning");
      setButtons(["OK"]);
      setCloseHandler("focusField");
    }
  }
}
```

> **Tip**
>
> The `initStream()` function should start at line 20 in the Actions panel. To see line numbers next to your code, click the Options menu in the top-right corner of the panel and choose View Line Numbers.

The code in Listing 10.4 checks the text property of the `streamName_txt` instance before any action is invoked upon the `stream_ns` object. If the user has not typed a name into the `streamName_txt` field, an instance of the `MessageBox` component displays on the stage, telling the user to specify a name in the field. When the user clicks the OK button in the `messageBox` instance, a function named `focusField()` is invoked (defined in the next step).

Most importantly, though, the `publish()` method now specifies the text property of the `streamName_txt` field and an "append" parameter, which tells the FlashCom server to record (or append) the stream to an FLV file.

4. Below the `initStream()` function, add the following `focusField()` function:

```
function focusField(){
    streamName_txt.text = "Type a stream name here.";
    Selection.setFocus(streamName_txt);
}
```

This code puts the text **Type a stream name here** into the `streamName_txt` field, and focuses the field for the user.

5. Save the document and test it (Ctrl+Enter or Command+Enter). If the user has a valid camera and microphone, the Flash movie jumps to the start frame, where the user can specify a stream name and begin publishing (and recording) the stream.

 You can find the completed file, `recordStream_100.fla`, in the `chapter_10` folder of this book's CD-ROM. You can copy and test this file from any location on your machine, provided that you have FlashCom server installed on that machine. If you are testing this movie with an external FlashCom server, be sure to change the URI of the application in the `connect()` method on frame 20 of the actions layer.

You can also add other enhancements to this movie, such as a ComboBox component instance, which allows the user to specify the stream type (`live`, `record`, or `append`). Also, you may want to change the SWF reference in the `loadMovieNum()` action on the `no_input` action frame, in order to load the enhanced playback file you create in the next section.

When you record a stream (FLV file), the file is saved in a default `streams` folder of your application. If you open the `broadcast` folder within the applications directory of your FlashCom server installation, you should see any recorded streams in the `streams/_definst_` folder, as shown in **Figure 10.21**.

If you connect to a specific instance of a FlashCom application, the stream files are saved in a separate subdirectory of the `streams` directory. For example, if your client-side ActionScript code specified the following URI:

```
app_nc = new NetConnection();
app_nc.connect("rtmp:/broadcast/10-11-2002");
```

then any recorded streams would be saved in a subdirectory named 10-11-2002 within the `streams` folder of the `broadcast` application. You can also create common stream locations that allow multiple applications to access and store streams to the same directory. You will learn more about this approach in Chapter 13.

Figure 10.21 By default, recorded streams are stored in a subfolder of the application's `streams` folder.

Creating a Movie that Plays Recorded Streams

In this section, you create a Flash movie that can play a named stream, as specified in the same type of Input text field you created in the last section.

Before you begin this exercise, locate the `playStream_100.fla` document you created earlier in this chapter. You can also find this file in the `chapter_10` folder of this book's CD-ROM.

TO SUBSCRIBE A MOVIE TO A RECORDED STREAM:

1. Open the `playStream_100.fla` document, and resave it as **playStream_101.fla** in the same location on your computer.

2. Open the Library panel (F11) for the current Flash document, and drag the `MessageBox` component from the Components panel into the Library panel.

3. Create a new layer named **streamName_txt**. On frame 1 of this layer, use the Text tool to create an Input text field named **streamName_txt** and the Static text **Stream name:**, just as you did in the previous section.

4. Select frame 1 of the actions layer, and add the highlighted lines of code shown in **Listing 10.5** to the initStream() function.

Listing 10.5 Subscribing the movie to a specific stream

```
function initStream(obj) {
    if(streamName_txt.text != ""){
        if (!obj.isSubscribing) {
            subStream_ns.play(streamName_txt.text, -2);
            videoWin.attachVideo(subStream_ns);
        } else {
            subStream_ns.play(false);
        }
    } else {
        _root.attachMovie("FMessageBoxSymbol", "messageBox", 1);
        with(messageBox){
            _x = 275 - (_width/2);
            _y = 200 - (_height/2);
            setTitle("No Stream Name Specified");
            setMessage("Please specify a name for the stream.");
            setIcon("warning");
            setButtons(["OK"]);
            setCloseHandler("focusField");
        }
    }
}
```

The code in Listing 10.5 works with the same structure as the record movie. If there isn't any text typed into the streamName_txt field, the MessageBox component is displayed on the stage with a message directing the user to specify a stream name. If the user has specified a stream name, the play() method is invoked on the subStream object, using the text within stream-Name_txt as the stream name. The start argument -2 is also prescribed, telling the FlashCom server to begin streaming the live data for the specified stream. If no live data is found, then recorded data (if available) will be streamed instead. If recorded data is not available, the Flash movie will subscribe to the named stream and wait for the stream to publish.

5. Now, add the `focusField()` function to frame 1 of the actions layer, just as you did in the previous section. The `focusField()` function is used as the close handler of the `MessageBox` instance:

```
function focusField(){
    streamName_txt.text = "Type a stream name here.";
    Selection.setFocus(streamName_txt);
}
```

6. Resave your Flash document and test it (Ctrl+Enter or Command+Enter). If you publish a stream with the `recordStream_100.swf` movie, you can specify the same stream name in this movie and play it.

You can find the completed file, `playStream_101.fla`, in the `chapter_10` folder of this book's CD-ROM.

PLAYING OTHER FLV FILES

You can create FLV files with Macromedia Flash MX, Sorenson Squeeze or Wildform Flix, and place them into a subdirectory of your application's streams directory. Once an FLV file is placed into a streams folder, the file can be played just like any other recorded stream. For example, you can record a presentation with your DV camcorder and transfer the footage to your computer, where you compress the footage as an FLV file in one of the aforementioned applications. Flash Communication Server MX automatically creates the necessary IDX file for an FLV file that you place into a streams folder. The IDX file is created the first time a user or application accesses the FLV file.

SUMMARY

- Before you build a FlashCom-enabled application, devise a production plan that clearly outlines the goals and structure of your application's functionality.

- Streams controlled and managed by a Flash Communication Server cannot be recompressed on the fly.

- An application must be defined in the `applications` directory of the Flash-Com server in order for a user to make a connection to the server.

- Make sure you have carefully reviewed all aspects of your application's use and functionality before you begin production in Flash MX.

- Consider the bandwidth requirements of your FlashCom-enabled application, examining the demands upon the server and upon each connected user.

- An empty embedded video object can display the live output from a user's camera or a subscribed stream.

- An application's name is referenced in the URI of the `NetConnection.connect()` method.

- Once a stream is publishing on the FlashCom server, other users can play or subscribe to the stream.

- One way of limiting the number of connections to a FlashCom server is by editing the `<MaxConnections>` node of the `Vhost.xml` configuration file.

- Flash UI components allow you to quickly integrate essential user interface elements into your Flash movie. The MessageBox component can display messages to your user and enable a user to choose options that affect the functionality of the application.

- By detecting specific events in the code property of information objects passed to `onStatus()` handlers for `NetConnection` and `NetStream` objects, an application can direct a stream to publish or play.

- A FlashCom server can record live streams to the application's `streams` folder. Once a connection is made to an application instance, a Flash movie can play that instance's stream files.

In This Chapter:

11 Sharing Text with Multiple Users

If you just read the last chapter, you may be thinking that Flash Communication Server MX can only benefit applications whose users have access to high-speed Internet connections. Granted, our sample application targeted an approximate bitrate of 144 Kbps. However, there's an entirely different aspect of FlashCom-enabled applications: remote SharedObject data. A Flash movie can connect to stored data within a FlashCom application, and, if any changes occur to that data while the user is connected to the application, the updated data is sent to all connected users. In this chapter, you will learn how to take advantage of the real-time data-sharing capability of remote SharedObjects powered by Flash Communication Server MX.

 Note The examples in this chapter require an installed version of Macromedia Flash Communication Server MX on your computer or another computer accessible to you over your network or the Internet.

UNDERSTANDING LOCAL AND REMOTE SHAREDOBJECT DATA

With the release of Flash Player 6, Flash movies can store and retrieve information with SharedObject data. There are two types of SharedObject instances in Flash MX ActionScript:

- **Local SharedObject instance**: You can enable a Flash movie to store data on the user's machine. This method of storage is similar to cookies that can be used in standard HTML pages in a Web browser. For example, a Flash movie can store a user's preferences in a local SharedObject (a SOL file) and access those preferences whenever the user comes back to the Flash movie in later visits (**Figure 11.1**). This data can only be stored and shared for a specific user's machine.

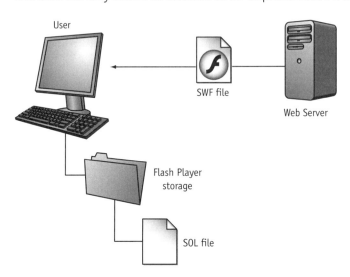

Figure 11.1 Flash movies served from any Web server can store data in a local SharedObject on the user's machine.

- **Remote** SharedObject **instance:** Using Macromedia Flash Communication Server MX, you can create applications that store and retrieve data within one or more server-side files. You can store an announcement message within a remote SharedObject file, and any user who connects to the FlashCom application will load and display the current announcement. More importantly, updates to this server-side data can be synchronized with connected clients. For example, you can design a chat application, which connects to a remote SharedObject to share text messages among users. When one user changes the data within the SharedObject (that is, sends a message to the server's application), any other user participating in the chat receives the new message because the user is connected to the same SharedObject instance (**Figure 11.2**). Another benefit of remote SharedObject data is that updates occur in real time without any reloading of the Flash movie or repeated timed executions of ActionScript functions. Prior to Flash Communication Server's release, a typical scenario for "real-time" information retrieval involved the use of polling functions, which checked an application server for data changes.

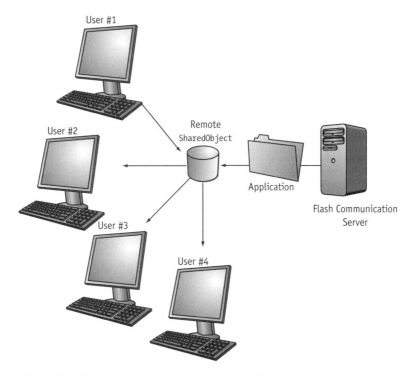

Figure 11.2 A user can broadcast a message to other connected users with a remote SharedObject within an application instance on a FlashCom server.

Both types of SharedObject instances can store information in basic data types, from String objects to Object objects to Array objects. As such, you store anything from the simplest information (such as a user's name) to the most complex object structures within SharedObject instances.

Also, SharedObject files are created or retrieved with the same ActionScript method of the SharedObject class. For example, the following code creates a local SharedObject container named userData if one doesn't already exist:

```
userData_so = SharedObject.getLocal("userData");
```

The same methodology applies to remote SharedObject files referenced in client-side ActionScript code. The following code creates a remote SharedObject named announcement if the data doesn't already exist:

```
announcement_so = SharedObject.getRemote("announcement", true);
```

In this line of code, you see an additional *persistence* argument, true. Unlike local SharedObject data, remote SharedObject data can persist for the duration of an application instance, or it can be saved permanently from one session to the next.

You can think of persistent remote SharedObject data as a mini-database. You could potentially store records, such as contact information, production information, and session tracking information within a remote SharedObject. The capability to synchronize this information with connected clients or other FlashCom applications (residing on separate servers) in real time allows you to create incredibly powerful data-transfer mechanisms.

While the majority of this chapter focuses on remote SharedObject connectivity, you will learn how to work with basic local SharedObject data in the next section. Some of the Flash Communication components, such as SimpleConnect, also use local SharedObjects to remember a user's login name.

Connecting to Local SharedObject Data

Storing data on a user's machine can be accomplished without a connection to a FlashCom server. By default, Flash Player 6 allows any given Web domain to store up to 100 KB of stored data on a user's machine. If you attempt to store more information than this amount, the Flash Player Security Settings dialog box displays and prompts the user to allow the Flash movie to store additional data. You can manually allow a domain to store more data by right-clicking (or Ctrl-clicking on a Mac) a Flash movie in Flash Player 6 and choosing Settings. In the second tab of this dialog box, named Local Storage, a user can adjust the amount of storage dedicated to a specific domain (**Figure 11.3**).

Figure 11.3 The Local Storage tab of the Flash Player Settings allows you to control how much storage is allocated to local SharedObject data.

Tip

Flash Player 6 recognizes the second level domain from which the Flash movie (SWF file) is loaded. Therefore, the storage limit applies to all Flash movies loaded from any third (or higher) domain name. For example, a Flash movie from `www.myDomain.com` and a Flash movie from `apps.myDomain.com` have a combined default limit of 100 KB of local storage.

In the following steps, you create a basic Flash movie that stores a user's name and password in a local `SharedObject`, if the user enables a CheckBox component instance.

To store data in a local SharedObject:

1. Create a new document in Macromedia Flash MX. Save the document as `local_so_100.fla`.

2. Rename Layer 1 to **labels**. Select frame 20 and choose Insert > Frame to add empty frames to the layer. You can also press the F5 key to add empty frames.

3. Select frame 1 of the labels layer, and assign a frame label of **login** in the Property inspector. Select frame 10, insert a keyframe (Insert > Keyframe, or F6), and assign a frame label of **start** (**Figure 11.4**).

Figure 11.4 Two frame labels added to the Main Timeline of the Flash document.

4. Make a new layer and name it textfields. On frame 1 of this layer, use the Text tool to add the Static text **Login frame** to the top left corner of the stage. On frame 10 of this layer, add a new keyframe (F6) and change the Static text to **Start frame**.

5. Go back to frame 1 of the textfields layer, and use the Text tool to add an Input text field, with an instance name of **userName_txt**. Make sure you enable the Show Border option for this field in the Property inspector. Add another Input text field with an instance name of **userPassword_txt**. Place this instance below the userName_txt instance. In the Line type menu of the Property inspector, choose Password (**Figure 11.5**). Then, add the Static text **User name:** and **Password:** to the left of the fields, respectively.

Figure 11.5 Create Input text fields for the user's name and password.

6. Create a new layer and name it **remBox**. On frame 1 of this layer, drag an instance of the CheckBox component from the Components panel to the stage. Place the instance below the Input text fields, and name the instance **remBox** in the Property inspector. In the Parameters area of the inspector, type **Remember my login information** in the Label field. Leave the other parameters with the default values. When you are finished, select frame 10 of this layer and add a new empty keyframe (F7)—the rem-Box instance should not be displayed on the start frame.

Note You may need to scale the remBox instance to accommodate the label text. Use the Free Transform tool to stretch the instance horizontally.

7. Make a new layer and name it **pushButtons**. On frame 1 of this layer, drag an instance of the PushButton component from the Components panel to the stage. Place this instance below the remBox instance, and name the PushButton instance **proceedButton** in the Property inspector. In the Label field of the Parameters area, type **Proceed**. In the Click Handler field, type **initMovie**. In the next step, you define the initMovie() function.

8. Add a new layer and name it **actions**. Select frame 1 of this layer, and open the Actions panel (F9). Type the following code (in Expert mode) into the Script pane:

```
function initMovie(){
    //insert actions for movie playback
    _root.gotoAndStop("start");
}
stop();
```

This code is invoked by the proceedButton instance, and tells the Main Timeline to jump to the start frame label. The stop() action, declared after the initMovie() function, makes sure the movie does not play beyond the first frame when the movie loads.

9. Select frame 10 of the pushButtons layer, and press the F6 key to add a new keyframe. Rename the PushButton instance on this frame to **jumpButton**, and change its Label value to **Jump to login**. Delete the Click Handler value. With this instance selected on the stage, open the Actions panel (F9). Add the following code to the instance:

```
on(press){
    _root.gotoAndStop("login");
}
```

While somewhat unconventional, you can add traditional on() handlers to PushButton instances, treating them as regular Button instances. When this instance is clicked, the Main Timeline jumps to the login frame label.

10. Now that you have the means to navigate between both frame labels, save your Flash document and test the movie (Ctrl+Enter or Command+Enter). When you click the Proceed button, the movie should jump to the start frame. When you click the Jump to login button, the movie should go back to the login frame. If you type some text into the Input text fields on the login frame, click the Proceed button, and then click the Jump to login button, the text you entered into the Input fields does not "stick" in the fields—the contents of any TextField instance are emptied whenever the instance is removed from the timeline. In the remaining steps, you add the ActionScript code to store the Input text field values in a local SharedObject.

11. Go back to the actions on frame 1 of the actions layer. Within the init-Movie() function, add the following highlighted line of code:

```
function initMovie(){

    //invoke the storeData() function to store the
    //user's name and password in a local SharedObject
    storeData();

    //insert actions for movie playback
    _root.gotoAndStop("start");
}
stop();
```

This code invokes the storeData() function when the user clicks the proceed-Button instance. In the next step, you define this function.

12. Beneath the initMovie() function, add the lines of code in **Listing 11.1**. This function checks the current state of the remBox check box and connects the movie to a local SharedObject file named userData. The function then sets two data values, userName and userPassword, to the text within the userName_txt and userPassword_txt fields, respectively. If the text fields are empty, no data is stored.

Listing 11.1 storeData() **function**

```
function storeData(){
    //check the state of the remBox check box
    var isChecked = remBox.getValue();
```

Listing 11.1 storeData() **function** *(continued)*

```
        //check the contents of both Input text fields
        var isPopulated = (userName_txt.text != "" && userPassword_txt.text
        → != "") ? true : false;

        //connect to the local SharedObject named "userData"
        userData_so = SharedObject.getLocal("userData");

        //Create/set the value of a variable named "userName"
        //to the text within the userName_txt field
        userData_so.data.userName = (isChecked && isPopulated) ?
        → userName_txt.text : null;

        //Create/set the value of a variable named "userPassword"
        //to the text within the userPassword_txt field
        userData_so.data.userPassword = (isChecked && isPopulated) ?
        → userPassword_txt.text : null;

        //Create/set the value of a variable named "remember"
        //to the current value of the remBox check box
        userData_so.data.remember = isChecked;
}
```

Notice that the userData_so object has a data property. This property **must** be addressed to declare variables and other stored data in a SharedObject instance created in client-side ActionScript.

13. Save your Flash document and test it. Type a user name and password into the respective Input fields, select the check box, and click the Proceed button. On the start frame, click the Jump to login button. Notice that the text fields revert to their original empty state. What's happening? While the data is being stored to the SharedObject, there currently is not any code retrieving the data from the SharedObject to be redisplayed in the Input text fields. To see the current data in the SharedObject, re-test your movie with the Control > Debug Movie command. In the Debugger panel, click the Continue button (the green play arrow). Select the _level0 timeline in the panel, and click the Variables tab. At the end of the list, you should see the userData_so object. When you expand the listing, you will see the current values stored in the SharedObject (**Figure 11.6**).

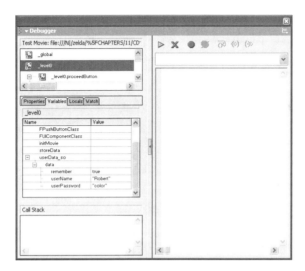

Figure 11.6 The Debugger panel shows you detailed information for variables within the Flash movie, including local `SharedObject` data.

14. Now, create a function named **checkData**. This function checks the contents of the `userData` local `SharedObject`. If the user enabled the `remBox` instance, the function retrieves the `userName` and `userPassword` values from `userData` and fills the Input text fields with the appropriate data. Select frame 1 of the actions layer, and add the code in **Listing 11.2** to the actions list:

Listing 11.2 checkData() **function**

```
function checkData(){

    //Create/connect to the local SharedObject named "userData"
    userData_so = SharedObject.getLocal("userData");

    //set a local variable named "isChecked" to the value of
    //the stored data named "remember"
    var isChecked = userData_so.data.remember;

    //if isChecked is equal to true
    if(isChecked){
```

Listing 11.2 checkData( ) **function** *(continued)*

```
            //set the text of the userName_txt field to the value
            //of the stored data named "userName"
            userName_txt.text = userData_so.data.userName;

            //set the text of the userPassword_txt field to the value
            //of the stored data named "userPassword"
            userPassword_txt.text = userData_so.data.userPassword;
        }

        //set the state of the remBox check box to
        //the value of isChecked (true or false)
        remBox.setValue(isChecked);
    }
    checkData();
```

15. Save your Flash document and test it. When you repeat the directions in step 13, the values you type in the Input text fields are retrieved whenever frame 1 of the movie plays. You can jump to the start frame and back to the login frame, and the values are retrieved. You can even close the Flash movie and re-test it, and the values will be displayed when frame 1 loads.

If you're curious to see the actual SOL file created by the Flash movie to store the local data, you can find the file in your operating system's preferences location. On Windows XP or 2000, you can find FSO files (listed by domain and filename of the SWF file that created it) in the following location:

```
C:\Documents and Settings\[Your User Name]\Application Data\Macromedia\Flash
Player\
```

If you're using Mac OS X, you can find SOL files in the following folder:

```
[Startup Disk]\users\[Your User Name]\Library\Preferences\Macromedia\Flash
Player\
```

Now that you have a basic understanding of how local SharedObject is stored and retrieved, you can explore the structure of remote SharedObject data within a FlashCom application.

Connecting to Remote SharedObject Data

Unlike local SharedObject data, which is stored on an individual user's machine as a SOL file, remote SharedObject data is stored within an application folder on a FlashCom server. By default, a remote SharedObject created within the default instance of an application is stored in a sharedobjects/_definst_ folder of the application folder. **Figure 11.7** shows a persistent remote SharedObject named announcement in an application named chat.

Figure 11.7 Remote SharedObject data is stored within FSO files on the FlashCom server.

In order to connect, send, and receive data with a remote SharedObject from client-side ActionScript, the following steps must occur:

1. A Flash movie creates a successful connection to the FlashCom application with a NetConnection object.

2. The movie then creates a client-side instance of the remote SharedObject, using the SharedObject.getRemote() method.

3. The client-side instance connects to the FlashCom application.

4. When the client-side instance of the remote SharedObject synchronizes with the actual data from the remote SharedObject on the server, data properties of the remote SharedObject can be accessed and changed.

In this section, you create a new application on your FlashCom server named chat and create a remote SharedObject named announcement within this application.

Note

The following steps assume that you are testing your Flash movie (SWF file) on the same server as your FlashCom server. You may need to change the URI used within `connect()` methods in order to make a successful connection to your installation of FlashCom server.

TO CONNECT A FLASH MOVIE TO A REMOTE SHAREDOBJECT:

1. On your FlashCom server, go to the `applications` directory. On a Windows server, the default development install location of this directory is

    `C:\Inetpub\wwwroot\flashcom\applications\`.

2. Create a new folder named **chat** within the `applications` folder.

3. Create a new Flash MX document in Macromedia Flash MX. Save the new document as `remote_so_100.fla`. If you are running your FlashCom server within the default `wwwroot` directory of Microsoft IIS, save the document to the same `chat` folder you created in step 2.

4. Rename Layer 1 to **actions**. Select frame 1 of this layer, and open the Actions panel (F9). Type the following code into the panel. You should already be familiar with creating connections to a FlashCom application as discussed in the previous chapter.

```
app_nc = new NetConnection();
app_nc.onStatus = function(info){
    if(info.code == "NetConnection.Connect.Success"){
        trace("---Successful connection to " + this.uri);
    } else if(info.code == "NetConnection.Connect.Failed"){
        trace("---No connection to " + this.uri);
    }
};
app_nc.connect("rtmp:/chat");
```

In the remaining steps, you create an Input text field into which you can type an announcement message. This message is stored in a remote SharedObject, and in the next section, you create a Flash movie that retrieves this information.

5. Create a new layer and name it **textfields**. On frame 1 of this layer, create a multiline HTML-enabled Input text field, capable of displaying at least five lines of text. Name this instance **announcement_txt** in the Property inspector (**Figure 11.8**).

Figure 11.8 Create an Input text field named announcement_txt.

6. Make a new layer and name it **storeButton**. On frame 1 of this layer, drag a PushButton component from the Components panel to the stage. Place the instance beneath the Input text field. In the Property inspector, name the instance storeButton. In the Parameters area of the inspector, specify a Label value of **Store Announcement** and a Click Handler of **storeData** (you define this function in step 10). Note that you may need to use the Free Transform tool to increase the width of the PushButton instance to correctly display the label.

7. Adjust the movie's code to disable or enable the storeButton, depending on the state of the connection to the FlashCom application. Select frame 1 of the actions layer, and insert the following highlighted code:

```
app_nc = new NetConnection();
app_nc.onStatus = function(info) {
```

```
  if (info.code == "NetConnection.Connect.Success") {
     trace("---Successful connection to " + this.uri);
     setupSO(this);
  } else if (info.code == "NetConnection.Connect.Failed") {
     trace("---No connection to " + this.uri);
     storeButton.setEnabled(false);
  }
};
storeButton.setEnabled(false);
app_nc.connect("rtmp:/chat");
```

In this revised code, a function named setupSO() is invoked when a successful connection is made to the chat application. This function is defined in the next step.

8. In the Actions panel code for frame 1 of the actions layer, add a few empty lines at the beginning of the existing code. On line 1, add the code in **Listing 11.3**, which defines the setupSO() function. This function creates a non-persistent remote SharedObject named announcement.

Listing 11.3 setupSO() **function**

```
1.  function setupSO(nc) {
2.     announcement_so = SharedObject.getRemote("announcement",
       →nc.uri, false);
3.     announcement_so.onSync = function(list) {
4.        trace("---announcement_so has synchronized");
5.        trace("The following list properties were returned:");
6.        for (var i in list) {
7.          for (var j in list[i]) {
8.             trace(i + ": " + j + " = " + list[i][j]);
9.          }
10.       }
11.       trace("---end synchronization messages");
12.    };
13.    announcement_so.connect(nc);
14.    storeButton.setEnabled(true);
15. }
```

In this code, several key concepts of remote SharedObject interactivity are introduced. In line 2, a connection is made to a remote SharedObject named announcement. The app_nc's connection URI (nc.uri) is referenced as the second argument of the getRemote() method. The third argument (false) specifies that the remote SharedObject is nonpersistent, which means that when the application unloads from the FlashCom server (that is, a short time after all users disconnect from the application), the announcement data is deleted.

Lines 3 through 12 set up an onSync() event handler for the announcement_so object. The onSync() handler is by far the most important handler that you can use with remote SharedObject data. This handler is invoked whenever the FlashCom server changes or updates data within the remote SharedObject. Any Flash movie (or user) that is connected to the same remote SharedObject receives this notification through the onSync() handler. The code in lines 4 through 11 simply send trace() messages to the Output window so you can see the changes that occur with this remote SharedObject. When the onSync() handler is invoked, an Array object is passed to the handler. Each index in the array represents a specific named data property within the remote SharedObject. The array element is actually an Object object with code, name, and oldValue properties.

Note   For more information on client-side remote SharedObject usage, refer to the Client-Side Communication ActionScript Dictionary PDF (named FlashCom_CS_ASD.pdf) on the Flash Communication Server MX installation CD-ROM. Alternatively, you can search for the term SharedObject in the Welcome to FlashCom HTML help pages (Window > Welcome to FlashCom) available in Macromedia Flash MX. Note that you must install the trial version, Personal, or Professional Edition of FlashCom on your computer to install the HTML help within Flash MX.

Line 13 establishes the connection to the remote SharedObject, using the reference to the app_nc (passed as the argument nc to the setupSO() function). You cannot make any changes or receive any updates to a remote SharedObject if you fail to make a connection to it on the FlashCom server.

Line 14 enables the storeButton instance on the stage. Remember, this instance was previously disabled. Once a successful connection is made with the app_nc object, a user can click the storeButton instance to make changes to the announcement remote SharedObject.

9. Save your Flash document and test it. If your Flash movie makes a successful connection to the chat application, you should see the following text
appear in the Output window:

```
---Successful connection to rtmp:/chat
---announcement_so has synchronized
The following list properties were returned:
0: code = clear
---end synchronization messages
```

The code string value of "clear" is returned to the onSync() handler of a
SharedObject instance when a Flash movie successfully connects to a nonpersistent remote SharedObject. "clear" can also be returned whenever all
the properties of a remote SharedObject have been deleted.

10. Now, you're ready to add the final function to this document: storeData(). This
function is already named as the click handler of the storeButton instance.
The purpose of this function is to copy the contents of the announcement_txt
instance to the remote SharedObject, announcement. Select frame 1 of the actions
layer, and define the following function after the setupSO() function:

```
function storeData() {
    announcement_so.data.message = announcement_txt.htmlText;
}
```

This function sets a message property within the announcement remote SharedObject to the text value of the announcement_txt instance. If you recall from
the previous section, the same data property must be addressed in the
client-side SharedObject instance in order to access properties of the actual
SharedObject on the server (or the user's machine).

11. Save your Flash document again and test it. You should see the same connect messages appear in the Output window (as shown in step 9). Now,
type some text into the announcement_txt field, and click the Store Announcement button. Once the FlashCom server receives the update, the following
additional text should appear in your Output window:

```
---announcement_so has synchronized
The following list properties were returned:
0: code = success
0: name = message
---end synchronization messages
```

Now, the `code` value returned to the first element (0) of the `list` array passed to the `onSync()` handler is `"success"`. This value is sent to the Flash movie that issued a change to a remote `SharedObject`. As you see in later examples, other Flash movies connected to the same remote `SharedObject` will receive the code value `"change"`. Furthermore, the first element of the `list` array has a `name` value of `"message"`, indicating the name of the property that was changed in the remote `SharedObject`.

12. To demonstrate how the `onSync()` handler interprets multiple changes, add a second Input text field to the document. On the textfields layer, create an HTML-enabled single line Input text field named **userName_txt**. Place this field between the `announcement_txt` field and the `storeButton` instance.

13. Go back to the `storeData()` function you defined in step 10. Add the following highlighted line of code to the function:

```
function storeData() {

    announcement_so.data.message = announcement_txt.htmlText;
    announcement_so.data.userName = userName_txt.htmlText;
}
```

This new line of code creates another property named `userName` in the remote `SharedObject`, announcement.

14. Save your document again and test it. Type some text into both text fields, and press the Store Announcement button. The following additional messages should appear in the Output window when the FlashCom server receives the updates:

```
---announcement_so has synchronized
The following list properties were returned:
1: code = success
1: name = userName
0: code = success
0: name = message
---end synchronization messages
```

As you can see, each property that was changed in the remote `SharedObject` is shown as a separate element (or index) within the `list` array returned to the `onSync()` handler. If you go back to the `announcement_txt` field and type some additional text into the field but leave the `username_txt` field as is, clicking the Store Announcement button results in the following messages in the Output window:

```
---announcement_so has synchronized
The following list properties were returned:
0: code = success
0: name = message
---end synchronization messages
```

This time, because the announcement_txt instance was the only field changed, the FlashCom server recognized that the userName property of the remote SharedObject remained unchanged. As such, the list array only reports the changed property name, "message".

You can find the completed document, remote_so_100.fla, in the chapter_11 folder of this book's CD-ROM.

You now understand how to connect to a remote SharedObject on a FlashCom server and how to change the properties of nonpersistent data. In the next section, you create a Flash document that displays the current values of the announcement remote SharedObject.

Synchronizing Data with Multiple Users

Once a Flash movie (or possibly server-side ActionScript code within a FlashCom application) creates and modifies information stored in a remote SharedObject, other Flash movies (or FlashCom applications) can be notified of the changes. In the following steps, you revise the Flash MX document from the previous section to retrieve information from a remote SharedObject.

Continue to use the same remote_so_100.fla document you created in the last section. You can also use the remote_so_100.fla file found in the chapter_11 folder of this book's CD-ROM.

TO RETRIEVE DATA FROM A REMOTE SHAREDOBJECT:

1. Open the remote_so_100.fla document in Macromedia Flash MX and re-save the document as **remote_so_retrieve_100.fla**.

2. For this movie, the storeButton instance and supporting ActionScript code can be removed. Delete the storeButton layer.

3. Select frame 1 of the actions layer, and open the Actions panel (F9). Delete the entire storeData() function. Remove the storeButton.setEnabled(false); lines of code from the actions list, found in the onStatus() handler for app_nc, the setupSO() function, and the code just before the app_nc.connect() method. Also, remove the storeButton.setEnabled(true); line of code within the setupSO() function.

4. Because this movie displays data from a remote SharedObject, change the Input text fields on the textfields layer to Dynamic text fields. Leave all other options with the text fields at the current settings.

5. Revise the setupSO() function to populate the correct TextField object with its matching data from the remote SharedObject. Add the following high-lighted lines of code to the setupSO() function:

```
function setupSO(nc) {
   announcement_so = SharedObject.getRemote("announcement", nc.uri,
   → false);
   announcement_so.onSync = function(list) {

      //debugging actions
      trace("---announcement_so has synchronized");
      trace("The following list properties were returned:");
      for (var i in list) {
         for (var j in list[i]) {
            trace(i + ": " + j + " = " + list[i][j]);
         }
      }
      trace("---end synchronization messages");

      //update TextField objects on the stage

      var listItems = list.length;

      for(var i = 0; i < listItems; i++){
         var name = list[i].name;
         var code = list[i].code;
         if(name == "message" && code == "change"){
```

```
        announcement_txt.htmlText = this.data.message;
      } else if(name == "userName" && code == "change"){
        userName_txt.htmlText = this.data.userName;
      }
    }
  };
  announcement_so.connect(nc);
}
```

The new `for` loop looks for specific name and code values. For example, when
the `name` value of one of the `list` elements is equal to `"message"`, and the `code`
value for the same element is equal to `"change"`, the `announcement_txt` field displays the HTML text stored in the `message` property of the `announcement` remote
`SharedObject`. The same operation is applied to the `userName_txt` field for
changes detected with the `userName` property of the `announcement` data.

Note

Objects within the `list` argument passed to a remote `SharedObject`'s `onSync( )` handler contain a `code` property. When you first synchronize a remote `SharedObject` without any data, the `code` property will report a `"clear"` value. However, if a persistent
remote `SharedObject` contains preexisting data (from a previous session), the `code`
property reports `"change"` during the first synchronization.

---

6. Save your document. Keep the current document open, and reopen the
original `remote_so_100.fla`. Choose File > Publish Preview > Default - (HTML)
to view the Flash movie in your default Web browser. When the Flash
movie loads, type some text into both Input text fields, and press the Store
Announcement button. Leave the Web browser window open, and switch
back to Flash MX. Choose the `remote_so_retrieve_100.fla` document. Test this
Flash movie using Control > Test Movie. As soon as the movie loads into
the Test Movie window, you should see the same text appear in the movie's
Dynamic text fields. If you go back to the Flash movie in the Web browser,
change the text in either field, and press the Store Announcement button,
the text in the other movie should update once again. You should also see
status messages in the Output window.

 You can find the completed document, `remote_so_retrieve_100.fla`, in the `chapter_11`
folder of this book's CD-ROM.

Because this example used a nonpersistent remote SharedObject, the data within the SharedObject is only stored within the application of the FlashCom server for the duration of the application session. By default, a FlashCom application instance unloads within 5 minutes from the time when the last client disconnects from the application instance. When the instance unloads, all nonpersistent remote SharedObject data is deleted. In the next section, you will learn how to enable a persistent remote SharedObject with the same example from this section.

Tip

FlashCom will delete idle application instances, shared objects, and streams at specific intervals. The process of removing these resources is called garbage collection. You can adjust the garbage collection time value (in minutes) within the <ApplicationGC> node of the server.xml configuration file, the time value (in minutes) within the <AppInstanceGC> node of the Vhost.xml document, and the idle time value (in seconds) within the <MaxAppIdleTime> node of the application.xml configuration file. These documents can be found in the conf folder of your FlashCom server installation directory. For a default installation of FlashCom on a Windows machine, use the following path:
C:\Program Files\Macromedia\Flash Communication Server MX\conf\.

Creating Persistent Remote SharedObject Data

As mentioned earlier, a remote SharedObject data can be stored indefinitely, if a *persistence* parameter in the SharedObject.getRemote() method is set to true. If you create a persistent remote SharedObject, you can access stored information from one application session to the next.

In this section, you modify the Flash MX documents created in the previous section to work with persistent data.

You can use the files you made in the previous section, or open the remote_so_100.fla and remote_so_retrieve_100.fla files from the chapter_11 folder of this book's CD-ROM.

TO CREATE PERSISTENT DATA WITHIN A REMOTE SHAREDOBJECT:

1. Open the remote_so_100.fla document, and resave it as **remote_so_101.fla**.

2. Select frame 1 of the actions layer and open the Actions panel (F9). In the setupSO() function, modify the following line of code:

   ```
   announcement_so = SharedObject.getRemote("announcement", nc.uri, true);
   ```

   Here, you change the *persistence* parameter from false to true. When the connection to the announcement SharedObject is made, the FlashCom server creates a permanent SharedObject file, named announcement.fso.

3. Save the document and test it. In the announcement_txt and userName_txt fields, type some text and press the Store Announcement button. The text within the fields is sent to the FlashCom application instance and stored in the announcement.fso file.

4. Close the remote_so_101.fla document, and open the remote_so_retreive_100.fla document. If you test remote_so_retrieve_100.fla, notice that the data you just stored is not loaded into the Flash movie— this version of the movie is looking for a nonpersistent remote SharedObject named announcement. In order to access the newly stored information, you need to change the SharedObject.getRemote() method in this movie as well.

5. Select frame 1 of the actions layer, and open the Actions panel (F9). Change the first line within the setupSO() function to:

   ```
   announcement_so = SharedObject.getRemote("announcement", nc.uri, true);
   ```

   Again, the *persistence* parameter is changed from false to true, in order to access the new persistent remote SharedObject named announcement.

6. Save your document as **remote_so_retrieve_101.fla** and test it. When the Flash movie loads, the text fields display the data you entered in step 3.

 You can find the completed files, remote_so_101.fla and remote_so_retrieve_101.fla, in the chapter_11 folder of this book's CD-ROM.

Try restarting your FlashCom server and loading the remote_so_retrieve_101.swf again. The same data is loaded into the text fields. Data within a persistent remote SharedObject is saved until you delete the FSO file stored in the application's sharedobjects folder, or until you create client-side or server-side Action-Script that deletes the data from the remote SharedObject.

PERSISTENT AND NONPERSISTENT REMOTE SHAREDOBJECTS

A persistent remote SharedObject has a separate namespace within a FlashCom application from a nonpersistent remote SharedObject. As such, it is feasible to have two remote SharedObjects with the same name within the same application instance. The following code creates a persistent and nonpersistent SharedObject named users, where app_nc represents a connection to the FlashCom application instance:

```
userStored_so = SharedObject.getRemote("users", app_nc.uri, true);
userStored_so.connect(app_nc);
userTemp_so = SharedObject.getRemote("users", app_nc.uri, false);
userTemp_so.connect(app_nc);
```

While each SharedObject must have a unique client-side instance name (such as user-Stored_so and userTemp_so), the two remote SharedObjects, the persistent users and the temporary users, exist separately within the FlashCom application instance. If possible, you should avoid using such a procedure to avoid confusion of the data that exists within each SharedObject.

Sharing Data Between Applications and Instances

You can also create remote SharedObject data in server-side ActionScript code, written in ASC files within each application on your FlashCom server. This functionality allows you to share stored data from one application (or application instance) with another application instance. For example, you could design a chat room application that needed to access an announcement message that's available for all instances of the chat room application. Therefore, when the specific instance of a chat room started, its server-side ActionScript code could connect to the default instance of the chat room application and retrieve the announcement message (**Figure 11.9**).

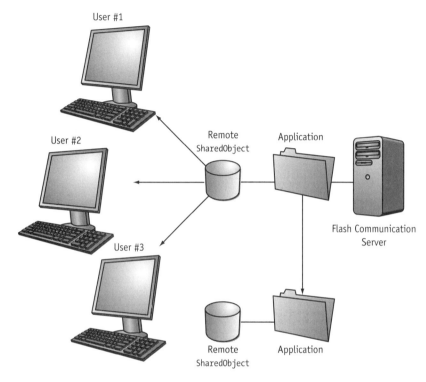

Figure 11.9 You can connect data from one application instance to another instance on the same (or different) FlashCom server.

Xref

In the "Utilizing Multiple Application Instances" section of this chapter, you will learn how to connect to one application instance's SharedObject data from another instance of the same application.

MAKING A BASIC CHAT APPLICATION

Of course, you can use remote SharedObject data for more than just simple announcement messages. Because you can synchronize remote SharedObject data with each connected client, you can use remote SharedObjects to broadcast messages in real-time. A perfect example of this functionality is a text chat application, where each connected user can see who's logged into the chat and can send text messages to the group of connected users. You will learn how to create a basic chat application in this section. Chat applications can be an effective low-bandwidth means of communicating with customers in a technical or customer support environment. With the help of Flash graphics and UI elements, you can create fun and easy-to-use applications that improve your customer's experience of your Web site and services.

Defining the Application

Before you begin to create the client-side and server-side files for the basic chat application, you should establish goals for the application:

- Allow each user to login to the application, specifying a preferred alias or name.

- If the user fails to provide a name, display an alert box providing more detailed instructions.

- Allow each user to connect to or disconnect from the application

- When the user connects to the application, update the list of users to show who's currently connected to the application.

- Allow each user to send a message to the group of connected users. This message can contain basic HTML markup tags for formatting or linking purposes.

- When a user enters a chat, display the current chat history in the new user's chat window.

- When a user leaves the chat, remove the user's name from the list of connected users.

In the following sections, you implement each of these goals, starting with the basic login interface.

Creating the Client-Side Login Elements

The first objective for the basic chat application is to design the login area of the Flash movie. Each user is required to specify a name, which is passed to the FlashCom application. In this section, you create an Input text field and the necessary functions to connect to the chat application.

Before you begin, make sure you have created a chat folder in your FlashCom's applications directory. Also, copy the following AS files from the chapter_10 folder of this book's CD-ROM to the location of your local FLA files: getMovieSize.as, movieclip_center.as, and showMessageBox.as.

TO CREATE A LOGIN FOR THE CHAT APPLICATION:

1. Create a new document in Macromedia Flash MX. Save the document as **basic_chat_100.fla**.

2. Rename Layer 1 to **textfields**. On frame 1 of this layer, use the Text tool to create a single line Input text field named **userName_txt**. Place the field in the top left corner of the stage. Add the Static text **Name:** to the left of the field, as shown in **Figure 11.10**.

Figure 11.10 Add an Input text field named userName_txt.

3. Create a new layer, and name it **connectButton**. On frame 1 of this layer, drag an instance of the PushButton component from the Components panel to the stage. Place the instance to the right of the userName_txt field. In the Property inspector, name the new instance **connectButton**. In the Label field, type **Connect**. In the Click Handler field, type **initConnect**. This button initializes the connection to the chat application on the FlashCom server.

4. Switch the view in the Components panel to the Flash UI Components Set 2. Drag an instance of the MessageBox component from the panel to the

stage. After an instance appears on the stage, delete the instance. The initConnect() function defined in the next step will dynamically attach an instance of the MessageBox symbol if the user fails to type a name into the userName_txt field.

Note

The MessageBox component was placed on the stage and then deleted in order to add the component to the movie's library, where it can be accessed via ActionScript code (as shown in the showMessageBox.as document). You cannot drag components from the Components panel directly to the Library panel.

---

5. Make another layer, and name it **actions**. Place this layer at the top of the layer stack. Select frame 1 of the actions layer, and add the code in **Listing 11.4**:

Listing 11.4 initConnect() **function**

```
1.   #include "showMessageBox.as"
2.   #include "getMovieSize.as"
3.   #include "movieclip_center.as"
4.
5.   function initConnect(obj) {
6.      var label = obj.getLabel().toLowerCase();
7.      if (label == "connect") {
8.         if (userName_txt.length > 0) {
9.            app_nc = new NetConnection();
10.           app_nc.onStatus = function(info) {
11.              var startPos = info.code.lastIndexOf(".")+1;
12.              var keyword = info.code.substr(startPos);
13.              if (keyword == "Success") {
14.                 trace("---Connected to " + this.uri);
15.                 initClient(this);
16.              } else if (keyword=="Failed" || keyword=="Closed") {
17.                 trace("---No connection to application");
18.                 closeClient();
19.              }
20.           };
21.           app_nc.connect("rtmp:/chat", userName_txt.text);
22.        } else {
23.           var title = "Missing Login Name";
24.           var message = "Please type your name in the Name field.";
25.           var icon = "warning";
```

Listing 11.4 initConnect() **function** *(continued)*

```
26.         var buttons = ["OK"];
27.         var buttonWidth = 100;
28.         var sizeW = 275;
29.         var sizeH = 125;
30.         var closeHandler = "focusField";
31.         showMessageBox(title, message, icon, buttons, buttonWidth,
            → sizeW, sizeH, closeHandler);
32.       }
33.    } else {
34.      app_nc.close();
35.    }
36. }
```

In lines 1-3, several AS files (explained in Chapter 10) are included with the frame actions. These files are necessary for the showMessageBox() function shown on line 31.

In the initConnection() function, the Flash movie establishes or breaks a connection with the chat application on the FlashCom server. As you have seen in past examples, the obj argument passed to this function represents a reference to the PushButton instance that invoked the function. In this case, obj represents the connectButton instance. In line 6, the label of the instance is retrieved. If the label is equal to "connect" (line 7) and the user-Name_txt field is not empty (line 8), the Flash movie creates a new connection to the chat application.

Notice in line 21 that the connect() method passes the text from the user-Name_txt field to the chat application. You can pass values to the application.onConnect() event handler within the server-side ActionScript code by specifying additional values after the rtmp URI in the connect() method. (You will learn more about this aspect of server-side coding in the next section.) If a successful connection is made (line 13), the initClient() function is invoked (discussed in step 6). If a connection fails or is closed by the user (line 16), the closeClient() function is invoked (line 18).

If the userName_txt field is empty, the else statement in lines 22-32 is executed. A MessageBox component instance is displayed, instructing the user to enter a name in the Name field (userName_txt). The MessageBox instance uses the function `focusField()` as a close handler. This function is discussed in step 7.

If the lowercase label of the `connectButton` is not "`connect`", then lines 33-35 execute. The label of the `connectButton` is switched to "`Disconnect`" in the `initClient()` function (step 6). When the user clicks the `connectButton` with a "`Disconnect`" label, the connection to the `chat` application is closed (line 34). When the `onStatus()` handler (lines 10-20) detects the "`Closed`" keyword, the `closeClient()` function is invoked (step 6).

6. Once a connection to the `chat` application is made, the `onStatus()` handler of the `app_nc` object invokes an `initClient()` function. For now, all this function needs to accomplish is to set the label of the `connectButton` to "`Disconnect`". Similarly, the `onStatus()` handler invokes the `closeClient()` function when the user presses the Disconnect button or when the movie fails to establish (or keep) a connection with the `chat` application. The `closeClient()` function resets the label of the `connectButton` instance to "`Connect`".

   In frame 1 of the actions layer, add the following functions after the existing code:

   ```
   function initClient(nc){
      connectButton.setLabel("Disconnect");
   }
   function closeClient(){
      connectButton.setLabel("Connect");
   }
   ```

7. In the same block of code, define the `focusField()` function, which is used as the close handler for the MessageBox component instance.

   ```
   function focusField(){
      userName_txt.text = "Type name here";
      Selection.setFocus(userName_txt);
      MovieClip.prototype.useHandCursor = true;
   }
   ```

   This function puts the text "`Type name here`" into the `userName_txt` field, and focuses the field for the user. Note that the `useHandCursor` prototype property is set back to `true` here as well. The `showMessageBox()` function (defined in the `showMessageBox.as` file) hides the hand cursor for all `MovieClip` objects.

8. Save your Flash document, and test it (Ctrl+Enter or Command+Enter). Type your name into the userName_txt field, and press the connectButton instance. If the connection is successful, the Output window displays the appropriate trace() message from the onStatus() handler.

You can find the completed document, basic_chat_100.fla, in the chapter_11 folder of this book's CD-ROM.

Right now, nothing terribly exciting is happening with either the client Flash movie or the chat application on the FlashCom server. In the next section, you will learn how to define the preliminary server-side ActionScript code for the chat application.

Setting Up the main.asc File

Once the Flash movie client interface has the login elements, you're ready to build the server-side ActionScript file (an ASC file) that loads when the user connects to the chat application.

DEFINING THE main.asc DOCUMENT

Whenever a FlashCom application loads, the FlashCom server looks for a file named main.asc in the application's directory. The main.asc file contains the initial server-side ActionScript code necessary for the application to perform. The main.asc file can also load other ASC files using the server-side ActionScript load() function.

ASC files can be created with any text editor. Of course, if you use Macromedia Dreamweaver MX, you enjoy the benefit of code hints and syntax coloring, just as you experience in Macromedia Flash MX.

Tip

Macromedia recommends that you save ASC files with UTF-8 text encoding. Most text editors, including Window's Notepad or Mac OS X's TextEdit, allow you to save a text file with UTF-8 encoding.

WORKING WITH THE Client AND Application OBJECTS

The primary objects that you use in server-side ActionScript code are the Client and Application objects. These objects allow you to retrieve and set information for each connected user (the Client object) and to describe how the FlashCom application behaves (the Application object).

Note There are several methods, properties and event handlers that can be used with the Client and Application objects. Throughout this book, you will learn how to employ many of these code features in your FlashCom projects.

DEFINING THE onAppStart() HANDLER

When the first user connects to a FlashCom application, the application.onApp-Start() handler within the main.asc file is invoked. In order for the chat application to function properly for multiple users, the following objectives need to be met:

- A nonpersistent remote SharedObject named users is created when the application loads. Each user's name and ID number (discussed next) are stored within this remote SharedObject.

- A base ID number is established. Each user is assigned a unique ID number in the onConnect() handler (discussed in the next section). The onAppStart() handler sets the starting value for the ID number. When each user connects, the value of the number increases.

Now, you're ready to create the onAppStart() handler in an ASC file.

Note While we recommend that you use Macromedia Dreamweaver MX for its ease of use, the following steps can be performed with any text editor.

TO CREATE THE onAppStart() HANDLER FOR THE CHAT APPLICATION:

1. In Macromedia Dreamweaver MX, choose File > New. In the New Document dialog box, choose Other in the Category pane and ActionScript Communications in the Other pane (**Figure 11.11**). A new ASC document will open, with the text // ActionScript Communications Document on line 1 of the document.

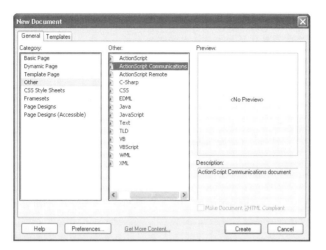

Figure 11.11 You can create specific document types in Dreamweaver MX.

2. Type the following code on lines 3 through 7:

```
3.  application.onAppStart = function(){
4.      trace("---chat instance " + this.name + " started");
5.      this.users_so = SharedObject.get("users", false);
6.      this.idNum = 0;
7.  };
```

Note

Do not type the line numbers into your actual code. The numbers shown here are references to the actual line numbers of the Dreamweaver document.

When the chat application loads, the trace() action outputs a message to the Live Log of the Communication App Inspector (discussed later in this chapter). This trace() action includes the specific instance name of the application (this.name, which represents application.name). Later in the chapter, you use named instances of the chat application to allow multiple chat rooms.

On line 5, a SharedObject instance named users_so is created within the scope of the application object. Note that the syntax for creating (or retrieving) a SharedObject in server-side ActionScript is different than client-side Action-Script—SharedObject.get() is used instead of SharedObject.getRemote().

Line 6 sets a variable named idNum to 0. As each user connects to the application instance, the value of idNum will increase. (The actual process of

incrementing the value occurs in the onConnect() handler, discussed in the
next section.)

3. Save your ASC file as **main.asc**, in the chat folder of your FlashCom's applications directory. Each FlashCom application can have its own main.asc file.
Leave the document open as you continue with the next section.

DEFINING THE onConnect() HANDLER

Once the chat application has initialized for the first time, the application is
ready to accept a connection from each user. In past FlashCom-enabled applications, no server-side scripting was necessary for the application's functionality.
If an application doesn't have a main.asc file and/or an application.onConnect()
handler, FlashCom automatically allows clients to connect to the application.
With the chat application, however, you want to keep track of each user that
connects. If you remember, the client-side ActionScript code passes the text
value from the userName_txt field to the chat application as a parameter. The following objectives will be met using the onConnect() handler:

- Apply the user's name to a Client object variable named userName.

- Assign a unique user ID to the client.

- Update the data within the users SharedObject (controlled via the users_so
  instance) with the user's unique ID and name.

- Allow the user to maintain a connection with the chat application.

In the following steps, you translate these tasks into specific server-side
ActionScript code.

TO IMPLEMENT THE ONCONNECT() HANDLER:

1. In the main.asc document you created in the last section, add the following
code to lines 9-15:

```
9.  application.onConnect = function(newClient, userName){
10.     newClient.userName = userName;
11.     newClient.id = "u" + this.idNum++;
12.     this.users_so.setProperty(newClient.id, userName);
13.     this.acceptConnection(newClient);
14.     trace("---Connected " + userName + ", id = " + newClient.id);
15. }
```

Line 9 declares the onConnect() handler for the application object. The first argument of the handler refers to an instance of the client object automatically passed to the handler. In this example, this parameter is named newClient. Any remaining parameters of an onConnect() handler refer to additional arguments that are passed to the application via the connect() method in the client-side ActionScript code. In this example, userName is a parameter that represents the text value of the userName_txt field.

Line 10 uses the userName value as the value of a property named userName in the newClient object.

Line 11 creates a unique ID string for the user (represented as the newClient object). Here, the current value of the idNum variable (declared in the onAppStart() handler) is concatenated with the letter "u". Therefore, the first user to connect to the application receives an idNum value of "u0". The value of idNum is then increased by 1. In this way, the next user that attempts a connection will receive a different ID string, such as "u1", "u2", "u3", and so on.

Line 12 creates a new property in the users SharedObject data, accessed through the users_so instance created in the onAppStart() handler. The new property has the same name as the unique ID created in line 11. The user-Name parameter is then used as the value of this new property. Note that the setProperty() method is used for server-side ActionScript code—you cannot use the data property of a SharedObject instance as you do in client-side ActionScript code. This same data, however, can (and will) be accessed in the Flash movie's client-side ActionScript code later in this example.

Line 13 allows the client to maintain a connection to the application instance. At this point, the Flash movie's onStatus() handler for the app_nc object receives the info.code value of "NetConnection.Connect.Success".

Tip

You can also deny a connection to a user by employing the rejectConnection() method of the Application object. For example, if you wanted to allow only five client connections, you could check the number of users stored within the users_so instance. If the number of users was less than five, then an allowConnection() method is used. Otherwise, the rejectConnection() method is used.

Line 14 passes the user's name and ID string to the Live Output window of the Communication App Inspector. You will learn how to monitor this information in the next section.

2. Resave your main.asc document. Make sure the document is being saved to the chat folder within your FlashCom applications directory.

 You can find the completed version of this file, main_100.asc, in the chapter_11 folder of the book's CD-ROM. If you want to use this file directly in your chat folder, you will need to rename a copy of this file to main.asc.

Now you're ready to test the server-side ActionScript code using the Communication App Inspector accessible from Macromedia Flash MX.

Using the Communication App Inspector

When you install Macromedia Flash Communication Server MX, the installer looks for a copy of Macromedia Flash MX on the system. If a copy is found, the installer adds new interface and help items to Flash MX. One of these enhancements is the Communication App Inspector, which can be opened by choosing Window > Communication App Inspector in Flash MX. This panel allows you to connect to a FlashCom server and monitor the connections, streams, and Shared Objects to any loaded application.

Tip

If you didn't install Flash Communication Server on the Windows machine that has your copy of Flash MX, you can run the FlashCom Server installer (or the trial installer) and choose the Custom install option to specify only the authoring components and help files. If you're using the Macintosh version of Flash MX, you can run the Flash-Com MX Authoring Installer located on the Flash Communication Server MX CD-ROM. If you don't have a purchased copy of FlashCom, refer to Appendix B for more information regarding Macintosh and the FlashCom server.

In the following steps, you will learn how to use the Communication App Inspector to monitor the trace() messages from the main.asc document you created in the last section.

To use the Communication App Inspector with your application:

1. After you have saved your main.asc document to the chat folder on your FlashCom server, go back to your basic_chat_100.fla document in Flash MX.

2. Open the Communication App Inspector by choosing Window > Communication App Inspector. The inspector displays in a detached window, as
shown in **Figure 11.12**. In the Host field, type the domain name of your
FlashCom server. If you have installed FlashCom on the same machine as
your Flash MX application, you can specify localhost. You also need to type
the user name and password that you supplied during the FlashCom
installation procedure. Select the Remember Connection Data and/or the
Automatically Connect check boxes if you'd prefer to store the information
and/or make a connection to your FlashCom server, respectively, each time
you open the inspector.

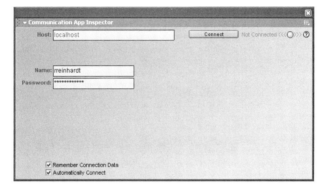

Figure 11.12 You can connect to your FlashCom server directly in Flash MX with the
Communication App Inspector.

Tip

The interface for the Communication App Inspector is actually a SWF file created by
Macromedia's engineering team. The SWF file makes use of the admin API Action-
Script for Flash Communication Server MX. For more information on the admin API,
read the Server Management ActionScript Dictionary PDF, available at
www.macromedia.com/support/flashcom/administration/admin_api_manual/.

3. Click the Connect button. Once a successful connection is made to the
server, the inspector displays the Active Application Instances list. In this
area of the inspector, you can view any FlashCom applications that are
currently running on the server. You can also invoke an application
instance in the App/Inst: field. Type the application name **chat** into this

field, and click the Load button (**Figure 11.13**). If the application is found, the default instance, chat/_definst_, displays in the Active Application Instances list (**Figure 11.14**). You can now monitor activity within this application instance of chat.

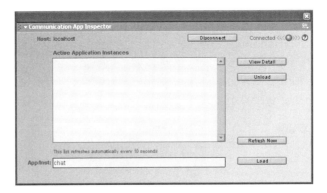

Figure 11.13 You can load a specific application by typing its name in the App/Inst: field of the Communication App Inspector.

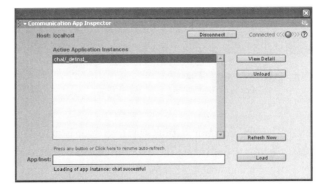

Figure 11.14 Once an application loads on the FlashCom server, its instance name is displayed in the Active Application Instances list.

4. With the chat/_definst_ item selected, click the View Detail button. Now, you can view information about the activity within the chat instance. Click the Shared Objects tab, and you should see the Shared Object named users, which you created in the onAppStart() handler of the main.asc document. Select the users list item to access its statistics. Currently, one user is connected to this remote SharedObject—the server application instance has initiated the Shared Object and is considered a user; no Flash client is actually connected to the application instance yet. Also, there isn't any data being stored within the Shared Object, as the Properties value reads 0 (**Figure 11.15**).

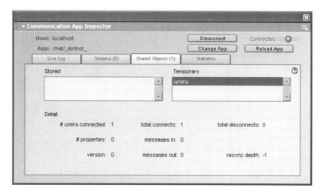

Figure 11.15 The Communication App Inspector allows you to access details for each SharedObject in the FlashCom application instance.

5. Leave the Communication App Inspector window open, and go back to the basic_chat_100.fla document. Choose Control > Test Movie and specify a user name in the userName_txt field. When you click the Connect button, the onConnect() handler of the chat application adds the user name as the value of a property named after the unique ID string assigned to the user. If you go back to the Communication App Inspector, the users SharedObject now shows a Properties value of 1. Note that the user count is still 1—the client-side code within the Flash movie does not specify a connection yet to the remote SharedObject.

6. Click the Live Log tab of the Inspector. You should see the trace() message from the onConnect() handler displayed, as shown in **Figure 11.16**. In order to see the trace() message from the onAppStart() handler, you need to reload the FlashCom application while you're viewing the application instance details in the Inspector. Click the Reload App button in the Inspector, and click OK in the Alert dialog box. When the application instance reloads, the Live Log displays server status messages along with the trace() message from the onAppStart() handler (**Figure 11.17**). If you look back at the SWF file shown in the Test Movie window, the client detects the broken connection to the

application and reverts the connectButton label to "Connect". The Output window should also display the trace() message from the onStatus() handler of the app_nc object.

```
---No connection to application
```

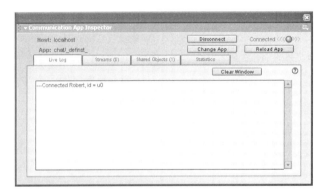

Figure 11.16 The Live Log tab displays the current trace() messages of the application instance.

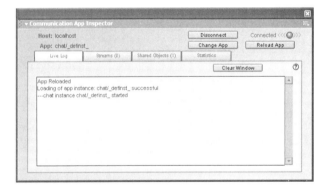

Figure 11.17 To view all of the trace() messages from the application instance, click the Reload App button in the Inspector.

You can continue to explore the Communication App Inspector as you build this example in the forthcoming sections. If you're experiencing difficulties with your server-side ActionScript code, the Inspector can help you debug the application.

USING THE NETCONNECTION DEBUGGER

You can also use the NetConnection Debugger to monitor connections between a Flash movie and a FlashCom application. On frame 1 of your Flash MX document, add the following action:

```
#include "NetDebug.as"
```

This directive tells Flash MX to include this AS file when the movie is tested or published. Make sure that you have installed the FlashCom authoring components and/or the Flash Remoting components for Flash MX before you attempt to use this directive.

Before you test your movie, choose Window > NetConnection Debugger to open its window. When you test the movie and make a connection to the FlashCom application, the NetConnection Debugger reports information related to the transaction in both the Summary and Details tabs. **Figure 11.18** shows the rtmp connection made from the basic_chat_100.swf client to the chat application.

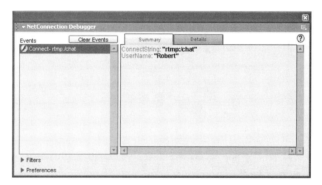

Figure 11.18 The NetConnection Debugger can be used to monitor the connection between a Flash movie and a FlashCom server.

Be sure to remove the #include "NetDebug.as" line from your document before you publish your final version of the movie. You should not include this code for a production-ready SWF file that you intend to upload to your Web server.

Constructing a List of Connected Users

Once the user connects to the chat application, the list of users currently logged into the chat should be visible. In this section, you access the remote SharedObject named users from client-side ActionScript code to build the list of users in a ListBox component instance.

To BUILD A LIST OF CONNECTED USERS:

1. Open the basic_chat_100.fla document you created in previous sections, and resave the document as **basic_chat_101.fla**.

2. Create a new layer, and name it **userList**. On frame 1 of this layer, drag an instance of the ListBox component from the Components panel to the stage. Place the instance to the left side of the stage, below the login elements. In the Property inspector, name this instance **userList**.

3. Select frame 1 of the actions layer, and open the Actions panel (F9). Add the following highlighted lines of code to the initClient() function:

```
function initClient(nc){

    connectButton.setLabel("Disconnect");
    users_so = SharedObject.getRemote("users", nc.uri, false);
    users_so.onSync = function(list) {
        userList.removeAll();
        for (var i in this.data) {
            userList.addItem(this.data[i]);
        }
    };
    users_so.connect(nc);
}
```

When the app_nc connects to the chat application, the initClient() function is invoked. At this point, the Flash movie can connect to the users remote SharedObject. More importantly, though, the onSync() method of the users_so instance updates the userList instance (the ListBox component) with the data from the users remote SharedObject. The addItem() method of the List-Box component allows you to add list items. In the loop, the variable i refers to all of the named properties within the users remote SharedObject. The value of each property (this.data[i]) is then added as a new list item.

Tip

You can also add further ListBox methods to the onSync() handler. For example, you can use the sortItemsBy() method to reorder the list items. The following line of code can be added after the for in loop of the onSync() handler to sort the users alphabetically:

```
userList.sortItemsBy("label", "ASC");
```

4. Save your Flash document, and choose File > Publish Preview > Default - (HTML) to view the Flash movie in your Web browser. When the Flash movie loads, type your name into the userName_txt field, and press the Connect button. When the Flash movie connects to the chat application, the client-side users_so instance synchronizes with the users SharedObject in the chat application, and the userList instance displays your name as a list item. Leave the Web browser window open, and go back to Flash MX. Use Control > Test Movie to view the SWF file. Type a different name into the userName_txt field, and press the Connect button. The userList instance displays both names, one from each connected Flash movie (**Figure 11.19**).

Figure 11.19 The userList instance displays the name of each connected user.

 You can find the completed file, basic_chat_101.fla, in the chapter_11 folder of this book's CD-ROM.

 At this point, the userList instance does not remove the names of users who disconnect from the application. In the "Cleaning Up the User List" section later in this chapter, you will learn how to update the userList instance whenever changes are made to the users_so remote SharedObject data.

Sending Text Messages among Clients

After each user has connected to the chat application, users should be able to communicate with each other by sending text messages to the group of connected users. There are a few ways broadcasted text messages can be sent to all connected clients in a FlashCom application. In this section, you will learn how to use the call() method of the client-side NetConnection object and a custom method of client-side SharedObject instances in order to send messages to connected users.

UNDERSTANDING THE call() METHOD OF NETCONNECTION OBJECTS

The call() method of the NetConnection object allows a Flash movie to invoke the named method of a Client object in server-side ActionScript code. By calling a server-side method, you can execute server-side ActionScript that returns or passes information back to the Flash movie that invoked the method, or send information to other Flash clients or FlashCom applications. For example, if you want to return a user's IP address to his Flash movie, you can call a method in server-side ActionScript to look up and return this information. First, you define a method for a Client object in the main.asc document of the FlashCom application. You can access the Client object in a variety of ways.

```
Client.prototype.getIP = function(){
   return this.ip;
}
or
application.onConnect = function(newClient){
   newClient.getIP = function(){
      return this.ip;
   };
   this.acceptConnection(newClient);
};
```

Both of these examples add a method named getIP() to a Client object that is accessible by a Flash movie's client-side ActionScript code. The following code can be added to a Flash movie to retrieve the user's IP address:

```
storeIP = new Object();
storeIP.onResult = function(ipNum){
   trace("The client's IP address is " + ipNum);
};
```

```
app_nc = new NetConnection();
app_nc.onStatus = function(info){
   if(info.code == "NetConnection.Connect.Success"){
      this.call("getIP", storeIP);
   }
};
app_nc.connect("rtmp:/chat");
```

When the call() method is invoked in the onStatus() handler of the app_nc
object, the getIP() method of the Client object is executed. The second
parameter of the call() method, storeIP, is a reference to the object whose
onResult() handler is invoked when the getIP() method returns data to the
Flash movie. In this example, the getIP() method returns the IP number to the
client. When the IP number information is received by the onResult() method
of the storeIP object, the IP number (represented by ipNum) is displayed in the
Output window.

Tip

Do not try to use the call() method in client-side ActionScript until a successful
connection has been made to the FlashCom application. If a Flash movie invokes a
call() method to a FlashCom application before a successful connection, the application will not receive the event.

In the basic chat example, you use the call() method to allow a user to send a
text message to all connected users of the application instance. Before you
tackle that code, though, you need to know how to use custom methods of
SharedObject instances. The call() method for the basic chat application will
work in tandem with a custom method of the users_so instance declared in
client-side ActionScript code.

Understanding Custom Methods of SharedObject Instances

Just as you can add custom methods to server-side Client objects, you can
add named methods to a SharedObject instance in either client- or server-side
ActionScript code. Instead of using the call() method to invoke these custom
methods, you use the send() method of the SharedObject class. For example, if
you want to display each user's name in the chat_txt field when each user connects to the chat application, you can use the send() method to inform each
client. The following code establishes a SharedObject instance named users_so,

which connects to a nonpersistent remote SharedObject named users and creates a method named displayUser():

```
users_so = SharedObject.getRemote("users", app_nc.uri, false);
users_so.displayUser = function(userName){
   chat_txt.htmlText += "<B>" + userName + "</B> has joined the chat.\n";
};
user_so.connect(app_nc);
```

The displayUser() method is only invoked when a client or application invokes a
send() method specifying "displayUser". The following code can be added to the
client-side ActionScript code when the Flash movie successfully connects to
the application:

```
app_nc = new NetConnection();
app_nc.onStatus = function(info){
   if(info.code == "NetConnection.Connect.Success"){
      users_so.send("displayUser", userName_txt.text);
   }
};
app_nc.connect("rtmp:/chat");
```

This example of the send() method passes the text from a text field named
userName_txt to the displayUser() method of each connected client. This text is
then handled as the userName argument of the displayUser() method. If a user
named Joe connects to the application, the displayUser() method adds the following HTML text to the chat_txt field:

Joe has joined the chat.

In the next section, you combine a call() method and a send() method to
notify all clients of a sent message.

ADDING THE ELEMENTS TO THE CLIENT MOVIE

You begin by adding new text fields to the Flash MX document, and adding
the call() and send() methods to the client-side ActionScript code.

Continue to use the basic_chat_101.fla document, which you created, in the previous section. You can also use the basic_chat_101.fla document located in the chap-
ter_11 folder of this book's CD-ROM.

To Construct the Chat Window:

1. Open the basic_chat_101.fla document, and resave the document as **basic_chat_102.fla**.

2. On the textfields layer, create a new Dynamic text field with the Text tool. Make this field large enough to accommodate several lines of text in order to display the chat messages sent among the connected users. Place this field to the right of the userList instance. In the Property inspector, name the TextField instance **chat_txt**, and enable the Selectable, HTML, and Show Border options (**Figure 11.20**). Choose Multiline in the Line type menu as well.

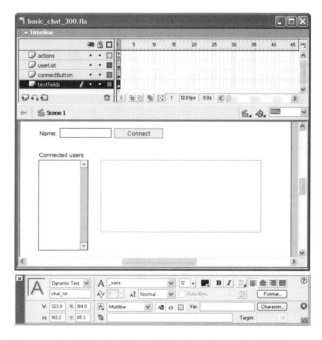

Figure 11.20 Create a Dynamic text field named chat_txt.

3. From the Components panel, drag an instance of the ScrollBar component to the right edge of the chat_txt instance. When you drop the instance on top of this edge, the ScrollBar instance should expand to the height of the text field. (If it doesn't, repeat the drag over the right edge of the field.) In the Property inspector, name this instance **chatScroller**.

4. Underneath the chat_txt instance, create a new Input text field with the Text tool. This field should only accommodate one line of text. In the Property inspector, name the instance **message_txt** and choose Single line in the Line type menu. Disable the HTML option, and enable the Show Border option (**Figure 11.21**).

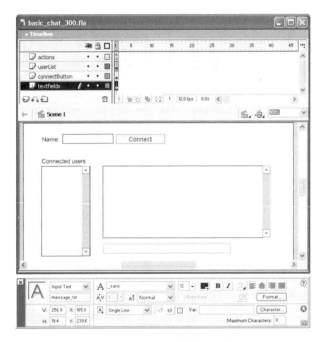

Figure 11.21 Add an Input text field named message_txt.

5. Create a new layer named **sendButton**. On frame 1 of this layer, drag an instance of the PushButton component from the Components panel to the stage. Place this instance to the right of the message_txt field. In the Property inspector, name the instance **sendButton**. In the Label field, type **Send**. In the Click Handler field, type **initMessage**. You can use the Free Transform tool to resize the width of the instance (**Figure 11.22**).

6. Now, you're ready to add the client-side ActionScript code to enable the items you just created. Select frame 1 of the actions layer, and open the Actions panel (F9). After the existing code, add the ActionScript code in **Listing 11.5**.

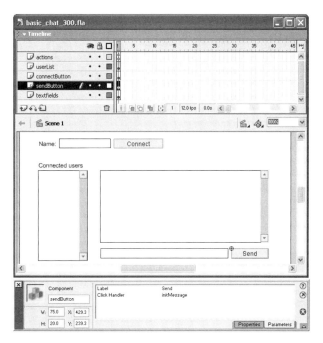

Figure 11.22 The sendButton instance allows the client to send a message to the Flash-
Com application instance.

Listing 11.5 initMessage() **function**

```
function initMessage(){
   if(message_txt.length > 0){
      trace("---Client called sendMessage() on server");
      app_nc.call("sendMessage", null, message_txt.text);
      message_txt.text = "";
   }
}
message_txt.onKeyDown = function(){
   if(Key.getCode() == Key.ENTER && this.length > 0){
      initMessage();
   }
};
Key.addListener(message_txt);
chat_txt.htmlText = "";
```

The initMessage() function is invoked when the user clicks the sendButton instance. If the user has typed some text into the message_txt field, a server-side method named sendMessage() is invoked, passing the text value from the message_txt field. For this operation, you specify a return object parameter of null—the sendMessage() method of a server-side Client object invokes a SharedObject send() method to broadcast the message to all connected clients.

Tip

You could also construct this example to work without a call() method, by using the send() method directly within the initMessage() function. In an effort to show you how application data can be accessed, though, we have combined both methods for this example.

An onKeyDown() method is also defined for the message_txt instance. If the user presses the Enter or Return key and has added some text to the message_txt field, the initMessage() function is invoked. With this listener in place, the user can press the Enter key to send messages, instead of clicking the sendButton instance.

7. Save your Flash document.

Currently, you can't test the functionality of the initMessage() function because you haven't defined the sendMessage() method of the server-side Client object. In the next section, you will learn how to create this method.

CREATING THE SERVER-SIDE sendMessage() METHOD

With the client-side code in place, you can now proceed to add the sendMessage() method to the server-side ActionScript code.

TO SEND MESSAGES FROM THE FLASHCOM APPLICATION:

1. In Macromedia Dreamweaver MX (or your preferred text editor), open the main.asc document located in the chat folder of your FlashCom applications directory.

2. Add the following highlighted code to the onConnect() handler:

```
application.onConnect = function(newClient, userName){

    newClient.userName = userName;
    newClient.id = "u" + this.idNum++;
```

```
     this.users_so.setProperty(newClient.id, userName);
     this.acceptConnection(newClient);
     trace("---Connected " + userName + ", id = " + newClient.id);

     newClient.sendMessage = function(msg){
        trace("--sendMessage() invoked on server by " + this.userName);
        msg = "<B>" + this.userName + ":</B> " + msg + "\n";
        application.users_so.send("receiveMessage", msg);
     };
}
```

The sendMessage() method is defined as a custom method of a Client object, represented by the newClient instance. The sendMessage() method uses one argument, msg, which represents the HTML text typed by the user in the message_txt field. The userName variable stored in the newClient object is appended in bold (<B></B>) to the value of msg, followed by a backslash pair, \n, for a new line. The value of msg is then specified as the argument of the receiveMessage() method, referenced in the send() method of the users_so object. Any client (or application instance) that has subscribed to the users remote SharedObject will receive the broadcasted message.

3. Save the main.asc document.

You can find this revision to the main.asc document in the main_101.asc document located in the chapter_11 folder of this book's CD-ROM.

You're nearly ready to test the new chat functionality of the Flash client. In the next section, you define the receiveMessage() method for the client-side instance of the users SharedObject, users_so.

CREATING THE CLIENT-SIDE receiveMessage() METHOD

When one user sends a message, invoking the sendMessage() method of the Client object in the FlashCom application, the receiveMessage() method of any SharedObject instance subscribed to the users remote SharedObject is invoked. In this section, you add the receiveMessage() method to the client-side Action-Script code.

To receive a message from the FlashCom application:

1. In the basic_chat_102.fla document, select frame 1 of the actions layer and open the Actions panel (F9). In the initClient() function, add the following highlighted code:

```
function initClient(nc){
    connectButton.setLabel("Disconnect");
    users_so = SharedObject.getRemote("users", nc.uri, false);
    users_so.onSync = function(list) {
        userList.removeAll();
        for (var i in this.data) {
            userList.addItem(this.data[i]);
        }
    };
    users_so.receiveMessage = function(msg) {
        chat_txt.htmlText += msg;
        updateScroll();
    };
    users_so.connect(nc);
}
```

When the receiveMessage() method is invoked, the msg text sent by the sendMessage() method is added to the existing contents of the chat_txt field as HTML text. The updateScroll() function, described in the next step, is then invoked to make sure the text is visible in the field.

2. After the last function declaration on frame 1 of the actions layer, add the updateScroll() function referenced in the receiveMessage() method.

```
function updateScroll(){
    chat_txt.scroll = chat_txt.maxscroll;
    chatScroller.setScrollTarget(chat_txt);
    chatScroller.setScrollPosition(chat_txt.maxscroll);
}
```

When the updateScroll() function is invoked, the scroll property of the chat_txt field is set to its maximum value, chat_txt.maxscroll. To make sure that the ScrollBar component instance (chatScroller) doesn't override this change, the scroll position of the chatScroller is set to the maxscroll value as well.

3. Save the Flash document. Before you test the client and server code, you may need to restart the chat application. Open the Communication App

Inspector. Once you log in to the server, if you see the chat/_definst_ instance listed in the Active Application Instances list, you need to select the instance and click the Unload button in the Inspector.

4. Run the Flash movie in two different locations to test the new chat functionality. Create the first client by choosing File > Publish Preview > Default - (HTML). When the Flash movie loads in a Web browser window, type a name into the userName_txt field and click the Connect button. Once the name appears in the userList instance, leave the browser window open and go back to Flash MX. There, choose Control > Test Movie to run another instance of the Flash movie. Repeat the same login procedure, specifying a different name. Now, type a message in the message_txt instance and click the Send button. The message should appear in the tested movie's chat_txt instance, preceded by that client's user name. Go back to your Web browser window. You should see the same text presented in that client's chat_txt instance as well. In the Web browser client, type a message in the message_txt field, and press the Enter (or Return) key. Again, the message should appear in both clients.

The completed document, basic_chat_102.fla, can be found in the chapter_11 folder of this book's CD-ROM.

Enabling a Chat History

When each user connects to the chat application, the user may be entering into a chat in progress, where other users have already messaged each other. In such a situation, it would be useful to keep a log of all of the current sessions' messages. These messages would then be sent to a client at the time of connect. In a previous section, you learned how to use the client-side call() method of the NetConnection object to invoke custom methods of the Client object in server-side ActionScript. In this section, you will learn how to do the exact opposite: use the server-side call() method of the Client object to invoke a custom method of a client-side NetConnection object. When a successful connection is made to the chat application, the chat_txt field is updated to show the current history of the chat.

MODIFYING THE SERVER-SIDE ACTIONSCRIPT CODE

You start by adding a new history property to the Application object. This history property stores each message that is sent by any user during the application session.

To add a history to the chat application:

1. Open the `main.asc` document in the `chat` folder of your FlashCom's applications directory. Add the following highlighted line of code to the `onApp-Start()` handler:

```
application.onAppStart = function(){
   trace("---chat instance " + this.name + " started");
   this.users_so = SharedObject.get("users", false);
   this.idNum = 0;
   this.history = "";
}
```

When the application instance first loads, the `history` property of the instance is set to an empty string.

2. Add the following highlighted lines of code to the `onConnect()` handler:

```
application.onConnect = function(newClient, userName){
   newClient.userName = userName;
   newClient.id = "u" + application.idNum++;
   this.users_so.setProperty(newClient.id, userName);
   this.acceptConnection(newClient);
   trace("---Connected " + userName + ", id = " + newClient.id);

   newClient.sendMessage =function(msg){
      trace("---sendMessage() invoked on server by " + this.userName);
      msg = "<B>" + this.userName + ":</B> " + msg + "\n";
      application.users_so.send("receiveMessage", msg);
      application.history +=msg;
   };

   newClient.call("receiveHistory", null, this.history);
}
```

When the client Flash movie invokes the `sendMessage()` method from the client-side `call()` method, the text from the user's `message_txt` field is passed as the `msg` argument. This argument, which is slightly modified in the `sendMessage()` method to include the user's name in bold formatting, is then added to the current value of the application instance's `history` property.

3. Save your `main.asc` document.

You can find this version of the `main.asc` document as `main_102.asc` in the `chapter_11` folder of this book's CD-ROM. If you want to use this file in your application, make a copy of it to the `chat` folder of your FlashCom's `applications` directory, and rename the file `main.asc`.

INITIALIZING THE HISTORY FOR EACH CLIENT

Now that the application instance is keeping track of the chat history, you can enable the Flash movie to access this stored history when the client connects to the application instance.

Continue to use the `basic_chat_102.fla` document you created in previous sections of this chapter. You can also find this file in the `chapter_11` folder of this book's CD-ROM.

TO INITIALIZE A CLIENT'S HISTORY:

1. Open the `basic_chat_102.fla` document, and resave the document as **basic_chat_103.fla**.

2. Select frame 1 of the actions layer, and open the Actions panel (F9). In the `initConnect()` function, add the following highlighted code. Note that only the first half of the function is shown and the `onStatus()` code is truncated; the remaining code in the function remains unchanged.

```
function initConnect(obj) {
    var label = obj.getLabel().toLowerCase();
    if (label == "connect") {
        if (userName_txt.length > 0) {
            app_nc = new NetConnection();
            app_nc.onStatus = function(info) {
                ...
            };
            app_nc.receiveHistory = function(history){
                chat_txt.htmlText = history;
                updateScroll();
            };
            app_nc.connect("rtmp:/chat", userName_txt.text);
        } else {
            ...
```

When the server-side call() method is invoked in the onConnect() handler, the receiveHistory() method is specified. At this time, the new client's receiveHistory() method of the app_nc object is invoked. The history argument represents the value of the history property stored within the application instance. This htmlText property of the chat_txt is set to this value, and the updateScroll() function (described in a previous section) refreshes the chat_txt field to make sure the last entries are visible.

Tip

When a Client object's call() method specifies a method name, only the current client receives the message from the server. In this way, the call() method of the Client object differs from the send() method of a SharedObject, in which all connected users receive the same broadcast.

3. Save your Flash document. Prepare the client for testing by checking the chat application status in the Communication App Inspector. If an instance is running, unload it. Then, repeat the procedure of testing the client and application functionality in a Web browser window and a Test Movie window. Before you connect with a second client, send a message from the first client. When you connect with another client, the history of the chat should appear in the chat_txt field.

The completed document, basic_chat_103.fla, can be found in the chapter_11 folder of this book's CD-ROM.

Cleaning Up the User List

The last objective for the basic chat application is to notify the users remote SharedObject when a user leaves the chat. The user's unique ID string should be removed from the SharedObject. When this removal occurs, the users_so instance within the remaining connected clients will automatically synchronize and update the items in the userList instance.

To remove a disconnected user from the SharedObject:

1. In Dreamweaver MX, open the main.asc document in the chat folder of your FlashCom's applications directory.

2. Add the following onDisconnect() handler after the existing code:

Caution

Do not put this code within the onAppStart() or onConnect() handlers. The onDisconnect() handler should be defined as soon as the application instance loads the main.asc document. If you created the onDisconnect() handler within another handler, there's a good chance the method would not be available when the client actually disconnects.

```
application.onDisconnect = function(oldClient){
    trace("---Disconnected " + oldClient.userName + ", id = " +
    ➝ oldClient.id);
    this.users_so.setProperty(oldClient.id, null);
};
```

The onDisconnect() handler is invoked when the user clicks the Disconnect button, which invokes the app_nc.close() method. The trace() message is displayed in the Live Log of the Communication App Inspector (if open). The user's id value, specified as a named property of the users remote SharedObject, is set to null. A value of null deletes the property from the SharedObject.

3. Save the main.asc document.

4. Open the basic_chat_103.fla document in Macromedia Flash MX. Resave the document as **basic_chat_104.fla**.

If you did not complete the basic_chat_103.fla document in the previous section, you can find the same file in the chapter_11 folder of this book's CD-ROM.

5. Because the Flash client-side ActionScript code already detects changes to the users SharedObject (via the users_so instance), you don't need to add any additional code to the onSync() handler of the users_so instance. However, you do need to clear the userList instance when the client disconnects—the disconnected user should no longer see the list of connected users. Select frame 1 of the actions layer, and open the Actions panel (F9). Add the following highlighted line of code to the closeClient() function:

```
function closeClient(){
    connectButton.setLabel("Connect");
    userList.removeAll();
}
```

6. Save your Flash document. Reload the chat application (if necessary) in the Communication App Inspector. Proceed to test the client and application functionality with a Web browser window and a Test Movie window. Login with each client, and send a message from each client. Then, click the Disconnect button within one of the clients. That client should disconnect from the chat application, and the userList instance should no longer display any connected users. In the remaining connected client(s), the userList instance should update its items to show only the connected user(s).

 You can find the completed document, basic_chat_104.fla, in the chapter_11 folder of this book's CD-ROM. You can also find the revisions to the main.asc document in the main_103.asc document of the same folder.

Once you complete this section, you have finished the basic chat application. You can continue to work on the Flash client movie, adding enhanced graphics and fonts to suit the style or branding for a project.

UTILIZING MULTIPLE APPLICATION INSTANCES

Many chat applications have the capability to segregate discussions into distinct groups, usually called chat rooms. As discussed previously, a FlashCom application runs as an instance on the server. If you do not specify an application instance name when you connect to an application from a Flash movie, FlashCom creates a default instance of the application named _definst_. You have already seen this instance name in the Communications App Inspector, with your previous basic chat application.

You can, however, name a specific instance of a FlashCom application in the connect() method of a NetConnection object by adding a forward slash (/) and a string value after the application's name in the URI parameter. The following code connects to an instance named general of the chat application:

```
app_nc = new NetConnection();
app_nc.connect("rtmp:/chat/general", userName_txt.text);
```

 For demonstration purposes, the onStatus() handler for the app_nc object has been omitted. Always include an onStatus() handler for every NetConnection object.

You can pass additional parameters, such as userName_txt.text, to application instances, just as you did with the default instance in previous exercises. The relationship between an application instance and the default application instance is very similar to the relationship between a MovieClip instance and its parent symbol in the Flash library. Every application instance inherits the same characteristics of the default instance. As such, all of the code from the main.asc document for an application is invoked for every instance of the application. Each instance, however, has its own scope on the FlashCom server, just as one MovieClip instance's characteristics are unique and separate from another MovieClip instance of the same symbol.

In the next section, you will learn how to create new application instances of the chat application.

Specifying an Application Instance

To add the capability of connecting to a named instance of the chat application, you will add an interface element, an Input text field, to the Flash movie that allows the user to type a specific instance name (or room name). The text value of this field is then used as the application instance name in the URI of the connect() method for the app_nc object.

Continue to use the basic_chat_104.fla document, which you created earlier in this chapter. You can also find this file in the chapter_11 folder of this book's CD-ROM.

To CONNECT TO A SPECIFIC INSTANCE OF THE CHAT APPLICATION:

1. Open the basic_chat_104.fla document, and resave it as **multiroom_chat_100.fla**.

2. On frame 1 of the textfields layer, duplicate the userName_txt field (Edit > Duplicate) and name the new instance **roomName_txt** in the Property inspector. Place this instance directly below the userName_txt field, and add the Static text **Room:** to the left of the field. You may need to move the other items on the stage in order to accommodate the new text field (**Figure 11.23**).

3. Select frame 1 of the actions layer, and open the Actions panel (F9). Add the following highlighted lines of code to the initConnect() function. Note that some of the code from this function has been omitted from the following listing, as indicated with the "..." characters.

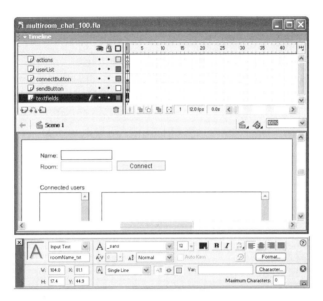

Figure 11.23 The user can specify a room name in the roomName_txt field.

Note

Be sure to **replace** the existing app_nc.connect("rtmp:/chat", userName_txt.text);
line with the app_nc.connect(appInstance, userName_txt.text); line shown in the following code.

```
function initConnect(obj) {
    var label = obj.getLabel().toLowerCase();
    if (label == "connect") {
        if (userName_txt.length > 0) {
            app_nc = new NetConnection();
            app_nc.onStatus = function(info) {
                ...
            };
            app_nc.receiveHistory = function(history){
                ...
            };
            var appURI = "rtmp:/chat/";
            var appInstance = (roomName_txt.length > 0) ? appURI +
            ➞ roomName_txt.text : appURI;
            app_nc.connect(appInstance, userName_txt.text);
        } else {
            ...
```

This code creates a local variable named appURI, which stores the path to the default instance of the chat application. If the user typed some text into the roomName_txt field, the text value from the field is concatenated to the appURI value, and set as the value of a local variable named appInstance. If the user left the field empty, the value of appInstance is set to the value of appURI. appInstance is then used as the URI of the connect() method for the app_nc object.

4. Save your Flash document, and open the Communication App Inspector. Log in to your FlashCom server to view the Active Application Instances list. Leave the Inspector open, and test the movie. Type a user name and a room name into the respective fields, and click the Connect button. The Inspector displays the new instance of chat in the list (**Figure 11.24**).

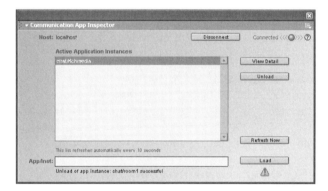

Figure 11.24 The Communication App Inspector displays the
new application instance name.

The completed document, multiroom_chat_100.fla, can be found in the chapter_11 folder of this book's CD-ROM.

For this example, no changes were necessary for the main.asc document of the chat application. You can run several Flash clients with this current example, each connecting to specific chat instances (or chat rooms). The discussion from one chat instance cannot be viewed from another chat instance.

Tracking Active Application Instances

The Flash client can now connect to a specific instance of the chat application. However, how will a user know which chat rooms are currently available? Will the user need to create a new room for others to join, or have other users

already gathered in a certain room? In this section, you create a new remote
SharedObject that is stored in the default instance of the chat application. A connection to this new SharedObject is made as soon as the Flash client loads, and
the SharedObject reports all of the currently active instances for the chat application. To do this, you modify the main.asc code for the chat application.

Continue to modify the existing main.asc document that you created in previous sections. You can also use the main_103.asc document from the chapter_11 folder of this
book's CD-ROM.

To track active application instances:

1. Open the main.asc document in Dreamweaver MX or your preferred text editor.

2. Add the following highlighted code to the onAppStart() handler of the
   application object:

   ```
   application.onAppStart = function(){
      trace("---chat instance " + this.name + " started");
      this.users_so = SharedObject.get("users", false);
      this.idNum = 0;
      this.history = "";

      if(this.name.toLowerCase().indexOf("_definst_") == -1){
         this.trackInstance();
      }
   };
   ```

   This new code checks the lowercase name of the application instance for the
   text "_definst_". Only the default instance name contains this text string. If
   the application instance is not the default instance, the instance name
   should be stored in a new remote SharedObject. The trackInstance() method of
   the Application object, discussed in the next step, performs this task.

3. After the onDisconnect() handler in the main.asc document, add the code in
   Listing 11.6. Note that the line numbers are relative to this code alone, not
   to the entire main.asc document.

The placement of the trackInstance() method can occur anywhere within the
main.asc document. For organizational purposes, custom methods of the application
object are declared after the event handler methods of the application object.

Listing 11.6 trackInstance() **function**

```
1.  application.trackInstance = function(){
2.    trace("--trackInstance() invoked from " + this.name);
3.    this.default_nc = new NetConnection();
4.    this.default_nc.onStatus = function(info){
5.      if(info.code == "NetConnection.Connect.Success"){
6.        trace("---Connected to default instance");
7.        application.rooms_so = SharedObject.get("rooms", false,
      → this);
8.        application.rooms_so.onSync = function(list){
9.          for(var i in list){
10.            if(list[i].code == "clear"){
11.              var startPos = application.name.indexOf("/")+1;
12.              application.instanceName =
              → application.name.substr(startPos);
13.              this.setProperty(application.instanceName,
              → "active");
14.            }
15.          }
16.        };
17.      } else if (info.code == "NetConnection.Connect.Failed"){
18.        trace("---No connection to default instance");
19.      }
20.    };
21.    this.default_nc.connect("rtmp://myFlashComServer.com/chat");
22. };
```

This method creates a server-side NetConnection object named default_nc (line
3). This object connects to the default instance of the chat application (line
21). More importantly, though, this connection allows a specific application
instance to access data that is stored in the default instance of the chat
application. Specifically, in lines 7-16, a server-side SharedObject instance
named rooms_so connects to a nonpersistent remote SharedObject named
rooms, located in the default instance. When a Flash client creates a new
instance of the chat application, the trackInstance() method stores the
instance's name in the rooms remote SharedObject (line 13). Note that lines 11
and 12 locate the actual instance name within the complete name of the
application instance. The name property of the application object returns the
application's name followed by a forward slash and the instance name, such
as "chat/room1". Because the rooms SharedObject data will be used to show the
active rooms (or instances) to the user, the "chat/" prefix is removed.

You must modify line 21 to include the complete URI to your FlashCom server. You cannot use relative URI references in the server-side NetConnection object's connect() method. For example, the following URIs will **not** work:

```
rmtp:/chat
rtmp://localhost/chat
```

You need to include the FlashCom's domain name or IP address in the URI, such as rtmp://fcs.mxbook.com/chat or rtmp://127.0.0.1/chat.

4. The application instance should also remove its name from the rooms SharedObject data after the last user has left that chat room. You can use the onDisconnect() event handler of the application object to invoke server-side ActionScript code when the last client (that is, user) disconnects from an application instance. Add the following highlighted code to the onDisconnect() method of the main.asc document.

```
application.onDisconnect = function(oldClient){
    trace("---Disconnected " + oldClient.userName + ", id = " +
    ➝oldClient.id);
    this.users_so.setProperty(oldClient.id, null);
    if(this.clients.length == 0 &&
    ➝this.name.toLowerCase().indexOf("_definst_") == -1){
        this.removeID = setInterval(this.removeInstance, 60000);
    }
};
```

This code works in a similar fashion to the onAppStart() method additions in step 2. If there are no other clients connected to the application instance and the application instance's lowercase name does not contain the text "_definst_", the setInterval() function invokes a method named removeInstance() of the application object 60 seconds after the last user disconnects. The removeInstance() method is described in the next step.

Tip

An application instance typically unloads within 3 to 5 minutes from the time when the last client disconnects from the application instance. While you can adjust the timeout of the setInterval() function to your preferred wait time, make sure this time does not exceed the unload interval. When the wait time is reached, the application instance name is removed from the rooms SharedObject data. For more information about unloading of application instances, refer to the earlier note at the end of the "Synchronizing Data with Multiple Users" section earlier in this chapter.

5. After the `trackInstance()` method, add the following code.

```
application.removeInstance = function(){
   trace("---removeInstance() invoked from " + this.name);
   application.rooms_so.setProperty(application.instanceName, null);
   clearInterval(application.removeID);
};
```

This code addresses the same property of the `rooms_so` instance created in the `trackInstance()` method. Here, however, the `instanceName` property is set to `null`, which deletes the instance's name from the `rooms` remote `SharedObject`. The `clearInterval()` function stops the `setInterval()` function, identified by `removeID`, from invoking further iterations.

6. Save your `main.asc` document.

You can find these revisions to the `main.asc` document in the `main_104.asc` document in the `chapter_11` folder of this book's CD-ROM. If you use this document, make sure to change the URI of the `default_nc` NetConnection object to reflect the IP address or domain name of your FlashCom server.

You can test this code in the Communication App Inspector in Flash MX. After you have logged in to your FlashCom server, you can specify an instance name in the App/Inst: field of the Inspector. For example, if you type **chat/room1** in this field and click the Load button, the FlashCom server creates an instance named room1 of the chat application (`chat/room1`). You can view the instance's details to see its connection to the `rooms` remote `SharedObject`. If you want to see all of the `trace()` messages from the code you created in this section, click the View Details button with the instance name selected. In the details section of the Inspector, click the Reload button. The Live Log now displays all of the `trace()` messages from the `main.asc` document.

Tip

When you load the named instance of the `chat` application, you will also see the `chat/_definst_` instance appear in the Active Application Instances list. Remember, the named instance creates a new `NetConnection` object that connects to the default instance. As such, you will see two instances display in the Inspector.

Displaying Active Application Instances in the Client

Once each chat instance registers its name into the `rooms` remote `SharedObject`, you can enable the Flash client to display the list of instances to the user. The user should be able to see this list before the user actually connects to a specific room; as such, a separate NetConnection object is made to connect to the rooms SharedObject. In this section, you create the interface elements and client-side ActionScript code necessary to tap the data from the rooms SharedObject.

Continue to use the multiroom_chat_100.fla document you created earlier in this chapter. You can also find this file in the chapter_11 folder of this book's CD-ROM.

To DISPLAY ACTIVE APPLICATION INSTANCES:

1. Open the multiroom_chat_100.fla document in Flash MX, and resave this document as **multiroom_chat_101.fla**.

2. Create a new layer and name it **roomList**. On frame 1 of this layer, drag an instance of the ComboBox component from the Components panel to the stage. In the Property inspector, name this instance **roomList**. On the textfields layer, add the Static text **Active Rooms:** above the instance. You may want to edit and reorganize the other text fields, as shown in **Figure 11.25**.

Figure 11.25 The data from the rooms remote SharedObject will populate the roomList instance with label names.

3. Select frame 1 of the actions layer, and open the Actions panel (F9). After the last function declaration, add the following getRooms() function:

```
function getRooms(){
    default_nc = new NetConnection();
    default_nc.onStatus = function(info){
        if(info.code == "NetConnection.Connect.Success"){
            trace("---Connected to default instance");
            rooms_so = SharedObject.getRemote("rooms", this.uri);
            rooms_so.onSync = function(list){
                roomList.removeAll();
                for(var i in this.data){
                    roomList.addItem(i);
                }
            };
            rooms_so.connect(this);
        } else if(info.code == "NetConnection.Connect.Failed"){
            trace("---No connection to default instance");
        }
    };
    default_nc.connect("rtmp:/chat");
}
```

This function creates a new NetConnection object named default_nc, and it performs the same task as the default_nc server-side object created in the chat application's main.asc document. This connection uses the default instance URI ("rtmp:/chat") to access the rooms remote SharedObject, which tracks all of the chat instance names. Whenever a new instance name is added to this SharedObject, the onSync() handler of the rooms_so instance is invoked, passing all of the room's property names to the roomList instance.

Tip

In this example, you do **not** want to retrieve the value of each named property in the SharedObject. The names of each property are the labels you want to display to the connected user.

4. Once the getRooms() function is defined, the Flash movie needs to invoke the function as soon as the movie loads. (The Connect button in the user interface is used to connect to a specific instance of chat, not necessarily the default instance.) At the end of the actions list for frame 1 of the actions layer, add the following code:

```
getRooms();
```

5. Save your Flash document, and test it (Ctrl+Enter or Command+Enter). As soon as the movie loads, the Output window should display the trace() message indicating a successful connection to the default instance of the chat application. Type a user name and a room name in the respective fields, and click Connect. The roomList instance should automatically display the new chat instance name (**Figure 11.26**).

 You can find this version of the Flash client, multiroom_chat_101.fla, in the chapter_11 folder of this book's CD-ROM.

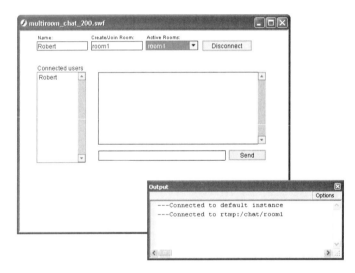

Figure 11.26 The roomList instance displays the name of the room to which you are connected. As other users create new rooms, other names will populate the list.

Connecting to a Specific Application Instance

While the roomList instance of the ComboBox component displays the current list of rooms (or chat instances), selecting a room name in the combo box does not connect the user to the chosen room. In this section, you finish the multiroom chat application by enabling elements within the interface.

 Continue to use the multiroom_chat_101.fla document from the last section. You can also find this file in the chapter_11 folder of this book's CD-ROM.

To CONNECT THE CLIENT TO A SPECIFIC APPLICATION INSTANCE:

1. Open the `multiroom_chat_101.fla` document in Flash MX, and resave the document as **`multiroom_chat_102.fla.`**

2. On the textfields layer, create a Dynamic text field named `currentRoom_txt`. This field is used to display the name of the chat room that a user joins. Add the Static text **Current room:** to the left of the field, as shown in **Figure 11.27**. You may need to move other interface elements on the stage to accommodate these new text fields.

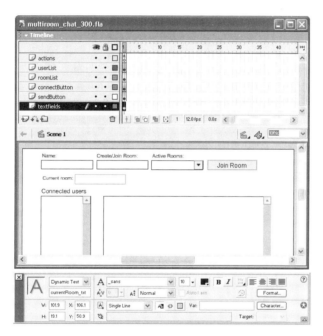

Figure 11.27 The `currentRoom_txt` field displays the current instance name of the chat application.

3. Select the `roomList` instance on the stage, and open the Property inspector. In the Change Handler field, type **setRoom**. The `setRoom()` function is discussed later in step 5.

4. Select the `connectButton` instance. In the Property inspector, change the Label field to **Join Room**. This text makes the functionality of the button clearer to the user.

5. Now you're ready to modify the client-side ActionScript code in order to add more functionality to the Flash movie. Start by creating the setRoom() function. This function is used as the new change handler for the roomList instance. Select frame 1 of the actions layer, and open the Actions panel (F9). Insert the code in **Listing 11.7** after the getRooms() function.

Listing 11.7 setRoom() **function**

```
1.  function setRoom(obj){
2.      var label = obj.getSelectedItem().label;
3.      if(label != roomName_txt.text){
4.          if(app_nc.isConnected){
5.              trace("---New room name selected while connected to
                → another room");
6.              var title = "Join another chat room?";
8.              var message = "You have selected a new chat room. Click
                → the \"Switch Rooms\" button to join a new room, or
                → click the \"Don't switch\" button to stay in the
                → current room.";
9.              var icon = "warning";
10.             var buttons = ["Switch rooms", "Don't switch"];
11.             var buttonWidth = 100;
12.             var sizeW = 320;
13.             var sizeH = 225;
14.             var closeHandler = "switchRooms";
15.             showMessageBox(title, message, icon, buttons, buttonWidth,
                → sizeW, sizeH, closeHandler);
16.         } else {
17.             roomName_txt.text = label;
18.             initConnect(connectButton);
19.         }
20.     }
21. }
```

When the user chooses an item in the roomList instance, the setRoom() function is invoked. The obj argument of this function represents an object reference to the roomList instance. In line 3, the chosen item's label value is compared to the text value of the roomName_txt field. If the text and the label do **not** match, then lines 4-19 are executed. If the values do match, then nothing happens when the user chooses an item in the roomList instance. In line 4, the isConnected property of the app_nc object is tested. If isConnected is true, the user is already connected to another chat instance and is attempting to switch rooms. Lines 5-15 set up the parameters for a MessageBox instance, just as you have done in previous exercises and chapters. Here, the user is warned that the user is about to leave the current chat room. The MessageBox instance presents two buttons, one, labeled "Switch rooms" and another labeled "Don't switch." When the user clicks either button, the switchRooms() function is invoked. The switchRooms() function is set as the close handler for the MessageBox instance in line 14, and is discussed in step 6.

If the user is not currently connected to a chat instance, lines 16-19 execute. Here, the roomName_txt field displays the chosen label name (line 17). In line 18, the initConnect() function is invoked, passing an object reference to the connectButton instance. In this manner, the initConnect() function executes as if the user clicked the connectButton instance directly.

6. Now define the switchRooms() function. This function is the close handler for the MessageBox instance displayed to the user if the user is already connected to a chat room when an item is selected in the roomList instance. Add the following code after the setRoom() function declaration:

```
function switchRooms(messageBox, buttonIndex){
    if(buttonIndex == 0){
        app_nc.close();
        roomName_txt.text = roomList.getSelectedItem().label;
        initConnect(connectButton);
    }
    MovieClip.prototype.useHandCursor = false;
}
```

The switchRooms() function is passed two arguments from the MessageBox instance: an object reference to the MessageBox instance itself and the index number of the button in the MessageBox instance that was clicked by the user. If the user pressed the button labeled "Switch rooms," the buttonIndex argument has a value of 0, as it is the first button named in the buttons array passed to the showMessageBox() function (see step 5). If the user presses this button, the connection to the current chat instance is closed. Then, the text property of the roomName_txt field is set to the current selected item's label in the roomList instance, and the initConnect() function is invoked, just as lines 17 and 18 from the setRoom() function described.

7. In the remaining steps, you modify the look and feel of other interface elements. While these steps are not required to enable the functionality of

the roomList instance, the enhancements provide more visual information to the connected user. The next modifications are made to the userName_txt, roomName_txt, and currentRoom_txt fields. When a user is connected to a specific chat room, the userName_txt and roomName_txt should be disabled in order to prevent the user from accidentally typing into these fields. You use the TextFormat object to make two colors: a light gray, indicating a disabled state, and black, indicating an enabled state.

Select frame 1 of the actions layer, and add the following code at the end of the actions list:

```
dimTextColor = new TextFormat();
dimTextColor.color = 0x999999;
regTextColor = new TextFormat();
regTextColor.color = 0x000000;
```

This code creates two TextFormat objects. The dimTextColor object, with a color property value of 0x99999, will be used to convert the color of the userName_txt and roomName_txt to a light gray when the user connects to a chat instance. The regTextColor object, indicating a solid black color, is used to revert the same fields' color to black when the user leaves a room.

8. To efficiently toggle the functionality of the userName_txt and roomName_txt fields, create a function named enableInput(). Place the code for this function after the switchRooms() function declaration.

```
function enableInput(list, isEnabled){
   var listLength = list.length;
   var fieldType = isEnabled ? "input" : "dynamic";
   var colorType = isEnabled ? regTextColor : dimTextColor;
   for(var i=0;i<listLength;i++){
     with(list[i]){
        type = fieldType;
        selectable = isEnabled;
        setTextFormat(colorType);
     }
   }
}
```

This function takes two arguments, list and isEnabled. list represents an Array object indicating which fields should be enabled or disabled. isEnabled is a Boolean value indicating whether the text fields should be active (true) or inactive (false) for user input. If the fields should be active, the fields' type property is set to "input". Otherwise, the type is set to `dynamic` (preventing the user from typing into the field). If `isEnabled` is true, the color of each field is set to black. Otherwise, the color of each field is set to gray, indicating an inactive field.

9. The last step is to modify the `userName_txt`, `roomName_txt`, and `currentRoom_txt` fields when the user connects or disconnects from a `chat` instance. Add the following highlighted lines of code to the `initClient()` and `closeClient()` functions in frame 1 of the actions layer. Note that some of the code within these functions has been omitted, denoted by the ... characters.

```
function initClient(nc){
    connectButton.setLabel("Leave room");
    users_so = SharedObject.getRemote("users", nc.uri, false);
    users_so.onSync = function(list) {
        ...
    };
    users_so.receiveMessage = function(msg) {
        ...
    };
    users_so.connect(nc);
    var startPos = nc.uri.lastIndexOf("/")+1;
    currentRoom_txt.text = nc.uri.substr(startPos);
    enableInput([userName_txt, roomName_txt], false);
}
function closeClient(){
    connectButton.setLabel("Join Room");
    userList.removeAll();
    chat_txt.text = "";
    enableInput([userName_txt, roomName_txt], true);
}
```

In the `initClient()` function, the label of the `connectButton` instance is changed to "Leave Room", instead of "Disconnect". Also, the `currentRoom_txt` field's text value reflects the newly connected application instance name. The `enableInput()` function is then invoked, passing an array that includes the `userName_txt` and `roomName_txt` object references, as well as a Boolean `false` argument, indicating that these fields should be converted to dim-colored Dynamic text fields.

In the `closeClient()` function, the label of the `connectButton` instance is reverted to "Join Room". Once again, the `enableInput()` function is invoked, passing the same text field array with a Boolean `true` argument. The text fields are then set back to Input text fields, with black-colored text.

10. Save your Flash document. You're ready to test the movie. You may want to connect to your FlashCom server with the Communication App Inspector to monitor the progress of the movie. Test or publish the Flash movie, and log in to the chat application with two or more clients. If you type a user name and a room name in the respective fields and click the Join Room button, the roomList instance should update with the new instance name. The userName_txt, roomName_txt, and currentRoom_txt fields should now change to reflect the new connection. In other clients, you can choose the new instance name as an item in the roomList instance, and the Flash client will automatically connect to that instance.

Tip

The completed document, multiroom_chat_102.fla, can be found in the chapter_11 folder of this book's CD-ROM. You look for further enhancements to this exercise on this book's Web site at www.mxbook.com.

SUMMARY

- A local SharedObject can save data from a Flash movie on a user's machine. By default, Flash Player 6 allows any second-level domain name to store up to 100 KB of data on a user's machine.

- A remote SharedObject saves data within an application on a Flash Communication Server.

- A remote SharedObject has a *persistence* parameter, which designates whether the data is stored beyond the application's session.

- Local SharedObject data is stored within SOL files located in a Flash Player folder for each user of a computer.

- Remote SharedObject data is stored within FSO files located in a SharedObjects folder of the application's folder on the FlashCom server. By modifying the server's XML configuration files, you can change this default folder name and/or location.

- In client-side ActionScript, the data property of a SharedObject instance allows you to change or read the named properties and values of a local or remote SharedObject. In server-side ActionScript, the SharedObject.getProperty() and SharedObject.setProperty() methods are used to accomplish these same tasks.

- When a remote SharedObject property value changes, any subscribers to that SharedObject receive a list of changed elements, handled by the onSync() method of the named SharedObject instance.

- FlashCom applications can use server-side ActionScript to access remote SharedObject data located within different FlashCom servers (or from different application instances).

- Each application on a FlashCom server can have its own main.asc document. This document contains the server-side ActionScript code that loads when an application instance is started.

- There are several event handler methods for the Application object in server-side ActionScript code, such as onAppStart(), onConnect(), and onDisconnect(). Each of these handlers can invoke other server-side functions and methods to communicate with connected clients.

- You can pass additional parameters to the onConnect() handler for the Application object by specifying the parameters after the URI of the connect() method for a client-side NetConnection object.

- The Communication App Inspector in Flash MX allows you to monitor the activity of FlashCom application instances.

- The call() method of the client-side NetConnection object enables a Flash movie (SWF file) to invoke a custom named method of a Client object within server-side ActionScript code.

- You can define named methods for client- or server-side SharedObjects that can be invoked with a send() method from another SharedObject instance subscribed to the same remote SharedObject.

- FlashCom application instances inherit the same functionality as the default instance of the application. The code within the main.asc document for an application is loaded for each new instance of the application.

- To connect to a specific instance of a FlashCom application, add the instance name to the end of the application's URI in the connect() method, such as rtmp:/chat/myroom.

- When you use a server-side NetConnection object, the URI for the connect() method must include the full domain name (or IP address) of the Flash-Com server, even if the connection is made to another instance on the same server.

In This Chapter:

12 Directing Streams Between Clients

If you read the previous two chapters, you should have a fairly comfortable knowledge of SharedObject and NetStream objects. You're now ready to build more complex FlashCom applications, which can provide customized multi-user functions. In this chapter, you learn how to build a talk show application. This application allows a speaker (or host) to control and moderate a live multi-user chat, complete with shared text, audio, and video.

In order to build the application, you need to have access to a FlashCom server. Preferably, you should have a Developer installation of the FlashCom server on the same machine you are using to create the Flash documents.

AN OVERVIEW OF THE APPLICATION

Unlike examples discussed in previous chapters, the talk show application will be built primarily from the Communication Components set. While these components can be used with little or no client- or server-side ActionScript, you learn how to enhance the capabilities of these components, enabling them to work more dynamically.

For an overview of the Communication Components, read Chapter 6.

Throughout this chapter, you build a talk show application with the following features:

- Each user can login to an application named talkshow on the FlashCom server, with the help of the SimpleConnect component.

- The login screen of the Flash client allows the user to decide his role in the presentation, as a viewer or a speaker.

- In order to participate as a speaker (or host), the user must login separately, in a new window. Only one user can be the active host of the application.

- In viewer mode, the user can see the login names of other connected users in an instance of the PeopleList component. Each user can freely send text messages to all connected users by way of the Chat component. If a viewer would like the opportunity to send audio/video to all connected users, he can also send a request to the speaker for audio/video access.

- In speaker mode, the user has the same functionality provided in viewer mode. Additionally, the user can immediately send the audio and/or video from his connected camera and microphone to the other connected users. This capability is provided by the AVPresence component. The speaker can also select another user's name in the PeopleList component, and create an AVPresence component for that user. When that user begins to send audio and/or video, the remaining users will see the streamed audio/video from the selected user.

Before you learn how to use the Communication Components, you create the Flash document (FLA file) with a basic timeline structure to establish the login, viewer, and speaker screens.

 To see this application working in a live development environment, visit www.mxbook.com/v1/ch12/.

Setting up the Main Timeline of the Flash Client

To get a sense of the client application structure, create the shell timeline for the Flash MX document (FLA file). This timeline should separate each section (or screen) of the presentation, clearly delineating the login screen from the viewer and speaker modes of the application.

TO CONSTRUCT THE BASIC CLIENT FRAMEWORK:

1. In Macromedia Flash MX, create a new document. Save the document as `talkshow_100.fla`.

2. Rename Layer 1 to **labels**. Select frame 30 of this layer, and press the F5 key (or choose Insert > Frame) to add additional frames.

3. Create the three sections for the application. Select frame 1 of the labels layer. In the Property inspector, specify a frame label of `login`. On frame 10, add a keyframe (F6) and assign a frame label of `viewer`. On frame 20, add another keyframe and label it `speaker`.

4. Make a new layer, and name it **actions**. Using the Actions panel, add `stop()` actions to frames 1, 10, and 20, inserting new keyframes where necessary.

5. Create a new layer, and name it **heading**. On frame 1 of this layer, use the Text tool to add the Static text **Login to application**. Place this text in the top-left corner of the stage.

6. On frame 10 of the heading layer, insert a new keyframe (F6). Change the Static text on this frame to **Participate in the discussion**.

7. On frame 20 of the heading layer, insert another keyframe (F6), and change the text to **Control the AV presentation**.

8. Save the document.

 You can find the completed version of this document, `talkshow_100.fla`, in the `chapter_12` folder of this book's CD-ROM.

Now that you have constructed the basic framework of the Flash client movie, you're ready to setup the application on your FlashCom server.

Preparing the FlashCom Application

In order to use the capabilities of a FlashCom server, you need to create a distinct application space on the server—just as you have done in previous chapters.

TO CREATE THE TALKSHOW APPLICATION:

1. On the computer where you installed the Flash Communication Server MX software, locate the `applications` directory. If you chose a default Developer Install of FlashCom on a Windows machine and you are running Microsoft IIS, the path to the `applications` directory should be

`C:\inetpub\wwwroot\flashcom\applications`

You can also locate the path of your `applications` directory by viewing the `<AppsDir>` node of the `Vhost.xml` file, which is located in the `conf` folder of your FlashCom installation.

2. In the `applications` directory, create a new folder named `talkshow`.

Remember the location to the `talkshow` folder. In the following sections, you create server-side ActionScript code that is saved in this folder.

 Tip To test your new `talkshow` application, login to your FlashCom server with the Communication App Inspector in Flash MX. Once connected, type **talkshow** into the `App/Inst:` field of the inspector. If you can connect to the application, then you created the `talkshow` folder in the proper location. For more information on this inspector, read Chapter 11.

ADDING YOUR FIRST COMMUNICATION COMPONENTS

As outlined in the previous section, the talk show has three screens: login, viewer mode, and speaker mode. In this section, you will create the elements of the interface that remain constant throughout each section of the client movie. Throughout the process, you are introduced to some of the Communication Components. In later sections, you will add dynamic elements that are created and presented to each connected user when and where necessary.

 In order to build the user interface described in this section, make sure you have installed the latest Communication Components for Macromedia Flash MX. You can download the free components at the following location: www.macromedia.com/software/flashcom/download/components

 If you downloaded and installed the Communication Components from Macromedia's site prior to November 13th, 2002, you will need to install the latest download at the URL in the previous note. The new Communication Components contain updated client- and server-side ActionScript code. This chapter utilizes these latest enhancements.

Understanding the SimpleConnect Component

The SimpleConnect component provides a fast and easy way to connect a Flash movie to a FlashCom application. The component essentially creates a NetConnection object for your Flash movie, and connects other Communication Component instances or custom objects to your FlashCom application. **Figure 12.1** shows the SimpleConnect as it appears on the stage of a Flash document in Flash MX.

Figure 12.1 The SimpleConnect component.

The component provides an Input text field, into which the user can type his name (or alias). The Login button is somewhat superfluous. The Flash movie automatically tries to connect to a FlashCom application as soon as the component instance appears in the movie during runtime. The user can manually click the Login button or press the Enter key (if focus is within the login text field) to attempt a connection.

Note

If the user wants to change the login name after a connection is made, he can enter a new login name and press the Login button (or press the Enter key) to update the user's name on the FlashCom server.

The SimpleConnect component also uses a local SharedObject to remember the user's login name. If the user types a name into the field and/or the Flash movie successfully connects to the FlashCom server, then the name is saved on the user's machine in a local SharedObject for later visits.

TO VIEW THE PARAMETERS OF THE SIMPLECONNECT COMPONENT:

1. Create a new temporary Flash document, separate from the talkshow_100.fla document you created in the last section.

2. In this new document, drag an instance of the SimpleConnect component from the Components panel to the stage. (In the Component panel, you need to change the displayed set to Communication Components to see the SimpleConnect component.)

3. Select the new instance on the stage, and open the Property inspector. The Parameters tab of the inspector shows two fields: Application Directory, and Communication Components. These parameters are discussed in the following sections.

APPLICATION DIRECTORY

This parameter of the SimpleConnect component declares the URI to the FlashCom application. The value specified in this field must start with an rtmp: declaration, in the form of

    rtmp:/applicationName

or

    rtmp://serverDomainName/applicationName

If you prefer to dynamically control the URI value, you can omit the value from the Property inspector and declare it in ActionScript code. Once you name a SimpleConnect instance, you can control the URI value by addressing the `appDirectory` property of the instance. For example, the following code sets the URI of a SimpleConnect instance named `login_mc`:

```
login_mc.appDirectory = "rtmp:/talkshow";
```

You can also control which instance of the FlashCom application to invoke. The SimpleConnect component looks for an `appInstance` variable on the parent timeline of the SimpleConnect instance. If you placed a SimpleConnect instance on the Main Timeline of your Flash movie (_root), then you can declare the `appInstance` on the _root, and the instance applies that value to the connect URI. The following code tells a SimpleConnect instance named `login_mc` to connect to the `chat` application instance named `"room1"`:

```
login_mc.appDirectory = "rtmp:/chat";
_root.appInstance = "room1";
```

This code essentially builds the URI, `rtmp:/chat/room1`, for the SimpleConnect instance. The `appInstance` technique is usually reserved for cases where you want to pass the instance name via the HTML document that loads the Flash movie. Any variables passed to a Flash movie by way of the FLASHVARS parameter in HTML are declared on the _root timeline of the Flash movie. For example, the following <OBJECT> and <EMBED> tags create an `appInstance` variable with a value of `room1`. Note that most standard attributes and parameters of these tags have been omitted in this example.

```
<OBJECT ... >
<PARAM NAME="movie" VALUE="main.swf">
<PARAM NAME="flashvars" VALUE="appInstance=room1">
<EMBED SRC="main.swf" FLASHVARS="appInstance=room1" ...>
</EMBED>
</OBJECT>
```

For the `talkshow` application, you will assign a static URI value directly in the Parameters area of the Property inspector for the SimpleConnect instance. The application's URI will not require dynamic changes or separate instance names.

COMMUNICATION COMPONENTS

This parameter of the SimpleConnect component allows you to specify other objects that require a `NetConnection` object (or connection to the FlashCom application). If you click this field in the Parameters area of the Property inspector, a Values dialog box is displayed. **Figure 12.2** shows the names of sample objects and instances. Click the plus (+) button to add new entries.

Use the minus (-) button to remove a selected item from the Values list. The up and down arrow buttons allow you to re-order the items in the list.

Figure 12.2 The Values dialog box specifies the other components (or objects) that should connect to the FlashCom application.

The object or instance name specified in as a Value item must exist on the same parent timeline of the SimpleConnect instance. For example, if you placed the SimpleConnect instance on the Main Timeline (_root), the name of the object referenced in the Values dialog box must exist on _root as well.

All names specified in the Values dialog box are interpreted as string data types. As such, do not specify paths to object names that do not exist on the same timeline as the Simple Connect instance.

When the SimpleConnect instance displays within a Flash movie, the instance makes a connection to the FlashCom application (or instance) specified in the Applications Directory field. When a successful connection is made, the Simple-Connect instance processes each name in the Communication Components list (which is actually an array). Specifically, the SimpleConnect passes its NetConnection object (named nc) to the connect() method of each named object in the list.

If you examine the internal ActionScript on any of the Communication Components, you will discover a connect() method within the #initclip and #endinitclip code of the component.

Later in this section, you learn how to add instance and object names to the Communication Components list for a SimpleConnect instance.

Connecting to the FlashCom Application

Once you have created the talkshow directory in your FlashCom server's applications directory, you're ready to begin adding Communication Components to your Flash client movie.

TO ADD THE SIMPLECONNECT COMPONENT TO THE CLIENT MOVIE:

1. Open the talkshow_100.fla document you created earlier in this chapter, and resave the document as **talkshow_101.fla**. (You can close the temporary practice document from the previous section.)

2. Create a new layer and name it **login_mc**.

3. Select frame 1 of the login_mc layer, and drag an instance of the Simple-Connect component from the Components panel to the left corner of the stage, just below the heading text. With the instance selected, open the Property inspector and name the instance login_mc. In the Application Directory field, type **rtmp:/talkshow** (**Figure 12.3**).

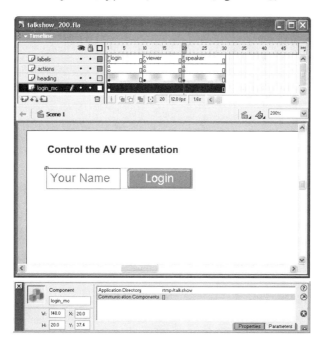

Figure 12.3 The login_mc instance connects to the talkshow application.

Note

If you are running the FlashCom server on a different server than the Web server delivering the Flash movie (SWF file), declare an absolute URI that specifies the FlashCom server's domain name.

4. Save the Flash document.

5. Before you can test the Flash movie, you need to enable the SimpleConnect component framework within the FlashCom application named talkshow. All of the Communication Components require one simple line of server-side ActionScript code in order to initialize properly with an application. In Macromedia Dreamweaver MX (or your preferred text editor), create a new ActionScript Communications document. On line 1 of this document, type the following code:

```
load("components.asc");
```

The load() action does exactly what it says: it loads another ASC file into the application. In this example, the components.asc file, which is located in the scriptlib folder of your FlashCom server, loads the component framework necessary for all Communication Components to function.

Tip

If you open the components.asc file in Macromedia Dreamweaver MX (or any text editor), you can find the references to other ASC files that are loaded for the component framework. Each Communication Component has its own ASC file associated with its functionality.

6. Save the text document as **main.asc** in the talkshow folder of your FlashCom server's applications folder.

7. Now, go back to the talkshow_101.fla document in Macromedia Flash MX. Open the Communication App Inspector, and login to your FlashCom server. If an instance of the talkshow application is currently running, unload the instance. Leave the inspector open, and test the talkshow_101.fla document by choosing Control > Test Movie. As soon as the movie loads, click the Refresh Now button in the Communication App Inspector. You should see the default instance (_definst_) of the talkshow application displayed in the Active Application Instances list.

You can find the completed document, talkshow_101.fla, in the chapter_12 folder of this book's CD-ROM. You can also find a version of the main.asc file as main_100.asc in this location.

If the Flash movie is not connecting to the talkshow application, double check the Application Directory value for the login_mc instance. Make sure you have the talkshow application folder created on the FlashCom server listed in the URI.

Adding More Components

Now you will see just how easy it is to "share" the NetConnection object initialized by the SimpleConnect instance. All of the Communication Components can be used with the SimpleConnect instance. You add the ConnectionLight and SetBandwidth components to the Flash client in this section.

ConnectionLight

This component allows a user to view the connection status to a FlashCom application. This small icon graphic can display three colors:

- **Green:** This color indicates a successful connection to the FlashCom application.

- **Yellow:** This color indicates that the latency between the Flash movie and the FlashCom application has exceeded the value specified in the component's parameters. (You will learn more about latency is just a moment.)

- **Red:** This color indicates that the Flash movie could not connect to the FlashCom application or that the Flash movie has been disconnected from the FlashCom application.

The ConnectionLight component also displays detailed information about the bitrate and latency values between the Flash movie and the FlashCom application. If the user clicks the connection icon graphic, a tooltip-like window will float over the Flash movie, as shown in **Figure 12.4**.

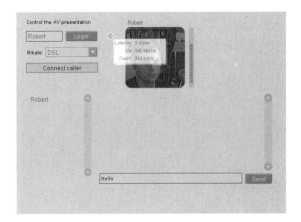

Figure 12.4 The ConnectionLight component can display vital
network statistics for your FlashCom application.
(Note that the Flash movie area around the display
box is intentionally dimmed for emphasis.)

The information window shows the current latency value and the Up and
Down bitrates (in Kbps or bps). Latency is the delay (in milliseconds) between a
packet being sent from one client and that packet being received by another
client. In the case of a FlashCom-enabled Flash movie, latency is the amount of
time that elapses when a packet is sent from the Flash movie and received by
the FlashCom application (or vice versa). For any real-time communication
over the Internet, latency values should be as small as possible while bandwidth (or throughput) should be as high as possible. Latency values can be
affected by a number of factors, including the physical distance between the
client and server and the amount of traffic being sent to and from the server.

Tip

You can use the information provided by the ConnectionLight component to see how
much bandwidth your FlashCom-enabled Flash movie is consuming. This is particularly helpful when you want to limit data rates for slower target bitrates, such as
dial-up modem users. The ConnectionLight component itself cannot limit throughput. You must adjust the parameters of the actual object or component instance
that's sending or receiving the data (e.g. the AVPresence component).

In the following steps, you add the ConnectionLight component to the talk
show client.

To add the ConnectionLight component to the client movie:

1. Open the `talkshow_101.fla` document that you created in the last section. Save this document as **talkshow_102.fla**.

2. Create a new layer, and name it **connLight_mc**.

3. On frame 1 of this new layer, drag an instance of the ConnectionLight component from the Components panel to the stage. Place the instance to the right of the `login_mc` instance. With the instance selected, open the Property inspector. Name the instance **connLight_mc**. Do not change the default values in the Parameters area of the inspector (**Figure 12.5**).

Figure 12.5 The connLight_mc instance is placed to the right of the login_mc instance.

Note

The measurement interval value (in seconds) controls how often the component polls the data being sent between the Flash client and the server. The latency threshold value (in seconds) determines the limit for the yellow warning level. If the latency value exceeds this value, the icon graphic switches to yellow.

4. In order for the connLight_mc instance to monitor the activity of the talkshow application, the instance must be connected to the application instance. Select the login_mc instance on the stage. In the Property inspector, click the Communication Components field. In the Values dialog box, click the plus (+) button. In field 0, type **connLight_mc** (**Figure 12.6**). Click OK to close the dialog box.

Figure 12.6 The conn-Light_mc instance name is added to the Values list for the Communication Components field of the login_mc instance.

5. Save your Flash document, and test it. If the movie successfully connects to the talkshow application, the ConnectionLight instance turns green.

 You do not need to add any additional server-side ActionScript code to the main.asc file for the talkshow application. The components.asc file automatically loads the framework necessary for all Communication Components to function properly.

SETBANDWIDTH

This component can adjust the bitrates of several Communication Components, particularly the AVPresence component, which will be used in the talk-show application. When the SetBandwidth component is added to a Flash movie, the user can select a preferred bitrate setting (in a combo box menu) that matches his Internet connection speed (**Figure 12.7**). By default, the component has four speed options, as shown in **Table 12.1**. The bitrate of each of the first three options (Modem, DSL, and LAN) can be specified in the Parameters area of the Property inspector.

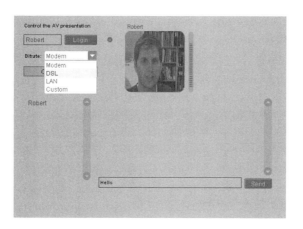

Figure 12.7 The SetBandwidth component allows the user
to choose a preferred bitrate.

TABLE 12.1 SetBandwidth Default Bitrates

SETTING	UPLOAD BITRATE	DOWNLOAD BITRATE
Modem	33 Kbps	33 Kbps
DSL	128 Kbps	256 Kbps
LAN	10,000 Kbps	10,000 Kbps
Custom	User specified	User specified

Note

The Custom setting can only be viewed at runtime. This option allows the user to specify a custom upload and/or download bitrate.

In the following steps, you add the SetBandwidth component to the talk show client.

To add the SetBandwidth component to the client movie:

1. Open the `talkshow_102.fla` document that you created in the previous section.

2. Make a new layer, and rename it **speedList_mc**. On frame 1 of this layer, drag an instance of the SetBandwidth component from the Components panel to the stage. Place the instance below the `login_mc` instance. In the

Property inspector, name this instance **speedList_mc**. Do not adjust the values in the Parameters area.

3. Using the Text tool, add the Static text **Bitrate:** to the left of the speedList_mc instance (**Figure 12.8**).

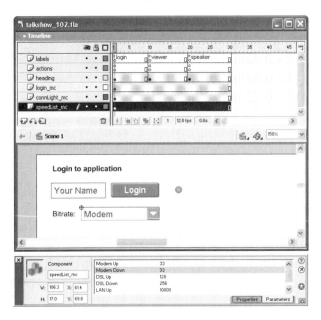

Figure 12.8 The Static text and speedList_mc instance are placed below the login_mc instance.

4. Add this instance's name to the Communication Components list for the login_mc instance. Select the login_mc instance, and, in the Property inspector, click the Communication Components field. In the Values dialog box, click the plus (+) button. In field 1, type **speedList_mc**, as shown in **Figure 12.9**.

Figure 12.9 The name of the speedList_mc instance is added to the Values list.

5. Save the Flash document. You do not need to test the Flash movie at this time, because there are no Communication Components on the stage that can display changes controlled by the SetBandwidth instance, speedList_mc.

 You can find the completed document, talkshow_102.fla, in the chapter_12 folder of this book's CD-ROM.

NAVIGATING THE CLIENT

The Communication Components allow your Flash movies to efficiently interact with a FlashCom application. However, the primary application logic for the talk show functionality must be custom built, in both the client (the Flash movie) and the server-side ActionScript code. In this section, you add the navigation elements that allow the user to choose either the viewer or speaker mode.

Enabling the Viewer Mode

In viewer mode, a user can participate in the talk show by sending text messages to the group of connected users and by sending a request to the host (also known as the speaker) to have access to an audio/video stream. Later in this chapter, you add other Communication Components to enable these capabilities. Right now, you need to create a button on the login frame label that moves the user to the viewer frame label.

To construct the viewer mode:

1. Open the talkshow_102.fla document, and resave the document as **talkshow_103.fla**.

2. Create a new layer and name it **viewerButton**. On frame 1 of this layer, drag an instance of the PushButton component from the Components panel to the stage. (You may need to switch the current component set to Flash UI Components first.) Place this instance below the speedList_mc instance, as shown in **Figure 12.10**. In the Property inspector, name this instance **viewerButton**. In the Label field of the Parameters tab, type **Participate in the discussion**. In the Click Handler field, type **initViewer**. To accommodate the

length of the button's label, use the Free Transform tool to extend the width of the instance.

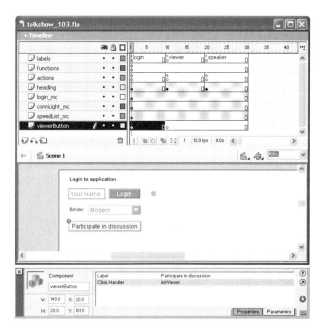

Figure 12.10 The `viewerButton` instance is positioned below
the `speedList_mc` instance.

3. The `viewerButton` instance should only be visible on the `login` frame of the client movie. Therefore, select frame 10 of the viewerButton layer and press the F7 key (or choose Insert > Blank Keyframe) to add an empty keyframe.

4. Now, create the `initViewer()` function, which was specified as the viewer-Button instance's Click Handler in step 2. Create a new layer and name it **functions**. Select frame 1 of the functions layer, and open the Actions panel (F9). Add the following code:

```
function initViewer(obj) {
  _root.gotoAndStop("viewer");
}
```

This code simply moves the timeline to the `viewer` frame label when the `viewerButton` instance is clicked.

> **Note**
>
> While the `obj` argument of the `initViewer()` function is not used by this specific application, we include it here to remind you that an object reference to the Push-Button instance is passed to the Click Handler. This functionality allows you to easily reference the instance invoking the handler without directly referring to the instance's name in the handler's code.

5. The user should be able to navigate to the `viewer` frame label only if a successful connection has been made to the FlashCom application. As such, the `viewerButton` instance should be disabled when the movie first loads. After the SimpleConnect component (that is, the `login_mc` instance) connects to the `talkshow` application, the `viewerButton` instance should be enabled. To disable the component instance on load, select frame 1 of the actions layer and add the following code:

```
viewerButton.setEnabled(false);
```

6. To enable the `viewerButton` instance after a successful connection, create an object that can monitor the connection status, just as the ConnectionLight component does. In fact, you can borrow the same methods of the ConnectionLight component and use them to change the enabled state of the `viewerButton` instance. Select frame 1 of the actions layer, and open the Actions panel (F9). Add the following highlighted code:

```
checkButtons = {};
checkButtons.connect = FCConnectionLightClass.prototype.connect;
checkButtons.onCheckInterval =
➞ FCConnectionLightClass.prototype.onCheckInterval;
checkButtons.showGreen = function(){
   viewerButton.setEnabled(true);
};
viewerButton.setEnabled(false);
stop();
```

Here, you create an object named `checkButtons`, which copies the `connect()` and `onCheckInterval()` methods from the `FCConnectionLightClass` created by the ConnectionLight component. The ConnectionLight component also uses a `showGreen()` method, which is invoked by the `onCheckInterval()` method when a successful connection is made. The `showGreen()` method of the `checkButtons` object enables the `viewerButton` instance.

7. Add a reference to the checkButtons instance to the Communication Components list parameter for the login_mc instance. Select the login_mc instance, and click the Communication Components field. In the Values dialog box, click the plus (+) button to add a new value. In field 2, type **checkButtons**, as shown in **Figure 12.11**. When the login_mc instance connects to the talkshow application, the instance invokes the connect() method of each object referenced in the Communication Components list parameter. Therefore, the connect() method you defined for the checkButtons object will be invoked when a successful connection is made.

Figure 12.11 A reference to the checkButtons object is added to the Values list.

8. Save your Flash document, and test it. When the Flash movie loads and successfully connects to the talkshow application, the viewerButton instance is enabled. Click the button, and the timeline jumps to the viewer frame label.

Later in this chapter, you will add more elements to the viewer frame label that enable multi-user interactivity.

Enabling the Speaker Mode

The speaker mode of the talk show client allows a user to control, which user(s) can open an audio/video stream that all users of the application can see. Because this capability assumes a level of administration and responsibility, you will restrict access to the speaker mode. In the scope of this chapter, true authentication measures will not be constructed. However, you learn how to setup the Flash movie client to use a separate login box for the speaker mode.

Xref

To learn more about using Flash Remoting to authenticate a user, read Chapter 14.

To begin construction of the speaker mode:

1. Open the `talkshow_103.fla` document that you created in the previous section. Create a new layer and name it **speakerButton**. Select frame 10 of this layer and press the F7 key to add an empty keyframe, just as you did for the viewerButton layer.

2. Select the `viewerButton` instance, and copy it (Edit > Copy). Choose frame 1 of the speakerButton layer, and paste the copied instance. Move the copied instance just below the original `viewerButton` instance. In the Property inspector, change the instance name to **speakerButton**. In the Parameters tab, change the Label value to **Access speaker login** and the Click Handler value to **speakerLogin**. See **Figure 12.12**.

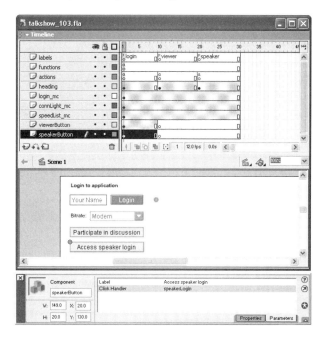

Figure 12.12 The `speakerButton` instance is placed below the `viewerButton` instance.

3. Now, you need to add a login box that will appear on the stage of the Flash movie when the user clicks the `speakerButton` instance. A login Movie Clip symbol has already been made for you, which you can copy into this Flash document. Open the `speakerPanel.fla` document from the `chapter_12` folder

of this book's CD-ROM. Drag the speakerPanel symbol from this document's library to the library of the talkshow_103.fla document. This symbol has two Input text fields and a PushButton instance. The PushButton instance invokes a checkLogin() function (found on frame 1 of the actions layer in this symbol), which moves the Main Timeline to the speaker frame label.

Note

Do not place an instance of the speakerPanel symbol on the stage. In a later step, you add an instance to the stage with ActionScript code.

4. In previous chapters, you learned how to use the MessageBox component to quickly add dialog boxes to a Flash movie. A similar component is the DraggablePane component, also available in the Flash UI Components Set 2. You can think of this component as the "shell" of the MessageBox component. The DraggablePane component allows you to insert a custom symbol from the movie's library into a pop-up window. In the talk show client, you place the speakerPanel symbol (copied in the last step) into an instance of the DraggablePane component. In order to use this component, though, you need a copy of it in the document's library. At this time, drag the DraggablePane component from the Components panel to the stage of the talkshow_103.fla document. Because you only need the component in the document's Library panel (F11), delete the DraggablePane instance from the stage. (The DraggablePane symbol will still exist in the Flash UI Components folder of the document's library.).

5. Now, you're ready to create a function that dynamically adds instances of the DraggablePane component and the speakerPanel symbol to the client movie. This function, named speakerLogin, is invoked when the user clicks the speakerButton instance. Select frame 1 of the functions layer, and add the code shown in Listing 12.1 after the existing initViewer() function:

Listing 12.1 speakerLogin() **function**

```
function speakerLogin() {
   var title = "Speaker Login";
   var content = "speakerPanel";
   _root.attachMovie("FDraggablePaneSymbol", "speakerPane", 1);
   with (speakerPane) {
      setPaneTitle(title);
      setPaneMaximumSize(250, 160);
```

Listing 12.1 speakerLogin() **function** *(continued)*

```
        setPaneMinimumSize(250, 160);
        setContentSize(250, 140);
        setResizable(false);
        setScrollContent(content);
        setScrolling(false);
        _x = 20;
        _y = 175;
    }
}
```

This code uses the attachMovie() method of the MovieClip object to add an instance of the DraggablePane component (which uses a linkage identifier of FDraggablePaneSymbol) to the stage. The local variable named content is set equal to the linkage identifier of the speakerPanel symbol. This variable is then used as the argument of the setScrollContent() method. For more information about the DraggablePane's methods, you can look up each method in the Reference panel of Flash MX.

6. Now, you need to control the enabled state of the speakerButton instance, just as you did with the viewerButton instance. Add the following highlighted lines of code to frame 1 of the actions layer:

```
checkButtons = {};
checkButtons.connect = FCConnectionLightClass.prototype.connect;
checkButtons.onCheckInterval =
→ FCConnectionLightClass.prototype.onCheckInterval;
checkButtons.showGreen = function(){
    viewerButton.setEnabled(true);
    speakerButton.setEnabled(true);
};
viewerButton.setEnabled(false);
speakerButton.setEnabled(false);
stop();
```

7. Save your Flash document, and test it (Control > Test Movie). After the Flash movie successfully connects to the FlashCom application, both the viewerButton and speakerButton instances are enabled. When you click the speakerButton instance, a speakerPanel instance appears in an instance of the DraggablePane component (**Figure 12.13**). When the user clicks the Login button in this pane, the Flash movie jumps to the speaker frame label.

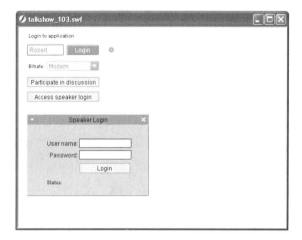

Figure 12.13 When the user clicks the speakerButton instance, the DraggablePane component displays with an instance of the speakerPanel symbol.

 You can find the completed document, talkshow_103.fla, in the chapter_12 folder of this book's CD-ROM.

As mentioned earlier, the speakerPane instance does not perform any validation on the text entered into the Input text fields. After you have read Chapter 14, you may want to come back to this example to add similar authentication methods to the talk show client movie.

INITIALIZING THE CHAT

Once the user has a means to choose an area of the talk show client, the Flash movie can offer other user interface elements necessary for that area's functionality. In this portion of the chapter, you will learn how utilize other Flash-Com-enabled components in the client. The following Communication Components are added to the client movie:

- **PeopleList component:** This component retrieves a remote SharedObject that stores the names (and user IDs) of all connected users. This list of users is automatically updated and displayed in a list box within the component.

- **Chat component:** This component allows a user to view and send messages to all connected users. The server-side ASC file for this component automatically stores the ongoing history of a chat.

- **AVPresence component:** By far one of the most powerful components, the AVPresence component's functionality is two-fold: it can either enable a user to start sending audio and/or video to a FlashCom application, or it can display the audio and/or video sent from another user. Later in this section, you will learn how to use both capabilities.

Connecting More Communication Components

A user who enters either the viewer or speaker modes of the talk show client should be able to view the list of connected users and send text messages to other connected users. In the following steps, you add the PeopleList and Chat components to the Flash movie.

TO ADD THE PEOPLELIST AND CHAT COMPONENTS TO THE CLIENT MOVIE:

1. Open the `talkshow_103.fla` document from the last section. Resave this document as **talkshow_104.fla**.

2. Create a new layer, and name it **peopleList_mc**. Select frame 10 of this layer, and press the F7 key to add an empty keyframe.

3. With frame 10 of the `peopleList_mc` layer selected, drag an instance of the PeopleList component from the Components panel to the stage. (You may need to switch the active set to the Communication Components first.) Place this instance near the left edge of the stage, as shown in **Figure 12.14**. Name the instance **peopleList_mc**. This component does not have any custom parameters.

Note

You can use the Free Transform tool to resize the `peopleList_mc` instance to accommodate your preferences.

4. Repeat steps 2 and 3 for the Chat component, naming the new layer and instance **chat_mc**. When you are finished, your document should resemble **Figure 12.15**.

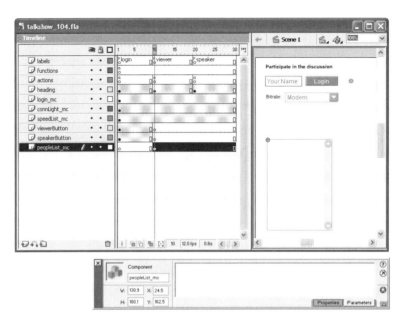

Figure 12.14 Place the peopleList_mc instance near the left edge of the stage.

 Note You may want to create some additional artwork to provide a border or frame around these component instances.

Figure 12.15 The chat_mc instance is positioned to the right of the peopleList_mc instance.

5. Now, you need to connect this new component instances to the same Net-Connection object that the login_mc instance uses. At first glance, it may seem feasible to add the new instance names to the Communication Components list parameter of the login_mc instance (as you have done in previous sections of this chapter). However, because these components do not appear on the same frame as the login_mc instance, this approach will not work. Rather, you create ActionScript code that invokes the connect() methods of each instance, when the user navigates to either the viewer or speaker frame labels. Select frame 1 of the functions layer, and add the following function after the existing code:

```
function initChat(nc) {

   chat_mc.connect(nc);
   peopleList_mc.connect(nc);
   login_mc.fcComponents.push("chat_mc");
   login_mc.fcComponents.push("peopleList_mc");
}
```

In steps 6 and 7, you create the code that invokes the initChat() function. The function uses one argument, nc, which represents the NetConnection object created by the login_mc instance. This object is passed to the connect() methods of the chat_mc and peopleList_mc instances.

Once the components are connected to the talkshow application, the instances should continue to be updated by any changes that occur to the user's name or connection status. To do this, the instance names must be added to the fcComponents array of the SimpleConnect component instance (login_mc). The push() method of the Array object inserts each instance name into the fcComponents array.

6. Invoke the initChat() function on the viewer frame label. Select frame 10 of the actions layer, and open the Actions panel (F9). Add the following high-lighted code:

```
initChat(login_mc.main_nc);
stop();
```

Each instance of the SimpleConnect component has an internal NetConnec-tion object reference named main_nc. This object reference is passed as the argument of the initChat() function when the Flash movie jumps to the viewer frame label.

Tip

The SimpleConnect component also creates an internal `NetConnection` object named `nc`. You can use either the `main_nc` or `nc` reference in your ActionScript code.

7. Add the same code from step 6 to frame 20 of the actions layer. The same components should initialize when the user chooses the speaker mode.

8. Save the Flash document, and test it. Type your name into the SimpleConnect field, and click the Login button. Click either the `viewerButton` or the `speakerButton` instance to test the new components.

Caution

Do not use the Enter key in Test Movie mode unless you have chosen Control > Disable Keyboard Shortcuts while testing the movie. The Enter key is mapped to the Play and Stop shortcuts (Control > Play or Control > Stop) in Test Movie mode and will make your movie's main timeline play or stop from the current frame.

You can find the completed document, `talkshow_104.fla`, in the `chapter_12` folder of this book's CD-ROM.

Opening the Speaker Stream

You're now ready to add the AVPresence component to the Flash client movie. This component enables a user to either send or receive an audio/video stream. If you place a fixed instance of the AVPresence component in the viewer mode, any user can take a hold of that stream and begin publishing with it. In the controlled environment of the talk show presentation, the host (or speaker) should be the only user capable of determining who gets a stream to publish. As such, you need to build a system where passive participants are presented an AVPresence component only when authorized users have been granted permission to publish. If a user is already publishing a stream with a given instance of the AVPresence component, then no other participant can use that stream.

In the next section, you learn how to control the speaker's instance of the AVPresence component.

CREATING THE SPEAKER'S INSTANCE OF THE AVPRESENCE COMPONENT

When the user chooses the speaker mode, the user should have an audio/video stream available to publish to the `talkshow` application. This stream will automatically be displayed to other participants once publishing begins. In the following steps, you learn how to add the AVPresence component to the speaker screen.

To add the AVPresence component to the speaker mode:

1. Open the `talkshow_104.fla` document you completed in the previous section, and resave the document as **talkshow_105.fla**.

2. Add the AVPresence component to the Flash document. Because you can't drag a component directly into the Library panel of the document, drag the AVPresence component from the Components panel to the stage. As soon as you have an instance on the stage, delete the instance. You only need the component in the movie's library, so that it is accessible by ActionScript code.

Tip

Each Communication Component has a linkage identifier that starts with the prefix "FC" and ends with the suffix "Symbol". You can view the linkage identifiers by expanding the Library panel's width, to expose the Linkage column.

3. In order to determine how instances of the AVPresence component should be handled, you need to let the Flash movie know which mode the user has chosen. Create a global variable named `viewerMode` that uses a Boolean value. If the user is on the `viewer` frame label, `viewerMode` equals `true`. If the user is on the `speaker` frame label, `viewerMode` equals `false`. Select frame 10 of the actions layer, and open the Actions panel (F9). Add the following highlighted line of code:

```
_global.viewerMode = true;
initChat(login_mc.main_nc);
stop();
```

4. Select frame 20 of the actions layer, and open the Actions panel (F9). Add the following highlighted line of code:

```
_global.viewerMode = false;
initChat(login_mc.main_nc);
stop();
```

5. Create a function that adds the AVPresence component to the stage, specifically for the speaker's audio/video stream. You'll add more code to

this function in the next section to enable the same stream for other participants. Select frame 1 of the functions layer, and add the following code after the existing functions:

```
function showSpeaker(isEnabled) {
   trace("showSpeaker("+ isEnabled + ") invoked");
   if (isEnabled) {
      _root.attachMovie("FCAVPresenceSymbol", "speakerWin_mc", 2,
      →{_x:225, _y:30});
      if (!viewerMode){
         speakerWin_mc.setUsername(login_mc.username);
      }
      speakerWin_mc.connect(login_mc.main_nc);
      login_mc.fcComponents.push("speakerWin_mc");
   }
}
```

The showSpeaker() function uses one argument, isEnabled. This argument determines if the AVPresence component is added or removed from the Flash movie. This code only adds an instance named speakerWin_mc to the stage. In a later section, you learn how to remove the instance from other participants' movies when the speaker stops publishing.

When an instance of the AVPresence component is added to the stage with the attachMovie() method, an initObject with the following parameters is specified:

{_x:225, _y:30}

This code positions the speakerWin_mc instance at the X, Y coordinates of 225, 30, which is to the right of the ConnectionLight instance.

Note

You enable the speakerWin_mc instance for participants in the next section. Right now, you are only enabling the instance for the host (or speaker) of the talk show client movie.

Note that the setUsername() method of the AVPresence component is invoked for the new instance. This method lets the server-side FlashCom application know the name of the user who publishes an audio/video stream with the component instance. This method only needs to be invoked for the speaker's instance; therefore, the viewerMode value is tested. The remaining code connects the instance to the FlashCom application and adds the instance's name to the fcComponents array, just as you did with the peopleList_mc and chat_mc instances.

6. Go back to frame 20 of the actions layer, and open the Actions panel (F9). Add the following highlighted line of code to the existing list of actions:

```
_global.viewerMode = false;
showSpeaker(true);
initChat(login_mc.main_nc);
stop();
```

When the user navigates to the speaker frame label, the showSpeaker() function is invoked with a true argument, adding the speakerWin_mc instance of the AVPresence component to the stage.

7. Save your Flash document, and test it. After you login to the FlashCom application, click the Access speaker login button and click the Login button in the DraggablePane instance. As soon as the movie jumps to the speaker frame label, the speakerWin_mc instance of the AVPresence component should appear on the stage. (You will also see the trace() message from the showSpeaker() function appear in the Output window of Flash MX.) If you click the Send Audio/Video text in the component, the Flash Player asks you for permission to access your camera and microphone. Click Allow to see your camera's image and your microphone's output display in the instance, as shown in **Figure 12.16**.

Figure 12.16 The speaker mode of the client can now display the AVPresence component.

The completed document, `talkshow_105.fla`, can be found in the `chapter_12` folder of this book's CD-ROM.

DISPLAYING THE AVPRESENCE COMPONENT FOR PARTICIPANTS

In order for each connected user to detect when the speaker begins publishing a stream with the AVPresence component, the `talkshow` application needs a mechanism that can notify every connected user when publishing on the speaker's stream is detected. In this section, you create a remote `SharedObject` that handles this task. In the previous section, the `showSpeaker()` function created the `speakerWin_mc` instance of the AVPresence component. This instance creates a stream whose name is based on the instance's name. The server-side ActionScript code for the AVPresence component (loaded by the `components.asc` document) names this stream with the following syntax:

```
FCAVPresence.instanceName.av
```

Caution

This naming convention is used by the second release of the Communication Components. As we indicated earlier in this chapter, make sure you have downloaded and installed the latest Communication Components from Macromedia's Web site in order to complete the talk show application successfully. The original AVPresence component used a `soName` parameter, available in the Property inspector, to name the stream and `SharedObject` created by the component. The `soName` parameter is no longer designated directly in the Property inspector for later releases of the AVPresence component.

For the talk show example, the speaker's instance is named `speakerWin_mc`. Therefore, the stream name of this instance is `FCAVPresence.speakerWin_mc.av`. A remote `SharedObject` named `broadcastNotifier` will monitor this stream's activity. Both the `talkshow` application and each connected Flash movie client will subscribe to this `SharedObject`, detecting any changes that occur to its properties. When the speaker starts publishing on the stream named "FCAVPresence.speakerWin_mc.av", a property of `broadcastNotifier` named `speakerBroadcast` will be set to `true`. When the speaker stops publishing, this property will be set to `false`. In the following steps, you learn how to implement this structure in the `main.asc` document of the `talkshow` application and the Flash MX talk show client document.

To present the speaker's stream to other participants:

1. In Macromedia Dreamweaver MX (or your preferred text editor), open the main.asc document located in the talkshow folder of your FlashCom server's applications directory. (You created this document earlier in this chapter.)

2. After the existing line of code, add the server-side ActionScript code shown in Listing 12.2. Note that the line numbers shown are specific to the new lines you are inserting. You should already have a load() function declared within the main.asc document prior to this new code.

Listing 12.2 The onAppStart() **handler of the** application **object**

```
1.  application.onAppStart = function(){
2.     this.broadcastNotifier_so =
       → SharedObject.get("broadcastNotifier");
3.     this.checkStream = function(info){
4.        if(info.code == "NetStream.Play.PublishNotify"){
5.           application.broadcastNotifier_so.setProperty(this.id,
             → true);
6.        } else if (info.code == "NetStream.Play.UnpublishNotify"){
7.           application.broadcastNotifier_so.setProperty(this.id,
             → false);
8.        }
9.     };
10.    this.speakerStream = Stream.get("temp_1");
11.    this.speakerStream.id = "speakerBroadcast";
12.    this.speakerStream.onStatus = this.checkStream;
13.    this.speakerStream.play("FCAVPresence.speakerWin_mc.av");
14. };
```

In line 1, you declare the onAppStart() handler for the talkshow application. This entire handler (lines 1-14) is invoked when the first instance of the talkshow application loads.

In line 2, the application object creates (or connects to) a non-persistent remote SharedObject named broadcastNotifier. The instance name of this object is broadcastNotifier_so.

Lines 3-9 create a checkStream() method for the application object. This method will be used in line 12 as the onStatus() handler for a server-side Stream object. The functionality of this method is discussed in just a moment.

Line 10 creates a server-side Stream object named speakerStream. This object makes a new stream named temp_1. This new stream will be a copy of the FCAVPresence.speakerWin_mc.av stream.

Line 11 creates an id property for the speakerStream object. This property is set to speakerBroadcast, indicating which mode the speakerStream object is monitoring. This property is referenced in the checkStream() method.

Line 12 sets the onStatus() handler of the speakerStream object to the check-Stream() method declared in lines 3-9.

In line 13, the speakerStream object subscribes to the FCAVPresence.speaker-Win_mc.av stream. Any events that occur on the FCAVPresence.speakerWin_mc.av stream can now be detected on the temp_1 stream.

Note You can't subscribe directly to the FCAVPresence.speakerWin_mc.av stream in line 10, because doing so would prevent the speakerWin_mc instance of the AVPresence component from publishing. There can only be one publisher assigned to a stream at any given time.

When the speaker begins publishing on the FCAVPresence.speakerWin_mc.av stream, lines 4 and 5 are invoked and a property named speakerBroadcast (returned by the id property) is set to true. This value, in turn, will be sent to all other Flash clients that are subscribed to the broadcastNotifier remote SharedObject. When the speaker stops publishing on the FCAVPres-ence.speakerWin_mc.av stream, lines 6 and 7 are invoked. The speakerBroadcast property is then set to false. Later in this section, you implement these property values in client-side ActionScript code.

Note The AVPresence component also creates a remote SharedObject named FCAVPresence.speakerWin_mc.av. You cannot create an additional SharedObject instance that connects to this data. Only one client-side or server-side SharedObject instance can connect to a remote SharedObject. The components.asc document (and subsequent ASC files that it loads) already creates a server-side instance that monitors the activity on FCAVPresence.speakerWin_mc.av. As such, you will not be able to create an additional SharedObject instance that can monitor the same remote Share-dObject data. That is why you create a completely separate remote SharedObject named broadcastNotifier in this step.

3. Save the `main.asc` document, and go back to Macromedia Flash MX.

4. Open the `talkshow_105.fla` document from the previous section, and resave it as **talkshow_106.fla**.

5. Select frame 1 of the functions layer, and open the Actions panel (F9). Add the following highlighted lines of code to the existing `initChat()` function:

```
function initChat(nc) {
    chat_mc.connect(nc);
    peopleList_mc.connect(nc);
    login_mc.fcComponents.push("chat_mc");
    login_mc.fcComponents.push("peopleList_mc");
    broadcastNotifier_so = SharedObject.getRemote("broadcastNotifier",
    ➥nc.uri, false);
    broadcastNotifier_so.onSync = function(list) {
        for (var i in list) {
            if (list[i].name == "speakerBroadcast") {
                if (viewerMode)
                    showSpeaker(this.data.speakerBroadcast);
            }
        }
    };
    broadcastNotifier_so.connect(nc);
}
```

This code creates a client-side `SharedObject` instance named `broadcastNotifier_so`, which connects to the same remote `SharedObject`, `broadcastNotifier`, created by the server-side `application` object. The `onSync()` handler detects any changes to the property named `speakerBroadcast`. If `viewerMode` is set to `true` (that is, if the user chooses the `viewer` mode), the `showSpeaker()` function is invoked, passing the value of the `speakerBroadcast` property as the `isEnabled` argument. Therefore, when the speaker begins publishing on the `FCAVPresence.speakerWin_mc.av` stream, `showSpeaker()` will be invoked on all connected clients whose `viewerMode` is set to `true`.

6. If the speaker stops publishing, the same `onSync()` handler of the `broadcastNotifier_so` instance is invoked, and `speakerBroadcast`'s value will equal `false`. As such, the `showSpeaker()` function needs an `else if` condition to invoke when isEnabled is equal to `false`. Add the following highlighted lines of code to the existing `showSpeaker()` function on frame 1 of the functions layer:

```
function showSpeaker(isEnabled) {
    trace("showSpeaker("+ isEnabled + ") invoked");
    if (isEnabled) {
      _root.attachMovie("FCAVPresenceSymbol", "speakerWin_mc", 2,
      → {_x:225, _y:30});
      if (!viewerMode)
         speakerWin_mc.setUsername(login_mc.username);
      speakerWin_mc.connect(login_mc.main_nc);
      login_mc.fcComponents.push("speakerWin_mc");
    } else if (viewerMode) {
      speakerWin_mc.removeMovieClip();
      for (var i = 0; i < login_mc.fcComponents.length; i++) {
        if (login_mc.fcComponents[i] == "speakerWin_mc") {
          login_mc.fcComponents_array.splice(i, 1);
          break;
        }
      }
    }
}
```

If isEnabled is set to `false` by the `onSync()` handler, the `else if` condition is tested. This block of code is only invoked for participants; the speaker's instance remains unaffected. If viewerMode is equal to `true`, the speakerWin_mc instance is removed. Because the speakerWin_mc instance is no longer present on the stage, the fcComponents array of the login_mc instance (that is, the SimpleConnect component) needs to be updated. The for loop searches each element of the array and removes the reference to the speakerWin_mc instance.

7. Save your Flash document. Before you test the movie, login to your Flash-Com server and unload any active instances of the talkshow application. Go back to the talkshow_106.fla document, and choose File > Publish Preview > Default - HTML. In your Web browser window with the published movie, login to the talk show client as a speaker. Click the Send Audio/Video text in the AVPresence component to begin publishing a stream. (If your microphone is active, you may want to mute it to prevent a feedback loop.) Leave the browser window open, and go back to Flash MX. Test the talk-

show_106.fla document using Control > Test Movie. In the Test Movie window, login to the talk show client as a viewer. As soon as the movie jumps to the viewer frame label, a new instance of the AVPresence component should appear, displaying the live audio/video stream from the speaker client.

 The completed document, talkshow_106.fla, can be found in the chapter_12 folder of this book's CD-ROM. A version of the main.asc document, named main_101.asc, can also be found in this location.

IDENTIFYING A UNIQUE CLIENT

The talk show client is nearly complete. Right now, your version of the application can open a stream for the speaker and present that stream to other connected users when the speaker begins to publish. There is one major capability left to add to the application: allowing the speaker to choose a user name in the PeopleList component and opening a second instance of the AVPresence component for that particular user.

While this task may appear somewhat simple, it requires a thorough understanding of how clients connect to an application and how the FlashCom server identifies each user. There is no built-in ability for remote SharedObjects to target a specific user with an update. Any update to a property of a remote SharedObject is broadcast to all clients connected to the remote SharedObject. As such, you need to create a process in which the speaker's Flash movie can invoke a method within the application's server-side ActionScript code that identifies the user the speaker has chosen.

Examining the Flash Communication Framework

You start your sleuthing by reviewing the server-side code for the PeopleList component. This code is contained within the people.asc document, which is located in the scriptlib/components folder of your FlashCom server. The people.asc document is automatically loaded by the components.asc document you have specified in the main.asc document for the talkshow application. Open the people.asc document in Macromedia Dreamweaver MX or your preferred text editor.

Note

If you chose the default Developer Install for the Windows version of Flash Communication Server MX, you can find the `people.asc` document in the following location: `C:\Inetpub\wwwroot\flashcom\scriptlib\components\`

At line 47, the following `connect()` method is declared:

```
FCPeopleList.prototype.connect = function( client ) {
   var cglobal = this.getClientGlobalStorage(client);
   var clocal = this.getClientLocalStorage(client);

   clocal.id = "u" + this.getClientID(client);
   this.users_so.setProperty(clocal.id, cglobal.username == null ?
   → " fc_lurker" : cglobal.username);
}
```

When a Flash movie client connects to the `talkshow` application, the instance name of the PeopleList component found in the client, `peopleList_mc`, becomes the name of a new `FCPeopleList` object for the client in server-side ActionScript. Each Communication Component can add properties to a global or local client storage object. Most of the Communication Components create a local identifier property named `id`. The value for this property is unique for each user. In the `connect()` method of the `FCPeopleList` class, this identifier is stored in the `users_so` instance of a remote `SharedObject`, which is also used by the client-side PeopleList component. This `SharedObject` populates the actual items in the client-side PeopleList component. Therefore, you have a means of matching a user to a specific user ID. You won't need to change the existing code of the `people.asc` document, but you will take advantage of the `getClientLocalStorage()` method to retrieve a user's ID string later in this section.

Tip

For further deconstruction of the global client storage object, review the `framework.asc` document in the `scriptlib` folder. This document is also loaded by the `components.asc` document. Also, the second release of the Communication Components contain a new server-side method, `getClientID()`, which you can use to retrieve a client's identifier.

Preparing a Caller Instance of the AVPresence Component

Just as the speaker requires an instance of the AVPresence component in order to stream audio and video to the other connected users, any participant who is given permission to stream by the speaker will require a unique stream as well. Perform the following steps to begin the process of enabling another instance of the AVPresence component for a chosen participant.

TO GIVE STREAMING PERMISSION TO ANOTHER PARTICIPANT:

1. In Macromedia Flash MX, open the `talkshow_106.fla` document that you created earlier in this chapter. Resave this document as `talkshow_107.fla`.

2. Recreate the same capabilities of the `showSpeaker()` function for another instance of the AVPresence component, and encapsulate the actions within a function named `showCaller()`. Select frame 1 of the functions layer, and open the Actions panel (F9). After the existing functions, add the code shown in Listing 12.3.

Listing 12.3 showCaller() **function**

```
1.  function showCaller(isEnabled, callerMode) {
2.      trace("showCaller(" + isEnabled + "," + callerMode + ")
        → invoked");
3.      if (isEnabled) {
4.          if (!callerWin_mc) {
5.              _root.attachMovie("FCAVPresenceSymbol", "callerWin_mc", 3,
                → {_x:375, _y:30});
6.              if (callerMode){
7.                  callerWin_mc.setUsername(login_mc.username);
8.              }
9.              callerWin_mc.connect(login_mc.nc);
10.              login_mc.fcComponents.push("callerWin_mc");
11.          }
12.      } else {
13.          callerWin_mc.removeMovieClip();
14.          for (var i = 0; i < login_mc.fcComponents.length; i++) {
15.              if (login_mc.fcComponents[i] == "callerWin_mc") {
16.                  login_mc.fcComponents_array.splice(i, 1);
17.                  break;
18.              }
19.          }
20.      }
21. }
```

Line 1 declares the showCaller() function with two arguments, isEnabled and callerMode. isEnabled determines if an AVPresence component instance is added or removed for the chosen caller, and callerMode (also a Boolean value) determines if the function is invoked for the caller (true) or a connected user who will watch the caller (false). The showCaller() function can be invoked by a server-side ActionScript method within the talkshow application (as you'll see in a later section) or by the onSync() handler of the broadcastNotifier_so instance, discussed in the next step.

If the isEnabled argument is set to true (line 3), lines 4 through 11 are processed. Line 4 checks to see if an instance of callerWin_mc already exists; this condition prevents the caller's AVPresence component from re-initializing when the stream begins to publish. Lines 5 through 10 perform the same functions as the equivalent code in the showSpeaker() function: a new instance, callerWin_mc, of the AVPresence component is created and connected to the talkshow application. There are two important distinctions from the showSpeaker() function: a different instance name, callerWin_mc, and a different X coordinate position for the instance. The caller's AVPresence component must have a unique instance name. Remember, the instance name is also used to form a unique stream name, FCAVPresence.callerWin_mc.av. (The speaker is already publishing on a stream named FCAVPresence.speakerWin_mc.av via an instance named speakerWin_mc.)

If isEnabled is set to false (line 12), lines 13 through 20 are processed. Again, just like the showSpeaker() function, the AVPresence instance is removed from the stage and the instance's name is deleted from the fcComponents array of the login_mc instance.

3. Now, the initChat() function must be updated to catch an additional property of the broadcastNotifier remote SharedObject. This property is named callerBroadcast and works in the same fashion as the speakerBroadcast property. Just as the speakerBroadcast property value is used as the isEnabled argument of the showSpeaker() function, the callerBroadcast property value is used as the isEnabled argument of the showCaller() function. Navigate to the initChat() function within frame 1 of the functions layer, and insert the following highlighted code. Note that much of the original code from

this function has been omitted in the listing below (denoted with the ... characters).

```
function initChat(nc) {
    ...
    broadcastNotifier_so.onSync = function(list) {
        for (var i in list) {
            if (list[i].name == "speakerBroadcast") {
                if (viewerMode)
                    showSpeaker(this.data.speakerBroadcast);
            }
            if (list[i].name == "callerBroadcast") {
                showCaller(this.data.callerBroadcast, false);
            }
        }
    };
    broadcastNotifier_so.connect(nc);
}
```

When a change to the `callerBroadcast` property is detected, the `onSync()` handler invokes the `showCaller()` function, passing the value of the `callerBroadcast` property as the `isEnabled` argument. As you learn in the next step, the `onSync()` handler is only used to control the AVPresence component of other participating users—not the instance of the actual caller. Therefore, the `callerMode` argument is always set to false within the scope of the `onSync()` handler.

4. The last code modification occurs within the `main.asc` document of the `talkshow` application. Open this document in Macromedia Dreamweaver MX (or your preferred text editor), and add the following highlighted lines of code:

```
application.onAppStart = function(){
    this.broadcastNotifier_so = SharedObject.get("broadcastNotifier");
    this.checkStream = function(info){
        if(info.code == "NetStream.Play.PublishNotify"){
            application.broadcastNotifier_so.setProperty(this.id, true);
        } else if (info.code == "NetStream.Play.UnpublishNotify"){
            application.broadcastNotifier_so.setProperty(this.id, false);
        }
    };
    this.speakerStream = Stream.get("temp_1");
```

```
    this.speakerStream.id = "speakerBroadcast";
    this.speakerStream.onStatus = this.checkStream;
    this.speakerStream.play("FCAVPresence.speakerWin_mc.av");

    this.callerStream = Stream.get("temp_2");
    this.callerStream.id = "callerBroadcast";
    this.callerStream.onStatus = this.checkStream;
    this.callerStream.play("FCAVPresence.callerWin_mc.av");
};
```

These lines of code create a new Stream object named callerStream. This object creates a stream named temp_2, which plays a copy of the FCAVPresence.caller-Win_mc.av stream published by the callerWin_mc instance of the AVPresence component. The id property of the callerStream object is set to callerBroadcast. This property value enables the onStatus() handler, checkStream, to set the correct property of the broadcastNotifier remote SharedObject. When the caller starts to send audio and/or video, the onStatus() handler of the callerStream object sets the callerBroadcast property to true. When the caller stops sending audio and/or video, the callerBroadcast property is set to false. When the client-side onSync() handler of the broadcastNotifier_so instance detects these changes, the showCaller() function is invoked with the respective isEnabled value.

5. Save the Flash document.

 The completed document, talkshow_107.fla, can be found in the chapter_12 folder of this book's CD-ROM. You can also find a version of the main.asc document, named main_102.asc, in this location.

At this juncture, you cannot test the capabilities of these new functions and objects. You have not enabled the speaker to choose a specific user from the PeopleList component. In the next two sections, you learn how to modify the client-side PeopleList component and enable the server-side ActionScript code of the talkshow application to locate a user that is selected by the speaker.

Altering the Client-Side PeopleList Component

In this brief section, you go under the hood of the PeopleList component in the Flash MX talk show client movie. As you learned a few sections back, the connect() method of the server-side FCPeopleList class creates a unique ID string for each client that connects to the FlashCom application. This ID string is then added as a new property to the remote SharedObject that the client-side PeopleList component uses to populate its list elements, displaying each user's name.

Note

The list box element within the PeopleList component is actually an instance of the ListBox component.

While the user's name can be helpful in an attempt to identify the user from other users, it may not be unique. More than one person could login to the application with the same name. In the following steps, you learn how to easily modify the client-side PeopleList component so that each user can be uniquely identified in ActionScript code.

To identify each user with the PeopleList component:

1. Open the talkshow_107.fla document from the last section, and resave this document as **talkshow_108.fla**.

2. Open the document's Library panel (F11), and open the Communication Components folder. Inside of this folder, double-click the PeopleList component symbol.

3. In the timeline of the PeopleList symbol, select frame 1 of the actions layer. Open the Actions panel (F9), and scroll down to line 46, which has the following code:

   ```
   this.owner.people_lb.addItem(this.data[i]);
   ```

   Change this code to:

   ```
   this.owner.people_lb.addItem(this.data[i], i);
   ```

   This line of code appears within a for in loop of the onSync() handler of the SharedObject instance responsible for populating the list box (people_lb) of the PeopleList component. The remote SharedObject for the PeopleList component stores only the names of each connected user, specified as the value of the user's ID string.

Note

The name of the remote SharedObject for this example is FCPeopleList.peopleList_ mc.users. The data of this remote SharedObject does not need to be altered. Rather, you simply need to create a way to access more of the existing data within the SharedObject.

For example, the remote SharedObject contains properties that resemble the following structure:

```
u0 = "Jane"
u1 = "Jeff"
u2 = "Sean"
```

The original code on line 46 only takes the values of each property (data[i]) to create a label property for each item in the list box. The label property value is what is actually displayed in a ListBox component. The modified code continues to make each value the label while using the property's *name* (represented in the for in loop as i) as the data property. The data property value of each element in the list box is not visible. It can, however, be accessed with other methods of the ListBox component.

4. Save the Flash document.

You can find this version of the Flash document, talkshow_108.fla, in the chapter_12 folder of this book's CD-ROM

In the next section, you use the newly added data value of each list box element to allow the speaker to choose a user that can be identified by server-side ActionScript code.

Choosing a Participant in Speaker Mode

Once the PeopleList component has been modified to allow access to each user's ID string, you can build an interface that the speaker can use to open a stream to a chosen caller. The process involves the following steps:

1. The speaker selects a user's name in the list box of the PeopleList component.

2. The speaker clicks a PushButton component instance to invoke a function that sends the user's ID string to a custom method of the Client object in server-side ActionScript code.

3. The custom method compares the sent ID string to the ID string for each connected user. When a match is found, the Client object method invokes a call() method for that client's movie, specifying the showCaller() method.

4. The recognized client movie invokes the showCaller() method, opening an instance of the AVPresence component for the chosen caller only.

5. When the caller starts to publish an audio/video stream, the showCaller() function of other connected Flash clients is invoked.

In the remaining two sections, you construct the remaining core features of the talk show presentation. The next section shows you how to create and enable a PushButton instance that allows the speaker to choose a user's name in the PeopleList component and send that user's ID to the talkshow application.

To CREATE A CALLER BUTTON FOR THE SPEAKER:

1. In Macromedia Flash MX, open the talkshow_108.fla document, and resave it as **talkshow_109.fla**.

2. Create a new layer and name it **connectCaller**. On this layer, you create a PushButton instance that enables the speaker to invoke a function that recognizes the currently selected caller in the PeopleList component. Select frame 20 of the callerButton layer, and press the F7 key to add an empty keyframe. On this frame, place an instance of the PushButton component below the speedList_mc instance (**Figure 12.17**). In the Property inspector, name the new PushButton instance **callerButton**. In the Label field, type **Connect caller**. In the Click Handler field, type **connectCaller**. You may want to extend the width of the instance using the Free Transform tool.

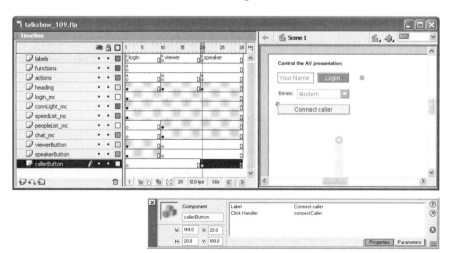

Figure 12.17 The callerButton instance is placed below the speedList_mc instance.

3. Define the `connectCaller()` function that is invoked when the speaker clicks the `callerButton` instance. Select frame 1 of the functions layer, and open the Actions panel (F9). Add the following code after the existing functions:

```
function connectCaller(obj) {
   var currentCaller = peopleList_mc.people_lb.getSelectedItem();
   var userID = currentCaller.data;
   login_mc.main_nc.call("requestCaller", null, userID);
}
```

This function creates a local variable named `currentCaller`, which retrieves the selected item of the `people_lb` ListBox component nested within the `peopleList_mc` instance. The `getSelectedItem()` method returns an object with `label` and `data` properties—the same `label` and `data` properties assigned to each item in the modified PeopleList component code.

A local variable named `userID` represents the `data` property of the `currentCaller` object. This value is then sent to a custom method named `requestCaller`, which will be created for a `Client` object in server-side ActionScript code in the next section. All client-side `call()` methods are invoked through a client-side `NetConnection` object. In the case of the talk show client, the `NetConnection` object is the `main_nc` object created by the SimpleConnect component, `login_mc`.

4. As you see in the next section, a server-side `Client` object will invoke another `call()` method specifying a custom method to be executed by the caller Flash movie. As such, you need to map the `showCaller()` function to the `main_nc` object, so that the function is accessible by a server-side `call()` method. Select frame 10 of the actions layer, and open the Actions panel (F9). Insert the following highlighted code:

```
_global.viewerMode = true;
login_mc.main_nc.showCaller = showCaller;
initChat(login_mc.main_nc);
stop();
```

This line of code simply creates a method named `showCaller()` for the NetConnection object, `main_nc`. The method invokes the same code used within the `showCaller()` function that you created earlier in this chapter.

5. Save your Flash document.

You can find the completed version of this document, `talkshow_109.fla`, in the chapter_12 folder of this book's CD-ROM.

You're almost ready to test the Flash movie and `talkshow` application. When the speaker clicks the `callerButton` instance, the `main_nc` NetConnection object invokes a custom method named `requestCaller` in server-side ActionScript code. In the next section, you define this method for the `talkshow` application.

TO CREATE THE REQUESTCALLER() METHOD OF THE CLIENT OBJECT:

1. In Macromedia Dreamweaver MX, open the `main.asc` document for the `talkshow` application.

2. After the existing code, add the `onConnect()` handler for the `application` object, shown in Listing 12.4.

Listing 12.4 The `onConnect()` **handler of the** application **object**

```
1.  application.onConnect = function(newClient){
2.     this.acceptConnection(newClient);
3.
4.     newClient.requestCaller = function(userID){
5.        trace("requestCaller() invoked with " + userID);
6.        var clientCount = application.clients.length;
7.        for(var i=0; i < clientCount; i++){
8.           var currentClient = application.clients[i];
9.           var clocal =
              → currentClient.FCPeopleList.peopleList_mc.
              → getClientLocalStorage(currentClient);
10.          if(clocal.id == userID){
11.             trace("user found: ID = " + clocal.id);
12.             currentClient.call("showCaller", null, true, true);
13.             break;
14.          }
15.       }
16.    };
17. };
```

As you learned in earlier chapters, the `onConnect()` method of the application object is invoked whenever a client attempts to connect to a Flash-Com application. The first argument of the `onConnect()` method always represents the Client object attempting to make a connection. In this example, the argument newClient is used as a Client object reference.

Line 2 allows the newClient object to connect to the talkshow application.

Lines 4 through 15 define the requestCaller() method for the newClient object. The argument userID represents the data property value sent by the speaker's Flash movie (see step 3 in the previous section). If you monitor the talkshow application with the Communication App Inspector in Flash MX, you can view the trace() message invoked in line 5. Line 6 declares a local variable named clientCount, which represents the number of Flash movie clients connected to the talkshow application.

Lines 7 through 15 perform an essential task: searching each Client object connected to the talkshow application and finding the one whose id property matches the id property sent from the speaker's Flash client. Line 8 addresses each Client object connected to the application, with the syntax applications.clients[i] Each client is represented in the clients array of the application object. In line 9, an object named clocal retrieves the local storage object created by the FCPeopleList class for the peopleList_mc instance. This object contains the id property of each client. If the id property from the clocal object matches the requested id property, then the showCaller() method of that client's NetConnection object is invoked (see step 4 of the previous section). With this process in place, only one client can receive the call() method specified in line 12.

Xref

See the sidebar at the end of this section for more information on using the new getClientID() method with FlashCom components and Client objects.

3. Save the main.asc document, and go back to the talkshow_109.fla document in Macromedia Flash MX.

4. Open the Communication App Inspector, and login to your FlashCom server. Unload any instances of the talkshow application that are currently running. Leave the inspector open, and publish preview the talkshow_109.fla document. In your Web browser window, login to the talk show client as a speaker, and begin publishing an audio/video stream. Go back to Flash MX, and test the talkshow_109.fla document (Control > Test Movie). Login to the client as a viewer, and be sure to change your user name. By default, the SimpleConnect component will load the same name that your speaker client is using. Click the Login button to accept the changed user name. Once both clients are logged in, go back to the speaker client. Select the user name of the viewer client in the PeopleList component, and click the callerButton instance. When you switch back to the viewer client, a new instance of the AVPresence component should be visible to the right of the speakerWin_mc instance. When you begin publishing in the viewer client, the speaker client should also display a new AVPresence instance.

USING GETCLIENTID() WITH THE REQUESTCALLER() METHOD

The second release of the Communication Components introduced a new method of the FCComponent class, getClientID(). You can find this method defined in the component.asc document, located in the scriptlib/components folder of your FlashCom server. getClientID() provides a universal approach to retrieving an identifier for each client connected to a FlashCom component. You could use the following revised requestCaller() method to identify a caller in the main.asc document of the talkshow application. The highlighted lines of code are added or modified lines.

```
newClient.requestCaller = function(userID){
   trace("requestCaller() invoked with " + userID);
   userNum = Number(userID.substr(1));
   trace("userNum = " + userNum);
   var clientCount = application.clients.length;
   for(var i=0; i < clientCount; i++){
      var currentClient = application.clients[i];
      var clientID =
      → currentClient.FCPeopleList.peopleList_mc.
      → getClientID(currentClient);
      if(clientID == userNum){
         trace("user found: ID = " + clientID);
         currentClient.call("showCaller", null, true, true);
         break;
      }
   }
};
```

Here, the number within the userID argument is extracted and stored within the userNum variable. This variable is compared to the number returned by the getClientID() method of the peopleList_mc component instance. If the two numbers match, the correct Client object has been found, and the showCaller() method of that client is invoked.

You will not be able to view the same camera output across two different desktop applications running the Flash client movie. For example, you can't access the camera output in Internet Explorer and the Test Movie environment of Flash MX simultaneously. If you want to test the output of your camera within two instances of the Flash client, open two browser windows instead of using one Web browser window and the Test Movie environment.

For more accurate testing, you may want to recruit a few friends who can test the FlashCom application with you.

You can find other readers online at www.mxbook.com or www.flashsupport.com. The Flash Communication Server forum on Macromedia's Web site also allows you to find other Flash developers. The Macromedia forums are listed at www.macromedia.com/ support/forums.

You can find the completed version of the main.asc document, named main_103.asc, in the chapter_12 folder of this book's CD-ROM.

Finalizing the Application

Now that the core features of the talk show client are operational, you can focus your attention on other capabilities that enhance the multi-user interactivity for all connected clients.

Allowing a Viewer to Request Access

Just as calls from listeners of a radio or TV talk show can be queued for the speaker, the talk show client should provide a means by which each viewer can let the speaker (or host) know he would like an opportunity to talk. In the following steps, you enable a PushButton instance for each user in the viewer mode.

To add a request button to the viewer mode:

1. In Macromedia Flash MX, open the talkshow_109.fla document you created in the last section. Resave this document as **talkshow_110.fla**.

2. Create a new layer, and name it **requestButton**. Insert empty keyframes on frames 10 and 20 of this layer.

3. On frame 10 of the requestButton layer, place an instance of the PushButton component. Position the instance just below the speedList_mc instance, as shown in **Figure 12.18**. In the Property inspector, name the new PushButton instance **requestButton**. In the Label field, type **Request AV access**. In the Click Handler field, type requestAccess.

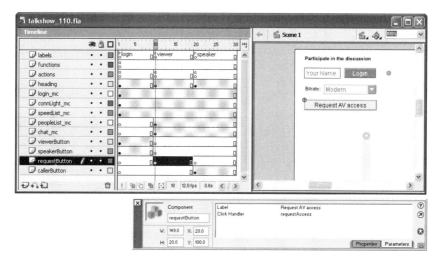

Figure 12.18 The requestButton instance is placed below the speedList_mc instance.

4. Define the requestAccess() function used by the requestButton instance. Select frame 1 of the functions layer, and open the Actions panel (F9). Add the following code after the existing functions:

```
function requestAccess(obj) {
  login_mc.main_nc.call("FCChat.chat_mc.sendMessage", null,
  → "---| Requesting call-in |---");
}
```

The requestAccess() function invokes a pre-built method of the server-side FCChat object for this movie's Client object. You do not need to add any further code within the talkshow application's main.asc document. This call() method is the same one used internally within the Chat component symbol.

Tip

If you double-click the Chat component in the document's Library panel, you can find a similar call() method within the frame 1 actions of the component's timeline.

5. Save the Flash document, and test it. Login to the Flash client as a viewer, and click the requestButton instance. The request text should appear in the Chat component, as shown in **Figure 12.19**.

Figure 12.19 When the user clicks the requestButton instance, a message is displayed to all users connected to the talkshow application.

This version of the client, talkshow_110.fla, can be found in the chapter_12 folder of this book's CD-ROM.

Limiting the Number of Speaker Logins

In the present state of the talk show client, it's feasible for more than one person to choose the speaker mode—even if authentication measures were employed. In the following steps, you will learn how to track a speaker's access to the client. If one person has already logged in as a speaker, then any other user who attempts to login as a speaker receives a message indicating that the speaker mode is already in use.

To limit the number of speaker logins:

1. Open the `talkshow_110.fla` document, and save it as **talkshow_111.fla**.

2. Create a Movie Clip symbol with text indicating the speaker mode is currently occupied. This symbol will be used by the DraggablePane instance created by the `speakerLogin()` function. For this example, you can use a prebuilt symbol, which is available on this book's CD-ROM. Open the `speakerBusy.fla` from the `chapter_12` folder of this book's CD-ROM, using the File > Open as Library command. Drag the speakerBusy symbol from this document's library to the Library panel of the `talkshow_112.fla` document.

3. Select frame 1 of the functions layer, and modify the `speakerLogin()` function with the following highlighted code:

```
function speakerLogin() {
  var speakerStatus = {};
  speakerStatus.onResult = function(isBusy) {
    trace("speakerStatus.onResult() invoked");
    trace("isBusy = " + isBusy);
    if (!isBusy) {
      var title = "Speaker Login";
      var content = "speakerPanel";
    } else {
      var title = "Speaker Logged In";
      var content = "speakerBusy";
    }
    _root.attachMovie("FDraggablePaneSymbol", "speakerPane", 1);
    with (speakerPane) {
      setPaneTitle(title);
      setPaneMaximumSize(250, 160);
      setPaneMinimumSize(250, 160);
      setContentSize(250, 140);
      setResizable(false);
      setScrollContent(content);
      setScrolling(false);
      _x = 20;
      _y = 175;
    }
  };
  login_mc.main_nc.call("checkSpeaker", speakerStatus);
}
```

In this modified version of the speakerLogin() function, you nest the existing code within an onResult() method of a speakerStatus object. The last line
of the function invokes a call() method to the talkshow application, specifying the method name checkSpeaker. You define the checkSpeaker() method
in step 5. This method returns a true or false value to the onResult()
method of the speakerStatus object. If another user currently occupies the
speaker mode, the isBusy argument of the onResult() method equals true,
and the speakerBusy symbol is displayed in the DraggablePane component. If the speaker mode is currently unoccupied, the isBusy argument
equals false, and the speakerPanel symbol is displayed.

4. As you will see in step 5, the checkSpeaker() method of the talkshow application will check the application object for a variable indicating whether a
user has logged on as the speaker. In order to let the application object
know a speaker has logged in, you need to call a separate method in the
talkshow application once the speaker has logged in. Select frame 20 of the
actions layer, and open the Actions panel (F9). Add the following highlighted code to the existing code:

```
_global.viewerMode = false;
showSpeaker(true);
initChat(login_mc.main_nc);
login_mc.main_nc.call("setSpeaker", null, true);
stop();
```

This new line of code invokes a Client object method named setSpeaker in
server-side ActionScript code, passing it a parameter of true. Note that this
method does not require an object to handle a result; therefore, null is
specified as the second argument of the call() method.

5. Now, you need to add the setSpeaker() and checkSpeaker() methods to the
newClient object in the server-side ActionScript code for the talkshow application. In Macromedia Dreamweaver MX, open the main.asc document for
the application. Add the following highlighted lines of code to the onCon-
nect() handler. Note that the code within the requestCaller() method has
been omitted for this listing.

```
application.onConnect = function(newClient){
    this.acceptConnection(newClient);
```

```
newClient.requestCaller = function(userID){
  ...
};

newClient.setSpeaker = function(isBusy){
  trace("setSpeaker() invoked");
  application.speakerStatus = isBusy;
  application.activeSpeaker = this;
  trace("status = " + application.speakerStatus);
};

newClient.checkSpeaker = function(){
  trace("checkSpeaker() invoked");
  trace("status = " + application.speakerStatus);
  return application.speakerStatus ? application.speakerStatus :
  ➞ false;
};

};
```

The setSpeaker() method of the newClient object tracks the status of a speaker. When this method is invoked by the Flash client movie, the isBusy argument is set to true. Therefore, a property named speakerStatus of the application object is set to true. This method also tracks the Client object (this) created for the speaker's connection.

The checkSpeaker() method simply returns the speakerStatus property of the application object. If no user has logged on as the speaker, then the speaker-Status property does not exist. Therefore, the ? : conditional operator is used to test the value (or existence) of the speakerStatus property. If it exists (or is already set to true), the method returns true. If the property does not exist (or is already set to false), the method returns false.

6. When the active speaker disconnects from the talkshow application, the speakerStatus property should be set to false and the activeSpeaker client should be cleared. You can accomplish these tasks in the onDisconnect() handler of the application object. Add the following handler after the existing code in the main.asc document:

```
application.onDisconnect = function(oldClient){
if(this.activeSpeaker == oldClient){
```

```
        this.speakerStatus = false;
        this.activeSpeaker = null;
    }
};
```

This code compares the oldClient object (a Client object) to the activeSpeaker object (also a Client object) that was established in the setSpeaker() method. If the two objects match, the speakerStatus property is set to false and the activeSpeaker object is set to null. When this code executes, another user can then login as a speaker.

7. Save the main.asc document, and go back to the talkshow_111.fla document in Flash MX.

8. Open the Communication App Inspector, and login to your FlashCom server. Unload any instances of the talkshow application that are currently running.

9. Publish preview the talkshow_111.fla document. When the movie loads into a Web browser window, login to the client as a speaker. (You don't need to start publishing audio/video.) Leave the browser window open, and switch back to Flash MX. Test the talkshow_111.fla document (Control > Test Movie), and try to login as a speaker. An instance of the speakerBusy symbol should appear in the DraggablePane component, as shown in **Figure 12.20**.

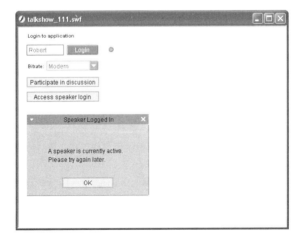

Figure 12.20 If another user occupies the speaker mode, an instance of the speakerBusy symbol is displayed in the DraggablePane component.

You can find a completed version of this document, `talkshow_111.fla`, in the `chapter_12` folder of this book's CD-ROM. The modified version of the `main.asc` document is saved as `main_104.asc` in the same location.

Xref

You may notice a message in the Live Log tab of the Communication App Inspector indicating Method not found (connect). This message does not affect the performance or functionality of the talkshow application. This is a status message returned by the Component Framework code of the FlashCom server.

Disconnecting a Caller

In order to offer the speaker complete control of the audio/video stream of a connected caller, the speaker should have the ability to remove the AVPresence component of the caller (and other connected users) at any point in time. In this section, you will learn how to add a property to the `broadcastNotifier` remote `SharedObject` to enable this level of control.

To add a disconnect button to the speaker mode:

1. Open the `talkshow_111.fla` document from the last section, and resave the document as **talkshow_112.fla**.

2. Modify the `connectCaller()` function to enable a toggle that can connect or disconnect a caller. Select frame 1 of the functions layer, and open the Actions panel (F9). Add the following highlighted lines of code to the `connectCaller()` function:

```
function connectCaller(obj) {
   var label = obj.getLabel();
   if (label == "Connect caller") {
      var currentCaller = peopleList_mc.people_lb.getSelectedItem();
      var userID = currentCaller.data;
      login_mc.main_nc.call("requestCaller", null, userID);
      obj.setLabel("Disconnect caller");
      broadcastNotifier_so.data.openStream = true;
   } else {
      broadcastNotifier_so.data.openStream = false;
   }
}
```

When the callerButton instance initializes, it has a label value of "Connect caller". When the speaker connects a chosen user, the label of the caller-Button instance (represented as the obj argument) is changed to "Disconnect caller". Then, a new property named openStream is declared in the broadcast-Notifier remote SharedObject. This property is set to true when the speaker opens an audio/video stream for a chosen caller. If the label of the caller-Button does not equal "Connect caller" when the connectCaller() function is invoked, the openStream property is set to false. In the next step, you learn how the openStream property is put into further action.

3. Now, you need to modify the onSync() handler of the broadcastNotifier_so instance to detect the changes made to the openStream property. Within the actions for frame 1 of the functions layer, locate the initChat() function, and add the following highlighted lines of code to the onSync() handler:

```
broadcastNotifier_so.onSync = function(list) {

    for (var i in list) {
        if (list[i].name == "speakerBroadcast") {
            if (viewerMode) {
                showSpeaker(this.data.speakerBroadcast);
            }
        }
        if (list[i].name == "callerBroadcast") {
            showCaller(this.data.callerBroadcast, false);
            if(!viewerMode && !this.data.callerBroadcast)
                callerButton.setLabel("Connect caller");
        }
        if (list[i].name == "openStream" && !this.data.openStream) {
            callerWin_mc.stopPublish();
            if (!viewerMode) {
                callerButton.setLabel("Connect caller");
            }
        }
    }
};
```

When the speaker chooses to disconnect a caller with an audio/video stream, the openStream property is set to false. When this change occurs, the onSync() handler invokes the stopPublish() method of the callerWin_mc instance. Because callerWin_mc is an instance of the AVPresence component, it has access to the prototype methods of the `FCAVPresence` class defined in the AVPresence component. The `stopPublish()` method tells the `callerWin_mc` instance to no longer publish a live audio/video stream to the FlashCom application. When the server-side ActionScript code detects the `unpublish` event, the `callerWin_mc` instance is removed via the client-side `showCaller()` function.

Note that the `callerBroadcast` detection has also been updated. If the caller freely chooses to stop publishing an audio/video stream, the label of the `callerButton` instance of the speaker's movie should be changed.

4. Save the Flash document. Test the Flash movie in two Web browser windows. One window should act as the viewer, while another is acting as the speaker. From the speaker client, select the user name from the viewer client in the PeopleList component, and click the `callerButton` instance. The label of the `callerButton` instance should change to "`Disconnect caller`". When the AVPresence component appears within the viewer client, click the `callerButton` instance again in the speaker client. The AVPresence component should no longer be available in the viewer client.

You can find the completed version of this document, `talkshow_112.fla`, in the `chapter_12` folder of this book's CD-ROM.

Clearing the Chat History

One of the problems you may have noticed with the talk show client is that the chat history is retained from each session, even if you unload any instances of the `talkshow` application or restart the FlashCom server. By default, the server-side `FCChat` class creates a persistent remote `SharedObject` to store the history of each chat message. In this section, you learn how to clear the chat history after the last user of each session disconnects from the `talkshow` application.

The `FCChat` class is created by the `chat.asc` server-side document, which is loaded by the `components.asc` document loaded at the beginning of the `talkshow` application's `main.asc` file. The `FCChat` class controls the client- and server-side behavior of the Chat component.

To remove the chat history when the last client disconnects:

1. In Macromedia Dreamweaver MX, open the main.asc document of the talk-show application.

2. Add the following highlighted lines of code to the onDisconnect() handler of the application object:

```
application.onDisconnect = function(oldClient){
  if(this.activeSpeaker == oldClient){
    this.speakerStatus = false;
    this.activeSpeaker = null;
  }
  if(this.clients.length == 0){
    oldClient.FCChat.chat_mc.clearHistory();
    this.speakerStream.play(false);
    this.callerStream.play(false);
    this.broadcastNotifier_so.close();
  }
};
```

When each client disconnects from the talkshow application, the length property of the application object's clients array is tested. The length property returns the number of elements within a given Array object. The clients array of the application object keeps track of each client connected to the application instance. When the last client disconnects, the length is equal to 0. At this point, the clearHistory() method of the FCChat class is invoked. This method sets the value of the history property of the chat's remote SharedObject to null. Therefore, the next time the talkshow application loads, the chat history will be empty.

This code also unsubscribes the speakerStream and callerStream objects from the AVPresence component streams and closes the connection of the broadcastNofifier_so instance. Performing these actions allows the FlashCom server to unload the application instance during the next garbage collection period. (For more information on garbage collection, refer to Chapter 11).

Tip

To learn more about the internal server-side ActionScript code for the Chat component, open the chat.asc document in Macromedia Dreamweaver MX. This document is located in the scriptlib/components/ folder of your FlashCom server.

3. Save the main.asc document, and go back to Macromedia Flash MX.

4. Open the Communication App Inspector, and login to your FlashCom server. Unload any instances of the talkshow application.

5. Test the talkshow_112.fla document that you created in the previous section. Login as a viewer or a speaker, and send a couple of messages with the Chat component. Close the test Flash movie, and re-test the document. When you log back into the client, the chat history is empty.

This version of the main.asc document is saved as main_105.asc in the chapter_12 folder of this book's CD-ROM.

Other Considerations

At this point, you've created a versatile talk show client and application. You can continue to add other features (or components) to the client. Here are some suggestions for further exploration:

- **UserColor component:** This simple Communication Component allows the user to designate a color for his text in the Chat and PeopleList components. This bit of functionality easily distinguishes one user from another.

- **Multiple callers:** You can rearrange the interface to accommodate more than one caller (or speaker). In order to accommodate multiple callers, you need to create a separate Connect/Disconnect button for each caller.

- **Chat archives:** The onDisconnect() handler of the server-side application object can be modified to send the chat history to a database when the last user disconnects.

Tip

Of course, you probably have your own ideas for taking this application further. You can continue your development by sharing your ideas and questions with other readers at mxbook.com.

SUMMARY

- The Communication Components set provides several pre-built user interface elements that can interact with a FlashCom server application.

- The SimpleConnect component connects a Flash movie client to a specific FlashCom application. Other Communication Components and custom objects can use the connection created by the component.

- The ConnectionLight component allows a user to quickly see the connection status to a FlashCom application, as well as view the network activity between a Flash movie client and the FlashCom application.

- The SetBandwidth component adjusts the bitrates of Communication Components that use audio and/or video streams. The user can choose a bitrate preset that best matches his connection speed.

- You can connect your own custom objects to the FlashCom application via the SimpleConnect instance. Such custom objects need to have a `connect()` method and must be added to the Communication Components list parameter (or the `fcComponents` array) for the SimpleConnect instance.

- The DraggablePane component allows you to insert a custom symbol from the movie's library into a pop-up Flash window.

- The PeopleList component provides a specialized ListBox component that displays the login name of each connected user to a FlashCom application.

- The Chat component allows users to freely communicate with one another using text messages.

- The AVPresence component enables a user to send or receive audio and video to and from a FlashCom application.

- The `fcComponents` array of the SimpleConnect component is the internal ActionScript reference to the Communication Components list parameter that you see in the Property inspector. You can take control of this list by inserting or removing elements from the `fcComponents` array.

- You may not want to provide unrestricted access to AVPresence component instances in a FlashCom application. In the talk show client, only a user in speaker mode can authorize the use of an AVPresence component by another connected user.

- Each of the Communication Components has unique server-side Action-Script objects, properties, and methods. Most Communication Components place client information in local and global client storage objects, which can be used in your own custom server-side ActionScript code.

- If you need to create custom capabilities for any Flash component, you can edit the internal ActionScript for the component. Be sure to thoroughly test the standard functionality of the component after any changes are made to the code. Most components use a highly intricate and intertwined system of functions, objects, and methods, and can be easily "broken."

- You can use the methods of client-side Communication Components for other interface elements, as the `requestAccess()` function demonstrated.

- By default, the history of messages stored by the Chat component is kept from one session to another. You can, however, delete the history by invoking the `clearHistory()` method of the `FCChat` class in server-side ActionScript code.

In This Chapter:

13 Creating a Stream Archive System

In this final chapter of Part III, you will learn how to create a FlashCom application and client that enable two users to conduct an audio/videoconference, which is recorded by the FlashCom application. A user can then open another client movie to watch any previously recorded session. Perhaps more than any other example in previous chapters, this application requires careful attention to the order of operations—when streams and SharedObject instances are invoked and how properties are stored and retrieved. Among other techniques presented in this chapter, the uses of proxied SharedObject data and common stream file locations are discussed.

Note

In order to build the application, you need to have access to a FlashCom server. Preferably, you should have a Developer installation of the FlashCom server on the same machine you are using to create the Flash documents.

AN OVERVIEW OF THE APPLICATION

The conference application you are about to build must solve several problems that have not been explored in previous chapters and exercises. Before you go any further with the material in this section, try out the conference application at the following URL:

www.mxbook.com/v1/ch13/

Before you enter the application, you may want to find another online friend who has a Webcam and a microphone and wants to participate in a chat with you. On the Web page at the book's Web site, click the conference recorder link. A Flash client movie (**Figure 13.1**) loads into the Web browser.

Two-Party Audio Video Conference :: Record

Conference Title: Mon Nov 4 22:22:03
Conference Room:
Proceed

NOTE: This call will be recorded and archived on this server.
If you do not want to be recorded, please exit the application.

When you click the Proceed button, you may be asked to allow
access to your camera and microphone. In the Flash Player
Settings dialog box, select "Allow" and click the "Close" button.

Figure 13.1 The conference recording client.

Two Input text fields are presented on the first screen, one from the conference's title and another for its room name (that is, the application instance's name). The title is preassigned with the current date. Type a room name into the appropriate field, and click the Proceed button.

Note You can only use alphanumeric characters and the underscore (_) character in the room name. All other characters are prohibited in the field. If you are conducting a conference with another person, make sure that person uses the same room name that you entered.

When the next screen loads (**Figure 13.2**), you see some familiar UI elements discussed in previous chapters and examples, such as the SimpleConnect, ConnectionLight, SetBandwidth, and AVPresence components. Type a login name in the SimpleConnect component and click the Login button. Choose your preferred bitrate in the SetBandwidth instance. If you want to change the title of the conference session, change the title in the field at the bottom of the movie and click the Change button. In either of the AVPresence components, click the Send Audio/Video text link. Your audio and video will begin to stream to the FlashCom application instance, and any other user connected to this application instance will see your audio/video stream. If you have another friend participating in the chat, instruct him to begin streaming with the other instance of the AVPresence component. After you have spent a few moments conversing, close the Flash movie and instruct your friend to do so as well.

Figure 13.2 The chat frame of the recording client.

Go back to the original URL (www.mxbook.com/v1/ch13/) and click the conference retrieval link. This Flash client movie (**Figure 13.3**) has only one screen, where you can choose a previously recorded conference session in a ComboBox component. If necessary, log in to the FlashCom application by typing your name into the SimpleConnect instance and clicking the Login button. Choose the title of your conference session from the ComboBox instance. The audio/video streams from your conference will begin to play in the respective video windows of the client. You can also view any other videoconference recorded by other users of the application.

Figure 13.3 The conference retrieval client.

Note   Streams recorded by public users of this example are frequently deleted from the FlashCom server used for the mxbook.com site. The degree of synchronization between the recorded streams largely depends on low latency values during the recording and playback of the streams. If the connection to the FlashCom server is slow, the two streams may play back with less-than- perfect synchronization.

While the operation of this Flash application may seem simple enough, several tasks must be accomplished in both client- and server-side ActionScript to accommodate these features. In the next two sections, you will examine the processes of this application.

Examining the User's Experience

To understand the goals of the application, each step of the application you tested in the last section is outlined. By looking at the tasks the user performs to interact with the application, you can better understand how to build the Flash client movie and FlashCom application code.

As with any multimedia project, the ability to define the process of a user interface is critical. Don't attempt to build an interface in any authoring tool until you have a plan. Even the most basic plan can save you hours, if not days or weeks, of development work. Granted, it's much simpler to deconstruct an existing example than it is to describe or map a concept from scratch. Most developers and UI designers create mock-ups in graphic design programs such as Macromedia FreeHand or Fireworks. You can even create paper mock-ups, with simple sketches of each user interface (or screen) within the application.

MAPPING THE CONFERENCE RECORDER PROCESS

Figure 13.4 illustrates the path a user takes to start a live conference session. This map begins to deconstruct the server-side operations within the Flash-Com application. The process involves two screens: a start screen where the user can specify a conference room and title, and a chat screen where the user can send and receive audio/video streams from another participant.

CHARTING THE CONFERENCE RETRIEVAL PROCESS

The process for the second user interface is shown in **Figure 13.5**. This Flash client movie allows the user to connect to a FlashCom application and choose a previously recorded conference session from a combo box. When the selection is made in the combo box, the AV streams are presented to the user.

Determining the Requirements

Now it's time to get down to brass tacks. You know what the application needs to do, but what factors do you need to consider to create such an application? What kind of application architecture do you need to construct that will allow several hundreds (if not thousands) of users to conduct chat sessions with one another?

Live Conference Recording Client

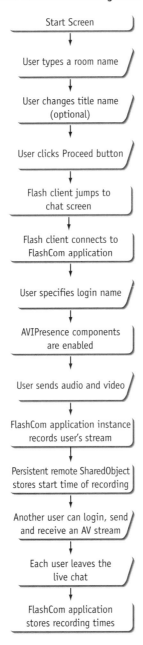

Figure 13.4 The process flowchart of the conference recording client.

Conference Retrieval Client

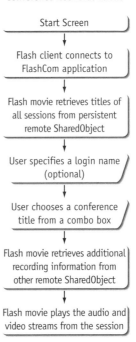

Figure 13.5 The process flowchart of the conference retrieval client.

MANAGING APPLICATION INSTANCES AND CONCURRENT SESSIONS

One of the objectives of this conference application is the ability to host several two-way chats for many simultaneous users. Therefore, each conference session needs its own application instance, just as you saw in the multiroom text chat example in Chapter 11. The name of the conference room is used as the instance name for the FlashCom application. While the conference recording client is engaged with one instance of the application, the default instance (_definst_) needs to be available for users who want to view previously recorded sessions. In the next section, you will learn how information recorded from each application instance can be accessible by the default instance of the FlashCom application.

Note

As you will learn later in this chapter, the actual name of the FlashCom application is conference. This name is referenced in the rtmp URI used in client- and server-side ActionScript code.

STORING INFORMATION FOR EACH SESSION

The conference retrieval client can retrieve the information for any recorded session. The retrieval client connects only to the default instance of the conference application on the FlashCom server. Hence, each recording session needs to save its information in a common namespace. For the conference application, the default application instance (_definst_) is designated as this namespace.

There are three persistent remote SharedObject instances created by server-side ActionScript for each recording session (or application instance). Each of these instances creates an FSO file stored in the sharedobjects/_definst_ folder of the conference application.

- **av_1_timeTracker_so:** This SharedObject instance creates a file that stores the recording information of the first user's AV stream. The details of the recording information are discussed in the next section. The name of the SharedObject FSO file is based on the following formula:

  application instance name + "_" + stream number + "_" + current date

  The instance name of the application is the same as the room name of the conference, and the stream number is either 1 or 2. The date information uses the following formula:

  year + "_" + month + "_" + day + "_" + hour + "_" + minute

For example, if a person using the left AVPresence component in the Flash client movie connected to the application, the instance named `family` starts sending an AV stream on October 31, 2002 at 7:21 PM, and the FSO file will have the following name:

`family_1_2002_10_31_19_21.fso`

- **av_2_timeTracker_so:** This `SharedObject` instance stores the recording information for the second user's AV stream. The second user is the person using the AVPresence component instance located on the right half of the Flash movie stage.

- **savedCalls_so:** When each user has disconnected from an instance of the `conference` application (that is, when the `application.clients.length` property is less than 1 or equal to 0), the application instance stores the conference title, date (as established by the previous date formula), length (in milliseconds), and instance name. This information is saved as a new property name in the remote `SharedObject` file, `savedCalls.fso`, created by the instance. The name of this property uses the following formula:

`application instance name + "_" + current date`

The information stored in the `savedCalls` data is loaded into the conference retrieval client as soon as it loads. When a user selects a conference title in the combo box, the appropriate time tracker data is loaded from the other two remote `SharedObjects`.

> **Note** Later in this chapter, you will learn about other temporary (non-persistent) remote `SharedObject` instances that are created to store other information used by the application instance.

Each instance of the `conference` application also records streamed audio and video from the AVPresence components to stored FLV files. You will learn more about the specific server-side ActionScript code to record streams later in this chapter. For now, it's important to understand that you can create virtual locations for stored streams on a FlashCom server. By default, if you create or record a stream within a specific application instance, the FLV file for that stream is saved within an instance folder of the `streams` folder for your application. For example, if you record a stream with a connection to the default instance of the conference application, the stream is saved in the following location:

```
applications/conference/streams/_definst_
```

If a Flash client movie wants to play a stream located in this folder, then the client must connect to the default instance of the application. If the movie is connected to another instance, only streams for that instance can be played. However, an XML configuration file for your FlashCom server allows you to specify virtual locations for stored streams. On your FlashCom server, locate the Vhost.xml file. With a default Windows installation of Flash Communication Server MX, this file is located in the following folder:

```
C:\Program Files\Macromedia\Flash Communication Server MX\conf
→ \_defaultRoot_\_defaultHost_\Vhost.xml
```

Open this XML file in Macromedia Dreamweaver MX or your preferred XML document editor. If you scroll down to the <VirtualDirectory> node, the inserted comments tell you that you can specify virtual locations for streams. Later in this chapter, you create the following virtual path in this node, which adds a callStream alias name to your server's configuration:

```
<Streams>callStreams;C:\Inetpub\wwwroot\flashcom\applications\conference
→ \callStreams</Streams>
```

Tip
The actual folder name in the physical path does not need to have the same name as the alias itself. You must restart your FlashCom server to register any newly added aliases.

Caution
When you create a virtual directory for a stream alias, you must specify the format aliasName;path. You need to provide a name for the stream alias, followed by a semi-colon (;) and the full path to the directory you want to use. You can use network paths as well, such as \\myLocalServer\myShareName\myFolder.

By adding this node to the <VirtualDirectory> node, you can make references to the callStreams alias in the stream name of a NetStream.publish() or Stream.get() method. For example, once the callStreams alias is created, the following client-side code creates an FLV file named myRecording in the callStreams folder of the

conference application, where nc represents a valid NetConnection object reference and myCamera represents a Camera object:

```
myStream_ns = new NetStream(nc);
myStream_ns.attachVideo(myCamera);
myStream_ns.publish("callStreams/myRecording", "record");
```

Regardless of the application or application instance to which the nc object is
connected, the myRecording.flv file is stored in the callStreams folder. This technique allows you to retrieve streams in the callStreams location from any application or application instance running on the FlashCom server. As such, you
can create several common folders and aliases for streams, allowing you to
save or play streams to and from other various locations, including networked
drives.

 Note As the Vhost.xml document's name suggests, stream aliases can be used by any
application on the current virtual host domain of the FlashCom server. The Professional edition of FlashCom server allows one server to manage several virtual
domains.

The intended purpose for saving SharedObject data in the _definst_ instance of
the conference application and stream files to the callStreams alias is to enable
the retrieval client movie to connect to just one application instance (_definst_
) to access information and streams for *any* recorded session. Regardless of the
name of the application instance that was responsible for creating the session, the default instance of the application can access streams recorded by
other application instances.

GATHERING INFORMATION FOR EACH SESSION

Most of the information stored in the three persistent remote SharedObjects
mentioned in the previous section is created within the server-side Action-
Script code of the conference application. Because a chat between two people
occurs in real time, the application must track when each person begins publishing a stream and when that stream is stopped. This tracking (and subsequent saved data) is necessary for the chat to be replayed at a later time by
the retrieval client.

In order to track the time, the application instance creates a property named startTime. This property is a Date object representing the time (in milliseconds) at which the first user clicks the Send audio/video text link within one of the AVPresence components—or more exactly, when the server first receives the stream from that user's client. The conference session's length and the specific recording times of each user's streams can be determined by subtracting startTime from a new Date object. The onStatus() handler of the server-side Stream objects is used to capture the start and stop "moments" of each user's stream. Each set of start and stop times is saved as a separate object within a recordTimes array stored in each user's respective time tracker SharedObject (discussed in the previous section). You will learn more about these specific operations later in this chapter.

The server-side ActionScript code of the conference application also borrows information from the temporary remote SharedObject that was created for the AVPresence components. Each of these objects stores the user's login name (as entered in the SimpleConnect component instance). The user's name is retrieved from the respective SharedObject and stored in the user's recordTimes array.

Xref

The FlashCom Component Framework was introduced in the last chapter. Many of the Communication Components create remote SharedObjects that allow the components to share information among connected users, application instances, and other Communication Components.

The recording client also provides a text field for the conference's title. This text is stored (and synchronized) via another temporary remote SharedObject named sessionName. Any time a user changes the text within the title field in the Flash client and clicks the Change button, a property named title within the sessionName data is updated. The value of the title property is saved in the savedCalls SharedObject at the end of the recorded session.

RETRIEVING INFORMATION FOR ARCHIVED SESSIONS

When the retrieval client movie first loads, the movie connects to the default instance (_definst_) of the conference application. Once a successful connection is made, the movie connects to savedCalls, the persistent remote SharedObject created (or modified) during a recorded session. Each named property of this object represents a recorded session, and the value of each property is an object with several other properties describing details of the session. One of these properties, confTitle, stores the title of the session (this value is actually retrieved from the SharedObject named sessionName, discussed in the previous section). The confTitle property from each session is used as the label property for each item in the ComboBox instance displayed in the retrieval client movie. The data property of each item is set to the respective property name of the savedCalls remote SharedObject. When a user selects a session's title in the combo box, this data property is used to retrieve the appropriate tracker SharedObject data for each recorded stream.

When the data for each user's recorded session is retrieved, a setInterval() function recreates the same timing mechanism used in the server-side Action-Script code. When the elapsed time of the client movie matches the start time of either user's recording session, the movie begins to play the saved stream. When the elapsed time matches the stop point of a user's recording, playback on that stream is stopped.

Note

During a recording session, a user can start or stop publishing as many times as he or she deems necessary. Each start and stop point is saved in the recordTimes array for each user.

DESIGNING THE LIVE CONFERENCE CLIENT MOVIE

As you learned at the beginning of this chapter, the conference recording and retrieval clients are two different Flash movies. You start by building the conference chat client, which allows two users to log in to a specific application instance, which records each user's audio/video stream.

Note

This section walks you through the steps necessary to make the Flash MX document that connects to the conference application. Later in this chapter, you will learn how to create the server-side capabilities required for this Flash client movie.

Creating the Start Screen

The first screen of the live chat client presents the user with two text fields in which the user can specify a conference title and room name. The client movie does not make a connection to the conference application until the user clicks a Proceed button, which moves the timeline to the chat frame label (discussed in the next section).

To build the start screen of the client movie:

1. On the machine that's hosting the FlashCom server, create a folder named **conference** in the applications folder. If you have the default Developer Install the FlashCom server on a Windows machine running IIS, the path to this folder should be the following:

   C:\Inetpub\wwwroot\flashcom\applications\conference

   Once the conference folder is created, connections can be made to this application on the FlashCom server.

2. Open Macromedia Flash MX and create a new document. Save this document as **confRecord_100.fla**.

3. Change the dimensions of this document to 425 × 300. Choose Modify > Document and enter the new dimensions in the Document Properties dialog box (**Figure 13.6**).

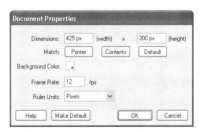

Figure 13.6
The dimensions of the Flash movie are changed in the Document Properties dialog box.

4. Rename Layer 1 to **labels**. On this layer, select frame 20 and press the F5 key (or Insert > Frame) to add more frames. Select frame 1 of the labels layer and label this keyframe **init** in the Property inspector. Select frame 10 and insert an empty keyframe (F7, or Insert > Blank Keyframe). Label this frame **chat**.

5. Create a new layer, and name it **heading**. Place this layer beneath the labels layer. On frame 1 of this layer, use the Text tool to add the Static text **Two-Party Audio Video Conference :: Record**. Place this text near the top edge of the stage. Make another layer named **frame** and create a rounded rectangle shape with the Rectangle tool, as shown in **Figure 13.7**.

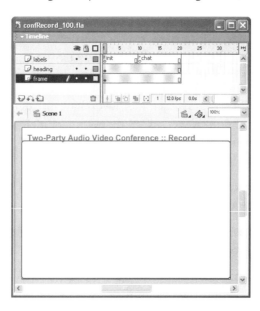

Figure 13.7
The Rectangle tool is selected, and the Round Rectangle Radius button in the toolbox is enabled to draw a rounded frame for a portion of the movie's stage.

6. Create another layer, and name it **textfields**. Place this layer underneath the heading and frame layers. Select frame 10 of the textfields layer, and press the F7 key to insert an empty keyframe.

7. Select frame 1 of the textfields layer. Using the Text tool, create an Input text field with an instance name of `confName_txt`. Enable the Show border option for this field, and set the Line type to Single line. Add the Static text **Conference Title:** to the left of the field (**Figure 13.8**).

8. Repeat step 7 for another Input text field with an instance name of `conf-Room_txt`. Place this field beneath the `confName_txt` instance (**Figure 13.9**). Enable the same options for this text field in the Property inspector. Add the Static text **Conference Room:** to the left of the field.

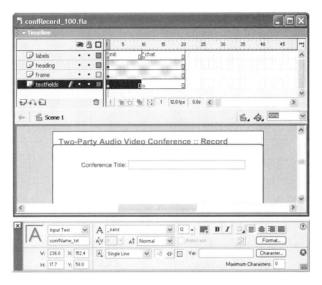

Figure 13.8 A confName_txt field is created and labeled with Static text.

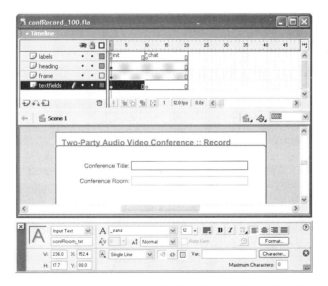

Figure 13.9 A confRoom_txt field designates the application instance name of the conference application.

Tip   You can optionally add the following Static text to alert the user to the purpose and functionality of the application: *This call will be recorded and archived on this server. If you do not want to be recorded, please exit the application*.

Note   When you click the Proceed button, you may be asked to allow access to your camera and microphone. In the Flash Player Settings dialog box, select "Allow" and click the "Close" button.

9. Create a new layer, and name it **proceedButton**. Place this layer underneath the textfields layers. Select frame 10 of the proceedButton layer, and press the F7 key to insert an empty keyframe.

10. Select frame 1 of the proceedButton layer, and drag an instance of the SimpleConnect component from the Components panel to the stage. You won't actually use the SimpleConnect component on this frame, but you will use the FCPushButton component that's nested within the SimpleConnect component. This component is a modified version of the regular PushButton component. Delete the SimpleConnect instance on the stage, and open the document's Library panel (F11). There, open the Communication Components folder, and then open the Communication UI Components folder. From this folder, drag the FCPushButton symbol from the Library panel to the stage. Position the new instance below the Input text fields. In the Property inspector, name this instance proceedButton. Assign a Label value of **Proceed** and a Click Handler value of setName (**Figure 13.10**).

11. Make a new layer and rename it **functions**. Place this layer underneath the labels layer. Define the setName() function, which is used as the click handler for the proceedButton instance. This function moves the playhead of the Flash movie to the chat frame label, if the Input text fields are not empty. If one of the fields is empty, the respective field displays a message to the user, and focus is directed to the field. The setName() function follows in Listing 13.1.

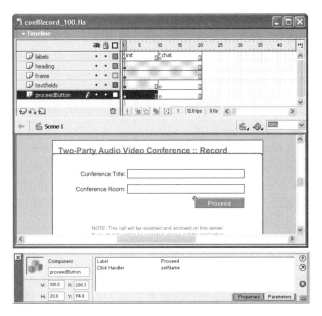

Figure 13.10 The proceedButton instance is placed below and to the right of the TextField instances.

Listing 13.1 setName() **function**

```
function setName(obj) {
    if (confName_txt.text != "" && confRoom_txt.text != "") {
        appInstance = confRoom_txt.text;
        confTitle = confName_txt.text;
        this.gotoAndStop("chat");
    } else if (confName_txt.text == "") {
        confName_txt.text = "Specify a title name for the conference.";
        Selection.setFocus(confName_txt);
    } else if (confRoom_txt.text == "") {
        confRoom_txt.text = "Type a name for the chat room.";
        Selection.setFocus(confRoom_txt);
    }
}
```

This code also creates two variables on the _root timeline: appInstance and confTitle. When you declare an appInstance variable on _root, its value is appended to the Application Directory value (that is, the connect URI) used by a SimpleConnect component instance. Later in this chapter, you will place a SimpleConnect instance on the chat frame, where the appInstance value is used. For this application, the text that the user types in the confRoom_txt field becomes the name of the application instance within the conference application on the FlashCom server. The confTitle variable stores the current text within the confName_txt field, so that the title can be redisplayed to the user on the chat frame.

Note	The setName() function is shown here with an obj argument. This argument is not actually used in the scope of the function. It's included to remind you that you can directly access a reference to the proceedButton instance as the argument of a click handler for a PushButton (or FCPushButton) instance.

12. Define a function that retrieves and formats the current date. This function is used to populate the confName_txt field with a new date when the movie loads. Select frame 1 of the functions layer, and open the Actions panel (F9). Add the following code after the existing setName() function:

```
function retrieveDate() {
    var currentDate = new Date().toString();
    currentDate = currentDate.substring(0, (currentDate.indexOf("GMT")
    → - 1));
    return currentDate;
}
```

13. Create another layer and rename it **actions**. Place this layer beneath the functions layer. On the init frame, you fill the confName_txt field with the current date and restrict the confRoom_txt field to accept only alphanumeric characters and the underscore character. In this way, you can prevent a user from typing an illegal instance name for the conference application into the confRoom_txt field. Select frame 1 of the actions layer, and open the Actions panel (F9). Add the following code:

```
confName_txt.text = retrieveDate();
confRoom_txt.restrict = "A-Za-z0-9_";
Stage.scaleMode = "noScale";
stop();
```

This code also sets the scaleMode of the Stage object to "noScale", which prevents the Flash movie from scaling above or below 100 percent of its original size (425 × 300). This line is optional and can be omitted.

14. Choose File > Publish Settings, and choose the HTML tab. In the Dimensions field, choose Percent. Leave the Width and Height values at 100 percent. This setting allows the Flash movie to center itself at original size (thanks to the noScale property set in the previous step) within the full area of the browser window. Now, choose the Formats tab and clear the Use default names check box. In the Filename field for the Flash format, type confRecord.swf. In the Filename field for the HTML format, type confRecord.html.

15. Save the Flash document and test it (Control > Test Movie). When the movie loads, the current date should display in the confName_txt field. Type a name into the confRoom_txt field and click the Proceed button. The movie should jump to the empty chat frame. You can retest this movie leaving one of the Input text fields empty to test the nested else if statements within the setName() function.

You can find the completed version of this document, confRecord_100.fla, in the chapter_13 folder of this book's CD-ROM.

If you inserted the Stage.scaleMode = "noScale"; line in step 13, try using File > Publish Preview > Default - (HTML) to view your Flash movie in a Web browser. Regardless of the size of the browser window, the Flash movie appears centered within the window, and the movie's dimensions remain fixed at 425 × 300.

Constructing the Chat Screen

Once the user has specified a room name (and modified the conference title, if desired), the user can begin to publish an AV stream to a specific instance of the conference application on the FlashCom server. On the chat frame, you will add the same Communication Components you learned in the last chapter. You will also create an Input text field that displays the conference's title. The user can change the title in this field, and update a remote SharedObject with this new title, so that any user connected to the same application instance can see the updated title.

Caution Before you begin this section, make sure you have downloaded the latest Communication Components from Macromedia's Web site at:

www.macromedia.com/software/flashcom/download/components

If you downloaded and installed the first version of the Communication Components (prior to November 13th, 2002), you will need to reinstall the latest download. This application will not function properly with the original AVPresence component from the first release.

To BUILD THE CHAT SCREEN:

1. Open the confRecord_100.fla document from the last section and save this document as **confRecord_101.fla**.

2. Create a Dynamic text field to display the current room name (that is, application instance name). Select the empty keyframe on frame 10 of the textfields layer. Use the Text tool to create the field and position the field below the heading text. In the Property inspector, name the instance **confRoom_txt**, enable the Selectable option, and disable the Show border option. Choose Single line in the Line type menu. (**Figure 13.11**)

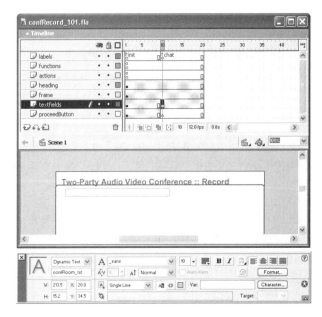

Figure 13.11 A new instance of the confRoom_txt field is created and placed at the top left of the stage.

3. Create a new layer and name it **login_mc**. Place this layer beneath the proceedButton layer. Select frame 10 of this layer and press the F7 key to insert
an empty keyframe. With frame 10 selected, drag an instance of the SimpleConnect component from the Components panel to the stage. Place the
instance below the confRoom_txt instance. In the Property inspector, name
the instance **login_mc**. In the Application Directory field, type the URI to
the FlashCom server hosting the conference application. If the FlashCom
server is running on the same IP and machine as the Web server hosting
the Flash client movie (SWF file), you can use the value **rtmp:/conference**. For
now, do not add any instance names to the Communication Components
list parameter. (**Figure 13.12**)

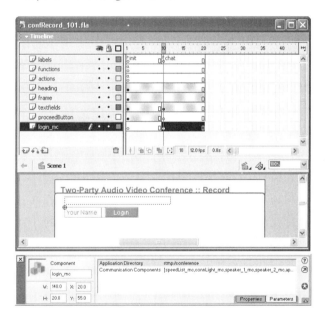

Figure 13.12 An instance of the SimpleConnect component.

4. Make a new layer named **connLight_mc**. Place this layer underneath the
login_mc layer, and add an empty keyframe on frame 10. With this frame
of the connLight_mc layer selected, drag an instance of the Connection-
Light component from the Components panel to the stage. Place the
instance to the right of the SimpleConnect instance. In the Property
inspector, name the instance **connLight_mc**. Do not change the default
parameters of this instance.

5. Create a layer named **speedList_mc** and place this layer below the conn-Light_mc layer. Insert an empty keyframe on frame 10 of the new layer. On this keyframe, drag an instance of the SetBandwidth component from the Components panel to the stage. Place the instance near the right edge of the stage (**Figure 13.13**). In the Property inspector, name the instance speedList_mc. Do not change the default parameters of the instance. On frame 10 of the textfields layer, add the Static text **Bitrate:** to the left of the speedList_mc instance.

Figure 13.13 An instance of the SetBandwidth component is placed to the right side of the stage.

6. Create a layer named **speakers** and move the layer below the speedList_mc layer. On frame 10 of the new layer, insert an empty keyframe and drag an instance of the AVPresence component to the stage. Place the instance in the left half of the movie's stage, below the other components. In the Property inspector, name the instance speaker_1_mc. Do not change the default parameters of the instance (**Figure 13.14**).

7. Select the speaker_1_mc instance from step 6 and duplicate it (Edit > Duplicate). Position the new instance to the right of the original, as shown in the **Figure 13.15**. Name the new instance speaker_2_mc.

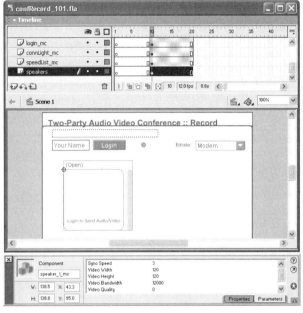

Figure 13.14 The speaker_1_mc instance of the AVPresence
component is placed on the left half of the stage.

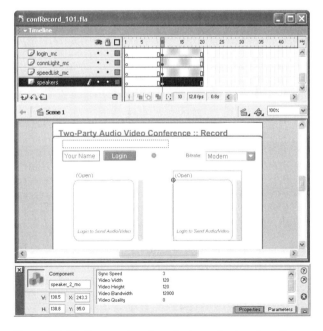

Figure 13.15 The speaker_2_mc instance is placed on the
right half of the stage.

8. Create an Input text field in which the user can change the title of the conference during the session. On frame 10 of the textfields layer, use the Text tool to create an Input text field instance named **confName_txt**. Use the same options as the original confName_txt field. Place this instance near the bottom edge of the stage, leaving a gap for another text field (discussed in the next step). Add the Static text **Title:** to the left of the confName_txt field (**Figure 13.16**). The text in this field is used to update a property of a remote SharedObject, discussed in steps 13 and 14.

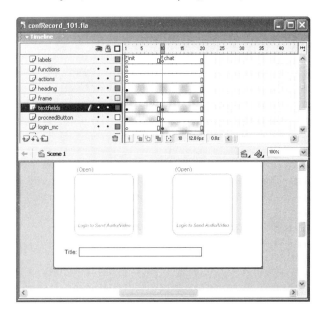

Figure 13.16 A new instance of the confName_txt field.

9. Make a text field that displays a notification regarding the update status of the remote SharedObject storing the conference's title information. On frame 10 of the textfields layer, create a Dynamic text field instance named **soStatus_txt**. Place this field below the confName_txt field. Disable the Show border option for this field (**Figure 13.17**).

10. Make a new layer named **updateButton**. Move the layer below the proceedButton layer. On frame 10 of the new layer, insert an empty keyframe and place another instance of the FCPushButton component to the right of the confName_txt field. In the Property inspector, name this new instance

updateButton. In the Parameters tab, assign a Label value of **Change**. In the Click Handler field, type `updateTitle`. Refer to **Figure 13.18**.

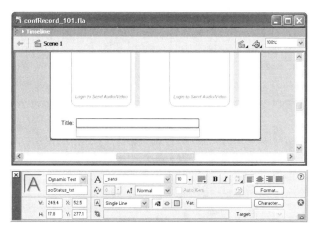

Figure 13.17 The soStatus_txt field displays notification messages to the user.

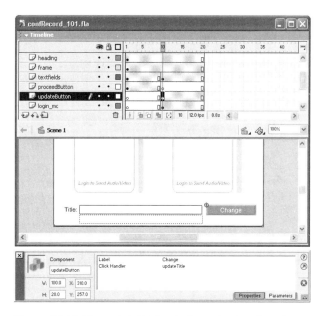

Figure 13.18 The updateButton instance is placed to the right of the confName_txt instance.

11. Now, add a sound asset to the movie's library. This sound plays when the remote `SharedObject` for the conference's title successfully updates. Choose Window > Common Libraries > Sounds. From this document's Library panel, drag a copy of the Plastic Button sound to the Library panel of the `confRecord_101.fla` document. Right-click (or Control-click on the Mac) the Plastic Button sound in the `confRecord_101.fla` document's Library panel, and choose Linkage. In the Linkage Properties dialog box, select the Export for ActionScript check box and change the Identifier value to **updateSuccess** (**Figure 13.19**). Click the OK button to accept the changes. This sound asset can now be dynamically attached and played with ActionScript code. You will use this linkage identifier in step 13.

Figure 13.19 A linkage identifier of updateSuccess
is assigned to the Plastic Button sound.

12. Add actions to the `chat` frame that insert the appropriate information into the `confRoom_txt` and `confName_txt` fields. Create an `Object` object that can use the `NetConnection` object from the SimpleConnect component. This object should create a client-side reference to a temporary remote `Shared-Object` named `sessionName`. This `SharedObject` stores the conference's title, as typed in the `confName_txt` field. Insert an empty keyframe on frame 10 of the actions layer. Select this frame and open the Actions panel (F9). Type the following code in the actions list:

```
initSO = {};
initSO.connect = function(nc) {
  sessionName_so = SharedObject.getRemote("sessionName", nc.uri,
  → false);
  sessionName_so.onSync = sessionSync;
  sessionName_so.connect(nc);
};
confName_txt.text = confTitle;
confRoom_txt.text = "Room: " + appInstance;
```

The connect() method of the initSO object is invoked by the SimpleConnect instance, login_mc. In step 14, you will add the name of the initSO object to the Communication Components list parameter of the login_mc instance. When the connect() method is invoked, the sessionName remote SharedObject data is linked to the sessionName_so instance. This instance's onSync() handler, sessionSync, is defined in the next step.

13. When the first user connects to the sessionName data, that user's title information should be assigned to a property of sessionName. If any user revises the text in the confName_txt field and clicks the Change button, the new title information should be shared with the other user. Select frame 1 of the functions layer and add the code in Listing 13.2 after the existing functions. Note that the line numbers shown with this code are relative; they do not refer to the actual line numbers in the Actions panel.

Listing 13.2 sessionSync() **function**

```
1.  function sessionSync(list) {
2.     for (var i in list) {
3.        trace(i + ": name: " + list[i].name + ", code: " +
          → list[i].code);
4.        if (list[i].code == "clear" && this.data.title == null) {
5.           this.data.title = confTitle;
6.        } else if (list[i].name == "title") {
7.           if (list[i].code == "change") {
8.              confName_txt.text = this.data.title;
9.              soStatus_txt.text = "Conference title changed.";
10.             var playSound = true;
11.          } else if (list[i].code == "success") {
12.             soStatus_txt.text = "Conference title updated.";
13.             var playSound = true;
14.          } else if (list[i].code == "reject") {
15.             soStatus_txt.text == "Change rejected by server.";
16.             var playSound = false;
17.          }
18.          if (playSound) {
19.             clickSound = new Sound(_root);
20.             clickSound.attachSound("updateSuccess");
21.             clickSound.start();
22.          }
23.          statusTimer = setInterval(clearStatus, 3000);
24.       }
25.    }
26. }
```

This function processes any changes or updates that occur to the session-Name data within the current instance of the conference application. Remember, such changes are reported as an Array object to the onSync() handler of a remote SharedObject instance.

If the conference title has not been added to the sessionName data, lines 4 and 5 are processed. A property named title is set to the text contents of the confName_txt field. This code is only invoked for the user who is the first to arrive on the chat frame. If the title property has already been set, lines 6-24 are processed.

Lines 7-10 are processed by any client that is receiving an update published by another user. The confName_txt field displays the new value of the title property, and the soStatus_txt field displays a notification message of "Conference title changed." A local variable named playSound is set to true, indicating that the Plastic Button sound should be played (lines 18-22).

Lines 11-13 are processed by the client movie that declared the new conference title in the sessionName data. Because this client (that is, the user) was the one that already typed a new title into the confName_txt field, no text changes need to occur in the confName_txt field. Only the soStatus_txt field needs to display a notification to the user that the server successfully received his update. Again, playSound is set to true to indicate that the Plastic Button sound should be played.

Lines 14-16 are processed by any client movie whose attempt to change the title property of the sessionName data was denied or rejected. The soStatus_txt field displays an error notification, and playSound is set to false. The Plastic Button sound is not played for this condition.

Tip You could add a second linked sound asset to the movie's library for the error (or reject) condition. In this situation, you would set playSound equal to the linkage ID of the appropriate sound to be played. Instead of using a static reference in the attachSound() method in line 20, you would use the playSound value.

If playSound was set to true in the previous code, the updateSuccess sound (that is, the Plastic Button sound) is played by the movie in lines 18-22.

After a notification message has been displayed to the user, the clearStatus() function is invoked within 3 seconds, as shown in line 23. The `clearStatus()` function clears the `soStatus_txt` field after the delay period has transpired. You will define the `clearStatus()` function in step 15.

14. Define the `updateTitle()` function used as the Click Handler for the `update-Button` instance. This function changes the `title` property of the `sessionName` remote `SharedObject` to match the text typed into the `confName_txt` field. Select frame 1 of the functions layer and open the Actions panel (F9). Add the following code after the existing functions:

```
function updateTitle(obj) {
    trace("updateTitle() invoked");
    sessionName_so.data.title = confName_txt.text;
}
```

15. Define the `clearStatus()` function invoked by the `onSync()` handler, `session-Sync`. This function is invoked three seconds after the notification text is displayed to each user in the `soStatus_txt` field. Select frame 1 of the functions layer and open the Actions panel (F9). Insert the following code after the last function:

```
function clearStatus() {
    trace("clearStatus() invoked");
    soStatus_txt.text = "";
    clearInterval(statusTimer);
}
```

16. Add all the object instance names requiring a `NetConnection` object to the Communication Components list parameter of the `login_mc` instance. Select the `login_mc` instance and click the Communication Components field in the Property inspector. In the Values list, add each instance's name as a new item (**Figure 13.20**).

Figure 13.20
The instance names of each object that requires a connection to the conference application are added to the Values list.

17. Save the Flash document. Before you can test the movie, you need to create a main.asc document for the conference application that enables the Communication Components.

18. In Macromedia Dreamweaver MX, choose File > New to create a new ActionScript Communications document. On line 1 of this document, type the following code:

```
load("components.asc");
```

This code loads the components.asc document when a new instance of the conference application runs. The components.asc document contains all the necessary server-side ActionScript code for the Communication Components to interact with one another.

Xref

For more information on the components.asc document, read the previous chapter.

19. Save the ASC document as a file named **main.asc** in the conference folder, located in the applications folder of your FlashCom server.

20. Switch back to the confRecord_101.fla document in Macromedia Flash MX. Test the movie (Control > Test Movie). When the movie loads, type a room name and click the Proceed button. On the chat frame, the connLight_mc instance should turn green once a connection is made to an instance of the conference application. Type a name into the text field of the login_mc instance and click the Login button. The AVPresence instances should then be enabled for your use. Test the movie in a Web browser on two different computers at the same time. While the conference application does not currently record any streams or save any permanent data, you should be able to conduct a live conference with two users in the Flash client movie.

You can find the completed version of this document, confRecord_101.fla, in the chapter_13 folder of this book's CD-ROM. A version of the main.asc document, named main_100.asc, is also in this location.

MANAGING STREAMS AND DATA IN THE FLASHCOM APPLICATION

Once the Flash client movie can engage two users in a live audio/video chat, you're ready to tap the power of the FlashCom server to record data and streams published by each participant. At this point, you may want to reread the overview of the application earlier in this chapter. You will create or modify the following ASC files in this section:

- `main.asc` : You created the first version of this document in the last section. The `main.asc` document is automatically loaded for each instance of a FlashCom application. The `main.asc` is responsible for loading the `components.asc` file, as well as the other documents in this list. The `application.onConnect()` and `application.onDisconnect()` handlers are the only methods directly defined in the `main.asc` file; all other methods of the application are defined in the other ASC files.

- `formdate.asc` : This document contains a method that returns the current date, formatted with the syntax described earlier in this chapter.

- `timer.asc` : This ASC document is responsible for creating and maintaining an instance timer, which tracks the amount of time an instance of the conference application has been running.

- `startup.asc` : This file contains the server-side ActionScript code that is initialized when the first user of an application instance connects to the FlashCom server. All remote `SharedObjects` and server-side `Stream` objects are created in the methods defined in this document.

- `shutdown.asc` : This ASC document defines the server-side methods that are invoked when the last user disconnects from an instance of the conference application. All connections to remote `SharedObjects` and server-side streams are closed.

In the following sections, you will build the server-side ActionScript code necessary for each of these documents.

Tip

While it's feasible to combine the code from all these individual ASC files into one large ASC document, you can more easily manage the scope of your FlashCom application by breaking the functionality into smaller files.

Initializing Each Instance of the Conference Application

When the first user connects to an instance of the conference application, several parameters need to be created; these help the session keep track of data associated with the streams published by each user. This data is later used to identify each stream for playback in the retrieval client.

RETRIEVING THE CURRENT DATE

One of the first tasks is to create a string that represents the current date, including the year, month, day of the month, hour, and minutes. In this section, you create a formDate() method for the application object to build this date identifier. The string is used in the names of persistent remote SharedObjects and saved streams.

TO ESTABLISH THE CURRENT DATE:

1. In Macromedia Dreamweaver MX, create a new ASC document. Save this document as **formdate.asc** in the conference folder of your FlashCom server.

2. Add the code in Listing 13.3 to the formdate.asc document.

Listing 13.3 formDate() **method**

```
1.   application.formDate = function(dateStamp) {
2.      var year = dateStamp.getFullYear();
3.      var month = dateStamp.getMonth() + 1;
4.      var day = dateStamp.getDate();
5.      var hour = dateStamp.getHours();
6.      var minute = dateStamp.getMinutes();
7.      minute = (minute < 10) ? ("0" + minute) : minute;
8.      hour = (hour < 10) ? ("0" + hour) : hour;
9.      day = (day < 10) ? ("0" + day) : day;
10.     month = (month < 10) ? ("0" + month) : month;
11.     var fullDate = year + "_" + month + "_" + day + "_" + hour + "_"
        → + minute;
12.     trace("fullDate = " + fullDate);
13.     return fullDate;
14. };
```

The formDate() method accepts a Date object instance as its only argument. From this Date object, the year, month, day, hour, and minute are extracted (lines 2-6). Lines 7-10 add a leading 0 to the value of each local variable, if the variable value is less than 10. Line 11 concatenates all the local variable values into one long string named fullDate. Each variable's value is separated by an underscore (_) character. The formDate() method returns this value (line 13) whenever the method is invoked.

3. Save the document.

 The completed formdate.asc document can be found in the chapter_13 folder of this book's CD-ROM.

ACCEPTING EACH CLIENT CONNECTION AND CONNECTING TO THE DEFAULT APPLICATION INSTANCE

Granted, the formDate() method has only been defined in the formdate.asc document. You have yet to implement the date string into other aspects of the conference application. In this section, you create the onConnect() handler of the application object. The onConnect() handler is responsible for setting up the application instance when the first user connects.

TO CONNECT AN APPLICATION INSTANCE TO THE DEFAULT INSTANCE:

1. In Macromedia Dreamweaver MX (or your preferred text editor), open the main.asc document that you created earlier in this chapter. This file should be located in the conference folder on your FlashCom server.

2. Enable the instance of the conference application to load the server-side code contained within the formdate.asc document you created in the previous section. Insert the following code after the existing code in the main.asc document.
```
load("formdate.asc");
```

3. Define the onConnect() handler for the application instance. This handler is invoked whenever a client connects to an instance of the conference application. Add the code in Listing 13.4 to the main.asc document. Note that the line numbers shown below are relative; the numbers are not intended to match those shown in the document.

Tip

The application object is a reference to the current instance of a FlashCom application. The FlashCom server automatically keeps track of each of the properties and methods associated with each instance of an application. When you see references to the application object in server-side code throughout this chapter, keep in mind that each instance has its own application object.

Listing 13.4 onConnect() **handler**

```
1.  application.onConnect = function(newClient) {
2.     this.acceptConnection(newClient);
3.     if (this.name.indexOf("_definst_") == -1 && !this.inited) {
4.        this.appName = this.name.substr(this.name.indexOf("/")
           → + 1);
5.        this.currentDate = this.formDate(new Date());
6.        trace("currentDate = " + this.currentDate);
7.        this.parentConn_nc = new NetConnection();
8.        this.parentConn_nc.onStatus = function(info) {
9.           trace("parentConn_nc: info.code = " + info.code);
10.          if (info.code == "NetConnection.Connect.Success") {
11.             trace("---Successful connection to default
                → instance");
12.             application.initSO(this);
13.             application.initStreams();
14.             application.inited = true;
15.          } else if (info.code ==
                → "NetConnection.Connect.Closed") {
16.             trace("---Default instance connection closed. All
                → SharedObjects should be cleared.");
17.             application.clearSharedObjects("/");
18.             application.inited = false;
19.          }
20.       };
21.       this.parentConn_nc.connect("rtmp://localhost/conference");
22.    }
23. };
```

Line 1 defines the onConnect() handler for the application object. This usage of the method only uses one argument, newClient, which represents the Client object connecting to the application instance. Line 2 allows the client to connect to the application instance; if this line were omitted, the client's request to connect would be rejected.

Line 3 checks the application instance name to which the client is connecting and checks the `inited` property of the application instance. If the application instance does not contain the text "_definst_" and if the `inited` property doesn't exist (or is equal to `false`), the code in lines 4-22 is processed. If the application instance is the default instance (_definst_), then this code should not be invoked. The default instance should only be directly accessed by the conference retrieval client, not the conference recording client. The conference retrieval client does not need to initialize the code in lines 4-22. The `inited` property tracks whether the code in lines 4-22 has been initialized. If a Flash client movie has already invoked this code for a given instance of the `conference` application, then another client connecting to the same instance should not invoke it.

Line 4 establishes a property named `appName`, which stores the instance name of the application. The `name` property of the `application` object returns the full name of the application instance. For example, the application name of the default instance of the `conference` application is "conference/_definst_". The `appName` property in line 4 extracts the string after the forward slash. The `app-Name` property is used to form the name of remote `SharedObjects` and stored streams.

Line 5 creates a property named `currentDate`, which is set to the string returned from the `formDate()` method. A new `Date` object is created as the argument of this method in line 5.

The most important aspect of the application instance's initialization occurs within lines 7-21. This code creates a server-side `NetConnection` object to the default instance of the `conference` application. Why? Even though each live conference session needs to occur within uniquely named application instances, the persistent remote `SharedObjects` and recorded streams from each session need to be saved in a common location. By creating a common location, or instance (such as the default instance), the conference retrieval client will know where to find data related to every session.

Line 21 specifies the URI of the new `NetConnection`. You can implicitly connect to the default instance of any FlashCom application by simply referring to the application name (that is, `conference`) without any additional instance name specified.

Note Depending on the setup of your FlashCom server, you may need to change the `localhost` server path to a fully qualified domain name. If the `localhost` is listening on the ports assigned to the FlashCom server, you shouldn't have a problem using the `localhost` name. However, you **cannot** use a relative path, such as `rtmp:/conference` with server-side `NetConnection` objects.

When a successful connection to the default instance is made, lines 10-14 are invoked. The `initSO()` and `initStreams()` methods of the `application` object are defined in the following sections. The `inited` property of the `application` object is also set to `true`, preventing the code in lines 3-22 from being processed by any other users who connect to the same instance.

4. Save the `main.asc` document.

This version of the `main.asc` document is saved as `main_101.asc` in the `chapter_13` folder of this book's CD-ROM.

CREATING THE INSTANCE'S SharedObjects

During the initialization of the application instance in the `onConnect()` handler, the instance creates a secondary connection to the default instance of the `conference` application. Once this connection is made, the `initSO()` and `initStreams()` methods of the `application` object are invoked. The `initSO()` method, discussed in this section, creates persistent and temporary remote `SharedObjects` for the conference session. The persistent `SharedObjects` are stored with the namespace of the default instance, defined by the `parentConn_nc` object.

TO CREATE THE SharedObjects:

1. In Macromedia Dreamweaver MX, create a new ActionScript Communications document. Save this document as **startup.asc** in the `conference` folder of your FlashCom server.

2. Define the `initSO()` method of the `application` object. This method is invoked once a successful connection is made to the default instance of the `conference` application. Add the code in Listing 13.5 to the `startup.asc` document:

Listing 13.5 initSO() **method**

```
1.   application.initSO = function(nc) {
2.     for (var i = 1; i <= 2; i++) {
3.         var avNum = "av_" + i;
4.         var soName = this.appName + "_" + avNum + "_" +
           → this.currentDate;
5.         this[avNum + "_timeTracker_so"] = SharedObject.get(soName,
           → true, nc);
6.         this[avNum + "_timeTracker_so"].onSync = this.syncTracker;
7.         this[avNum + "_so"] =
           → SharedObject.get("FCAVPresence.speaker_" + i +
           → "_mc.av", false);
8.     }
9.     this.savedCalls_so = SharedObject.get("savedCalls", true, nc);
10.    this.savedCalls_so.onSync = this.syncTracker;
11.    this.sessionName_so = SharedObject.get("sessionName", false);
12. };
```

Line 1 defines the initSO() method, specifying one argument, nc. The argument nc is the NetConnection object reference to the default instance, parentConn_nc. Line 2 iterates the code within lines 3-7 two times; because there are two users (or clients) that can participate in a live conference session, two sets of SharedObject references are created.

Line 3 creates a simple string value to refer to each user's stream (av_1 or av_2), which is also used in the names of persistent SharedObjects for the session as defined in line 4. The application instance's name and current date help to form the unique name of each persistent SharedObject.

Line 5 creates av_1_tracker_so and av_2_tracker_so, the persistent SharedObject instances that store the information for each user's stream. Note that the nc reference to the parentConn_nc object is specified as a parameter of the SharedObject.get() method. When you create a SharedObject within the space of another application instance, the SharedObject is called a *proxied* SharedObject.

Line 6 defines the onSync() handler for each proxied SharedObject created for the user streams. This method, syncTracker(), is defined in step 3.

Line 7 creates a reference to the SharedObject created by each user's AVPresence component. You retrieve the user's name from this SharedObject whenever a user begins to publish audio and/or video with the AVPresence component in the Flash client movie.

Line 9 creates another proxied persistent SharedObject named savedCalls. This data stores the general information from every recorded conference. The data within savedCalls is used by the conference retrieval client to populate the combo box. Line 10 sets the onSync() handler of this SharedObject to the syncTracker() method as well (defined in the next step).

Line 11 creates a reference to the sessionName SharedObject. If you recall, this is the name of the SharedObject in which the conference's title is stored from the conference recording client. Data from sessionName is later stored in the savedCalls SharedObject when the recording session has finished.

3. Define the syncTracker() method of the application object, which is used as the onSync() handler for the persistent remote SharedObjects created in the previous step. In the startup.asc document, add the code in Listing 13.6 after the existing code:

Listing 13.6 syncTracker() **method**

```
1.  application.syncTracker = function(list) {
2.      for (var i in list) {
3.          trace(i + ": name: " + list[i].name + ", code: " +
            → list[i].code);
4.          if (list[i].name == application.soPropName && list[i].code ==
            → "success" && application.clients.length < 1) {
5.              trace("closed savedCalls_so");
6.              //close savedCalls_so instance
7.              application.savedCalls_so.flush();
8.              application.savedCalls_so.close();
9.              //close client connection to default instance
10.             application.parentConn_nc.close();
11.         }
12.     }
13. };
```

The syncTracker() method handles the updates and changes for all the SharedObject instances in the application instance: av_1_tracker_so, av_2_tracker_so, and savedCalls_so. Actually, only lines 1 through 3 are invoked for all three instances. Line 3 outputs the messages from each synchronization cycle to the Live Log tab of the Communication App Inspector in Flash MX. Lines 4-11 are invoked for the savedCalls_so instance when the final update is made to the savedCalls data at the end of the conference session. At that time, the data written to savedCalls is saved (line 7), and the connection to this data is closed (line 8). In line 10, the connection to the default instance of the application instance, parentConn_nc, is also closed. You will learn more about how this code comes into play later in this chapter.

4. Save the startup.asc document. You will continue to add code to this document in the next section.

5. Go back to the main.asc document, and add the following highlighted line of code before the application.onConnect() handler. Note that only the first line of the onConnect() handler is displayed in the following code.

```
load("components.asc");

load("formdate.asc");
load("startup.asc");

application.onConnect = function(newClient){
   ...
```

The highlighted line of code loads the server-side ActionScript code from the startup.asc document when an instance of the conference application runs.

6. Save the main.asc document.

STARTING THE SERVER-SIDE Stream OBJECTS

Part of the initialization process involves the creation of two server-side Stream objects, one for each stream that can be published from each AVPresence instance in the conference recording client. When the recording client is on the chat frame, two streams are automatically set up by the AVPresence instances: FCAVPresence.speaker_1_mc.av and FCAVPresence.speaker_2_mc.av, the same names used for the SharedObject data. There are two possibilities for recording the stream published by the AVPresence component:

- Modify the client-side code of the AVPresence component to use a "record" or "append" parameter in its publish() method, instead of a "live" parameter. By doing this, you save the av_1 and av_2 streams in specific application instance folders of the conference application. This method only allows you to store two streams per instance at any given time. As such, if any users return to the same application instance, the previous streams will be overwritten and deleted.

■ Create a server-side Stream object that subscribes to (that is, plays) and records the stream published by the AVPresence component. Using the application instance's appName and currentDate properties, the server-side Stream object can have a separate and distinct name from the AVPresence stream. This stream "copy" can be saved in a common location, where all applications (and all application instances) can play the stream. Moreover, because each server-side Stream object has a unique name, users can return the same application instance to record new sessions, without losing the previous recordings within the instance.

Tip

This application only explores the capability of Stream objects to copy and record the data from another publishing stream. Server-side Stream objects are incredibly versatile and can be used to create self-running playlists and to manage streams to which users have access.

In this next section, you will start the process of implementing method #2 for the conference application.

To CREATE A METHOD THAT INITIALIZES THE SERVER-SIDE STREAMS:

1. In the startup.asc document, define the initStreams() method of the application object. This method is invoked from the onStatus() handler of the parentConn_nc object initialized in the onConnect() handler of the application object (see the main.asc document). The initStreams() method creates two server-side Stream objects that subscribe to the stream names published by the AVPresence components in the conference recorder Flash movie. After the existing code in the startup.asc file, add the lines of code in Listing 13.7:

Listing 13.7 initStreams() **method**

```
1.  application.initStreams = function(){
2.      // redirect a conference streams to new server streams
3.      for (var i = 1; i <= 2; i++) {
4.          var avNum = "av_" + i;
5.          var streamInstanceName = "stream_" + avNum;
```

Listing 13.7 initStreams() method *(continued)*

```
6.       var streamName = "callStreams/" + this.appName + "_" + avNum
    → + "_" + this.currentDate;
7.       this[streamInstanceName] = Stream.get(streamName);
8.       this[streamInstanceName].ref = avNum;
9.       this[streamInstanceName].onStatus = this.streamStatus;
10.      //start the default streams
11.      this[streamInstanceName].play("FCAVPresence.speaker_"+ i +
    → "_mc.av");
12.   }
13. };
```

When the initStreams() method is invoked, the for() loop in lines 3-12 creates two Stream objects. The instance names of these objects are stream_av_1 and stream_av_2. The actual stream name for each recorded FLV file is formed in line 6. Notice that this name starts with "callStreams/". This prefix designates a stream alias location, which you will define in the next section. A stream alias allows you to publish or store streams in a location that is accessible by all application instances running on the FlashCom server.

Line 7 creates the new stream and Stream object, and line 8 creates a property named ref for each Stream object. The ref property is a reference to the AVPresence stream name subscribed to by the respective Stream object. In line 11, the Stream instance subscribes to the AVPresence stream. For example, the stream_av_1 instance plays the stream named FCAVPresence.speaker_1_mc.av, which is published by the speaker_1_mc instance of the AVPresence component in the conference recording client.

Line 9 defines the onStatus() handler of each Stream object, using a method named streamStatus of the application object. You will create the streamStatus() method in the section "Monitoring Activity on the AVPresence Streams," later in this chapter.

2. Save the startup.asc document.

ADDING A STREAM ALIAS TO THE VHOST.XML DOCUMENT

The Vhost.xml configuration document of your FlashCom server controls many aspects of each virtual host running on the server. A virtual host is a specific domain name to which the FlashCom server responds. The Vhost.xml document controls the settings that are applied to each domain. One of the nodes, `<Vir-tualDirectory>`, allows you to create aliases for stream locations. An alias is a shortcut term that can be used in client- and server-side ActionScript to store streams in a specific location. In this section, you will create the `callStreams` alias referenced in the `initStreams()` method. All the streams (or FLV files) recorded by each session are stored in this common location.

To CREATE A STREAM ALIAS:

1. On your FlashCom server, locate the configuration files for Flash Communication Server MX. With a default installation of FlashCom on a Windows computer, the configuration files are stored in the following folder:

`C:\Program Files\Macromedia\Flash Communication Server MX\conf\`

2. Inside of the `conf` folder, open the `_defaultRoot_\_defaultVHost_` folder, and you will find the `Vhost.xml` file. Open this document in Macromedia Dreamweaver MX.

Note

If you are using FlashCom on an operating system other than Windows, locate the `Vhost.xml` in the `conf` folder on that machine. You may require specific administrator privileges to access and/or modify this document. Also, if you have configured more than one virtual host, open the `Vhost.xml` for the domain hosting the conference application.

---

3. In the `Vhost.xml` document, locate the `<VirtualDirectory>` node. An empty `<Streams></Streams>` node should already exist within this node. Add the following text between the `<Streams></Streams>` tags, replacing *path_to_conference_folder* with the full path to the `conference` folder of your FlashCom server:

`callStreams;path_to_conference_folder\callStreams`

For example, if you had chosen a default Developer Install FlashCom Server on a Windows server running IIS, the `<Streams>` node should contain the following text:

`callStreams;C:\Inetpub\wwwroot\flashcom\applications\conference\`
`→ callStreams`

4. Save the Vhost.xml document.

5. Create a **callStreams** folder in the conference folder of your FlashCom server.

6. To make the changes available immediately, restart your FlashCom server.

With this stream alias in place, you can now publish or play streams located in the callStreams folder from any application or application instance running from this virtual host on your FlashCom server. Specify the alias name followed by a forward slash (/) to the stream name parameter used in a publish() or play() method of a client-side NetStream object, or a get() or play() method of a server-side Stream object. Refer to the code added in step 1 of the previous section to see how the callStreams/ prefix is used with the server-side Stream objects of the conference application.

You can find a sample Vhost.xml document in the chapter_13 folder of this book's CD-ROM.

Monitoring Activity on the AVPresence Streams

After the application instance's SharedObjects and streams have been initialized, the application needs to know when a participant begins to publish a stream with one of the AVPresence components. This stream is recorded by the server-side Stream object that is subscribed to the publishing stream (FCAVPresence.speaker_1_mc.av or FCAVPresence.speaker_2_mc.av). However, the application must do more than record the stream. It needs to track the times at which recording started and stopped. In this section, you will learn how to track the recording time and enable the Stream objects to record the publishing streams.

TRACKING THE INSTANCE'S TIME

Because the conference recording session occurs in real time, you will need to create a technique that allows the FlashCom application to keep track of time, and more importantly, when each user sends audio/video with the AVPresence component. This information is saved in the data that is linked in the av_1_timeTracker_so, av_1_timeTracker_so, and savedCalls_so instances. The time tracker SharedObjects store the start time, stop time, and user name of each recording segment. A user can start and stop publishing as many times as he wants during a call. The savedCalls_so instance stores the overall length of the entire recording session, from the moment the first stream starts to the moment when the last user stops streaming and closes the Flash movie.

TO TRACK TIME WITHIN THE APPLICATION INSTANCE:

1. In Macromedia Dreamweaver MX, create a new ActionScript Communications document. Save this document as **timer.asc** in the conference folder of your FlashCom server.

2. Define a method of the application object that stores the time when the method is invoked. This method is only invoked once during the conference session, when the first user begins to publish a stream with an instance of the AVPresence component. (You will learn more about this stream detection in the next section.) At the beginning of the timer.asc document, add the following lines of code:

```
application.beginTimer = function() {
   this.startTime = new Date().getTime();
};
```

The startTime property of the application instance stores the current time, in milliseconds. This value is used as a baseline; throughout the recording session, new Date objects are created and compared to the startTime value.

3. Define a method of the application object that returns the number of milliseconds elapsed since the beginTimer() method was invoked. By subtracting the startTime value from a new Date object, you can determine how many milliseconds have elapsed. Add the following code after the begin-Timer() method in the timer.asc document:

```
application.fetchTime = function() {
   var currentTime = new Date().getTime();
   var elapsedTime = currentTime - this.startTime;
   return elapsedTime;
};
```

The fetchTime() method is invoked from code within the streamStatus() method, discussed in the next section.

4. Save the timer.asc document.

5. Go back to the `main.asc` document and add the code that will load the `timer.asc` document when the application instance starts. Insert the following highlighted line of code, before the `onConnect()` handler:

```
load("components.asc");

load("formdate.asc");
load("timer.asc");
load("startup.asc");

application.onConnect = function(newClient) {
    ...
```

6. Save the `main.asc` document.

DETECTING STREAM ACTIVITY

Now you are ready to add the code that determines when publishing has started or stopped over the `av_1` or `av_2` streams created by the AVPresence component instances. Remember, in the `startup.asc` document, you created two `Stream` instances—named `stream_av_1` and `stream_av_2`—that subscribe to the `av_1` and `av_2` streams, respectively. Any events that occur with the `av_1` and `av_2` streams are passed along to the `stream_av_1` and `stream_av_2` instances.

TO DETECT EVENTS OCCURRING WITHIN EACH STREAM:

1. Open the `startup.asc` document in Macromedia Dreamweaver MX.

2. Create the `onStatus()` handler, `streamStatus`, which is defined for each server-side `Stream` object in the `initStreams()` method from the `startup.asc` document. This handler records any audio/video published by each user to the respective server-side `Stream` object. Add the code in Listing 13.8 at the end of the `startup.asc` document:

Listing 13.8 `streamStatus()` **handler**

```
1.  application.streamStatus = function(info) {
2.     trace("---Current stream: " + this.ref);
3.     var currentTime = application.fetchTime();
4.     var currentTracker = application[this.ref + "_timeTracker_so"];
5.     if (!currentTracker.getProperty("recordTimes"))
6.        currentTracker.setProperty("recordTimes", new Array());
```

Listing 13.8 streamStatus() **handler** *(continued)*

```
7.    var timeArray = currentTracker.getProperty("recordTimes");
8.    trace(this.ref + " info.code = " + info.code + ", " +
      ➞ currentTime);
9.    if (info.code == "NetStream.Play.PublishNotify") {
10.      trace(this.ref + ": Publishing started.");
11.      this.record("append");
12.   } else if (info.code == "NetStream.Record.Start") {
13.      trace(this.ref + ": Recording started.");
14.      this.isRecording = true;
15.      if (!application.startTime){
16.         application.beginTimer();
17.         currentTime = application.fetchTime();
18.      }
19.      var currentUser = application[this.ref +
         ➞ "_so"].getProperty("speaker");
20.      trace("currentTime = " + currentTime + ", currentUser = " +
         ➞ currentUser);
21.      //save start time of recording in SO for stream
22.      timeArray.push({start: currentTime, user: currentUser});
23.      currentTracker.setProperty("recordTimes", timeArray);
24.   } else if (info.code == "NetStream.Play.UnpublishNotify") {
25.      trace(this.ref + ": Publishing stopped.");
26.      this.record(false);
27.   } else if (info.code == "NetStream.Record.Stop") {
28.      trace(this.ref + ": Recording stopped.");
29.      this.isRecording = false;
30.      //save stop time of recording in SO for stream
31.      timeArray[timeArray.length - 1].end = currentTime;
32.      currentTracker.setProperty("recordTimes", timeArray);
33.      if(this.callBack)
34.         application[this.callBack]();
35.   }
36. };
```

The streamStatus() method essentially checks the info.code value for each
message sent to the onStatus() handler of the av_1 and av_2 streams.
Because the stream_av_1 and stream_av_2 instances subscribe to these
stream names, any events that occur to the FCAVPresence.speaker_1_mc.av
and FCAVPresence.speaker_2_mc.av streams are directed to the streamStatus()
method.

Line 2 sends a trace() message to the Live Log of the Communication App Inspector, indicating which stream is currently receiving an event. Remember, the ref property was assigned to each Stream object in the initStreams() method.

Line 3 establishes a local variable named currentTime, whose value is retrieved from the fetchTime() method. This value, in milliseconds, indicates when the onStatus() handler (or streamStatus() method) was invoked.

Line 4 creates a local variable named currentTracker, representing the persistent SharedObject that is responsible for tracking the current stream's recording information. Using the ref property, the proper SharedObject instance is identified (that is, av_1_timeTracker_so or av_2_timeTracker_so).

Line 5 checks for the existence of a recordTimes array within the current-Tracker instance. If the array doesn't exist, line 6 creates a new empty array. This Array object stores the start time, stop time, and user name associated with each recording segment for the respective stream.

Line 7 creates a local reference, timeArray, which retrieves the current values in the recordTimes array of the currentTracker instance.

Lines 9-11 are invoked when publishing is detected on the stream. The server-side Stream instance begins to record the publishing stream from the respective AVPresence component stream (line 11).

Lines 12-23 are invoked when the recording initiated in line 11 actually begins. In line 14, a property named isRecording within the Stream instance is set to true. In line 15, the value of the startTime property is checked; if it doesn't exist, the beginTimer() method is invoked and the currentTime variable is retrieved from the fetchTime() method. Line 19 retrieves the value of the speaker property assigned to the SharedObject created by the AVPresence component (see the initSO() method in the startup.asc document). This value contains the string representing the user's login name as designated in the SimpleConnect instance of the recording client movie. In line 22, this value and the currentTime value retrieved in line 3 or line 17 are used to create the user and start properties, respectively, of an Object object added to the timeArray instance. Each start and stop process adds a new index to the user's recordTimes array in the appropriate time tracker SharedObject. In line 23, the recordTimes array is updated with the new values of the timeArray instance.

Lines 24-26 are invoked when a user stops sending audio and/or video with an AVPresence instance. In line 26, recording on the server-side Stream instance is stopped.

Lines 27-34 are processed when the Stream instance stops recording. The isRecording property is set to false (line 29), and the end property of the object at the last index of the timeArray instance is set to the currentTime value. The end property indicates the time at which recording stopped. In line 32, the updated timeArray value is applied to the recordTimes data. In lines 33 and 34, a callback handler is invoked if one has been set by the exit routine. This operation will be explored in the next section.

3. Save the startup.asc document.

You can find the completed version of the startup.asc document in the chapter_13 folder of this book's CD-ROM.

Shutting Down the Conference Session

So far, you've created the server-side ActionScript code necessary to initialize an application instance and record any published streams from the AVPresence component instances. When each user has logged out of the conference application instance or has closed the Flash movie, the application instance should save the conference session information to the savedCalls SharedObject and close all connections to the server-side NetConnection object, parentConn_nc, and other SharedObjects.

DETECTING THE LOGOUT OF THE LAST USER

The application instance follows a shutdown routine when the last user disconnects. In this section, you will begin the process of defining the methods of the application object that enable this routine.

To define the ONDisconnect()handler:

1. In Macromedia Dreamweaver MX, open the `main.asc` document from the `conference` folder of your FlashCom server.

2. Create an `onDisconnect()` handler for the `application` object. This method is automatically invoked by the application instance whenever a client disconnects from the instance. After the `onConnect()` handler of the `application` object, add the following code:

```
application.onDisconnect = function(oldClient) {
   trace("application.clients.length = " + this.clients.length);
   if(this.name.indexOf("_definst_") == -1 && this.clients.length < 1)
      this.exitApp();
};
```

If the application instance name (the `name` property) does not contain the text "_definst_" and the number of connected clients is less than 1, then another method named `exitApp` is invoked. With the conditions that are specified in the `if()` statement, the `exitApp()` method is only invoked when the last user connected to any instance *except* the default instance disconnects. You will define the `exitApp()` method in the next section.

3. Save the `main.asc` document.

Checking Activity on the Streams, Closing Connections, and Saving the Final Data

If indeed the last user is disconnecting from an application instance, the server-side `SharedObject`, `Stream`, and `NetConnection` objects should close their connections. You also need to account for the situation wherein a user closes or quits the Flash movie while he is publishing an AV stream. If one of the `Stream` objects is still recording when a participant disconnects, the stream needs to stop recording and save the stop time (as an `end` property in the `recordTimes` array) before the application instance starts to close any server-side connections.

To save the final session data after the last user disconnects:

1. In Macromedia Dreamweaver MX, create a new ActionScript Communications document. Save this document as **shutdown.asc** in the `conference` folder of your FlashCom server.

2. Create a function that checks the isRecording values of each stream. This function returns a true or false value. If either user's stream is recording at the time the last user closes the Flash movie client, tell that stream to stop recording. Add the code in Listing 13.9 to the shutdown.asc document:

Listing 13.9 checkStreams() **function**

```
1.  application.checkStreams = function(){
2.    for(var i = 1; i <= 2; i++){
3.      var currentStream = this["stream_av_" + i];
4.      if(currentStream.isRecording){
5.        var streamActive = true;
6.        currentStream.callBack = "exitApp";
7.        currentStream.record(false);
8.      }
9.    }
10.   return (streamActive) ? streamActive : false;
11. };
```

Lines 2-9 use a for loop to check each server-side Stream object, stream_av_1 and stream_av_2. Each instance is represented by the currentStream variable in line 3. If the isRecording property of the instance is true, a streamActive variable is set to true (line 5), and a callBack property is set to the string "exitApp" (line 6). This string represents the exitApp() method, which is described in the next step. If you recall from the streamStatus() method defined in the startup.asc document, each Stream instance checks for the existence of a callBack property when recording is stopped. By declaring the callBack property, the exitApp() method will be now be invoked by the streamStatus() method. The Stream instance stops recording in line 7. When the for loop completes, the checkStreams() method returns true (a stream was in the middle of recording) or false (the stream was not recording).

3. The checkStreams() method will be invoked by the exitApp() method, which is invoked when the last client disconnects from the current instance of the conference application (see the onDisconnect() handler in the previous section). After the checkStreams() method, add the code in Listing 13.10 to the shutdown.asc document:

Listing 13.10 exitApp() **method**

```
1.   application.exitApp = function(){
2.      if(!this.checkStreams()){
3.         trace("exitApp() invoked and checkStreams() returned false");
4.         var title = this.sessionName_so.getProperty("title");
5.         trace("title = " + title);
6.         this.sessionTitle = (!title) ? "(No name)" : title;
7.         this.checkTracker_1 =
           → this.av_1_timeTracker_so.getProperty("recordTimes");
8.         this.checkTracker_2 =
           → this.av_2_timeTracker_so.getProperty("recordTimes");
9.         this.closeSO();
10.        this.stream_av_1.play(false);
11.        this.stream_av_2.play(false);
12.        this.shutDownApp();
13.     }
14.  };
```

In line 2 of the exitApp() method, the checkStreams() method is invoked. If the method returns a false value, lines 3-12 are processed. If checkStreams() returns a true value, the streamStatus() method of the recording stream instance will reinvoke the exitApp() method.

Line 4 retrieves the current title property of the sessionName SharedObject. This is the SharedObject that each client can update by using the confName_txt field and the Change button in the recording client.

Line 6 creates an application instance property named sessionTitle, which is equal to the title property if one exists. If a title has not been created, a title of "(No name)" is used.

Lines 7 and 8 create references to the recordTimes array that stored each user's stream data. checkTracker_1 and checkTracker_2 are checked in the shutDownApp() method, discussed in step 5.

Line 9 invokes a method named closeSO(). As its name implies, this method is responsible for closing the connections for most of the server-side SharedObject instances. You will create the closeSO() method in the next step.

Lines 10 and 11 tell the server-side Stream instances to stop subscribing to the streams created by the client-side AVPresence components.

Line 12 invokes the shutDownApp() method, which will be described in step 5. This method saves the conference session's general information to the savedCalls SharedObject and begins the process of shutting down the remaining server-side SharedObject and NetConnection instances.

4. Define the closeSO() method, which is invoked by the exitApp() method. The closeSO() method is responsible for closing all the server-side SharedObjects instances, except savedCalls_so. This SharedObject instance is closed later in the process. After the exitApp() method declaration in the shutdown.asc document, add the following lines of code:

```
application.closeSO = function() {
    trace("closeSO() invoked");
    this.sessionName_so.close();
    for (var i = 1; i <= 2; i++) {
        var avNum = "av_" + i;
        this[avNum + "_timeTracker_so"].flush();
        this[avNum + "_timeTracker_so"].close();
        this[avNum + "_so"].close();
    }
};
```

This method closes the connection with the sessionName_so, av_1_timeTracker_so, av_2_timeTracker_so, av_1_so, and av_2_so instances. These instances were created (or initialized) in the initSO() method of the startup.asc document.

5. Define the shutDownApp() method, which is also invoked by the exitApp() method. The shutDownApp() method stores all the remaining session data in the savedCalls remote SharedObject. Add the code in Listing 13.11 to the shutdown.asc document, after the closeSO() method declaration:

Listing 13.11 shutDownApp() **method**

```
1.  application.shutDownApp = function() {
2.      trace("shutDownApp() invoked.");
3.      if(this.checkTracker_1.length > 0 || this.checkTracker_2.length
        ⟶ > 0){
4.          var sessionObj = {
5.              confTitle: this.sessionTitle,
6.              confDate: this.currentDate,
7.              confLength: this.fetchTime(),
8.              confInstance: this.appName
9.          };
```

Listing 13.11 shutDownApp() **method** *(continued)*

```
10.        this.soPropName = this.appName + "_" + this.currentDate;
11.        this.savedCalls_so.setProperty(this.soPropName, sessionObj);
12.    } else {
13.        this.savedCalls_so.close();
14.        this.parentConn_nc.close();
15.    }
16.    this.startTime = null;
17. };
```

If start and stop times were stored in either time tracker SharedObject instance, lines 4-11 are processed. A sessionObj instance is created, storing the sessionTime, currentDate, elapsed time, and application instance name values as properties of the object. This data is specific to each recording session, and the name for this data object must be unique. In line 10, a property named soPropName is formed, using the application instance name and the current date string. soPropName is then used as the name of a new property in the savedCalls data, which is connected by the savedCalls_so instance. The sessionObj data is specified as the value of the new property. As you will learn later in this chapter, the retrieval client uses each property name in the savedCalls data as a new item in a ComboBox component instance, so that a user can choose from a list of recorded sessions.

At this point, you may want to revisit the syncTracker() method code in the startup.asc document. This method has the following if statement:

```
if (list[i].name == application.soPropName && list[i].code == "success"
→ && application.clients.length < 1) {
    trace("closed savedCalls_so");
    //close remaining SharedObject instances
    application.savedCalls_so.flush();
    application.savedCalls_so.close();

    //close client connection to default instance
    application.parentConn_nc.close();
}
```

When the soPropName property is created in the shutDownApp() method and added to the savedCalls SharedObject data, the onSync() handler for the saved-Calls_so instance is invoked after the data update occurs. Remember, the onSync() handler uses the syncTracker() method. As such, the if statement evaluates to `true` when the `soPropName` data and `sessionObj` data have been added to the `savedCalls` `SharedObject`, and the last user has disconnected from the application instance. At this time, the connection created by the `savedCalls_so` and `parentConn_nc` instances can be safely closed.

Note You can also review the code in the `onConnect()` handler of the `application` object in the `main.asc` document. Any lingering `SharedObject` instances are closed in the `onStatus()` handler for the `parentConn_nc` instance, and the `inited` property of the application instance is set to `false`.

Back in the `shutDownApp()` method, lines 12-15 are invoked if neither user published any streams with the AVPresence component instances. The connections created with the `savedCalls_so` and `parentConn_nc` instances are closed.

In line 16, the `startTime` property is set to `null`. This property is reset for the next use of the application instance, just in case another pair of users connects to the instance before the FlashCom server unloads the instance (and all its properties).

6. Save the `shutdown.asc` document.

7. Go back to the `main.asc` document. Insert a `load()` action, indicating the name of the `shutdown.asc` file. Add the following highlighted line of code:

```
load("components.asc");

load("formdate.asc");
load("timer.asc");
load("startup.asc");
load("shutdown.asc");

application.onConnect = function(newClient) {
   ...
```

8. Save the `main.asc` document.

 You can find the `shutdown.asc` document in the `chapter_13` folder of this book's CD-ROM. The completed `main.asc` document is also in this location.

Testing the Conference Recording Client

You're ready to test all the server-side code that you have created in the previous sections. Make sure you have saved all the ASC files in the conference folder of your FlashCom server.

To quickly check the syntax of each ASC document for errors, you can copy and paste the ActionScript code into the Actions panel for a new temporary untitled Flash MX document. Create a new document (File > New) in Macromedia Flash MX, select the first frame of the timeline, and open the Actions panel (F9). Paste each ASC document's code into the panel, and click the Check Syntax button on the panel's toolbar. If an error is reported, the Output window will display some additional information about the error.

After you have checked each ASC document, restart your FlashCom server. In a Web browser, open the confRecord.html document created from the confRecord_101.fla document. Before you type a room name and click the Proceed button in the client, go back to Macromedia Flash MX and open the Communication App Inspector (Window > Communication App Inspector). In the inspector, log in to your FlashCom server. Go back to the Web browser containing the Flash client, type a room name, and click the Proceed button. If the ConnectionLight component instance turns green on the chat frame, your ASC documents did not contain any immediate syntax errors. If the light turns red, then it's likely that you have a syntax error in one of your ASC files for the conference application. If this occurs, you'll need to double-check your code.

Tip

Using the technique described earlier, copy and paste your ASC document's code into the Actions panel of a Flash MX document to check the syntax of your code.

Once you have a successful connection to an instance of the conference application, go to the Communication App Inspector, select the application instance name in the Active Application Instances list, and click the View Detail button. When the new details appear, leave the Live Log tab selected.

In the Web browser running the Flash client, make sure you have typed a name into the SimpleConnect instance and clicked the Login button. Start publishing a stream with the left AVPresence instance, speaker_1_mc. As the stream is publishing, look at the Live Log information in the Communication App Inspector. You should have data similar to the following trace() messages:

```
Publishing FCAVPresence.speaker_1_mc.av.---Current stream: av_1
```

```
elapsedTime = NaN
av_1 info.code = NetStream.Play.PublishNotify, NaN
av_1: Publishing started.
---Current stream: av_1
elapsedTime = NaN
av_1 info.code = NetStream.Record.Start, NaN
av_1: Recording started.
currentTime = 0, currentUser = Robert
elapsedTime = 0
0: name: recordTimes, code: success
```

As you can see, when the first onStatus() calls are made on the stream_av_1 instance, the elapsedTime value returns NaN because the startTime value has not been initialized yet. However, when recording begins, currentTime and elapsed-Time report values of 0. The last trace() message is from the syncTracker() method, which is reporting the new data added to the recordTimes array for the av_1_timeTracker_so instance.

In the Communication App Inspector details, you should also see four streams active in the Streams tab: the two from the client-side AVPresence component instance and the two server-side Stream instances that are subscribing to the client-side streams. The Shared Objects tab should show seven SharedObjects, three persistent (Stored) and four temporary (**Figure 13.21**). The names of the two-time tracker persistent SharedObjects will vary, depending on the instance name of the application and the current date.

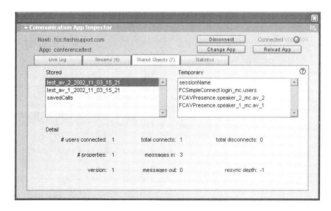

Figure 13.21 The Shared Objects tab of the Communication App Inspector reveals the names of persistent and temporary remote SharedObjects.

Go back to the Web browser with the Flash client movie. Stop sending audio and video with the left AVPresence component by clicking the red circle "X" in the lower-left corner of the component (you have to roll over this area first with the mouse for the circle to appear). When the video no longer appears in the instance, go back to the Communication App Inspector's Live Log tab. You should see information similar to the following data. Note that the `elapsedTime` values will be different in your tests.

```
---Current stream: av_1
elapsedTime = 501812
FCAVPresence.speaker_1_mc.av is now unpublished.
av_1 info.code = NetStream.Play.UnpublishNotify, 501812
av_1: Publishing stopped.
---Current stream: av_1
elapsedTime = 501859
av_1 info.code = NetStream.Record.Stop, 501859
av_1: Recording stopped.
0: name: recordTimes, code: success
```

Now, if you test the right instance of the AVPresence component in the Flash client movie, you should see data similar to the `trace()` messages of the `av_1` stream for the `av_2` stream name. When you close the Flash movie (or close the Web browser window), the Live Log window displays the `trace()` messages associated with the shutdown routine. Again, the time values will be different in your own tests.

```
application.clients.length = 0
exitApp() invoked and checkStreams() returned false
title = Sun Nov 3 15:21:14
closeSO() invoked
shutDownApp() invoked.
elapsedTime = 823458
---Current stream: av_1
elapsedTime = 1036366509100
av_1 info.code = NetStream.Play.Stop, 1036366509100
---Current stream: av_1
elapsedTime = 1036366509100
av_1 info.code = NetStream.Unpublish.Success, 1036366509100
---Current stream: av_2
elapsedTime = 1036366509100
av_2 info.code = NetStream.Play.Stop, 1036366509100
```

```
---Current stream: av_2
elapsedTime = 1036366509100
av_2 info.code = NetStream.Unpublish.Success, 1036366509100
0: name: test_2002_11_03_15_21, code: success
closed savedCalls_so
parentConn_nc: info.code = NetConnection.Connect.Closed
---Default instance connection closed. All SharedObjects should be
→ cleared.
```

If you see any errors reported in the Live Log output, check the syntax in your ASC documents again. If your code has introduced errors, you may see additional errors reported by server-side methods of Communication Component instances.

Once you have successfully tested the conference application by yourself, invite someone else to test the application with you. Check the Live Log output for errors while each person is publishing a stream.

BUILDING THE RETRIEVAL CLIENT

You've come a long way since the beginning of this chapter. You have created the Flash client movie, which publishes live streams from two participants, and you have developed the server-side ActionScript code necessary to record the streams and session information for each application instance. In this section, you will create the final element of the application: the retrieval client movie. This movie allows a user to view any previously recorded conference session, as you saw at the beginning of this chapter.

Creating the Interface

In the following steps, you will build the elements of the retrieval client interface. Most of this client's interface resembles the chat frame of the confRecord_100.fla document.

TO BUILD THE RETRIEVAL MOVIE INTERFACE:

1. In Macromedia Flash MX, create a new document (File > New). Save this document as **confRetrieve_100.fla**.

2. Change the document's width and height to match the recording client's dimensions. Choose Modify > Document, and specify a width of **425** px and a height of **300** px.

3. Copy the heading and frame artwork from the confRecord_101.fla document into the confRetrieve_100.fla document. Keep the artwork and text on individual layers, as shown in **Figure 13.22**. Change the Static text to **Two-Party Audio Video Conference :: Retrieval**.

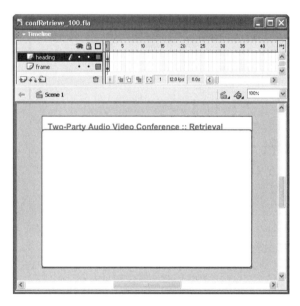

Figure 13.22 The heading and frame layers in the new document for the retrieval client are replicated.

4. Create a new layer named **login_mc**. On frame 1 of this layer, place an instance of the SimpleConnect component. Place the instance near the top-left corner of the stage (**Figure 13.23**). In the Property inspector, name the instance login_mc. In the Application Directory field, type the URI of the conference application on your FlashCom server. If the Flash movie and FlashCom application are hosted on the same server, type rtmp:/conference. Do not specify an application instance name in the URI.

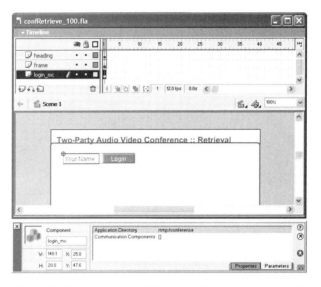

Figure 13.23 An instance of the SimpleConnect component is placed near the top-left corner of the stage.

5. Create a new layer named **connLight_mc**. On frame 1 of this layer, place an instance of the ConnectionLight component. Name this instance `connLight_mc` in the Property inspector. Place the instance to the right of the `login_mc` instance.

6. Make another layer, and name it **confList_cb**. On frame 1 of this layer, place an instance of the ComboBox component below the `login_mc` instance, as shown in **Figure 13.24**. This combo box displays the titles of every recorded session from the conference application. Name the new ComboBox instance `confList_cb` in the Property inspector. You may want to stretch the width of the instance with the Free Transform tool to accommodate long session titles.

7. Add a new layer named **textfields**. On frame 1 of this layer, use the Text tool to add the text **Choose a conference call in the list below:** above the `confList_cb` instance (**Figure 13.25**).

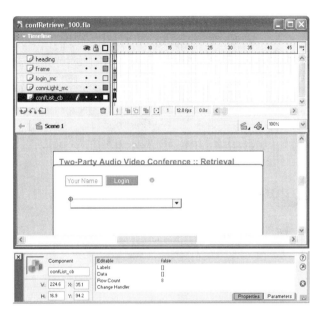

Figure 13.24 An instance of the ComboBox component is positioned below the `login_mc` instance.

Figure 13.25 Descriptive Static text is added above the `confList_cb` instance.

8. Now, you're ready to build the `MovieClip` objects that display the recorded streams from a session. Choose Insert >New Symbol (Ctrl+F8). Name the symbol **speakerWin**, choose the Movie Clip behavior, and click the OK button.

9. On the `speakerWin` timeline, rename Layer 1 to **userName_txt**. On frame 1 of this layer, use the Text tool to create a Dynamic text field with an instance name of `userName_txt`. Disable the Show border option for the field. Place the top-left corner of the field at the registration point of the symbol (0, 0). See **Figure 13.26**.

Figure 13.26 In the speakerWin symbol, a Dynamic text field named userName_txt is created.

10. Open the Library panel (F11) for the `confRetrieve_100.fla` document. In the options menu (located at the top-right corner of the panel), choose New Video. A new Embedded Video symbol appears in the panel. On the `speakerWin` timeline, create a new layer named **videoWin**. On frame 1 of this layer, drag an instance of the new Embedded Video symbol to the stage. Place the instance below the `userName_txt` field. In the Property inspector, name the instance `videoWin` and change the Width and Height values to 120. (These are the dimensions of the stream recorded by the AVPresence component.) See **Figure 13.27**.

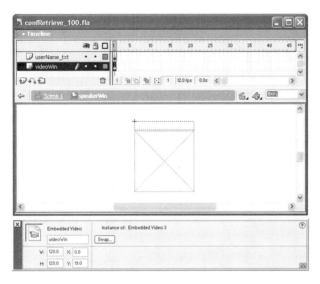

Figure 13.27 An instance of the Embedded Video symbol is placed below the userName_txt instance, and the dimensions of the instance are changed in the Property inspector.

11. Create a new layer named **frame**, and place this layer above the videoWin layer. On frame 1 of the frame layer, use the Rectangle tool to create a non-filled square above the videoWin instance. Assign the same dimensions to the square artwork in the Property inspector. Convert the artwork into a graphic symbol named **frame** (do not include the videoWin instance in the new symbol).

12. Go back to the Main Timeline (that is, Scene 1) of the confRetrieve_100.fla document. Create a new layer named **speaker_1_mc**. On frame 1 of this layer, drag an instance of the speakerWin symbol from the Library panel to the stage. Place the instance on the left half of the stage, below the confList_cb instance. Name the new instance **speaker_1_mc** in the Property inspector (**Figure 13.28**).

13. Create another layer and name it **speaker_2_mc**. Make a copy of the speaker_1_mc instance, and paste it in frame 1 of the speaker_2_mc layer. In the Property inspector, name the instance **speaker_2_mc**. Place the instance to the right of the speaker_1_mc instance.

14. The last interface elements for the retrieval client are two Dynamic text field instances that display the current running time of the recording session and the overall length of the recording session. Using the Text tool, create a Dynamic text field instance named confTime_txt on frame 1 of the textfields layer. Disable the Show border option for this field. Place the instance to the right of the speaker_2_mc instance. Duplicate the confTime_txt instance, and place the new copy below the original. Rename this instance **totalTime_txt** in the Property inspector. (**Figure 13.29**)

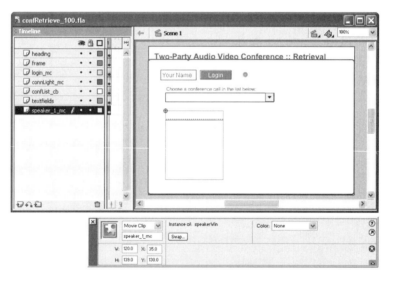

Figure 13.28 The speaker_1_mc instance is placed in the lower-left half of the stage.

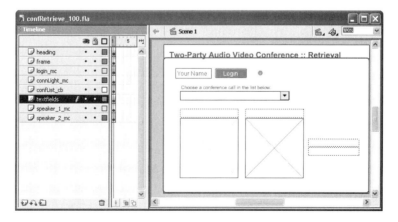

Figure 13.29 Two Dynamic text fields are created to display the elapsed time and total time of the conference session.

15. The user interface for the retrieval client is now complete. Save the document. Before you can use the client, you will create the client-side ActionScript code that retrieves the data from the recorded sessions.

The completed document, `confRetrieve_100.fla`, is located in the `chapter_13` folder of this book's CD-ROM.

Connecting to the savedCalls Data

When the retrieval client loads and establishes a connection to the default instance of the `conference` application, the `savedCalls` data created during prior recording sessions is available. In the following steps, you will enable the retrieval client to access the session data stored with the `savedCalls` `SharedObject`.

To connect to the savedCalls data:

1. Open the `confRetrieve_100.fla` document from the previous section, and save it as **confRetrieve_101.fla**.

2. Create a new layer, and name it **actions**. Place this layer at the top of the layer stack.

3. Construct an object that establishes a connection to the `savedCalls` data stored in the default instance of the `conference` application. This object should have a `connect()` method, so it can be easily integrated with the SimpleConnect component instance `login_mc`. Select frame 1 of the actions layer, and open the Actions panel (F9). Add the code in Listing 13.12 to the actions list:

Listing 13.12 Frame 1 actions of the retrieval movie

```
1.  Stage.scaleMode = "noScale";
2.  initSO = {};
3.  initSO.connect = function(nc) {
4.    savedCalls_so = SharedObject.getRemote("savedCalls", nc.uri,
      → true);
5.    savedCalls_so.onSync = function(list) {
6.      for (var i in list) {
```

Listing 13.12 Frame 1 actions of the retrieval movie *(continued)*

```
7.              trace(i + ": name:" + list[i].name + " code:" +
                → list[i].code);
8.              var propName = list[i].name;
9.              var itemLabel = this.data[propName].confTitle;
10.             confList_cb.addItem(itemLabel, propName);
11.         }
12.     };
13.     savedCalls_so.connect(nc);
14.     confList_cb.setChangeHandler("openSession");
15. };
```

Line 1 sets the scaleMode of the Stage object to "noScale", preventing the movie from scaling beyond 100 percent in a Web browser or the stand-alone player.

Line 2 creates the initSO object as an Object instance, and lines 3-15 define a connect() handler for the object. This handler will be invoked by the login_mc instance once a successful connection is made to the conference applica-tion. The argument nc represents the NetConnection object created by the login_mc instance.

In line 4, the nc argument is used to specify the location of the savedCalls data for the savedCalls_so instance. Lines 5-12 define the onSync() handler for this instance. Whenever an update to the savedCalls data occurs, the for loop in lines 6-11 adds each property name (propName) of the savedCalls SharedObject as the data property of a new item to the confList_cb instance. The confTitle property from each conference session is used as the label property (itemLabel) of each new item as well.

Line 13 connects the savedCall_so instance to the conference application.

Line 14 defines the change handler for the confList_cb instance. The change handler of a ComboBox instance is invoked when the user chooses an item in the drop-down menu. This handler, openSession(), will be discussed in the next section.

4. Add the names of the connLight_mc and initSO instances to the Communica-tion Components list parameter of the login_mc instance. Select the login_mc instance. In the Property inspector, click the Communication Components field to open the Values dialog box. In this box, add the instance names connLight_mc and **initSO** (**Figure 13.30**).

Figure 13.30
The instance names are added to the Communication Components list.

5. Save the Flash MX document and test it (Control >Test Movie). When the movie loads and successfully connects to the conference application, the confList_cb instance populates with the titles from each recorded session (**Figure 13.31**).

Figure 13.31
The confList_cb instance displays the confTitle property values stored in the savedCalls data.

The completed version of this document, confRetrieve_101.fla, can be found in the chapter_13 folder of this book's CD-ROM.

Retrieving Each Stream's Data

After the titles and property names from the savedCalls data have been added to the confList_cb instance, the user can choose one of the sessions from the list. When this selection has occurred, the retrieval client needs to access the two other persistent remote SharedObjects, the time trackers, which were created during the recording session. In the following steps, you will add the client-side ActionScript code necessary to retrieve this data.

To retrieve the tracking information for each stream:

1. In Macromedia Flash MX, open the `confRetrieve_101.fla` document created in the previous section and save it as **confRetrieve_102.fla**.

2. Create a new layer and name it **functions**. Place this layer at the top of the layer stack.

3. Define a function that can convert seconds into a time format of `mm:ss`, where `mm` represents minutes and `ss` represents seconds. This function is used to convert the running time and total time of each conference session to the `mm:ss` format. This time format is shown in the `confTime_txt` and `totalTime_txt` fields. Select frame 1 of this layer and open the Actions panel (F9). Add the code in Listing 13.13 to the actions list.

Listing 13.13 `calculateTime()` **function**

```
1.  function calculateTime(seconds) {
2.      var newTime = Math.floor(seconds);
3.      var newMinutesExact = newTime/60;
4.      var newMinutesWhole = Math.floor(newMinutesExact);
5.      var newSeconds = Math.floor((newMinutesExact -
        → newMinutesWhole)*60);
6.      if (newSeconds<10)
7.          newSeconds = "0" + newSeconds.toString();
8.      if (newMinutesWhole<10)
9.          newMinutesWhole = "0" + newMinutesWhole.toString();
10.     return newMinutesWhole + ":" + newSeconds;
11. }
```

The `calculateTime()` function takes one argument, `seconds`. In line 2, the seconds value is rounded down. In lines 3 and 4, the number of minutes is determined. In line 5, the difference between `newMinutesExact` and `newMinutesWhole` is used to determine the number of seconds remaining. Lines 6-9 add a leading 0 to each value if the value is less than 10. Line 10 returns the values in the `mm:ss` format.

4. Define the `openSession()` function, which is used as the change handler of the `confList_cb` instance. This function determines which item in the `confList_cb` instance was selected by the user, retrieves the data associated with the item's corresponding recorded session, and sets up the `NetStream` instances, which will play the recorded streams. After the `calculateTime()` function declaration, add the code in Listing 13.14.

Listing 13.14 openSession() **function**

```
1.   function openSession(obj) {
2.       var item = obj.getSelectedItem();
3.       var sessionObj = savedCalls_so.data[item.data];
4.       _global.confLength = sessionObj.confLength;
5.       totalTime_txt.text = "Length:\t" +
         → calculateTime(confLength/1000);
6.       var confDate = sessionObj.confDate;
7.       var confInstance = sessionObj.confInstance;
8.       var nc = login_mc.main_nc;
9.       for(var i=1; i<=2; i++){
10.          var speaker = "speaker_" + i;
11.          var avNum = "av_" + i;
12.          var basePath = confInstance + "_" + avNum + "_" + confDate;
13.          this[speaker + "_ns"] = new NetStream(nc);
14.          var speakerStream = this[speaker + "_ns"];
15.          speakerStream.pathToStream = "callStreams/" + basePath;
16.          speakerStream.pathToSO = basePath;
17.          this[speaker + "_mc"].videoWin.attachVideo(speakerStream);
18.          this[speaker + "_so"] =
             → SharedObject.getRemote(speakerStream.pathToSO, nc.uri,
             → true);
19.          var speakerSO = this[speaker + "_so"];
20.          speakerSO.num = i;
21.          speakerSO.onSync = speakerSyncHandler;
22.          speakerSO.connect(nc);
23.      }
24. }
```

The `openSession()` function uses one argument, `obj`, which represent the `confList_cb` instance. In line 2, an `item` variable points to the current item that the user selected in the combo box. Each item in a ComboBox instance is an `Object` instance, with `label` and `data` properties. In line 3, the `data` property of the `item` object is used to retrieve the session information stored in the `savedCalls SharedObject`. The local variable `sessionObj` represents the same information stored in the server-side `sessionObj` instance created in the `shutdown.asc` document.

In line 4, a global variable named confLength is created and assigned the value of the confLength property stored in the sessionObj instance.

In line 5, the totalTime_txt field displays the total minutes and seconds of the recording session. The confLength value is stored in milliseconds; therefore, the value is divided by 1000 and sent to the calculateTime() function.

In line 6, the date string, confDate, is retrieved from the sessionObj instance. Then, the instance name of the conference application that recorded the session is retrieved (line 7). The nc variable in line 8 points to the NetConnection object, login_mc.main_nc, of the SimpleConnect component. These values are used to create the persistent remote SharedObjects and NetStream instances, as shown in the for loop (lines 9-23). This for loop re-creates the objects similar to the server-side objects created during the recording session.

Line 14 creates the NetStream instances, one for each potential stream recorded by the AVPresence components in the recording client. In lines 15 and 16, two vital properties are created for each NetStream instance: pathToStream and pathToSO. These values indicate the stream and remote SharedObject names associated with each recorded stream. Line 17 attaches the streams to the videoWin instances inside of the speaker_1_mc and speaker_2_mc instances.

Line 18 creates the SharedObject instances, speaker_1_so and speaker_2_so. These instances connect to the time tracker data created by the server-side av_1_timeTracker_so and av_2_timeTracker_so instances during the recording session.

Line 20 sets a num property for each client-side SharedObject instance. This property indicates which stream number the instance represents.

Line 21 defines the onSync() handler for each SharedObject instance. The handler uses a function named speakerSyncHandler(), which will be discussed in the next step.

Line 22 establishes the actual connection to the SharedObject data within the default instance of the conference application.

5. Define the speakerSyncHandler() function, which is used as the onSync() handler for each stream's SharedObject instance. After the createStreams() function, add the code in Listing 13.15.

Listing 13.15 speakerSyncHandler() **function**

```
1.  function speakerSyncHandler(list) {
2.     var currentStream = _root["speaker_" + this.num + "_ns"];
3.     for (var i in list) {
4.         trace(i + ": name: " + list[i].name + " code: " +
           → list[i].code);
5.         if (list[i].name == "recordTimes" && list[i].code ==
           → "change") {
6.             currentStream.syncList = this.data.recordTimes.slice(0);
7.             startPresentation();
8.             this.close();
9.         }
10.    }
11.    if (this.data.recordTimes == null) {
12.        currentStream.syncList = [];
13.        startPresentation();
14.        this.close();
15.    }
16. }
```

When the connection to the SharedObject data for each instance is made
(see line 12 of the createStreams() function), the onSync() handler is invoked.
In line 2, a reference named currentStream is created, pointing to the appropriate NetStream object. Each SharedObject instance is matched to a NetStream
instance in the createStreams() function.

When the onSync() handler is invoked for the first time, the if conditions in
line 5 evaluate to true. At this time, each NetStream instance is assigned a
syncList property, which is a copy of the recordTimes array created for each
stream during the recording session.

In line 7, a function named startPresentation is invoked. This function
begins playback of each NetStream object. This function will be discussed in
the next section.

In line 8, the connection to the SharedObject data is closed. Once the
recordTimes information has been retrieved, the connection is no longer
necessary.

Lines 9-15 are processed if either stream does not have any recordTimes
data. This situation can occur if only one user logged into a conference session and published a stream. As you will learn in the next section, each

NetStream instance must have a syncList property in order for a session to begin playback via the startPresentation() function. Line 12 assigns an empty array to the syncList property of the NetStream instance, and line 13 continues to invoke the startPresentation() function. Line 14 then closes the connection to the SharedObject data.

6. Save the Flash MX document.

Playing a Recorded Session

You're approaching the final steps to complete the retrieval client. After each conference stream's recordTimes data has been accessed and assigned to its syncList property, all the data for the recorded session is available to begin playing the actual saved streams on the FlashCom server.

TO INITIATE PLAYBACK OF A RECORDED SESSION:

1. Continue to work with the confRetrieve_102.fla document from the last section. Now, define the startPresentation() function, which is invoked by each SharedObject instance's onSync() handler after the recordTimes data has been loaded. Select frame 1 of the functions layer and open the Actions panel (F9). After the speakerSyncHandler() function declaration, add the following code:

```
function startPresentation() {
  if (speaker_1_ns.syncList && speaker_2_ns.syncList) {
    startTime = getTimer();
    playID = setInterval(playStreams, 10);
  }
}
```

The if expressions check the existence of the syncList property on each NetStream instance. If both properties have been set, the nested code is processed. A variable named startTime is initialized, using the current time of the Flash movie as returned by the getTimer() function. The startTime variable serves the same role as the application.startTime property in the application instance; startTime creates a reference point to determine how much time has elapsed. Then, a function named playStreams is invoked with the setInterval() function. The playStreams() function is discussed in the next step. The ID for this interval is playID, and the playStreams() function is invoked every 10 ms to constantly track the time of the conference session.

2. Define the playStreams() function as shown in Listing 13.16, which constantly monitors the playback of the recorded streams and the elapsed time of the Flash retrieval client. After the startPresentation() function declaration, add the following code:

Listing 13.16 playStreams() **function**

```
1.   function playStreams() {
2.      var elapsedTime = getTimer() - startTime;
3.      confTime_txt.text = "Time:\t" + calculateTime(elapsedTime/1000);
4.      for (var i = 1; i <= 2; i++) {
5.         var currentStream = _root["speaker_" + i + "_ns"];
6.         var syncList = currentStream.syncList;
7.         var activeStart = syncList[0].start;
8.         var speakerWin = _root["speaker_" + i + "_mc"];
9.
10.        if (elapsedTime >= activeStart && syncList.length > 0) {
11.           currentStream.activeSeek = syncList.shift();
12.           currentStream.nextStop = currentStream.activeSeek.end;
13.           currentStream.checkStop = true;
14.
15.           var userName = currentStream.activeSeek.user;
16.           trace("userName = " + userName);
17.           speakerWin.userName_txt.text = userName;
18.
19.           var seekTime = (!currentStream.nextSeek) ? 0 :
              → currentStream.nextSeek;
20.           trace("speaker_" + i + "_ns seekTime = " + seekTime);
21.           currentStream.play(currentStream.pathToStream, seekTime);
22.        }
23.        if (currentStream.checkStop) {
24.           if (elapsedTime >= currentStream.nextStop) {
25.              trace("speaker_" + i + "_ns has paused or stopped.");
26.              currentStream.checkStop = false;
27.              currentStream.play(false);
28.              var activeSeek = currentStream.activeSeek;
```

Listing 13.16 playStreams() function *(continued)*

```
29.              currentStream.nextSeek = (activeSeek.end -
                 → activeSeek.start) / 1000;
30.            }
31.          }
32.        }
33.      if (elapsedTime >= confLength) {
34.          if(playID){
35.             clearInterval(playID);
36.             delete playID;
37.          }
38.          trace("---Conference session has finished playing.");
39.      }
40.      updateAfterEvent();
41. }
```

The purpose of the playStreams() function is to check the elapsed time of the conference playback and to control a speaker's stream whenever a start or stop time matches the elapsed time. In line 2, the elapsedTime variable is determined, by subtracting the startTime value from the current time retrieved by getTimer(). In line 3, the confTime_txt field is updated with this new value, and the calculateTime() function is used to format this time correctly.

Lines 4-32 use a for loop to compare the elapsedTime with the current start and stop values stored in the syncList array for each NetStream instance. In line 10, the elapsedTime value is compared to the activeStart value of the current stream. activeStart is determined in line 7, from the first index element of the current stream's syncList property.

If the elapsedTime value is equal to or greater than the activeStart value and elements remain in the syncList array, lines 11-21 are processed. In line 11, the current first index element of the syncList array is removed and set equal to an activeSeek property of the currentStream instance. The activeSeek property contains an object with start, user, and end properties, as saved in the recordTimes array during the live conference recording. A property named nextStop is added to the currentStream instance, indicating the time value when the stream should stop playing. A checkStop property is also added to the currentStream instance, indicating that an end value (via nextStop) should be checked in line 23.

In lines 15-17, the user property is retrieved form the current activeSeek property. This variable, userName, is then used to set the userName_txt field of the speakerWin instance (that is, either the speaker_1_mc or speaker_2_mc instance), which is determined in line 8.

In lines 19-21, playback of the recorded stream begins with a seek time determined by the existence (and value) of the NetStream instance's nextSeek property, which is set later in line 29. When the first recorded segment plays, the nextSeek property does not exist and seekTime is set to 0, which indicates the beginning of the stream. In line 21, the play() method is invoked on the NetStream instance, using the instance's pathToStream property as the name of the stream to play.

Lines 23-31 handle the detection of the stop time for each recording segment. If the checkStop property of the current NetStream instance has been set to true (as shown in line 13), the if statement in line 24 compares the elapsedTime value to the nextStop value of the NetStream instance. If elapsedTime is greater than or equal to the value of nextStop, lines 25-29 are processed. Here, the checkStop property is set to false (line 26), the stream stops playing (line 27), and the nextSeek point is calculated (lines 28 and 29).

Lines 33-39 are invoked if the elapsedTime value is greater than or equal to the length of the conference session, confLength. If this occurs, the setInterval() ID is cleared and deleted (lines 35 and 36).

The updateAfterEvent() function in line 40 allows faster execution of the setInterval() function and improves the time accuracy of the playStreams() function.

3. Now, you need to create a function, as shown in Listing 13.17, that can check whether a conference session had been retrieved and/or is still playing when the openSession() function is invoked by the confList_cb instance.

Listing 13.17 checkPlayback() **function**

```
function checkPlayback(){
    if(playID || startTime != null){
        clearInterval(playID);
        startTime = null;
        for(var i = 1; i<=2; i++){
```

Listing 13.17 checkPlayback() **function** *(continued)*

```
        var speaker = "speaker_" + i;
        delete _root[speaker + "_so"];
        with(_root[speaker + "_mc"]){
           videoWin.clear();
           userName_txt.text = "";
        }
        _root[speaker +"_ns"].close();
        delete _root[speaker + "_ns"];
     }
   }
}
```

If the playID variable exists or if startTime has a value other than null, the interval ID is cleared, and the startTime is set to null. Each speaker SharedObject is deleted, and each speakerWin instance is cleared. The NetStream instances are also closed and deleted.

4. Invoke the checkPlayback() function at the start of the openSession() function. Add the following highlighted line of code to the openSession() function. Note that only the first few lines of the function are shown; the rest of the function remains the same.

```
function openSession(obj) {

   checkPlayback();
   var item = obj.getSelectedItem();
   ...
```

5. Save the Flash document. You're now ready to test the Flash retrieval client. Choose File > Publish Settings, and in the Formats tab, clear the Use default names check box. Specify a Flash movie name of **confRetrieve.swf** and an HTML name of **confRecord.html**. Click OK. Now, choose File > Publish Preview > Default - (HTML). In the Web browser window, the retrieval client should show the titles of each recorded session. (You may want to run the record client a few times to add more recorded sessions.) Choose one of the sessions in the combo box. As soon as you release the mouse button after making the choice, the confTime_txt field begins to display the elapsed time of the session. One of the streams should begin to play in a speakerWin instance (**Figure 13.32**). When the session finishes, the confTime_txt field stops updating the elapsed time.

Figure 13.32
Recorded streams from an earlier session can now be viewed with the retrieval client.

You can find the confRetrieve_102.fla document in the chapter_13 folder of this book's CD-ROM.

As you have seen, the development of this application was not an easy or short task, despite the simplicity of some of the features as seen from the user's point of view. You now have an understanding of how detailed client-side and server-side operations complement one another to create a fully functional application.

EXTENDING THE POSSIBILITIES

You can continue to add functionality to the conference clients and application, or change the application's capabilities to work with other applications you have created. In this final section of the chapter, you can review some ideas to expand the potential of the conference application.

Authenticated Access

In the real world, you wouldn't likely want to leave bandwidth- and server-intensive applications available to anonymous visitors of your Web sites or Web-enabled interfaces. Using Flash Remoting routines, LoadVars, or other data-enabled ActionScript objects and methods, a Flash client can send user name and password information to an application server for login verification. Once the user is authenticated, the Flash client can access the URL of a FlashCom-enabled client.

Constructing authenticated user access is explored in more detail in Chapter 14.

Synchronization and Latency Problems

If you conduct several conference recording sessions and view the sessions with the retrieval client, you will likely witness streams that drift out of sync over time. The reason for this problem is latency. If either user's connection to the server is not fast enough to support the real-time transmission of audio and video data, or if the server's bandwidth is severely taxed, the accuracy of the recorded streams will suffer. Latency can also affect playback of recorded streams; if the viewer's connection speed is not fast enough, the data rate for each stream can become uneven, allowing one stream to receive more data than the other.

You can limit the severity of these problems in a few ways:

- Instruct participants to use the least-bandwidth-intensive setting in the SetBandwidth component instance. Unless you have modified the presets, the Modem setting uses the least amount of bandwidth.

- Use the conference application specifically for LAN-based environments where network latency becomes less of an issue.

- Track and store sync times in each stream as it records during the live conference session. During playback, compare the sync times across the streams. If one stream gets ahead of another, pause the faster stream until the other stream catches up. To store times in the recorded stream (that is, the FLV file), use the Stream.send() or NetStream.send() method to broadcast the sync times. Data sent over a live stream via the send() method is synchronously saved with the audio and video data of the recorded stream.

Look for updates and new versions of the conference application on the book's Web site at www.mxbook.com.

Session Data Storage

While recorded streams must be directly saved and accessed by client-side or server-side ActionScript within the FlashCom application, the data stored with the persistent remote SharedObjects for the conference application can be handled with Flash Remoting, an application server, and a data source. If you want to manage thousands of recorded sessions and users, you can store user information and the recording times data in a relational database. In this way, you can access this data with other non-Flash interfaces created in HTML with Macromedia Dreamweaver MX.

Removal of Stored Data

If you do not implement a separate data source for the session data of each recording session, you may want to create another Flash client movie, which allows you to delete streams and remote SharedObjects in the conference application. You can create an interface that allows you to choose a conference title and remove the associated time tracker SharedObjects and properties in the savedCalls SharedObject.

SUMMARY

- Before you build application code and a client interface, you should define the process of an application as it relates to the user interface.

- Each recording session stores three persistent remote SharedObjects: two time tracker SharedObjects and a savedCalls SharedObject. These objects save the recording times and conference session details.

- Stream aliases (or virtual directories) allow you to store recorded streams in common locations that are accessible by all applications and application instances running on a virtual host of the FlashCom server.

- The elapsed time of each application instance (from the time the first user publishes a stream) must be tracked in order to replay a recorded session in the retrieval client.

- As you learned with the server-side ActionScript code of the conference application, you can break up the methods of the application object across several ASC files. This procedure enables you to easily navigate and edit specific functions within your application.

- You can use server-side NetConnection objects to connect to other application instances on a FlashCom server. You can connect to an entirely different application and/or FlashCom server.

- To check the syntax of lengthy ASC documents, copy and paste the code from the ASC document into the Actions panel of Macromedia Flash MX. Click the Check Syntax icon on the panel's toolbar to locate any errors.

- Network latency can contribute to drifting synchronization of the recorded streams during playback. If possible, use the conference recording application within LAN environments. You can also explore more sophisticated synchronization by storing time data within each recorded stream, using the send() method of the NetStream (or Stream) object.

IV
Architecting a Comprehensive Application

In This Chapter:

14 Integration: Creating a Video Instant Messenger

It's time to put it all together. In previous chapters, you learned a great deal about the different elements used to build Rich Internet Applications with the Macromedia MX products.

In this chapter, you integrate this knowledge by creating a Video Instant Messenger application with database-driven user authentication and archiving. This multi-user application shows a practical example of everything in this book working in tandem, including:

- Complete Flash MX front end

- Flash Communication Server MX to record and publish video streams

- A relational DBMS, such as SQL Server or Microsoft Access

- ColdFusion Components to retrieve and update information in a database

- Flash Remoting

- Remote Shared Objects

- Local Shared Objects

- Server-side ActionScript

Note In order to build the application, you require a ColdFusion MX server and you also need to have access to a FlashCom server. Preferably, you should have a Developer installation of the FlashCom server on the same machine you are using to create the Flash documents.

An Overview of the Production Process

Although you've covered most of the knowledge necessary to go ahead with this chapter, there are still a few surprises in store, and we're taking a different approach to many of the previous chapters.

Before we begin, we need to define what we mean by a "video instant messenger." Rather than connecting two (or more) users together for a continuously streaming videoconference, we're going to build an application in which you only send a short duration of video and audio at a time. When you have something to say, you record and broadcast your video to the other participants in the conversation. Otherwise, you stay silent. This means that only the "conversation" is recorded and not the silence in between.

You can make the analogy that this method is similar to an Instant Messenger (IM) text application, such as ICQ, MSN or AIM. You don't send a continuous signal, only the "information packets" you want to send, whether they are text, audio, or video. You don't waste bandwidth by opening a continuous stream.

Note   In comparison, a video conferencing system is more analogous to a telephone call; everything, including the silence, is broadcast.

Instant messenger applications don't demand, nor expect, an instant response. When you send a message in an IM, there's no guarantee that the person hasn't gotten up to get a cup of coffee and missed the message. This requires that we build an application in which each user can "browse" through all the video messages that may come in while the user is taking a break, in the same way that IM applications allow you to browse previous text messages. Because the messages are all usually short and succinct, browsing through them shouldn't take much time.

No Components Here

Well, that's not quite true. This chapter does not use Flash Communication Components, but does use two of the standard Flash UI components, the Push-Button and the ListBox. At this point in your Flash career, we're not going to waste your time by instructing you how to create your own basic UI elements.

Although we recommend using the Flash Communication Components when suitable (as in Chapters 12 and 13) sometimes it's better to create the communication functionality from scratch rather than trying to adapt a particular component to your needs.

No FlashCom Rooms

When using Flash Communication Server MX, one common programming technique is to create "rooms" (application instances) under the application to allow multiple conversations at the same time. This is extremely useful in cases such as conferencing (as explained in previous chapters), but it doesn't really work for an instant messenger. In the IM example in this chapter, we want to keep track of interaction between *people*, not demand they create "rooms" for each conversation. So we're not going to use the "room" paradigm in this application.

Note

Although not utilized in this chapter, application instances *could* be practical in certain IM scenarios. Rather than requiring the users to create the rooms, the server would assign rooms dynamically to create one-on-one conversations between users.

The Example Site

Before launching into the application development, you should familiarize yourself with the finished example by going to the book's Web site at:

www.mxbook.com/v1/ch14/

At the Web site, a Flash client movie (**Figure 14.1**) loads into the Web browser requiring you to log in. For the example site, use any of the following usernames: *Robert*, *Simon*, *Toni*, or *Snow* and a password of *circuit*. Click the Log In button.

When the next screen loads (**Figure 14.2**), you see some familiar UI elements, including your own video visible in the lower portion of the screen and a list of users currently online.

Log In

Please log in.

```
simon
```
```
●●●●●●
```
☑ Remember my information

```
Log In
```

note for testing:
use *robert*, *simon*, *toni* or *snow* as the username
and *circuit* as the password

Figure 14.1 The Log In screen uses database tables to authenticate users.

In this application, video is not recorded or streamed automatically between users. To send a video message, **click and hold** the Record button to start recording.

Note You can think of clicking and holding the Record button as similar to a walkie-talkie or CB radio—press to speak, release when you're finished speaking. However, in this application, the message is only sent when the button is *released*. This is in contrast to the AudioConference component, described in Chapter 6, which attempts to send audio as real-time as possible to other connected users.

When you **release** the mouse button, the video stops recording. Your audio and video will begin to stream from the FlashCom application instance, and any other user connected to this application instance will see your audio/video stream. Also, the details of your stream (the time and your username) will display in the large list box. By default, your own messages do not play in your own window, but you can play your own messages by clicking on the relevant message details.

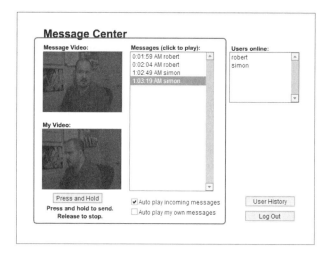

Figure 14.2 The Message Center allows users to send short video/audio streams to each other, and then records the details of these streams in a database.

If you have another friend participating in the chat, instruct her to log on under a different name. You can have multiple users in the same conversation at the same time. After you have spent a few moments conversing, click the User History button. A different section of the movie loads (**Figure 14.3**) where you can choose to view the history between yourself and any other user, regardless of whether they are currently online. Selecting any user will interrogate the database and bring back all the relevant message history ordered by date. Selecting a message will load and play that message.

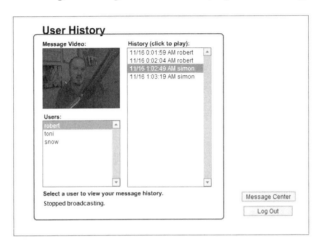

Figure 14.3 The User History section allows users to view their interactions with other users of the application.

Audience

For this example, we concentrate on the IM and archiving functionality, rather than the administrative functionality that would be necessary to administer an IM application with many thousands of participants. Consequently, we envision this application to be used in a limited environment, such as a small company, and implemented over controlled bandwidth: either a LAN or high-speed connections for any members of the workforce that are geographically distributed.

 This application could, of course, be extended to include additional functionality. Some suggestions for enhancing this application are covered at the end of the chapter.

Prerequisites

Again, our basic assumptions are that we will use Flash for the front-end client, ColdFusion components for the database queries, and Flash Remoting to join the two together. Any modern relational SQL-based database is practical. Also, an installation of Flash Communication Server MX is essential.

We're making the assumption that you have full access to the following programs from your development machine:

- Flash MX

- ColdFusion MX

- Flash Remoting Components

- Flash Communication Server MX

- A relational DBMS such as SQL Server or Microsoft Access

Flash Remoting Components, as described in the Flash Remoting chapter, are add-ons to Flash MX that are essential when building and testing Flash Remoting applications. If you installed ColdFusion MX after installing Flash MX, the Components will be installed automatically. Otherwise, download them from

www.macromedia.com/software/flashremoting/downloads/components/

This chapter example uses a ColdFusion MX installation using Internet Information Services (IIS).

If you specified the ColdFusion Web root folder in a non-standard location, or if you installed ColdFusion as a standalone Web server, please take that into account when following the exercises. Pay particular attention to the connection URL used for the Flash Remoting gateway.

MAPPING THE APPLICATION

Figure 14.4 illustrates the basic flow of the application, showing where the main processing and database interface elements belong. This flowchart begins to deconstruct the server-side operations within the application. The process involves three screens: the log in screen where the user is authenticated, the main message screen where the user can send and receive audio/video streams, and a user history screen where the user can select to view a variety of previous audio/video streams.

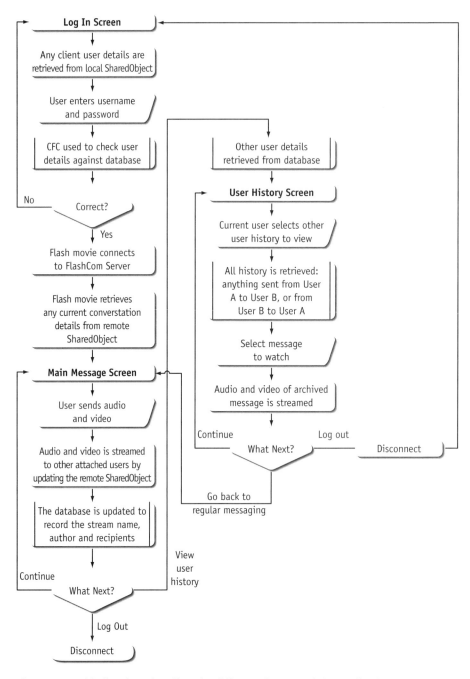

Figure 14.4 This flowchart describes the different elements of the application.

To implement and build the application, the steps we need to take are as follows:

- Define and create the database and data source.

- Write the ColdFusion components to manipulate the database.

- Create a Server-side ActionScript file to handle the connections to the Flash Communication Server.

- Create the Flash application Log In functionality, using a local `SharedObject` to save any client details and using a CFC to authenticate the user against the database.

- Create the Flash application Message Center functionality, connecting to the FlashCom server and accessing a remote `SharedObject` to determine any currently occurring conversation details. This section allows the user to send and receive video/audio streams and saves the details of any new message to the database.

- Create the Flash application User History functionality, connecting to the FlashCom server then retrieving all user history details from the database. This section allows the user to view recorded video/audio streams between the current user and any other user.

The process of mapping out the process aids in the first step of creating the database by making us consider what information needs to be stored for future use in later parts of the application.

CREATING THE DATABASE AND COLDFUSION MX DATA SOURCE

Although the information we need to store is quite abstract, we begin to concretize it into several fields as shown in **Table 14.1**. This is a brainstorming list of the different fields (or columns) that we need in the database. There is no order or grouping to the list—this is *before* the fields are split up into their constituent tables.

TABLE 14.1 FIELD LISTING FOR INSTANT MESSENGER APPLICATION

FIELD NAME	DESCRIPTION
User Name	The user name to allow logging in and also to attach to each video message.
User ID	A unique primary ID for each user.
User Password	The string of characters used for authentication.
Message Filename	A unique reference for future retrieval of the video stream.
Message Author	Who created the message? This should be stored as the user ID, so we can easily link messages to users. There is only one author per message.
Message Recipient	Who received the message? This should be stored as the user ID, so we can easily link messages to recipient users. There can be multiple recipients per message.
Message Date	The date the message was sent.

Thinking about what our database needs to accomplish will suggest ideas for the necessary fields, such as:

- We require users to log in; therefore we need to store usernames and passwords.

- We want to keep track of messages sent: we need to store message information, such as the date and the author.

- We're going to be broadcasting these messages at later times; therefore, we need to store the stream filename.

- We also want to know not only who sent the message, but also who the **recipients** were. There can be one or many users logged in to the conversation at the same time, so there can be multiple recipients.

This initial field listing suggests at least two database tables: users and messages. However, a little further thought presents a couple of problems with storing all message information in one table. The problem is this: we can store such information as the filename, author, and date in one database row, but if we start adding multiple recipient columns, we break the first normal form (1NF) rule of database design.

So as well as having a users table, we'll split up the message details into two tables: messages and message_recipients.

We need to store a unique filename for each video stream. This can serve as a unique key for the messages table. One possible way of creating a unique ID is to use a timestamp for the video stream file name. Timestamps are measured in milliseconds from Jan 1, 1970 and can be obtained by using the Date object. An example of a timestamp is:

```
1039766285859
```

Using a timestamp makes it very easy to determine the order of messages just by filename alone. We won't need to store separate date information for each message; we can take the timestamp and if need be, turn it back into a regular date. A possible problem would be that the different users could have different times (or even different time zones) on their individual machines, causing a conflict if we use the Flash client to obtain the timestamp. To bypass this, we'll create a server-side function to pull the timestamp from the Web server, not from the client.

It's possible (albeit unlikely) that two users might attempt to create a stream at the same millisecond, so we can add the username to each stream file-name, so the final streams will be saved in a unique format such as:

```
1039766285859_simon
```

The resulting filename can be used as the Primary key in the messages table, and as a foreign key on the recipients table.

The users table is basic and can be as simple as that described in **Table 14.2**. This definition even has a couple of additional columns, email and extension. These extra columns aren't necessary for the application itself and are just shown as an example of how extra columns are likely to be used.

TABLE 14.2 DATA MODEL FOR USERS TABLE

FIELD NAME	SAMPLE VALUE
User_id	1
UserName	Simon
Password	circuit
Email	simon@clingfish.com
Extension	1234

The data model for the messages table is also extremely simple, as shown in **Table 14.3**.

TABLE 14.3 DATA MODEL FOR MESSAGES TABLE

FIELD NAME	SAMPLE VALUE
Message_ID	1039766285859_simon
User_ID	1 (This is a foreign key to the users table)

The final data model for the message_recipients table only contains one more column, as shown in **Table 14.4**.

Although this looks very similar to the messages table, we don't use the message_id as the Primary key. This means we can store several rows for each message_id, each row corresponding to a separate recipient of the same message.

TABLE 14.4 DATA MODEL FOR MESSAGE_RECIPIENTS TABLE

FIELD NAME	SAMPLE VALUE
Message_Recipient_ID	1
Message_ID	1039766285859_simon (This is a foreign key to the messages table)
User_ID	2 (This is a foreign key to the users table)

 You can build this database in your chosen database system, or find the completed MS Access version of this database, videoIM.mdb, in the chapter_14 folder of this book's CD-ROM.

Creating the Relationships

We've built the tables, and referred to some foreign keys, but in all good database definitions, the relationships should be explicitly defined and referential integrity enforced. We have implemented the following relationships:

- A one-to-many relationship exists between users and messages: for every user there can be multiple messages. This relationship is on user_id.

- A one-to-many relationship exists between users and message_recipients: each user can be a recipient many times. This relationship is on user_id.

- A one-to-many relationship exists between messages and message_recipients: each message can relate to zero, one, or many recipients. This relationship is on message_id.

Creating the Data Source in ColdFusion MX

The next step is to create the data source in ColdFusion, in order that the Cold-Fusion components know to which database to point.

To create a data source, you must have access to the ColdFusion Administrator. If not, speak to your system administrator or ISP about getting a data source set up.

You can use the sample Microsoft Access database, videoIM.mdb, included in the chapter_14 folder on the accompanying CD. Copy it to a location on your hard drive, and make sure to turn off any read-only settings caused by copying from a CD-ROM.

To create the data source for the videoIM.mdb:

1. Open the ColdFusion MX Administrator

2. Select the Data Sources section under the Data & Services category.

3. In the Add New Data Source section, type a name for your new data source, such as videoIM and select the Microsoft Access driver. Click Add.

4. In the Microsoft Access Data Source dialog, select the Browse Server button for the Database File entry.

5. Navigate through the dialog box to the location of the poll.mdb file. Click Apply.

Creating the ColdFusion Component

There are five functionality requirements needed for the VideoIM application's ColdFusion Component:

- To authenticate the user (in the Log In section)

- To add new message author details to the database (in the Message Center section)

- To add new message recipient details to the database (in the Message Center section)

- To retrieve all user information from the database (in the User History section)

- To retrieve all history information of messages for a particular user (on the User History section)

First, we need to create the CFC.

To create the ColdFusion Component:

1. On the machine that's hosting the FlashCom server, create a folder named **videoIM** in the applications folder. If you have the default Developer Install of the FlashCom server on a Windows machine running IIS, the path to this folder should be the following:

   C:\Inetpub\wwwroot\flashcom\applications\videoIM

   Once the videoIM folder is created, connections can be made to this application on the FlashCom server.

2. If you're going to use Dreamweaver MX to create your ColdFusion MX code, open Dreamweaver MX, and define a ColdFusion site. Otherwise use your preferred text editor in the following steps.

3. In Dreamweaver, select File > New. The New Document dialog box appears.

4. Select the Dynamic Page category, and choose ColdFusion Component. Click Create. Dreamweaver creates a CFC shell. You can delete everything except the <cfcomponent> tags or, if you prefer, leave the existing example code to amend in the following steps.

5. Save this CFC file in the videoIM folder with a name of **videoIM.cfc**.

Now we need to add the identified functionality requirements. Let's take these one by one.

Logging in the Current User

The first method—let's call it checkUser—takes two parameters (username and password) from the Flash movie to check against the database.

Add the following CFFUNCTION declaration between the opening and closing CFCOMPONENT tags.

```
<cffunction name="checkUser" access="remote" returntype="query">
  <cfargument name="userNameParam" type="any" required="true">
  <cfargument name="userPasswordParam" type="any" required="true">
  <cfquery name="rsUser" datasource="VideoIM">
  SELECT * FROM users
      WHERE username = '#userNameParam#'
      AND password = '#userPasswordParam#'
  </cfquery>
  <cfreturn rsUser>
```

This is a fairly simple method with simple SQL. The </cffunction>line specifies the data source VideoIM that we created earlier to point to our database.

Adding Message Details to the Database

The second function—addMessage()—should accept two parameters: the name of the stream to save and the username. It should then insert these parameters directly into the messages table in the database.

Add the following code after the closing </cffunction> tag of the checkUser() function but before the closing </cfcomponent> tag:

```
<cffunction name="addMessage" access="remote" returntype="query">
  <cfargument name="streamname" type="any" required="true">
  <cfargument name="userid" type="any" required="true">
  <cfquery name="responseRecord" datasource="VideoIM">
  INSERT INTO messages (message_id, user_id)
      VALUES ('#streamname#', #userid#)
  </cfquery>
  <cfreturn responseRecord>
</cffunction>
```

Adding Recipient Details to the Database

The third function—addRecipient()—is called after the addMessage() function, as the recipient details refer to a message_id that should already exist. This function may be called several times, each adding a separate recipient to the database. The processing to handle this will be done in the Flash application.

Add the following code after the closing </cffunction> tag of the addMessage() function but before the closing </cfcomponent> tag:

```
<cffunction name="addRecipient" access="remote" returntype="query">
  <cfargument name="streamname" type="any" required="true">
  <cfargument name="userid" type="any" required="true">
  <cfquery name="responseRecord" datasource="VideoIM">
  INSERT INTO message_recipients (message_id, user_id)
      VALUES ('#streamname#', #userid# )
  </cfquery>
  <cfreturn responseRecord>
</cffunction>
```

Retrieving All Users from the Database

There are two functions used in the User History section of the Flash application. The first, getAllUsers(), should accept a parameter of user_id (which will be the ID of the current user) and then use that ID to find all other user details.

Add the following function code after the closing </cffunction> tag of the addRecipient() function:

```
<cffunction name="getAllUsers" access="remote" returntype="query">
  <cfargument name="userNameParam" type="any" required="true">
  <cfquery name="rsUser" datasource="VideoIM">
  SELECT * FROM users WHERE username<>'#userNameParam#'
  </cfquery>
  <cfreturn rsUser>
</cffunction>
```

The symbol "<>" is used in the line SELECT * FROM users WHERE username<>'#user-NameParam#' to find all users that aren't the current user.

Retrieving User History Details from the Database

The last function—let's call it `getUserHistory()`—should accept two parameters: the current user ID and another user ID. It then uses these two to find the details of any conversation that has occurred between the two. Importantly, we need the `message_id` field.

In plain English, we could phrase this request as: "Find all messages where the current user (user 1) was a sender, and the other user (user 2) was a recipient, **and** find all messages where the *other* user was the sender and the *current* user was the recipient."

It's hard to do this in one `SELECT` statement, but there is a way. (Actually, as is usual in SQL, there are several.) As ever in SQL, it's best to work incrementally. Taking the first part of the request: "Find all messages where the current user (user 1) was a sender, and the other user (user 2) was a recipient" we phrase this more succinctly as:

"Select the `message_id` from the `messages` table for the first user as long as the **same** `message_id` occurs in the `message_recipients` table for the second user."

We phrase the SQL as follows:

```
SELECT * from messages
WHERE user_id = (user 1 ID goes here)
AND message_id
IN (SELECT message_id from message_recipients WHERE user_id =
⸺(user 2 ID goes here))
```

This gets us half the results we want. But we also need the flipside: where user 2 was the sender and user 1 was the recipient. This looks exactly the same as the previous SQL, just exchange the placement of the user 1 and user 2 parameters. But that's two SQL statements, right?

Well, yes and no.

Using the SQL term `UNION` allows us to essentially create two (or more) SQL statements to create **one** set of results. This is used in the following code for the final ColdFusion Component function. Add the following code after the closing `</cffunction>` tag of the `getAllUsers()` function.

```
<cffunction name="getUserHistory" access="remote" returntype="query">
  <cfargument name="user1param" type="numeric" required="true">
  <cfargument name="user2param" type="numeric" required="true">
```

```
<cfquery name="rsHistory" datasource="VideoIM">
SELECT message_id from messages
    WHERE user_id = #user1Param#
    AND message_id
IN (SELECT message_id from message_recipients WHERE user_id = #user2param#)
UNION
    SELECT message_id from messages
    WHERE user_id = #user2param#
    AND message_id
IN (SELECT message_id from message_recipients WHERE user_id = #user1param#)
ORDER BY message_id
</cfquery>
<cfreturn rsHistory>
  </cffunction>
</cfcomponent>
```

Save and close the CFC. We're now ready to move on to the next stage of the application: building the server-side ActionScript.

CONSTRUCTING THE SERVER-SIDE ACTIONSCRIPT FILE

Before you can test the movie, you need to create a `main.asc` document for the `VideoIM` application. This document will be used to handle connectivity to FlashCom and the management and creation of remote SharedObjects.

1. In Macromedia Dreamweaver MX, choose File > New to create a new ActionScript Communications document.

Xref

For more information on the `main.asc` file, see Chapters 12 and 13.

2. Save the ASC document as a file named **main.asc** in the `videoIM` folder, located in the `applications` folder of your FlashCom server.

Application.onAppStart() Method

This method is fired off when the `videoIM` application starts. It issues a trace, which is visible in the Communications App Inspector, then creates a non-persistent SharedObject, `users`. The final line creates an index `idNum` to be used when connecting the users to the application.

Add the following code the `main.asc` file:

```
application.onAppStart = function(){
    trace("Video IM instance " + this.name + " has started");
    this.users_so = SharedObject.get("users", false);
    this.idNum = 0;
};
```

Application.onConnect() Method

The `application.onConnect()` method is fired off when any user attempts to connect to the `videoIM` application.

We mentioned earlier that we are going to use a timestamp to create a unique filename for each video stream and that we needed that timestamp to be generated by the server rather than on the client side. So the `onConnect()` method is an ideal place to create this functionality.

Add the following code to the `main.asc` file (don't add the line numbers).

```
1. application.onConnect = function(newClient, userName, userID){
2.     newClient.id = "u" + this.idNum++;
3.     this.users_so.setProperty(newClient.id,{uName: userName,uID: userID});
4.     this.acceptConnection(newClient);
5.     trace("--Connected " + userName + ", id = " + newClient.id);
6.
7.     // add a function to get a server-side timestamp
8.     newClient.getServerTime = function(){
9              var time = new Date();
10.             var timestamp = time.getTime();
11.             return timestamp;
12.     };
13. };
```

Note

Several code listings in this chapter use line numbers. They are used when the subsequent text needs to refer to specific lines for purposes of clarity and explanation. No line numbers should ever be typed in.

This code accepts three parameters from the Flash movie: the `newClient` client object, the `username` and `userID`. Line 3 creates an object in the `users_so` sharedObject, containing the `username` and `userID`. When the user signs on, we need to keep track of both the username (for cosmetic purposes) and the user ID (to update the database correctly.)

Line 4 accepts the connection to FlashCom and line 5 issues a trace reporting the connected client.

Lines 8-12 create a `getServerTime()` function. This will be called from the Flash application to obtain the correct timestamp when saving a video/audio stream. It creates a `Date` object on the server side and uses the `getTime` method to retrieve a timestamp.

Application.onDisconnect() Method

The `application.onDisconnect()` method is fired when FlashCom detects that a user has left the application. The `onDisonnect()` method only needs to do a couple of basic housekeeping tasks: First, to issue a trace to display the identity of the user being disconnected and second to remove the user from the remote sharedObject instance `users_so`. This means that any other users still using that sharedObject will automatically be updated with the fact that the user has left the application.

Add the following code to your `main.asc` file:

```
application.onDisconnect = function(oldClient){
    trace("--Disconnected " + oldClient.userName + ", id = " +
    → oldClient.id);
    this.users_so.setProperty(oldClient.id, null);
};
```

Close and save the `main.asc` file in your `videoIM` folder. We've now built the server-side functionality and can move on to the Flash application itself.

CREATING THE FLASH APPLICATION

As mentioned earlier, the Flash client can be split into three main sections of functionality: the login section, the message center and the user history section. We'll take each major part individually, but first let's create the basic Flash layout for the movie.

Creating the Flash Application Framework

As with the other applications in this book, this Flash movie will be divided into distinct sections to handle each major piece of functionality, each covering several frames for legible labeling and easy maintenance.

To create the Flash movie:

1. Open Macromedia Flash MX, and create a new document. Save this document as `videoIM_100.fla` in the `videoIM` folder in the `flashcom/applications` folder.

2. Rename Layer 1 to **labels**. On this layer, select frame 30 and press the F5 key to add empty frames.

3. Select frame 1 of the labels layer, and label this keyframe **login** in the Property inspector. Select frame 10, and insert an empty keyframe (F7). Label this frame **talk**. Insert another empty keyframe at frame 20 and label this frame **archive**.

4. Create a new layer, and name it **actions**. Put this layer above the labels layer. Then create four new layers: **components**, **fields**, **text**, and **art**. Position these below the labels layer. Create blank keyframes on these layers at frames 10 and 20. Your timeline should resemble **Figure 14.5**.

Figure 14.5 This displays the timeline of the Flash movie, showing the separation of different section across different frames.

5. Save the Flash document.

Creating the Login Page

This section allows the user to enter a username and password, then calling a ColdFusion component function to verify the user details and, if desired, store them in a local SharedObject to retain the details between site visits.

TO CREATE THE LOGIN PAGE:

1. On the first frame of the actions layer, add the following ActionScript:
   ```
   #include "NetServices.as"
   #include "NetDebug.as"
   #include "DataGlue.as"
   ```

   This includes the external ActionScript files necessary for Flash Remoting and debugging.

> **Note**
>
> The #include "NetDebug.as" line should be commented out once you have finished testing, as it adds unnecessary file size to a production Flash movie.

2. Add two Input text fields to frame 1 of the fields layer. Name them user-name_txt **and** userpassword_txt.

3. Add a PushButton component to frame 1 of the components layer. In the Property inspector, give it an instance name of login_btn, a Label of **Log In** and a Click Handler of doLogin.

4. On frame 1 of the components layer, drag an instance of the CheckBox component from the Components panel to the stage. Place the instance below the Input text fields, and name the instance remBox in the Property inspector. In the Parameters area of the inspector, type **Remember my information** in the Label field. Leave the other parameters with the default values

5. Above the input text fields, add a dynamic text field with an instance name of loginMessage_text. Type in a value of **Please Log In**.

6. You can add whatever arrangement and extras you like; the page should resemble **Figure 14.6**.

7. Save this file.

Figure 14.6 Use the suggested layout as a guide.

Next we'll add a function to pull any user details from a local SharedObject.

To CHECK THE LOCAL SharedObject:

On frame 1 of the actions layer, add the following code after the #include statements.

```
stop();

function checkData() {
   userData_so = SharedObject.getLocal("userData");
   var isChecked = userData_so.data.remember;
   if (isChecked) {
       userName_txt.text = userData_so.data.userName;
       userPassword_txt.text = userData_so.data.userPassword;
   }
   remBox.setValue(isChecked);
}
```

This function checks for a local SharedObject for the existence of any previously stored user login data, and if so, populates the fields with the data

The next piece of code handles the database authentication of the user details entered. This function, doLogin(), will be fired off when the Log In button is pressed.

TO AUTHENTICATE THE USER WITH FLASH REMOTING:

Add the code in Listing 14.1 to frame 1 of the actions panel, below the existing code:

Listing 14.1 doLogin() **function**

```
1.  function doLogin() {
2.    login_btn.setEnabled("false");
3.    if (inited == null) {
4.      inited = true;
5.      NetServices.setDefaultGatewayUrl("http://localhost/
       ↪ flashservices/gateway");
6.      gateway_conn = NetServices.createGatewayConnection();
7.      myService = gateway_conn.getService("flashcom.applications.
       ↪ videoIM.videoIM", this);
8.    }
9.    myService.checkUser(userName_txt.text, userPassword_txt.text);
10. }
```

Line 2 disables the Log In button so it can't trigger another call while an existing one is occurring. As is conventional with Flash Remoting, line 3 checks to ensure we haven't already performed this code. Line 5 sets the default URL, and line 7 links to the videoIM.cfc in the videoIM folder under the flashcom/applications folder.

The videoIM.videoIM section may seem repetitious, but it refers to the videoIM CFC in the videoIM folder.

 Note

If your Flash Remoting gateway is at a different location, or your videoIM.cfc file is not in the same folder structure as suggested, then line 5 and/or line 7 may need to be altered to reflect your own installation scenario.

Finally, line 9 calls the checkUser() function of the ColdFusion component, passing the values in the username and password input fields.

When the checkUser() function returns from the CFC, Flash will look for the checkUser_result() function to handle the result from the server.

Add the code in Listing 14.2 to frame 1 of the actions panel:

Listing 14.2 checkUser_result() **function**

```
1.  checkUser_result = function (rsUser_rs) {
2.     if (rsUser_rs.getLength()>0) {
3.        loginMessage_txt.text = "Thanks. ";
4.        var isChecked = remBox.getValue();
5.        var isPopulated = (userName_txt.text != "" &&
          → userPassword_txt.text != "") ? true : false;
6.        userData_so = SharedObject.getLocal("userData");
7.        userData_so.data.userName = (isChecked && isPopulated) ?
          → userName_txt.text : null;
8.        userData_so.data.userPassword = (isChecked && isPopulated) ?
          → userPassword_txt.text : null;
9.        userData_so.data.remember = isChecked;
10.       userName = userName_txt.text;
11.       userID = rsUser_rs.items[0].user_id;
12.       gotoAndStop("talk");
13.    } else {
14.       loginMessage_txt.text = "Login incorrect. Please try again";
15.       userName_txt.text = "";
16.       userPassword_txt.text =   "";
17.       login_btn.setEnabled(true);
18.    }
19. };
```

Line 1 declares that the function will return with a recordset rsUser_rs. In line two, this recordset is checked for a length of more than zero. This basically checks whether there was a successful result or not. If the recordset length is zero, there were no records found that matched the username and password entered. However, if the recordset is not zero, the username and password matched an entry in the database, and we can proceed.

Lines 4 through 9 store the successful user information in a local SharedObject. Line 10 and 11 store the username and user ID in variables that will be accessible to the rest of the Flash movie, and line 12 kicks the timeline forward to the message center section.

If the log in attempt was unsuccessful, line 14 sets an error message, while lines 15 and 16 clear out the input text fields, and line 17 makes the Log In button enabled again.

Finally, we add a couple of lines to make sure that whenever we land on this page, the Log In button is enabled, and the checkData() function is called to check the local SharedObject for stored user data. At the end of the actions panel for frame 1, add the following code:

```
login_btn.setEnabled(true);
checkData();
```

Creating the Message Center

This is the heart of the application. This section is responsible for the exchange of audio/video messages between users.

Before creating the page layout, take a look at an example in **Figure 14.7** of how this page is arranged. It's a fairly busy page with several instances of some symbols, so it's easier to show the page than describe the positioning of each component.

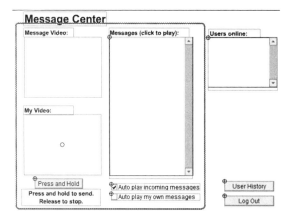

Figure 14.7 There are many components to the Message Center page, so use the suggested layout as a guide.

TO CREATE THE PAGE LAYOUT:

1. Select frame 10 of the components layer. Open the Library panel (F11) and choose New Video from the options menu. An embedded video library item appears. Drag out two instances of the embedded video symbol onto frame 10 of the components layer, one above the other.

Give the top symbol an instance name of `replay_video` and the lower one an instance name of `live_video`.

2. From the Components panel, drag out two instances of a `ListBox` component.

In the Property inspector, name the leftmost one `play_list`. Increase its width and height to 170 by 280, and in the Change Handler field, enter **play_click**. This ListBox should be positioned in the middle of the page.

Give the other ListBox component an instance name of `userList`. Leave the other values as default values. This component will show the other users currently online and should be positioned at the top-right quadrant of the page.

3. Add three `PushButton` components to frame 10 of the components layer.

In the Property inspector, give the first one an instance name of `record_btn`, and a Label of **Press and Hold.** This button does not need a Click Handler. Position this beneath the lower video symbol on the left.

In the Property inspector, give the second pushButton an instance name of `history_btn`, a Label of **User History** and a Click Handler of `doUserHistory`. Position this button at the lower right.

In the Property inspector, give the third button an instance name of `logout_btn`, a Label of **Log Out** and a Click Handler of `doLogout`. Position this button also at the lower right.

4. Drag two instances of the `CheckBox` component from the Components panel to the frame 10 of the components layer. Place the instances below the large list box.

Name the first checkbox instance `autoPlay_chk` in the Property inspector. In the Parameters area of the inspector, type **Auto Play Incoming Messages** in the Label field. Change the Initial value to **true**. Leave the other parameters with the default values.

Name the second checkbox instance `playMine_chk` in the Property inspector. In the Parameters area of the inspector, type **Auto Play My Own Messages** in the Label field. Leave the other parameters with the default values.

5. In the art and text layers, you can add static text fields around the components as an explanation. The final page should resemble **Figure 14.7.**

6. Save this file.

The next step is to add all the separate functions used by this page. The first
function to be declared is responsible for creating the connections to the
FlashCom server.

TO CREATE THE CONNECTIONS:

On frame 10 of the actions layer, add the code in Listing 14.3:

Listing 14.3 createStreams() **function**

```
1. function createStreams() {
2.    client_nc = new NetConnection();
3.    client_nc.onStatus = function(info) {
4.       trace("Level: "+info.level+" Code: "+info.code);
5.       if (info.code == "NetConnection.Connect.Success") {
6.          out_ns = new NetStream(client_nc);
7.          out_ns.setBufferTime(10);
8.          createSharedObjects();
9.       } else if (info.code == "NetConnection.Connect.Closed") {
10.         gotoAndStop("login");
11.      }
12.   };
13.   client_nc.connect("rtmp:/videoIM/", userName, userID);
14. }
```

Line 2 creates a new NetConnection object.

> **Note**
>
> The onConnect() function declared earlier in the main.asc file takes this information
> and updates a remote SharedObject with details of the new user that has just
> logged in.

Lines 3-12 specify the onStatus() function that will trace any status messages
from the NetConnection object.

Line 5 tests for a successful connection, and if so, line 6 creates a new NetStream
object soon to be used by our outbound video, and line 7 specifies a buffer

time of 10 seconds for the `NetStream` object. Line 8 calls the `createSharedObjects` function, which we'll write in a moment.

Line 9 tests for a closed connection, and takes the timeline back to the Login page.

Line 13 issues the connection call to the FlashCom server, naming the application and also passing the username and user ID that the user logged in with.

The next function—`createSharedObjects()`—has a fairly self-explanatory title. This function deals with two remote `SharedObjects`. `users_so` (which is updated by the `application.onConnect()` function in the `main.asc` file) stores details of each user currently logged on to the application. This information is used to update the ListBox to show current users.

The other `SharedObject instance`, `rec_so`, is another non-persistent `SharedObject` that stores information about the video messages being streamed between users in any currently occurring conversation.

To CREATE THE REMOTE sharedObjects:

Add the code in Listing 14.4 to frame 10 of the Actions panel:

Listing 14.4 createSharedObjects() **function**

```
1.  function createSharedObjects() {
2.    users_so = SharedObject.getRemote("users", client_nc.uri, false);
3.    users_so.onSync = function(list) {
4.      userList.removeAll();
5.      for (var i in this.data) {
6.        userList.addItem(this.data[i].uName, this.data[i].uID);
7.      }
8.    };
9.    users_so.connect(client_nc);
10.   rec_so = SharedObject.getRemote("messages", client_nc.uri, false);
11.   rec_so.onSync = function(list) {
12.     for (var i in list) {
13.       if (list[i].code != "clear") {
14.         var timeString = getTime(list[i].name.substring(0, 13));
15.         sendersName = list[i].name.slice(14);
16.         _root.play_list.addItem(timeString+" "+sendersName,
            → list[i].name);
```

Listing 14.4 createSharedObjects() **function** *(continued)*

```
17.            }
18.        }
19.        if (list.length > 1) {
20.            _root.play_list.sortItemsBy("data","ASC");
21.        }
22.        if (_root.autoplay_chk.getValue() && (sendersname != username)
           → && (list[i].code != "clear")) {
23.            playItem(play_List.getItemAt(play_list.getLength()-1).data);
24.        }
25.        if (_root.playMine_chk.getValue() && (sendersname == username)){
26.            playItem(play_List.getItemAt(play_list.getLength()-1).data);
27.        }
28.    };
29.    rec_so.connect(client_nc);
30. }
```

Lines 2-8 handle the users_so SharedObject. The onSync() function is declared to
detect when any update has been made to the SharedObject, such as a new user
connecting or a current user disconnecting. It then removes all entries from
the userList ListBox component and refreshes its values from the SharedObject.

Line 9 issues the essential code that connects the SharedObject to our current
NetConnection object.

The code handling the rec_so SharedObject is a little more involved. This SharedObject will be used much more often, as it changes every time someone sends a
message.

Lines 12-18 handle the refresh of the play_list ListBox component that displays
all the details of the messages going back and forth. However, the messages
are stored using a timestamp, which is not the friendliest of date formats. So
line 14 performs a substring to strip out the timestamp and pass it to a function called getTime(). This function, which we'll write in a moment (it isn't part
of Flash, although the name resembles the inbuilt method getTimer) takes the
timestamp and returns it in a more palatable format.

Line 15 determines the user name of whoever sent the message, and line 16 concatenates the formatted date and name into a text value to use to fill the ListBox.

Lines 19-21 handle the eventuality that when a new user connects, the onSync
method of the SharedObject may fire for multiple messages that have occurred.

To make sure the new user sees all the messages in their correct order, the onSync method uses the sortItemsBy method of the ListBox to sort by the time-stamp.

Lines 22-28 handle whether the new messages will automatically play when detected, and whether the current user's own messages will also automatically play. These are dependent on whether the checkboxes on the screen are checked or not. They both call a function, playItem(), which handles the playback of messages.

Finally, line 29 connects the rec_so SharedObject to the current NetConnection instance.

The next function should fire when the Record button is pressed. Because of the way we want the application to work (almost like a CB radio—press to speak, let go when finished speaking) that's *pressed*, not *released*, a normal Click Handler won't do the trick. We must assign a function to the onPress event of the button.

TO RECORD THE STREAM:

1. Add the code in Listing 14.5 to frame 10 of the actions layer.

Listing 14.5 record_btn.onPress() **function**

```
1. record_btn.onPress = function() {
2.    if (Record_btn.getLabel() == "Press and Hold") {
3.        in_ns.onStatus = null;
4.        in_ns.close();
5.        record_btn.setLabel("Release to Stop");
6.        ServerTimeObj = new Object();
7.        ServerTimeObj.onResult = function(timestamp) {
8.            out_ns = new NetStream(client_nc);
9.            out_ns.attachAudio(Microphone.get());
10.           out_ns.attachVideo(Camera.get());
11.           streamname = timestamp+"_" + userName;
12.           out_ns.publish(streamname, "record");
13.       };
14.        client_nc.call("getServerTime", ServerTimeObj);
15.    }
16. };
```

Line 2 tests the label of the button to make sure the press event has occurred on a button in its regular state. Lines 3 and 4 stop any currently playing stream and line 5 changes the button label.

Line 6 creates a new object to hold a Date object that will be passed back from the FlashCom server.

Lines 7-13 define a function to be fired off when the timestamp is returned from the server. This function then creates a new NetStream, attaches the output from the camera and microphone, and then begins publishing a stream (Line 12) using the concatenated timestamp and username for a unique stream name.

Now that the function has been created to handle the return from the server, line 14 then calls the getServerTime() function on the FlashCom server, as we need a server-side timestamp to create the name of our video stream.

So we've started to publish a stream. But at this point, we neither have a way to stop recording, nor to broadcast the information about this stream to both the shared objects and the database.

To do this, we define a function that will perform when the user releases the button. This function will both update the remote SharedObject and publish the message details to the database.

To save the recorded stream details:

Add the following code after the existing ActionScript:

```
1. record_btn.onRelease = function() {
2.    if (Record_btn.getLabel() == "Release to Stop") {
3.       out_ns.close();
4.       record_btn.setLabel("Press and Hold");
5.       _root.rec_so.data[streamname] = streamname;
6.       _root.rec_so.flush();
7.       myService.addMessage(streamname, userID);
8.    }
9. };
```

Line 5 adds a new entry to the rec_so SharedObject. When this happens, all the other users will sync to the new SharedObject and repopulate the play_list List-Box component with the new details.

Line 7 calls the addMessage() function of the CFC, passing the stream name and the user ID. This is all the CFC needs to know to add a new row to the messages table.

When the addMessage() function returns from the CFC, it will look for an addMessage_result() function in the Flash client. This is the perfect place to then issue as many calls as needed to the addRecipient() function, in order to add new rows for each user currently online.

To create the addMessage_result() function:

Add the following code after the existing ActionScript:

```
1. addMessage_result = function () {
2.    for (i=0; i<userlist.getLength(); i++) {
3.        if (userlist.getItemAt(i).data != userID) {
4.            myService.addRecipient(streamname,
              ⇥ userlist.getItemAt(i).data);
5.        }
6.    }
7. };
```

This loops around the current userList ListBox. This should be an accurate tally of the users currently online, as it is synched with the users_so remote SharedObject.

Line 3 checks to make sure we don't try to add ourselves as a recipient to a message. We can be sender or recipient but not both.

Line 4 calls the addRecipient() CFC function, passing the stream name and user ID. This function will then look for an addRecipient_result() function when it executes.

To create the addRecipient_result() Function:

There isn't one. Nothing needs to be done when the recipients are added except carry on as normal within the application. Just because the Flash client will automatically look for a function Name_result(), doesn't mean you always have to write one.

After the message has stopped recording, there are two ways in which it can be played: either automatically, when the sharedObject is updated with information about the new message, or manually, by clicking on the message name in the play_list ListBox.

TO PLAY THE SELECTED MESSAGE:

Add the following code after the existing ActionScript:

```
1. function playItem(playFileName) {
2.    in_ns.close();
3.    in_ns = new NetStream(_root.client_nc);
4.    in_ns.setBufferTime(10);
5.    in_ns.play(playFileName);
6.    replay_video.attachVideo(in_ns);
7.    replay_video.attachAudio(in_ns);
8. }
```

Line 2 closes any current NetStream object, and then a new NetStream is created to play the file name passed to the function. Lines 6 and 7 attach it to the replay_video instance.

The next small addition calls the playItem() function when the message entry is clicked in the play_list ListBox.

TO PLAY THE SELECTED MESSAGE WHEN SELECTED IN THE LISTBOX:

Add the following code after the existing ActionScript:

```
function playClick() {
    playItem(play_list.getSelectedItem().data);
}
```

The playClick() function is specified in the Property inspector as the Click Handler for the play_list ListBox.

The remaining buttons require fairly straightforward functionality, as they handle simple timeline and logging out operations.

TO MOVE TO THE USER HISTORY SECTION OF THE APPLICATION:

Add the following code after the existing ActionScript for when the user clicks the User History button:

```
function doUserHistory() {
    gotoAndStop("archive");
}
```

This forwards the timeline to the User History section.

The next function to add occurs when the Log Out button is pressed. It closes the connection and takes the user back to the Log In screen.

TO LOG OUT OF THE APPLICATION:

Add the following code after the existing ActionScript:

```
function doLogout() {
    client_nc.close();
}
```

When the client_nc object is closed, its onStatus method will be called. This was written in the earlier createStreams() function. When the close event occurs, the timeline is moved back to the Login page.

The last remaining function to add to this frame was mentioned earlier. The getTime() function takes the timestamp used as the stream name, and converts it into a more human-readable format.

TO CREATE THE getTime() FUNCTION:

Add the following code after the existing ActionScript:

```
function getTime(timestamp) {
    var time = new Date(timestamp);
    var hour = time.getHours();
    var minute = time.getMinutes();
    var second = time.getSeconds();
    var temp = ""+((hour>12) ? hour-12 : hour);
    temp += ((minute<10) ? ":0" : ":")+minute;
    temp += ((second<10) ? ":0" : ":")+second;
    temp += (hour>=12) ? " PM" : " AM";
    return temp;
}
```

The timestamp is the number of milliseconds since January 1, 1970, and is great for comparisons but poor for readability. However, the Date object in Flash understands timestamps perfectly, and by using standard Flash Date object manipulation, this function constructs a more-readable date to display in the application.

Finally, now that all these functions are declared, we finish the ActionScript on this frame by calling the functions to connect to the server and create the SharedObject instances. At this point, we also attach video to the live_video instance, so that each current user can make sure they look all spiffy before recording their messages.

To call the necessary functions:

Add the following code after the existing ActionScript:

```
live_video.attachVideo(Camera.get());
createStreams();
```

Save your movie.

Creating the User History Section

This section allows users to view any previous messages they have exchanged with another user. It doesn't allow communication, so we're not interested in who is currently online. We just need to be able to view the details stored in the database, and from that, play pre-recorded video streams.

Before creating the page layout, take a look at an example of how this page is arranged, in **Figure 14.8.**

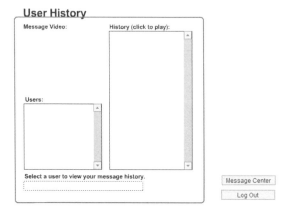

Figure 14.8 There are many components to the User History page, so use the suggested layout as a guide.

TO CREATE THE PAGE LAYOUT:

1. Select frame 20 of the components layer. From the Library, drag out an instance of the embedded video symbol. Give the top symbol an instance name of `history_video.`

2. From the Components panel, drag out two instances of a `ListBox` component.

In the Property inspector, name the leftmost one `allUser_list`. In the Change Handler field, enter **doSelectUser**. This ListBox should be positioned on the left-hand side of the page and will show all possible users.

Give the other ListBox component an instance name of `archive_list` and resize it to 170 pixels wide by 280 pixels high. Give it a Change Handler of **playClick**. Leave the other values as default values. This component should be positioned in the middle of the page.

3. Add two PushButton components to frame 20 of the components layer.

In the Property inspector, give the first one an instance name of `msgCenter_btn`, a Label of **Message Center**, and a Click Handler of **doMessageCenter**.

In the Property inspector, give the second pushButton an instance name of `logout_btn`, a Label of **Log Out** and a Click Handler of `doLogout`.

4. Add a dynamic text field with an instance name of **status_txt**.

Retrieving All User Details

The Flash client always knows who the current user is. In the User History section, we need to present a list of all the *other* users, in order to be able to retrieve a shared history between the current user and any other user.

When arriving at this section of the Flash movie, the functions are declared and then the `myService.getAllUsers()` CFC function is immediately called to retrieve the usernames of everyone who isn't the current user.

When the `getAllUsers()` function is completed on the server side, it returns to the Flash movie and the `getAllUsers_result()` function will be executed. It will be passed a recordset containing the user information.

This function is a perfect place to use the `DataGlue bindFormatStrings` method, part of the `DataGlue.as` file that should be included on frame 1 of the movie.

There are four parameters to the bindFormatStrings().

- The instance name of the UI component object

- The recordset name

- The recordset field to use to define the UI component labels

- The recordset field to use to define the UI component values

To POPULATE THE LISTBOX USING bindFormatStrings:

Add the following code to the actions layer of Frame 20:

```
getAllUsers_result = function (rsUsers) {
    DataGlue.bindFormatStrings(allUser_List, rsUsers, "#username#",
    ➞ "#user_id#");
};
```

This will populate the listbox with all the available users. In the last two parameters, the recordset field names are placed between pound signs (#).

When a user is selected in the ListBox, the doSelectUser() function is executed, passing the ID of the current user and of the selected user. This function will call the getUserHistory() CFC function, retrieving all the information for a user pair.

To SELECT ALL MESSAGES FOR A USER:

Add the following code after the existing ActionScript on the frame:

```
function doSelectUser() {
    status_txt.text = "Retrieving information... please wait...";
    archive_list.setEnabled(false);
    myService.getUserHistory(userID, allUser_list.getValue());
}
```

The function sets a status message on the stage.

As we can switch between different users on this page, it then temporarily disables the existing message ListBox to ensure nothing can be selected while fetching the new list of messages.

Next, the getUserHistory method is called, using the current user ID and the value of whatever user is currently selected in the allUser_list ListBox.

When the `getUserHistory` method returns from the server, the `getUserHistory_result()` function executes. This is the ideal place to perform the formatting necessary to turn the names of the streams from timestamps into readable dates before displaying them in the ListBox.

The best method to use for converting the timestamp is to use the other method in the `DataGlue` file, the `bindFormatFunction()` method. It takes three parameters:

- The UI component instance name

- The recordset name

- A reference to a function, which needs to return an object with two properties — `label` and `data`.

The named function will be automatically called once for each record in the recordset, and is where the actual formatting code is placed.

TO POPULATE THE LISTBOX USING `bindFormatFunction`:

Add the following code after the existing ActionScript:

```
getUserHistory_result = function (rsUserHistory) {
    status_txt.text = "User history retrieved.";
    archive_list.setEnabled(true);
    DataGlue.bindFormatFunction(archive_list, rsUserHistory, fnFormat);
};
```

The function named in the `bindFormatFunction` line, `fnFormat`, will be called for each record in the recordset and can perform its formatting tricks on it.

TO CREATE THE FORMATTING FUNCTION:

Add the following code after the existing ActionScript:

```
function fnFormat(rec) {
    var timeString = getTimeAndDate(rec.message_id.substring(0, 13));
    var sendersName = rec.message_id.slice(14);
    obj = new Object();
    obj.label = (timeString + " " + sendersName);
    obj.data = rec.message_id;
    return obj;
}
```

This function must return an object with label and data properties. This example does something similar to some earlier code, in that it strips out the timestamp from the message file name before calling another function (in this case, getTimeAndDate) to turn it into a more readable format.

The next function handles the playback of each selected message. It is very similar to the playItem() function in the main message center page, but needs to be redefined for this page, as the video symbols have different instance names.

TO PLAY THE SELECTED MESSAGE:

Add the following code after the existing ActionScript:

```
function playClick() {
   Status_txt.text = "Accessing";
   in_ns.onStatus = null;
   in_ns.close();
   in_ns = new NetStream(_root.client_nc);
   in_ns.onStatus = function(info) {
      // Handle errors and stream stopping
      if (info.level == "error" || info.code ==
      ➞ "NetStream.Play.Stop") {
         Status_txt.text = "Stopped broadcasting.";
      }
   };
   in_ns.setBufferTime(10);
   in_ns.play(archive_list.getSelectedItem().data);
   history_video.attachVideo(in_ns);
   history_video.attachAudio(in_ns);
}
```

When the current user has finished browsing past messages, they can either log out or return to the main message section. This simple function just takes the timeline back to the messaging section.

TO RETURN TO THE MESSAGE CENTER SECTION:

Add the following code after the existing ActionScript:

```
function doMessageCenter() {
   gotoAndStop("talk");
}
```

Creating the `getTimeAndDate()` Function

This function is very like the `getTime()` function used in the previous section, except we need a month and day. An instant messenger conversation typically just needs a time: if you're talking to someone, you know what day it is—but an archiving system would be of little use if all it could show us was the time of the message but not what day, month, or year it came from.

Add the following code after the existing ActionScript:

```
function getTimeAndDate(timestamp) {
    var time = new Date(timestamp);
    var month = time.getMonth();
    var day = time.getDate();
    var hour = time.getHours();
    var minute = time.getMinutes();
    var second = time.getSeconds();
    var temp = month + "/" + day + " " +((hour>12) ? hour-12 : hour);
    temp += ((minute<10) ? ":0" : ":")+minute;
    temp += ((second<10) ? ":0" : ":")+second;
    temp += (hour>=12) ? " PM" : " AM";
    return temp;
}
```

Calling the Necessary Functions

Finally, the last line on this page calls the CFC function to retrieve the user data and start the ball rolling. Add the following code:

```
myService.getAllUsers(username);
```

That's it! Save your page and test it.

Testing

The NetConnection Debugger and Communication App Inspector have been covered in great detail in earlier chapters, and they will be invaluable to you in testing and debugging this application.

Xref

The NetConnection Debugger is covered in Chapters 7, 8, and 9. The Communication App Inspector is covered in Chapters 12 and 13.

Where to Go From Here?

You should be able to gather from viewing this application that all video messages are recorded and stored on the server. This leads to several concerns:

- **Disk space:** Storing the collected video messages from many users over weeks or months of time is likely to lead to a great deal of space issues. In a small company, this wouldn't add up to much: disk space is cheap. But in a large company, it's an added concern.

- **Administrative needs:** After a time, you're likely to want to create some administrative screens so that the users themselves might be able to clear up their own streams, or be warned when their total disk space is approaching a set amount.

- **User issues:** The nature of this application assumes a small enough user group where there are not likely to be thousands of users, as the method we explored in this chapter only creates one "free-for-all" discussion area, where anyone currently logged on can join the same conversation as anyone else. An application with a higher user base would need to examine other options.

- **Lag time:** This application is more feasible when run within a LAN, as large lag times when dealing with multiple users across multiple bandwidths may unduly affect the application. This is of particular interest for this application, as the short nature of the messages mean they are extremely susceptible to any lag or delay in transmission.

- **Error checking:** While it's not absolutely necessary for the context of this prototype, in a live production environment, further error checking functionality would be necessary. Consult the example exercises in earlier chapters where error checking was specified for connections.

Summary

- This chapter explored an application that drew together all the different elements used in this book: Flash Remoting, Flash Communication Server,

ColdFusion Components, remote and local `SharedObjects`, together with relational database integration.

- User authentication is an ideal situation to use Flash Remoting to join the Flash application to a ColdFusion Component.

- The `main.asc` file can be used to perform housekeeping tasks on clients connecting and disconnecting to the application. It is also the place to create any functions that need to access server-side information, such as obtaining the server-side timestamp.

- As always, SQL is a much underused aspect of many Web sites, but when used properly can negate the need for a lot of complex programming. In this chapter, the UNION keyword was shown as a way to collate two (or more) SQL statements into one result.

- Functions called in ColdFusion components will attempt to run a `functionName_result()` callback function in the Flash client after they execute. This is the ideal place to run any operations on recordsets returned from the database.

- A timestamp shows the number of milliseconds since January 1, 1970, and is very useful for creating unique identification numbers. It is doubly useful if you also need to store date or time information.

- The `DataGlue.as` file is installed as part of the Flash Remoting install, and makes it easy to assign dynamic data to UI components, with the `bindFormatStrings` and `bindFormatFunction` methods.

- When your movies are complete and tested, you should remove the included `netDebug.as` file, as it is not needed for production movies.

We hope this book has been of help to you in learning to build Rich Internet Applications. Please consult the book's Web site, `www.mxbook.com` for more information about the development of Rich Internet Applications using the Macromedia MX tools.

Good Luck!

V
Appendixes

A Typical Bandwidth Consumption by Streams

One of the most exciting aspects of building applications with Flash Communication Server MX is streaming audio and video. As you learned in Chapter 10, streams can demand a large portion of bandwidth from both the Flash-Com server and the user running the Flash client. You can use this appendix to look up the bitrates used by default Camera and Microphone objects as well as the audio/video-enabled Communication components.

Use the following list as a guide to each table:

- Table A.1 provides a list of common connection speeds available to devices and computers connected to the Internet or a LAN (**L**ocal **A**rea **N**etwork). Use this table to help you determine the maximum bandwidth available to your FlashCom-enabled applications. The values in the Practical Speed column are approximately 67 percent of the Theoretical Speed column values.

- Table A.2 shows you the bitrates of the audio portion of a published (or subscribed) stream. You can use the `setRate()` method of the `Microphone` object to control the quality (and therefore, the bitrate) of an audio stream. The following code creates a `Microphone` object and sets its rate to 11 kHz:

```
user_mic = Microphone.get();
user_mic.setRate(11);
```

> **Note**
>
> The 1-minute transfer column is provided in Tables A.2 and A.3 to help you gauge how much server bandwidth is required for such streams. Most ISPs or hosting providers allow a limited amount of megabytes (or gigabytes) to be transferred per month from a given Web server account. Additional fees are usually levied if your Web site (or a Rich Internet Application running on your site) consumes additional bandwidth.

- Table A.3 provides sample values that can be used with the `setQuality()` method of the `Camera` object. This method allows you to control the maximum bandwidth that the video portion of a stream is allowed to use. When you invoke this method, you should specify both of the method's arguments, `bandwidth` and `frameQuality`. The `bandwidth` parameter is the bytes per second limit for the stream, while `frameQuality` controls the compression applied to the video. If you specify 0 for the `bandwidth` value, the Flash movie attempts to use all of the available bandwidth of the user's connection for the video stream. A value of 0 for the `frameQuality` attribute allows the Flash movie to vary the compression depending on the available bandwidth. You can set a fixed limit for the `bandwidth` value (such as those shown in Table A.3) as well as a fixed `frameQuality` value from 1 to 100, with 1 being the most compression (worst quality) and 100 being no compression (best quality). The following code limits a user's `Camera` object stream to 32 Kbps with a quality setting of 50 (medium quality):

```
user_cam = Camera.get();
user_cam.setQuality(4096, 50);
```

Note
If the specified `bandwidth` value cannot achieve the quality set by the `frameQuality` argument, then the Flash movie adjusts the frame rate of the video stream to reach the desired quality. If the `frameQuality` is exceedingly high and the `bandwidth` value is extremely low, the video portion of the stream will likely appear very choppy and slow (less than 1 fps).

■ Table A.4 shows the default settings of the SetBandwidth component. This component can be used in conjunction with other components, such as the AVPresence component, to control the quality and bitrate of an audio/video stream.

TABLE A.1 BITRATES AND CONNECTION SPEEDS

CONNECTION SPEED	THEORETICAL SPEED	PRACTICAL SPEED	PRACTICAL BITRATE
14.4 Kbps*	1.8 KB/sec	1.2 KB/sec*	9.6 Kbps
19.2 Kbps	2.4 KB/sec	1.6 KB/sec	12.8 Kbps
28.8 Kbps*	3.6 KB/sec	2.3 KB/sec*	18.4 Kbps
56 Kbps*	7 KB/sec	4.7 KB/sec*	37.6 Kbps
128 Kbps	16 KB/sec	10.7 KB/sec	85.6 Kbps
256 Kbps	32 KB/sec	21.4 KB/sec	172 Kbps
384 Kbps	48 KB/sec	32 KB/sec	257 Kbps
864 Kbps	108 KB/sec	72 KB/sec	579 Kbps
1 Mbps	128 KB/sec	86 KB/sec	686 Kbps
10 Mbps	1,280 KB/sec	858 KB/sec	6,861 Kbps
11 Mbps	1,408 KB/sec	943 KB/sec	7,547 Kbps
100 Mbps	12,800 KB/sec	8,576 KB/sec	68,608 Kbps

Note
The entries marked with an asterisk are values displayed in the Debug menu of the Test Movie (or Debug Movie) environment of Macromedia Flash MX.

TABLE A.2 `Microphone.setRate()` BITRATES PER STREAM

SAMPLING RATE	BITRATE	1 MINUTE TRANSFER
5 kHz	11.2 Kbps	84 KB
8 kHz (default)	16.4 Kbps	123 KB
11 kHz	22.4 Kbps	168 KB
22 kHz	44.9 Kbps	337 KB
44 kHz	89.4 Kbps	671 KB

TABLE A.3 `Camera.setQuality()` BITRATES PER STREAM

bandwidth VALUE (IN BYTES PER SECOND)	BITRATE	1 MINUTE TRANSFER
0	Maximum available	N/A
4096	32 Kbps	240 KB
8192	64 Kbps	480 KB
16384 (default)	128 Kbps	960 KB
24576	192 Kbps	1,440 KB (1.4 MB)
32768	256 Kbps	1,920 KB (1.88 MB)

TABLE A.4 DEFAULT BITRATES FOR THE SETBANDWIDTH COMPONENT

CONNECTION SPEED	UP	DOWN
Modem	33 Kbps	33 Kbps
DSL	128 Kbps	256 Kbps
LAN	10,000 Kbps	10,000 Kbps

The AVPresence component, when used without the SetBandwidth component, uses a video bitrate of 12,000 bytes per second, or 11.7 KB/sec (93.75 Kbps). The default audio sampling rate for both the AVPresence and AudioConference components is 8 kHz.

For up-to-date information on bandwidth strategies and techniques for FlashCom applications, check the book's Web site at www.mxbook.com.

B Online Appendixes

In an effort to provide the latest information regarding Macromedia MX software, we have created a set of online appendixes that you can download from the book's Web site at www.mxbook.com. These documents are briefly described in this appendix and are available as PDF files, which can be viewed using the free Adobe Acrobat Reader.

 Note You can download the latest Acrobat Reader from www.adobe.com/products/ acrobat/readermain.html.

DEVELOPING RICH INTERNET APPLICATIONS ON A MACINTOSH

Even though the Macromedia MX server products are not available for the Apple Macintosh operating system, you can build Rich Internet Applications using the Mac versions of Macromedia Flash MX and Dreamweaver MX. This online appendix walks you through the process of accessing non-Macintosh server resources as you develop and test applications.

PLANNING DEVELOPMENT AND PRODUCTION ENVIRONMENTS

All the exercises and projects described in this book can be created and tested with the trial versions of Macromedia's MX family of products installed on your own machine. But how do you take a Rich Internet Application from a development environment into a live production environment? In this online appendix, you will learn how to set up MX server products on a local area network and how to move your applications to live production servers. We'll also provide information about third-party vendors that specialize in MX-enabled server hosting.

DEBUGGING RICH INTERNET APPLICATIONS

Each Macromedia MX product has one or more tools available to access the processes of client- or server-side scripts within your Rich Internet Application. This appendix will help you troubleshoot problems you may encounter during the development of an application. From the Debugger panel in Flash MX to the Results panel in Dreamweaver MX, you will learn how to narrow your search for problems that affect the performance of your application.

Look for updated product news, tips, and discussion forums at the book's Web site at www.mxbook.com.

Index